Evidence Illustrated

Cases to Illustrate
How All the Rules Work

Evidence Illustrated

Cases to Illustrate How All the Rules Work

John Norman Scott
Professor of Law
Thomas M. Cooley Law School

A Division of LEARNING PUBLICATIONS, INC.
HOLMES BEACH, FLORIDA

Evidence Illustrated: Cases to Illustrate How All the Rules Work

ISBN 1-55691-181-5

©2000 by John Norman Scott

All Rights reserved. No part of this book may be reproduced or transmitted in any form or by any means, electronic or mechanical, including photocopying and recording, or by any information or retrieval systems, without permission in writing from the publisher.

A division of **Learning Publications, Inc.**
5351 Gulf Drive
P.O. Box 1338
Holmes Beach, FL 34218-1338

Printing: 5 4 3 2 1   Year: 4 3 2 1 0

Text and Cover designed by Image Creative Group, Lansing, MI

Printed in the United States of America

TABLE OF CONTENTS

Foreword xiii

Chapter One: Article I General Provisions 1
101, 1101	United States v. Monsanto (CA 2 1991)	1
102, 608(b)	United States v. Opager (CA 5 1979)	2
103(a)(1), (d), 404(b)	People v. Dunham (Mi App 1977)	4
103(a)(2)	Fox v. Dannenburg (CA 8 1990)	5
103(c)	United States v. Sutherland (CA 5 1981)	6
103(d), 403	Rojas v. Richardson (CA 5 1983)	7
104(a)	United States v. Campbell (CA 5 1996)	8
104(a), 804(b)(2)	Green v. State (Tx Cr App 1992)	10
104(a)(b), 412(b)	United States v. Platero (CA 10 1995)	11
104(b), 901(a)	Ricketts v. City of Hartford (CA 2 1996)	13
105	Government of Virgin Islands v. Mujahid (CA 3 1993)	15
106	United States v. Sutton (CA DC 1986)	16

Chapter Two: Article II Judicial Notice 19
201(b)	Barber v. Ponte (CA 1 1985)	19
201(B)	Griswold v. Commonwealth (Va App 1995)	20

Chapter Three: Article III Presumptions in Civil Actions and Proceedings 21
301	United States v. Ahrens (CA 8 1976)	21
301	In re the Yoder Company (CA 6 1985)	22
302	Monger v. Cessna Aircraft Company (CA 8 1987)	24

Chapter Four: Article IV Relevancy and Its Limits 25
401	Knapp v. State (In 1907)	25
401	State v. Brewer (Me 1985)	26
401, 403	State v. Kotsimpulos (Me 1980)	27
401	Higgins v. Hicks Co. (CA 8 1985)	28
401, 403	Bunion v. Allstate Insurance Co. (ED Pa 1980)	29
401, 403	Ponder v. Warren Tool Corp. (CA 10 1987)	30
401, 403	Hines v. Joy Manufacturing Co. (CA 6 1988)	31
401	Kelly's Auto Parts, No. 1, Inc. v. Boughton (CA 6 1987)	32
401, 403	Murphy v. Cincinnati Insurance Co. (CA 6 1985)	33
401, 403	People v. Mills (Mi 1995)	35
401, 403, 702	People v. Collins (Ca 1968)	36
403	Old Chief v. United States (US 1997)	38
404(a)(1), 405(a)	United States v. Gilliland (CA 10 1978)	39

404(a)(2)	Perrin v. Anderson (CA 10 1986)	40
404(a)(2), 405(a)	State v. Bazan (NM 1977)	42
404(a), 405(a), 610	Government of Virgin Islands v. Petersen (CA 3 1977)	43
404(a)(2), 405(a)	State v. Carlson (Oh App 1986)	44
404(b)	United States v. Fuller (CA 8 1989)	45
404(b	People v. Oliphant (Mi 1976)	46
404(b)	State v. Garfole (NJ 1978)	48
404(b), 408	Johnson v. Hugo's Skateway (CA 4 1991)	50
404(b)	United States v. Krezdorn (CA 5 1981)	51
404(b)	United States v. Buckhart (CA 10 1972)	52
405(a)	United States v. Bright (CA 5 1979)	53
405(a)	Securities and Exchange Commission v. Peters (CA 10 1992)	54
405(b)	Panas v. Harakis (NH 1987)	56
405(b)	State v. Woodson (WV 1989)	57
405(b)	Rocky Mountain Helicopters, Inc. v. Bell Helicopters Textron, Inc. (CA 10 1986)	58
405(b)	Mintle v. Mintle (Wy 1988)	59
405(b)	United States v. Keiser (CA 9 1995)	60
406, 404(b)	Halloran v. Virginia Chemicals, Inc. (NY 1977)	62
406	French v. Sorano (Wi 1976)	63
406	Charmley v. Lewis (Or 1986)	64
406	Progressive American Insurance Company v. Kurtz (Fl App 1987)	66
407	Muzyka v. Remington Arms Co. Inc. (CA 5 1985)	67
407	Boeing Airplane Co. v. Brown (CA 9 1961)	68
407	Hartman v. Opelika Machine and Welding Company (Fl App)	69
408	Ramada Development Co. v. Rauch (CA 5 1981)	70
408	Bhandari v. First National Bank of Commerce (CA 5 1987)	71
408	Freidus v. First National Bank (CA 8 1991)	72
408	Hudspeth v. Commissioner of Internal Revenue (CA 9 1990)	73
408	United States v. Gonzalez (CA 2 1984)	74
409	Home Insurance Company v. Spears (Ar App 1979)	75
410	United States v. Robertson (CA 5 1976)	76
410	United States v. Hare (CA 8 1995)	77
401, 410	United States v. Biaggi (CA 2 1990)	78
411	Dobbins v. Crain Brothers, Inc. (WD Pa 1976)	79
411	Charter v. Chleborad (CA 8 1977)	80
411	Morrissey v. Welsh Co. (CA 8 1987)	81
411	Miller v. Szelenyi (Me 1988)	82
411, 103(c)	Kozlowski v. Rush (Id 1992)	83
412	Doe v. United States (CA 4 1981)	85
412	United States v. Saunders (CA 4 1991)	87
412	United States v. Cardinal (CA 6 1986)	89

412	Judd v. Rodman (CA 11 1997)	91
413, 403	United States v. Guardia (CA 10 1998)	93
414, 403	United States v. Sumner (CA 8 1997)	94
414, 403	United States v. LeCompte (CA 8 1997)	95

Chapter Five: Article V Privileges 97

501, 5th Am.	United States v. Balsys (US 1998)	97
104(a), 501	United States v. Zolin (US 1989)	98
501	United States v. Oloyede (CA 4 1992)	99
501	United States v. Liebman (CA 3 1987)	100
501	In re Grand Jury Subpoena (CA 5 1991)	101
501	United States v. Tedder (CA 4 1986)	102
501	Swidler & Berlin v. United States (US 1998)	103
501	Upjohn Co. v. United States (US 1981)	105
501	Trammel v. United States (US 1980)	106
501	United States v. Byrd (CA 7 1984)	108
501	Jaffee v. Redmond (US 1996)	109

Chapter Six: Article VI Witnesses 111

601	State v. Roman (Me 1993)	111
601	State v. Warden (Ka 1995)	112
601	Brand v. Brand (CA 2 1986)	113
602, 601	United States v. Peyro (CA 8 1986)	115
602	McCrary-El v. Shaw (CA 8 1993)	116
602	United States v. Valdez (CA 5 1984)	117
603	United States v. Fowler (CA 5 1979)	119
604	United States v. Mayans (CA 9 1994)	120
605	Fox v. City of West Palm Beach (CA 5 1967)	121
605	United States v. Maceo (CA 5 1991)	122
606(a)	State v. Aaron (NM 1984)	123
606(b)	United States v. Swinton (CA 8 1996)	124
606(b)	United States v. Straach (CA 5 1993)	126
607, 403	United States v. Bratton (CA 5 1989)	127
607	Battle v. United States (CA DC 1965)	128
607	Henderson v. DeTella (CA 7 1996)	129
607	Wilmington Trust Co. v. Manufacturers Life Insurance Co. (CA 5 1980)	130
607	United States v. Buchanan (CA 10 1989)	131
607, 401, 403	United States v. Abel (US 1984)	132
607	United States v. Lindstrom (CA 11 1983)	133
607	Collins v. Wayne Corp. (CA 5 1980)	135
607, 6th Am.	Delaware v. Van Arsdall (US 1986)	136
607, 608(b)	United States v. DiPaolo (CA 2 1986)	137

608, 403	Barnier v. Szentmiklosi (CA 6 1987)	138
607, 608(b)	Chnapkova v. Koh (CA 2 1993)	140
608(a)	United States v. Malady (CA 8 1966)	141
608(b), 405(a)	United States v. Davenport (CA 9 1985)	142
609(a), 403	Radtke v. Cessna Aircraft Co. (CA 8 1983)	143
609(a)(1)	United States v. Sanders (CA 4 1992)	144
609(a)(1)	Wilson v. City of Chicago (CA 7 1993)	145
609(a)(1)	United States v. Swanson (CA 8 1993)	147
609, 410	United States v. Sonny Mitchell Center (CA 5 1991)	148
609(a)(2)	United States v. Toney (CA 5 1980)	149
609(a)(2)	State v. Ellis (Ne 1981)	150
609(b)	United States v. Daniel (CA 5 1992)	151
607, 609(d)	Davis v. Alaska (US 1974)	152
610	Mauldin v. Upjohn Company (CA 5 1983)	153
610	Firemen's Fund Insurance Company v. Thien (CA 8 1995)	154
611(a)	Berroyer v. Hertz (CA 3 1981)	155
611(b)	Bishop v. State (Ok Cr App 1978	156
611(b)	United States v. Taylor (CA 8 1979)	157
612	Wilson v. State (Ar 1982)	158
612	R.A.B. v. State (Fl App 1981)	159
612, 501	Samaritan Health Services, Inc. v. Superior Court (Az 1984)	161
613	People v. Petersen (Ca App 1972)	163
613, 801(d)(2)(B)	Doyle v. Ohio (US 1976)	165
613(b)	United States v. McLaughlin (CA 9 1981)	166
614(b)	United States v. Hickman (CA 6 1979)	167
615	Burke v. State (De 1984)	168
615	State v. Burdge (Or 1983)	169

Chapter Seven: Article VII Opinions and Expert Testimony 171

701	Smith v. Praegitzer (Id 1988)	171
701	State v. Salazar (Mn 1980)	172
701	United States v. Robinson (CA 4 1986)	172
701	Loof v. Sanders (Ak 1984)	173
701	Lewis v. State (De 1980)	174
701	United States v. Anthony (CA 10 1991)	175
701	Burlington Northern Railroad Co. v. State of Nebraska (CA 8 1986)	176
702	United States v. Amaral (CA 9 1973)	177
702	United States v. De Soto (CA 7 1989)	177
702	United States v. 77,819.10 Acres of Land More or Less (CA 10 1981).	178
702	Daubert v. Merrell Dow Pharmaceuticals, Inc. (US 1993)	179

703	State v. Henze (Ia 1984)	181
703	Carter v. Wiese Corporation (Ia App 1984)	182
704	Redman v. Ford Motor Company (SC 1969)	183
705	State v. Allison (NC 1983)	184
705	Forehead v. Galvin (Ne 1985)	185
706	State v. Archambeau (SD 1983)	186

Chapter Eight: Article VIII Hearsay 189

801(a)	In re Dependency of Penelope B. (Wa 1985)	189
801(c)	United States v. Emmons (CA 10 1994)	190
801(c), 801(d)(A), (B)	Smedra v. Stanek (CA 10 1951)	191
801(c)	Local 512, Warehouse & Office Workers Union v. National Labor Relations Board (CA 9 1986)	192
801(c), 801(d)(2)(E)	United States v. Alosa (CA 1 1994)	193
801(d)(1)(A), 613	Van Hattan v. State (Ak App 1983)	194
801(d)(1)(B)	Tome v. United States (US 1995)	195
801(d)(1)(C)	State v. Barela (NM 1982)	196
801(d)(2)(A)	Beamon v. State (Wi 1980)	197
801(d)(2)(A), (C)	Cameron County v. Velasquez (Tx App 1984)	198
801(d)(2)(A)	State v. Maniccia (Ia App 1984)	199
801(d)(2)(B)	Saudi Arabian Airline Corporation v. Dunn (Fl App 1983)	200
801(d)(2)(B)	United States v. Monks (CA 9 1985)	201
801(d)(2)(B)	United States v. Wiseman (CA 1 1987)	203
801(d)(2)(c)	Covington v. Sawyer (Oh App 1983)	204
801(d)(2)(D)	Pzeradski v. Rexnord, Inc. (Mi App 1982)	205
810(d)(2)(D)	Scientific Applications, Inc. v. Delkamp (ND 1981)	206
801(d)(2)(D)	United States v. Santos (CA 2 1967)	207
801(d)(2)(D)	Burkey v. Ellis (ND Al 1979)	208
801(d)(2)(E)	State v. Yslas (Az 1984)	209
801(d)(2)(E)	Williamson v. State (Ak App 1986)	210
801(d)(2)(E)	Bergeron v. State (Wi 1978)	211
6th Amendment	White v. Illinois (US 1992)	212
803(1)	First State Bank of Denton v. Maryland Casualty Co. (CA 5 1990)	213
803(1)	Hewitt v. Grand Truck Western Railroad Co. (Mi App 1983)	214
803(1)	State v. Case (NM 1984)	216
803(2)	Lewin v. Miller Wagner & Co., Ltd. (Az App 1986)	217
803(2)	United States v. Napier (CA 9 1975)	218
803(2)	Cole v. Tansy (CA 10 1991)	219
803(3)	Mutual Life Insurance Co. v. Hillmon (US 1892)	220
803(3)	State v. Auble (Ut 1988)	221
803(3)	State v. Nye (Me 1988)	222
803(3)	People v. Carlson (Co 1986)	223

803(4)	Bulthuis v. Rexall Corporation (CA 9 1985)	224
803(4)	State v. Justiniano (Wa App 1987)	225
803(4)	United States v. Iron Shell (CA 8 1980)	226
803(4)	State v. Moen (Or 1990)	227
803(5)	United States v. Picciandra (CA 1 1986)	229
803(5)	State v. Thompson (Ia 1986)	230
803(6)	United States v. Hayes (CA 10 1988)	231
803(6)	Thirsk v. Ethicon (Co App 1983)	232
803(6)	United States v. Catabran (CA 9 1988)	233
803(6)	Palmer v. Hoffman (US 1943)	234
803(6), (7)	Sheyenne Valley Lumber Co. v. Nokleberg (ND 1982)	235
803(6), (8)(B), (C)	State v. Rivera (De Super 1986)	237
803(8)(C)	Beech Aircraft Corp. v. Rainey (US 1988)	238
803(8)	United States v. Versaint (CA 3 1988)	239
803(8)(B)	United States v. Puente (CA 5 1987)	240
803(9)	State v. Gould (Mt 1985)	242
803(10)	Bardacke v. Dunigan (NM 1982)	243
803(11)	Hall v. Commissioner of Internal Revenue (CA 9 1984)	244
803(12)	Matuszewski v. Pancoast (Oh App 1987)	245
803(13)	Matter of Estate of Egbert (Mi App 1981)	246
803(14), (15)	Compton v. WWV Enterprises (Tx App 1984)	247
803(14), (15)	Greycas, Inc. v. Proud (CA 7 1987)	248
803(15)	Compton v. Davis (D Wy 1985)	249
803(16)	Moore v. Goode (WV 1988)	251
803(16), 901(b)(8)	Threadgill v. Armstrong World Industries, Inc. (CA 3 1991)	252
803(17)	Garvey v. O'Donaghue (DC App 1987)	254
803(18)	Molkenbur v. Hart (Mn App 1987)	255
803(18)	State v. Rangitsch (Wa App 1985)	256
803(19)	United States v. Allen (CA DC 1992)	257
803(20)	Goodover v. Lindey's, Inc. (Mt 1988)	258
803(21)	State v. Johnson (Me 1981)	259
803(21)	Ferguson v. State (Ok Cr App 1984)	260
803(22)	Safeco Insurance Company of America v. McGrath (Wa App 1986)	261
803(23)	Grant Brothers Construction Co. v. United States (US 1914)	262
804(a)(1)	People v. Rosenthal (Co App 1985)	263
804(a)	Cummiskey v. Chandris, S.A. (SD NY 1989)	264
804(b)(1)	United States v. Salerno (US 1992)	265
804(b)(1)	Lohrmann v. Pittsburgh Corning Corp. (CA 4 1986)	266
804(b)(2)	Shepard v. United States (US 1933)	267
804(b)(2)	People v. Siler (Mi App 1988)	269
804(b)(3)	Sackett v. Atyeo (Mi App 1996)	270
801(c), 804(b)(3)	State v. Saunders (Oh App 1984)	271

804(b)(3)	United States v. Salvador (CA 2 1987)	272
804(b)(3)	Williamson v. United States (US 1994)	273
804(b)(4)	People v. Raffaelli (Co App 1985)	274
804(b)(5)	United States v. Mastrangelo (CA 2 1982)	275
Mi R E 803A	People v. Hammons (Mi App 1995)	277
805	United States v. Portsmouth Paving Corporation (CA 4 1982)	278
805	Hart v. O'Brien (CA 5 1997)	280
806, 613(b)	Smith v. Fairman (CA 7 1988)	281
806, 613(b)	United States v. Wuagneux (CA 11 1988)	282
806, 608(a)	United States v. Lechoco (CA DC 1976)	284
807	Dallas County v. Commercial Union Assurance Co. (CA 5 1961)	285
807	United States v. Trujillo (CA 10 1998)	287

Chapter Nine: Article IX Authentication and Identification 289

901(a)	United States v. Whitaker (CA 7 1997)	289
901(a)	Graham v. State (In 1970)	290
901(a)	United States v. Harrington (CA 9 1991)	290
901(b)(1)	State v. Kroeplin (ND 1978)	292
901(b)(2)	State v. Stotts (Az 1985)	293
901(b)(3)	State v. Reasoner (Az App 1987)	294
901(b)(4)	United States v. Wilson (CA 8 1976)	296
901(b)(4)	State v. Best (Az App 1985)	297
901(b)(5)	State v. West (NC 1986)	298
901(b)(6)	State v. Hamilton (Mt 1980)	299
901(b)(7), 803(8)	Garcia v. Gloor (CA 5 1980)	300
901(b)(8)	Lockwood v. AC & S, Inc. (Wa App 1986)	301
901(a), (b)(9)	United States v. Rembert (CA DC 1988)	302
902(1)	United States v. Moore (CA 8 1977)	304
902(2)	United States v. Combs (CA 9 1985)	305
902(3), (4)	United States v. Doyle (CA 2 1997)	307
902(4)	United States v. Dancy (CA 5 1988)	309
902(5)	Silverman v. Barry (D DC 1986)	310
902(6)	Snyder v. Whittaker Corp. (CA 5 1988)	311
902(7)	United States v. Alvarez (CA 9 1992)	311
902(8)	United States v. M'Biye (CA DC 1981)	312
902(9)	United States v. Little (CA 8 1977)	313
902(10)	United States v. Sturman (CA 6 1991)	313
903	McQueeney v. Wilmington Trust Company (CA 3 1985)	314

Chapter Ten: Article X Contents of Writings, Recordings and Photographs 317

1001(1)	Seiler v. Lucasfilm, Ltd. (CA 9 1987)	317
1001(2), (3)	United States v. Leight (CA 7 1987)	319
1001(3), (4), 1003	United States v. Rangel (CA 8 1978)	321
1002	United States v. Humphrey (CA 5 1997)	322
1002	United States v. Fagan (CA 5 1987)	323
1002	United States v. Sliker (CA 2 1984)	324
1002	R & R Associates, Inc. v. Visual Scene, Inc. (CA 1 1984)	324
1003, 1001(4)	United States v. DiMatteo (CA 11 1983)	326
1004	Neville Construction Company v. Cook Paint and Varnish Company (CA 8 1982)	327
1005	United States v. Rodriguez (CA 5 1975)	328
1006, 803(6)	Ford Motor Company v. Auto Supply Company, Inc. (CA 8 1981)	329
1006	United States v. Johnson (CA 9 1979)	330
1007	B.D. Click Company, Inc. v. United States (Ct Cl 1980)	332
1008	Fox v. Peck Iron and Metal Company, Inc (Bkrtcy, SD Cal 1982)	333

Index and Tables 335
 Index 337
 Table of Cases 343
 Table of Rules 349

FOREWORD

This is a new kind of "casebook." Its only purpose is to help the future (or new) practitioner grasp the ways the Rules of Evidence are actually applied in real courtrooms — how they work.

Evidence Illustrated was written out of a need I have felt most keenly as a teacher of Evidence for over a dozen years.

I have taught from several original-judicial-text (edited-full-text) casebooks, and my students have found them all both too lengthy and, curiously, too "patchy" to be efficient. (I mean, if you have to read ten full-length cases on the top four hearsay exceptions, who has time for all the nuances of public records, much less documents affecting an interest in property?) By the time law students take Evidence they are pretty familiar with the all-important task of struggling to extract relevant principles from the excess of verbiage presented by most judicial opinions. In my experience a great many students just don't read the full-text cases, instead seeking shortcuts in outlines, canned briefs, audio tapes, and the like — even in the classrooms of fairly demanding Socratic-style teachers. Moreover, almost all traditional casebooks are necessarily limited to the "high spots," leaving coverage to the hornbooks or, by default, to the student outlines. And, frankly, many spend needless expanses of print on rather esoteric academic concerns of scant practical consequence.

And yet teaching Evidence instead from the Federal Rules, from treatises and hornbooks, even from the excellent student-oriented summaries, omits something vital that students need (and even acknowledge they need!) — a fact-rich real-world context for the major issues of each rule. This is where *Evidence Illustrated* comes in. Instead of too-brief three- or five-line "problems" abstracted from cases, or (as often) re-imagined from cases, this book presents whole cases, or at least the relevant evidentiary dimensions of whole cases, but *summarized* for accessibility and efficiency. Written in plain English and designed to be "user-friendly," the case summaries of *Evidence Illustrated* are fashioned for students who want to know how the law of Evidence works. And coverage can be more complete as well, because no one case summary goes more than a couple of pages. (A student might even be able and willing to read a few more than once!)

The cases included in *Evidence Illustrated* range from the ubiquitous "classics" (e.g., *Hillmon, Palmer, Davis, Upjohn, Dallas County, Knapp, Collins* et. al.) to the essential new (e.g., *Tome, Old Chief, Jaffee,* et. al.) to the obscure — including a fair sampling of state cases, since some 38 states have adopted Evidence codes closely based on the Federal Rules. The editorial decisions as to what cases and issues to include were strictly the author's own, although it is readily admitted that many if not most of the fine, existing original-text casebooks include a few cases I might not have stumbled upon if I hadn't seen them in their editions, and which delighted me too much for their illustrative promise and/or their vivid fact patterns for me to omit them.

A cautionary note for both student and teacher: This book is not a "study guide" nor a set of canned briefs: it is not geared for use **with** any one existing casebook, nor **in place** of one assigned. It is meant to be used *as* a primary casebook of sorts, albeit a more efficient one, with the advantages noted above, or at least as supplemental reading with rules-based texts. It goes without saying that students are encouraged to go to the original text of any of the cases summarized herein if curiosity moves them.

ACKNOWLEDGMENTS

I would like to thank my secretaries extraordinaire, Alicia Paape, for getting me started, and Cynthia Brown, for getting me finished; my gifted research and editorial assistant Mindy Fox, Fead Class graduate of the Thomas M. Cooley Law School, May 1999, for helping me get it right; the administration of the Thomas M. Cooley Law School for granting me sabbatical leave during most of 1998 so I could complete this project; my Evidence students for a dozen years at Cooley for showing me the need for a book like this; my good friends Edsel and Ruth Erickson of LP Law/Learning Publications for their courage, vision and expertise; my wife Donna for looking the other way for a year or more while this project adversely possessed our dining room table; and my four excellent kids, Bobby, Caren, Gordie and Teddy for excusing their dad's frequent distractions and preoccupations during the length of the project. Thanks to all — now let's party!

CHAPTER ONE
Article I – General Provisions

FRE 101, 1101 – Evidence Rules Need Not Be Followed in Pretrial Hearing on Continuation of Restraint of Assets Subject to Forfeiture on Conviction

Rule 101. Scope

These rules govern proceedings in the courts of the United States and before the United States bankruptcy judges and United States magistrate judges, to the extent and with the exceptions stated in Rule 1101.

Rule 1101. Applicability of Rules

(a) Courts and Judges. These rules apply to the United States district courts, the District Court of Guam, the District Court of the Virgin Islands, the District Court for the Northern Mariana Islands, the United States court of appeals, the United States Claims Court, and to United States bankruptcy judges and United States magistrate judges, in the actions, cases, and proceedings and to the extent hereinafter set forth. The terms "judge" and "court" in these rules include United States bankruptcy judges and United States magistrate judges.

(b) Proceedings Generally. These rules apply generally to civil actions and proceedings, including admiralty and maritime cases, to criminal cases and proceedings, to contempt proceedings except those in which the court may act summarily, and to proceedings and cases under title 11, United States Code.

(c) Rule of Privilege. The rule with respect to privileges applies at all stages of all actions, cases, and proceedings.

(d) Rules Inapplicable. The rules (other than with respect to privileges) do not apply in the following situations:

(1) Preliminary Questions of Fact. The determination of questions of fact preliminary to admissibility of evidence when the issue is to be determined by the court under Rule 104.

(2) Grand Jury. Proceedings before grand juries.

(3) Miscellaneous Proceedings. Proceedings for extradition or rendition; preliminary examinations in criminal cases; sentencing, or granting or revoking probation; issuance of warrants for arrest, criminal summonses, and search warrants; and proceedings with respect to release on bail or otherwise.

UNITED STATES v. MONSANTO
924 F.2d 1186 (2d Cir. 1991)

A July 1987 indictment charged Peter Monsanto with multiple RICO,[1] narcotics, CCE,[2] and firearms violations. The indictment also alleged that Monsanto owned a home, an apartment and $35,000 in cash that were all subject to forfeiture because they were derived

---

[1] Racketeer Influenced and Corrupt Organizations Act.
[2] Continuing Criminal Enterprise Act.

from narcotics offenses.[3] The U.S. District Court for the Southern District of New York granted the government's request for an ex parte restraining order barring Monsanto "from directly or indirectly transferring or encumbering the home or the apartment." A month later Monsanto moved to vacate or modify the restraining order so he could use the assets to obtain an attorney, contending that to continue the order "would impermissibly interfere with his qualified sixth amendment right to counsel of choice." The district court denied Monsanto's motion, and he appealed.

After several appeals and remands, including a ruling by the U.S. Supreme Court, at long last the case was back in the Second Circuit Court of Appeals on this question. The court adopted an earlier panel's ruling that "after an ex parte, post-indictment, pretrial restraining order is entered... 'a pre-trial adversary hearing is required where the question of attorney's fees is implicated.'"

Pursuant to the forfeiture statute, which provides that at such a hearing the court "may receive and consider... evidence and information that would be inadmissible under the Federal Rules of Evidence," the court remanded to the district court for such a hearing and held that the Rules would not apply, "thus allowing the use of hearsay testimony and precluding unwarranted exposure of government witnesses."

FRE 102, 608(b) – Requirement of Fairness Can Sometimes Shade Strict Applicability of Specific Rule of Evidence

> **Rule 102. Purpose and Construction**
> These rules shall be construed to secure fairness in administration, elimination of unjustifiable expense and delay, and promotion of growth and development of the law of evidence to the end that the truth may be ascertained and proceedings justly determined.
>
> **Rule 608. Evidence of Character and Conduct of Witness**
> *(b) Specific Instances of Conduct.* Specific instances of the conduct of a witness, for the purpose of attacking or supporting the witness's credibility, other than conviction of crime as provided in Rule 609, may not be proved by extrinsic evidence. They may, however, in the discretion of the court, if probative of truthfulness or untruthfulness, be inquired into on cross-examination of the witness (1) concerning the witness's character for truthfulness or untruthfulness, or (2) concerning the character for truthfulness or untruthfulness of another witness as to which character the witness being cross-examined has testified....

UNITED STATES v. OPAGER
589 F.2d 799 (5th Cir. 1979)

A jury in the federal district court for the Southern District of Florida convicted Patricia Lynn Opager of possession of cocaine, possession with intent to distribute, and distribution of cocaine after they heard about what the appellate court called her "regrettable mistake of selling a pound of 90.4% pure cocaine to three buyers, two

---
[3] Under the Comprehensive Forfeiture Act of 1984, 21 U.S.C. §853.

of whom happened to be law enforcement officers and the third a government informant and acquaintance of Opager." She was sentenced to 4½ years' imprisonment, to be followed by three years of special parole.

On her appeal to the Fifth Circuit Court of Appeals she raised several issues, principally one concerning limits that had been placed on her attempts to impeach the informant, Phillip Posner. Opager had tried to establish an entrapment defense, testifying that Posner pressured her into the sale she was charged with. On rebuttal, "Posner testified to show Opager's 'predisposition' to sell cocaine. He stated that he had observed her engage in cocaine transactions in the past. On cross-examination, Posner explained that he had worked at a beauty salon (the Clipper) with defendant in 1974 and again in 1976 and that during both times he had seen her use and sell cocaine." Opager presented five character witnesses regarding Posner's bad character for truth-telling under Rule 608(a). She then attempted to introduce business records from the salon (canceled checks, appointment books, tax forms, etc.) to prove that she and Posner had not worked together in 1974. "The District Court ruled that the records were inadmissible under [Rule] 608(b) as extrinsic evidence of a specific instance of conduct introduced to discredit the witness's testimony."

The appellate court reversed Opager's conviction, ruling that excluding the business records was prejudicial error for two reasons. First, the court held that the ban on extrinsic evidence in Rule 608(b) did not apply because the records were not being offered just for impeachment: "In this case, we are convinced that the records were not offered for such a purpose. The documents show and would permit the jury to find that, contrary to Posner's testimony, Posner and Opager did not work together in 1974 and that therefore Posner did not witness any of the drug transaction he described as occurring at that time. Thus, the records do more than indicate Posner's capacity to lie, about which five witnesses had testified. Instead, as Opager's counsel strenuously argued at trial, the records were introduced to disprove a specific fact material to Opager's defense."

Moreover, the court seemed to take some instruction from a case that presents what was believed to be an even more direct "confrontation between Rule 608(b) and the basic purpose of the federal rules as evidenced by [Rule]102." That case[4] contained the following observation: "We believe that the ultimate purpose of the rules of evidence should not be lost by a rigid, blind application of a single rule of evidence. Individual rules of evidence, in this instance Rule 608(b), should not be read in isolation, when to do so destroys the purpose of ascertaining the truth. This is especially so when a witness directly contradicts the relevant evidence which Rule 608(b) seeks to exclude."

That led the Fifth Circuit panel here to hold, "Rule 608(b) should not stand as a bar to the admission of evidence introduced to contradict, and which the jury might find disproves, a witness's testimony as to a material issue of the case.

"The fact that the business records might have the incidental effect of proving Posner a liar does not affect their admissibility as relevant evidence. In countless cases where facts are in dispute, one party may be able overwhelmingly to disprove the testimony of a prior witness. To exclude under Rule 608(b) the latter otherwise relevant evidence, as the government would have us do today, would completely divorce legal proceedings from the truth seeking process."

---

[4] *United States v. Batts*, 558 F.2d 513 (9th Cir. 1977).

Now, it may well be that neither *Batts* nor *Opager* presents a genuine need to override the direct import of Rule 608(b) in order to "ascertain the truth" in a fair, just manner. But it is almost certainly true that the "Purpose and Construction" Rule, Rule 102, influenced both courts in deciding whether the contradiction was a material fact in itself or was merely the collateral impeachment of the witness's general credibility contemplated (and restricted) by Rule 608(b).

FRE 103(a)(1), (d), 404(b) – To Preserve Issue of Introduction of Conduct Testimony on Appeal, Accused Must Object to It at Trial and Demonstrate Its Prejudice to Him

> **Rule 103. Rulings on Evidence**
> *(a) Effect on Erroneous Ruling.* Error may not be predicated upon a ruling which admits or excludes evidence unless a substantial right of the party is affected, and
> *(1) Objection.* In case the ruling is one admitting evidence, a timely objection or motion to strike appears of record, stating the specific ground of objection, if the specific ground was not apparent from the context;...
> *(d) Plain Error.* Nothing in this rule precludes taking notice of plain errors affecting substantial rights although they were not brought to the attention of the court.
> **Rule 404. Character Evidence Not Admissible to Prove Conduct; Exceptions; Other Crimes**
> *(b) Other Crimes, Wrongs, or Acts.* Evidence of other crimes, wrongs, or acts is not admissible to prove the character of a person in order to show action in conformity therewith. It may, however, be admissible for other purposes, such as proof of motive, opportunity, intent, preparation, plan, knowledge, identity, or absence of mistake or accident, provided that upon request by the accused, the prosecution in a criminal case shall provide reasonable notice in advance of trial, or during trial if the court excuses pretrial notice on good cause shown, of the general nature of any such evidence it intends to introduce at trial.

PEOPLE v. DUNHAM
559 N.W.2d 360, 220 Mich. App. 268 (1997)

In response to routine questions from a divorce mediator in the Clinton County, Michigan Friend of the Court's office, the six-year-old daughter of Russell Percy Dunham made statements that led to his being charged with first degree criminal sexual conduct. At Dunham's jury trial in St. Johns, the young victim testified and pursuant to a Michigan hearsay exception corresponding to what many states call the "tender years exception" (Mich. R. Evid. 803A, "Hearsay Exception; Child's Statement About Sexual Act"),[5] her statements to the mediator were introduced into evidence over defense objection. The prosecution also introduced evidence of Dunham's "prior bad acts" (unspecified in the report) and of "threats he made to the victim's mother." Dunham was convicted,

---
[5] See *People v. Hammons, infra* p. 328, for a more complete discussion of the so-called "tender years" hearsay exception.

and sentenced to twenty to thirty years' imprisonment. He appealed.

The Michigan Court of Appeals affirmed. The court noted that the defense failed to object to the introduction of the "prior bad acts" and "threats" testimony, so that under Michigan's version of Rule 103(a)(1), Dunham's counsel "failed to preserve these issues." The court went on to consider points most closely aligned with Rules 103(a) and 103(d): "Further, we are not persuaded that the alleged error, if any, was decisive to the outcome of the case. Defendant has not established the prejudice necessary to avoid forfeiture of this unpreserved issue.... Further, it appears the evidence concerning defendant's conduct toward the victim was relevant to explain her delay in reporting the alleged abuse, and at least some of the evidence concerning conduct toward the victim's mother was relevant to the mother's reason for leaving the marital home, an issue addressed by defendant."

FRE 103(a)(2) – Offer of Proof May Consist of Putting Proffered Witness on Stand for Preview of Actual Testimony or of Counsel's Specific Summary of Its Anticipated Contents

---

Rule 103. Rulings of Evidence

(a) Effect of Erroneous Ruling. Error may not be predicted upon a ruling which admits or excludes evidence unless a substantial right of the party is affected, and

(1) Objection. In case the ruling is one admitting evidence, a timely objection or motion the strike appears of record, stating the specific ground of objection, if the specific ground was not apparent from the context; or

(2) Offer of Proof. In case the ruling is one excluding evidence, the substance of the evidence was made known to the court by offer or was apparent from the context within which questions were asked.

Once the court makes a definitive ruling on the record admitting or excluding evidence, either at or before trial, a party need not renew an objection or offer of proof to preserve a claim of error for appeal.

FOX v. DANNENBERG
906 F.2d 1253 (8th Cir. 1990)

Junior college roommates Derek Fox and Todd Dannenberg were involved in a one-car wreck on I-35 on their way back to Centerville, Iowa from Manhattan, Kansas, where they had visited Fox's girlfriend at Kansas State University. The car left the road, struck large rocks and then hit the concrete pillar supporting the Vivion Road overpass. Fox and Dannenberg were thrown from the car. Fox died three days later of head injuries; Dannenberg was badly injured, but survived.

Fox's father brought a wrongful death action against Dannenberg. Dannenberg testified he was asleep in the passenger's seat at the time of the accident. Fox's expert witnesses were prevented from testifying that from the "damage to the car, the position the car was in and the path it took during the accident, and the boys' injuries, it could be determined within a reasonable degree of engineering certainty that Dannenberg was driving the car at the time of the accident." The trial judge in the Western District of Missouri said plaintiff's engineering experts were "not competent to state an expert opinion on who was driving because neither one had medical training." Dannenberg's expert testified that it was impossible to tell who was driving based on what was known. The jury verdict was for Dannenberg, and Fox appealed.

Fox claimed it was error to preclude his experts from testifying. Dannenberg argued Fox had not preserved this issue for appellate review because he had "failed to put the expert witnesses on the stand to elicit the proffered testimony" by way of an offer of proof under Rule 103(a)(2). But the Eighth Circuit Court of Appeals first held that the issue had been properly preserved when counsel stated specifically what testimony was expected from the experts. "Putting a proffered witness on the stand is not the only way to adequately make an offer of proof. It is also sufficient for counsel to 'state with specificity what he or she anticipates will be the witness's testimony....' That was accomplished in this case. Thus, we may review this issue." The court then held that under Rule 702 the experts proffered by Fox should have been allowed to testify. The verdict was reversed and the case remanded.

FRE 103(c) – Jury Should Not Be Shown Materials Not Admitted Into Evidence

> **Rule 103. Rulings on Evidence**
> *(c) Hearing of Jury.* In jury cases, proceedings shall be conducted, to the extent practicable, so as to prevent inadmissible evidence from being suggested to the jury by any means, such as making statements or offers of proof or asking questions in the hearing of the jury.

UNITED STATES v. SUTHERLAND
656 F.2d 1181 (5th Cir. 1981)

El Paso Municipal Court Judge Glen Sutherland was alleged to have conspired with Edward Maynard and Grace Walker to conduct a ticket-fixing scheme, and all three were charged with conspiracy to violate the federal Racketeer Influenced and Corrupt Organizations (RICO) Act.

At trial the government was permitted over defense objection to introduce into evidence low quality audio tapes (and transcripts of the tapes, some containing translations of portions of the conversations that were conducted in Spanish) of conversations between Maynard and "individuals who posed as persons seeking help on traffic tickets each had received."

On appeal of their convictions, one point among many raised concerned the authentication of the tapes and the transcripts. The Fifth Circuit Court of Appeals affirmed the convictions, and upheld the admissibility of the tapes themselves: "The government introduced the testimony of Terry Youngblood, an F.B.I. agent, and of Edward Ortega, an El Paso policeman, who together supervised the audio tapings at issue; both Youngblood and Ortega testified at some length," and Maynard was identified.

The appellate court, however, agreed with

the defense that the transcripts of the tapes were not sufficiently authenticated to be seen by the jury. No testimony was presented that the transcripts were "accurate reproductions of the taped conversations," nor that the Spanish-English translations were accurate. The government argued that the transcripts "were not evidence at all, but were merely 'aides' given to the jury to help them follow the tapes," and were not even "submitted to the jury, along with other evidence, for their considerations during deliberations." The court said that, on the contrary, "a transcript is evidence of what is recorded on an audio tape, just as the tape is evidence of what was said in the original conversation," and said its use is "analogous to the use of expert testimony as a device aiding a jury in understanding other types of real evidence." And the court said that showing the jury "inadmissible evidence, e.g., an unauthenticated transcript" is directly contrary to Rule 103(c).

(However, the court held the error in admitting the transcripts did not prejudice the defendants in light of other evidence of the contents of the tapes.)

FRE 103(d), 403 – Allowance of Opponent's Use of "Illegal Alien" Slur Was Plain Error, Causing Mistrial Even When Party Failed to Object

> **Ruling 103. Rulings on Evidence**
>
> *(a) Effect of Erroneous Ruling.* Error may not be predicated upon a ruling which admits or excludes evidence unless a substantial right of the party is affected, and
>
> *(1) Objection.* In case the ruling is one admitting evidence, a timely objection or motion to strike appears of record, stating the specific ground of objection, if the specific ground was not apparent from the context;...
>
> *(d) Plain Error.* Nothing in this rule precludes taking notice of plain errors affecting substantial rights although they were not brought to the attention of the court.
>
> **Rule 403. Exclusion of Relevant Evidence on Grounds of Prejudice, Confusion, or Waste of Time**
>
> Although relevant, evidence may be excluded if its probative value is substantially outweighed by the danger of unfair prejudice, confusion of the issues, or misleading the jury, or by considerations of undue delay, waste of time, or needless presentation of cumulative evidence.

ROJAS v. RICHARDSON
703 F.2d 186 (5th Cir. 1983)

A horse named Jet unseated ranch-hand Paulino Izaguirre Rojas, and he suffered severe injuries. He sued M and R Cattle Company and its partners, Kenneth McGee and Robert Richardson, in a diversity action in federal court for the Eastern District of Texas, claiming Jet had not been properly broken to saddle riding, and that the horse was equipped with a dangerous bridle. The defendants claimed contributory negligence on the part of Rojas.

During closing argument, defense counsel made the following remarks: "I hope – I hope that you don't, because Mr. Rojas is an alien, give him any more benefit than you would any United States citizen who comes in this Court. If the situation were reversed and you or I were in Mexico – were illegal aliens in Mexico – I would hope Mexico would open up their Courts, would open up their job market, would open up their public schools, would open up their State hospitals, as we have in this country for Mr. Rojas. Certainly he is – I'm not saying we shouldn't do those things, but he shouldn't be entitled to any extra benefits because he is an illegal alien in this country than would any other citizen of the United States be entitled." Rojas' counsel did not object to this reference. The jury returned a verdict for defendants.

Rojas appealed, claiming the "illegal alien" references were so prejudicial that their use amounted to plain error.[6] The Fifth Circuit Court of Appeals agreed and reversed. "These remarks prejudiced the jury on two counts. First, by introducing irrelevant and unproven allegations that Rojas was an illegal alien, the defense clearly was appealing to the prejudice and bias of members of the jury on the basis of national origin.... Even counsel's single reference to the incendiary, derogatory expression 'illegal alien' is prejudicial. Finally, the allegation that Rojas was in the country illegally is unsupported in the record." The appellate court concluded that the trial court's instruction to the jury that "all persons are equal before the law" was not adequate to correct the plain error of allowing the reference in the first place.

―――――●―――――

FRE 104(a) – Trial Court Can Consider Inadmissible Evidence in Determining Whether Attorney-Client Privilege Has Been Waived

> **Rule 104. Preliminary Questions**
>
> *(a) Questions of Admissibility Generally.* Preliminary questions concerning the qualification of a person to be a witness, the existence of a privilege, or the admissibility of evidence shall be determined by the court, subject to the provisions of subdivision (b). In making its determination it is not bound by the rules of evidence except those with respect to privileges.

UNITED STATES v. CAMPBELL
73 F.3d 44 (5th Cir. 1996)

William Gibbs Campbell, Jr. was the general partner of a Texas limited partnership, 3700 WFA Limited, which owned the Wakeforest Apartments. The partnership filed a petition to reorganize in bankruptcy under Chapter 11 in June 1986. Thirteen months later, "Campbell wrote a check for $96,000 to the Partnership from the First City Bank account of Wakeforest Management Company, a separate business entity from the Partnership. At the time Campbell wrote the check, the First City Bank account of Wakeforest Management Company had a balance of $301.73. The check was deposited into the Partnership's account at Allied Bank. Later, the $96,000 check was returned unpaid for insufficient funds.

---

[6]Counsel for Rojas spent considerable effort trying to argue that failure to object during closing argument was excused because they had made – and lost – a motion *in limine* to bar testimony or references to Rojas's status as a "wetback" or "illegal alien." Their Rule 103(d) argument was almost certainly "Plan B," given the extreme infrequency with which courts in civil cases find "plain error" in the absence of objection.

"On the same day, Campbell arranged a wire transfer of $56,000 from the Partnership's Allied Bank account to the Guadalupe County Abstract Company's account at the Nolte National Bank of Seguin ('Nolte Bank'). Campbell's accountant recorded the $56,000 payment to the Nolte Bank account on Campbell's personal ledger, not on the business records of the Partnership.

"Campbell used the $56,000 he had transferred from the Partnership's Allied Bank account to pay off a $47,000 real estate note on his personal residence at 284 Turtle Lane in Seguin, Texas."

Later in 1987 the bankruptcy was converted to a Chapter 7 liquidation. The court-appointed trustee, Lowell T. Cage, discovered the wire transfer and formally inquired of Campbell about its authorization. When Cage received no reply, Campbell was charged with bankruptcy fraud.

At Campbell's Southern District of Texas fraud trial, the government called Barbara M. Rogers, the attorney for the Partnership who had signed the original bankruptcy petition, to testify as a witness. Campbell objected, citing the attorney-client privilege. The government's position was that Rogers was not Campbell's personal attorney, and that in any event the bankruptcy trustee, Cage, had waived the privilege on behalf of the partnership. Campbell argued that the trustee lacked the authority to waive the partnership's privilege. The trial judge made a Rule 104(a) factual determination that the privilege never applied to Campbell personally, that Rogers was engaged solely by the partnership, and that a letter from Cage to Rogers waived the attorney-client privilege as to the partnership. The jury convicted Campbell, and he appealed.

The Fifth Circuit Court of Appeals affirmed. On the question of the attorney-client privilege, the court held the trustee has full authority to act on behalf of a limited partnership, "an inanimate entity that can act only through its agents," and that that authority extended to waiving the attorney-client privilege.

The appellate court went on to hold that the trial court was acting properly when it took into consideration, in determining whether the privilege had been waived under Rule 104(a), "a letter from Cage to Rogers in which Cage acknowledged waiving the attorney-client privilege on behalf of the Partnership."[7] Since under Rule 104(a) "the court is not bound by the rules of evidence in determining a preliminary question such as the existence of a privilege," the court could properly consider the Cage letter "even if the letter was hearsay not within any exception."

(The court then, in a gesture that certainly does nothing to advance the law of evidence, held the letter admissible under the residual exception, Rule 807, with no explanation at all.)

---

[7] Although the court's opinion is no model of clarity on the point, it seems that the letter "acknowledging" the waiver was not the waiver itself, or else the letter would be admissible as a (non-hearsay) verbal act, see *Local 512, Warehouse & Office Workers Union v. NLRB, infra* p. 192.

FRE 104(a), 804(b)(2) – Factual Finding Whether Victim Believed He Was Dying for Determination of Admissibility of Victim's Hearsay Statements Is for Trial Judge to Make

> **Rule 104. Preliminary Questions**
>
> *(a) Questions of Admissibility Generally.* Preliminary questions concerning the qualification of a person to be a witness, the existence of a privilege, or the admissibility of evidence shall be determined by the court, subject to the provisions of subdivision (b). In making its determination it is not bound by the rules of evidence except those with respect to privileges.
>
> **Rule 804. Hearsay Exceptions; Declarant Unavailable**
>
> *(a) Definition of Unavailability.* "Unavailability as a witness" includes situations in which the declarant —
>
> (4) is unable to be present or to testify at the hearing because of death or then existing physical or mental illness or infirmity;...
>
> *(b) Hearsay Exceptions.* The following are not excluded by the hearsay rule if the declarant is unavailable as a witness:
>
> *(2) Statement Under Belief of Impending Death.* In a prosecution for homicide or in a civil action or proceeding, a statement made by a declarant while believing that the declarant's death was imminent, concerning the cause or circumstances of what the declarant believed to be impending death.

GREEN v. STATE
840 S.W.2d 394 (Tex. Cr. App. 1992)

In an attempted robbery on February 13, 1985 of a Dyer Electronics store in San Antonio, Norman Evans Green, accompanied by Harold Bowens, shot 18-year-old clerk Timothy Adams three times with a .38 caliber Winchester handgun. The bullets had been manually altered, with an "X" cut into the nose for "a more rapid expansion of the bullet upon impact, resulting in faster killing power." Adams talked to a Dyer manager, an EMS supervisor and a police officer before he died. He told them he was dying and that he had been shot during a robbery attempt by the two black men that he and store manager Gerry Rickhoff had seen hanging around the store earlier. Green was convicted of capital murder and sentenced to death. (The disposition of charges against Bowens is not mentioned in the report.)

One of the thirteen points of error Green raised in his appeal to the Texas Court of Criminal Appeals concerned the admissibility of testimony about what Adams said about being shot. Under the "dying declarations" exception to the prohibition against hearsay evidence,[8] the Texas counterpart to Federal Rule of Evidence 804(b)(2) requires that such statement be made at a time when the declarant believes his death is imminent. Green contended the proof that Adams knew he was dying was not sufficient for the trial judge to make the preliminary finding necessary under rule 104(a) to allow the hearsay testimony to be admitted, especially because "the emergency medical technician on the scene made statements to the victim that were designed to alleviate his fear of dying."

---

[8]See *Shepard v. United States*, and *People v. Siler, infra* pp. 267-269.

The appellate court affirmed Green's conviction and death sentence[9] and specifically upheld the admissibility of the victim's dying descriptions of the robbery and shooting. "Here the victim expressly stated to witnesses, 'I'm dying.' The trial court could readily have accepted that the victim, the declarant of the statements, did, in fact, believe that death was imminent" under Rule 104(a). The trial court had to make a preliminary finding of fact — that Adams knew or believed he was about to die from his wounds — before the witnesses who spoke with Adams could testify about what he had said. The Texas appeals panel held the trial court was "justified" in so finding from the evidence on the record.

FRE 104(a),(b), 412(b) – Determination Whether Victim of Alleged Rape Had Pre-Existing Sexual Relationship with Third Party as Accused Claimed Was for Jury to Make

Rule 104. Preliminary Questions

(a) Questions of Admissibility Generally. Preliminary questions concerning the qualification of a person to be a witness, the existence of a privilege, or the admissibility of evidence shall be determined by the court, subject to the provisions of subdivision (b). In making its determination it is not bound by the rules of evidence except those with respect to privileges.

(b) Relevancy Conditioned on Fact. When the relevancy of evidence depends upon the fulfillment of a condition of fact, the court shall admit it upon, or subject to, the introduction of evidence sufficient to support a finding of the fulfillment of the condition.

Rule 412. Sex Offense Cases; Relevance of Alleged Victim's Past Sexual Behavior or Alleged Sexual Predisposition

(a) Evidence Generally Inadmissible. The following evidence is not admissible in any civil or criminal proceeding involving alleged sexual misconduct except as provided in subdivisions (b) and (c):

(1) Evidence offered to prove that any alleged victim engaged in other sexual behavior; and

(2) Evidence offered to prove any alleged victim's sexual predisposition.

(b) Exceptions.

(1) In a criminal case, the following evidence is admissible, if otherwise admissible under these rules:

(A) evidence of specific instances of sexual behavior by the alleged victim offered to prove that a person other than the accused was the source of semen, injury or other physical evidence;

(B) evidence of specific instances of sexual behavior by the alleged victim with respect to the person accused of the sexual misconduct offered by the accused to prove consent or by the prosecution; and

(C) evidence the exclusion of which would violate the constitutional rights of the defendant.

…

(c) Procedure to Determine Admissibility.

(2) Before admitting evidence under this rule the court must conduct a hearing in camera and afford the victim and parties a right to attend and be heard. The motion, related papers, and the record of the hearing must be sealed and remain under seal unless the court orders otherwise.

---

[9] Dr. Robert Bux, who conducted the Adams autopsy, said one of the bullets inflicted a chest wound that must have been delivered while Adams was already bent over or squatting down.

UNITED STATES v. PLATERO
72 F.3d 806 (10th Cir. 1995)

As Susan Francis was accompanying her co-worker, Vernon Laughlin, out of Gallup in September, 1992, they allegedly were pulled over by security guard Ferlin Platero, who acted as though he was a police officer. Platero checked them both out, then told Laughlin he would give him a break this time, to "take a hike." Telling Francis he was taking her in for drunk driving, Platero was alleged to have raped her twice and forced her to have oral sex in the car. He then returned her to her car, where Laughlin testified he saw Francis still trying to fix her clothes and button her blouse. Platero was charged with three counts of aggravated sexual assault, a federal crime because it took place on the Navajo Reservation. Platero said the sex he had with Francis was consensual, and that she made up the rape story to cover up a sexual relationship with Laughlin and to keep it from her husband.

Before trial Platero filed a motion under Rule 412(b) to introduce evidence of Susan Francis's alleged past sexual behavior with Laughlin "in order to show that Francis had a motive to fabricate the rape allegations against Platero." At the hearing held pursuant to Rule 412(c)(2), Francis and Laughlin both testified that "their relationship turned from friendship to intimacy after the rape," not before. Laughlin's former girlfriend, Anna Mike, said, however, that she thought they'd been having an affair for a couple of years. (By the time of trial they were living together.) The district judge excluded the evidence of the relationship under Rule 412(a)(1).

Platero was convicted, and appealed. The Tenth Circuit Court of Appeals remanded for a factual determination whether there was a pre-existing sexual relationship between Francis and Laughlin. "On remand, the district judge found that the testimony of Anna Mike was not credible and the testimony of the other witnesses was credible. On the basis of his own credibility determinations, the judge concluded that no sexual relationship existed between Laughlin and Francis at the time of the sexual assault. Finding no factual predicate for allowing cross-examination regarding the relationship between Francis and Laughlin, the judge let stand the conviction for aggravated sexual assault." Platero appealed once again.

While the second appeal was pending, Congress amended Rule 412 in a number of ways, including elimination of language that formerly lay at the feet of the trial judge the task of determining whether a "condition of fact" had been fulfilled to determine if proffered evidence was relevant. Despite its own earlier order, the Tenth Circuit panel reversed the conviction and remanded, holding that to allow the judge to determine the existence of the prior sexual relationship between Laughlin and Francis amounted to letting the judge, rather than the jury, determine whether a defense is true or false. "Here, the district judge's decision on remand was based on his determination of the witnesses' credibility, and had the effect of barring Platero from presenting evidence which if believed by the jury could have damaged Francis's credibility as a witness and possibly have caused the jury to disbelieve Francis's testimony entirely. The judge's decision under the old version of Rule 412(c)(2) therefore impinged on Platero's right to trial by jury."

The court went on to hold that it was Rule 104(b), not 104(a), that applied to this situation. "Where there is... a question of relevancy depending on a condition of fact, like the relationship issue here, that question goes to the jury for a determination, not to the judge." The trial judge's sole function is "to determine only the presence of sufficient evidence to support a finding by the jury" that the factual pre-condition exists. The sexual relationship question in this case is a "'relevancy conditioned on fact' question under Rule 104(b) as opposed to a preliminary question of admissibility of the type enumerated in Rule 104(a) (e.g., qualification of a witness, existence of a privilege). When the trial judge here made the conclusive finding on relevancy conditioned on fact (the relationship issue) adversely to Platero, this ran counter to" several cases demonstrating the differences between Rule 104(a) and 104(b).

FRE 104(b), 901(a) – To Exclude Audiotape on Authentication Grounds, Court Must Make Finding That No Rational Juror Could Have Decided Defendant's Voice Was That on Tape

---

Rule 104. Preliminary Questions

(a) Questions of Admissibility Generally. Preliminary questions concerning the qualification of a person to be a witness, the existence of a privilege, or the admissibility of evidence shall be determined by the court, subject to the provisions of subdivision (b). In making its determination it is not bound by the rules of evidence except those with respect to privileges.

(b) Relevancy Conditioned on Fact. When the relevancy of evidence depends upon the fulfillment of a condition of fact the court shall admit it upon, or subject to, the introduction of evidence sufficient to support a finding of the fulfillment of the condition.

Rule 901. Requirement of Authentication or Identification

(a) General Provision. The requirement of authentication or identification as a condition precedent to admissibility is satisfied by evidence sufficient to support a finding that the matter in question is what its proponent claims.

RICKETTS v. CITY OF HARTFORD
74 F.3d 1397 (2d Cir. 1996)

A police chase of robbery-and-assault suspect Timothy Moore through Hartford, Connecticut caught up with Moore. Several officers beat on him for a few minutes just after the chase crossed a soccer field where Weldon L. Ricketts was coaching a youth team. Ricketts got involved, inquiring why the officers were beating Moore. Depending on whose testimony is given credit, Ricketts either approached the officers quickly or calmly, quietly or angrily shouting, "This is not right," and "Why are you doing this?" The ensuing physical struggle and the beating of Ricketts by police was described variously as well: "Either just as Ricketts arrived, or after an exchange with the officers, or after Ricketts was told or threatened repeatedly not to interfere with Moore's arrest, several officers turned upon Ricketts and wrestled him to the ground. While most of the witnesses testified that the officers beat Ricketts just as they were beating Moore (punching and kicking him, and hitting him with their nightsticks), one witness testified that Ricketts flailed his arms and kicked his legs in an effort to escape, and another suggested that the beating was less severe than Moore's and responded to Ricketts' struggling. In addition, one witness testified that the same officers who beat Moore were the ones who beat Ricketts, while others stated that perhaps one, two, or three of those officers were joined by other officers. Similarly, one witness testified that the officers beat Ricketts for about three minutes, while another stated that the officers beat him for two minutes, another for one minute, and yet another for twenty-five to thirty seconds while Ricketts struggled and resisted arrest.

"Witnesses also related that while Ricketts was being beaten, several officers crossed the street to the soccer field and verbally abused the onlooking crowd. [Officer Paul] Cherniack allegedly said '[y]ou people are such animals,' and another officer allegedly called one of the onlookers a 'black nigger bastard.' In addition, some of the witnesses testified that after Moore and Ricketts had been taken away, several officers performed 'high-fives,' that is, they slapped their palms against one another's."

Ricketts, who like Moore is black, filed a §1983 action against the City of Hartford and eleven police officers, all but one of whom are white, all of whose badge numbers he claimed to remember during the beating.

At trial Ricketts sought to introduce a tape recording of a radio transmission between the police dispatcher and the officers chasing Moore that contained the words, "Run him over." Ricketts contended Officer Rob Davis said the words, and "shortly thereafter became the chief aggressor against Ricketts." The trial court sustained the defendants' objection to the tape after listening to it in camera, holding that here was no authentication that it was Davis's voice saying the key words. (When the matter came up in Ricketts' post-trial motion for a new trial, the district court reiterated the lack of authentication of Davis's voice and also held that the tape was, in any event, "irrelevant to the question whether the police used excessive force against Ricketts.")

The jury found for the defendants, and Ricketts appealed. The Second Circuit Court of Appeals affirmed the verdict but held that the trial judge had not applied Rule 104(b) properly in deciding to exclude the tape recording. "The comparison of a tape-recorded voice and the voice of a witness is primarily a matter for the jury... The district court's determination that it 'was not satisfied that the voice on the tape was that of Davis,' is inconsistent with these principles. So long as a jury is entitled to reach a contrary conclusion, it must be given the opportunity to do so. The tape reveals that the dispatcher was engaged in an exchange with an officer who was pursuing Moore and identified himself as unit 124. At one point during the exchange, the dispatcher said '[d]on't give up Rob,' a probable reference to Rob Davis. A short time thereafter a voice said: 'Run him over.' Moreover, Ricketts testified that Davis said later at the hospital: '[I]f he had his way he wouldn't chase the kid [Moore], he ... would have run him over with the car.' Although we do not have the benefit of having heard Davis testify, given these facts, and that the jury did hear him testify, we believe that the district court erred in excluding the tape on authentication grounds without making a finding that no rational juror could have concluded that Davis made the statement at issue," the standard applicable under Rule 104(b). The court held the error to be harmless, however, in light of the vigorous cross-examination of Davis and the other officers, and that the jury was made aware that someone in the police department had said the offending words.

FRE 105 – Codefendant's Guilty Plea Not Admissible to Prove Accused's Guilt, But Is Admissible (With Limiting Instruction) on Question of Witness's Credibility

> **Rule 105. Limited Admissibility**
> When evidence which is admissible as to one party or for one purpose but not admissible as to another party or for another purpose is admitted, the court, upon request, shall restrict the evidence to its proper scope and instruct the jury accordingly.

GOVERNMENT OF THE VIRGIN ISLANDS v. MUJAHID
990 F.2d 111 (3d Cir. 1993)

Abdul Mujahid, also known as George Bennett, and Claudette Fielteau, his girlfriend, were charged with two counts of rape in the first degree in connection with an assault upon Mary Joe Bernard in September, 1991. Bernard, who knew the defendants, went out with them to an isolated beach in their truck. She testified that when Mujahid accused her of "making a move" on Fielteau, he threatened to drown her, raped her in the pickup's back seat, raped her again in deep water, then took her to his house where she showered and Fielteau gave her a change of clothes. Bernard said Fielteau helped undress her in the car and held one of her legs while Mujahid raped her.

Fielteau plead guilty to aiding and abetting an unlawful sexual contact and agreed to testify against Mujahid. At trial in the District Court of the Virgin Islands, she corroborated Bernard's testimony against Mujahid, although she testified she did not actually see Mujahid having sex with Bernard. Mujahid denied having sex with her. When the government was questioning Fielteau on direct examination, the matter of the plea agreement, her plea of guilty, and the pendency of her sentence were all explored. Mujahid's trial attorney did not object to the introduction of evidence of his co-defendant's plea of guilty. On appeal of his conviction, however, Mujahid argued the court should not have admitted testimony about Fielteau's guilty plea without a "cautionary" or limiting instruction.

The Third Circuit Court of Appeals held, "It is well-established that a co-defendant's guilty plea is not admissible to prove the defendant's guilt... However, a guilty plea may be admitted for other, permissible purposes, such as bringing to the jury's attention facts bearing upon a witness's credibility... We have held that a co-defendant's guilty plea is admissible, for example, to rebut a defense assertion that a witness was acting as a government agent when he engaged in the activities forming the basis of his guilty plea, ...to dampen anticipated attacks on the credibility of a government witness and foreclose any suggestion that the government was concealing evidence, ...and to respond to a defense attack on the credibility of a government witness.

"In this case, the government referred to Fielteau's guilty plea in its opening statement and elicited testimony from her regarding the plea during direct examination. The government never informed the district court of its reasons for introducing the guilty plea. Because the record lacks evidence of prosecutorial misconduct, we assume that the government had the sole legitimate motive that is possible on this record: to dampen an anticipated defense attack on Fielteau's credibility.

"While a co-defendant's guilty plea may be admissible on the issue of credibility, the district court must instruct the jury regarding the limited purpose for which that evidence may be used. An instruction is necessary because admission of a co-defendant's guilty plea can be extremely prejudicial to the defendant, given the natural human tendency to assume that if an aider and abettor is guilty, the principal must also be guilty. The instruction to the jury must deal precisely with the issue of how the guilty plea evidence can and cannot be used... At very least, the district court should instruct the jury that a co-defendant's guilty plea is no proof whatsoever of the defendant's guilt...

"The government argues that the district court gave a curative instruction to the jury. We disagree. The district court instructed the jury to be very cautious when evaluating the credibility of a witness who entered into a plea agreement because she might be motivated to lie... The court also instructed the jury never to convict a defendant based on the unsupported testimony of such a witness unless they believe it beyond a reasonable doubt. These instructions do not specifically address the evidentiary use of Fielteau's guilty plea. The jury was never informed that Fielteau's guilty plea could not be considered evidence of Mujahid's guilt. We therefore cannot regard the instruction as curative.

"The district court erred by allowing the jury to be informed of the guilty plea without a cautionary instruction. However, because the defendant's trial counsel failed to object or to request a cautionary instruction, we can reverse only if the district court committed plain error,"[10] which it did not find.

Although the Rule speaks of there being a "request" for a limiting instruction, this case demonstrates that sometimes such an instruction is treated as mandatory, even if not requested.

FRE 106 – If Court Admits Incriminating Portions of Tape Recordings, Exculpatory Portions Should in Fairness Be Admitted Too, Regardless of Other Rules Excluding Them from Evidence

> **Rule 106. Remainder of or Related Writings or Recorded Statements**
>
> When a writing or recorded statement or part thereof is introduced by a party, an adverse party may require the introduction at that time of any other part or any other writing or recorded statement which ought in fairness to be considered contemporaneously with it.

UNITED STATES v. SUTTON
801 F.2d 1346 (D.C. Cir. 1986)

Robert Sutton, in the business of reselling crude oil, and Mark Sucher, an employee of the U.S. Department of Energy, were convicted along with several others in a complex scheme to bribe federal officials to obstruct a DOE investigation of Sutton's companies for noncompliance with price regulations and to obtain confidential information about DOE settlement negotiations. Sutton was sentenced to four

---

[10] See FRE 103(a)(1), Fed. R. Crim.P. 52(b).

years' imprisonment, five years' probation and to pay a $105,000 fine, and Sucher got two years in prison, three years' probation, and a $15,000 fine. They appealed.

One issue raised in Sucher's appeal concerned conversations he had with other conspirators that were taped. The government introduced portions of the tapes in which Sucher is heard discussing his potential criminal exposure, revealing his "consciousness of guilt." Sucher sought to admit other portions of the same tapes under Rule 106, the "rule of completeness." Those portions show Sucher saying he is unsure what two other participants in the scheme know or might tell investigators, that he has "always had a history of cooperating with people," that he "certainly never took any money from Shelley," i.e., Shelley Kolbert, a DOE Office of Special Counsel administrator, and that he doesn't "know if I'm in trouble or not." The district court had excluded these portions as inadmissible hearsay, "exculpatory extra-judicial statements as to a past fact."

The District of Columbia Circuit Court of Appeals considered the question to pose more properly a Rule 106 issue even if the evidence was plainly inadmissible under other rules: "Rule 106 can adequately fulfill its function only by permitting the admission of some otherwise inadmissible evidence when the court finds in fairness that the proffered evidence should be considered contemporaneously. A contrary construction raises the specter of distorted and misleading trials, and creates difficulties for both litigants and the trial court."

The appellate court observed, "Rule 106 explicitly changes the normal order of proof in requiring that such evidence must be 'considered contemporaneously' with the evidence already admitted." As to procedure and sequencing, the court noted, "the most sensible course is to allow the prosecution to introduce the inculpatory statements. The defense can then argue to the court that the statements are misleading because of a lack of context, after which the court can, in its discretion, permit such limited portions to be contemporaneously introduced as will remove the distortion that otherwise would accompany the prosecution's evidence. Such a result is more efficient and comprehensible, and is consonant with the requirement" of Rule 102 that the Rules be construed to promote fairness, efficiency, and growth of the law of evidence. "Moreover, under this approach the trial court can focus solely on issues of distortion and timing as mandated by Rule 106. The trial court has a wide range of discretion to expeditiously structure the inquiry, as the judge did in this case by requiring Sucher's attorney to point to specific passages of the transcript that ought to have been admitted to avert the distorting effect of the portions already introduced by the government. In addition, the provision of Rule 106 grounding admission on 'fairness' reasonably should be interpreted to incorporate the common-law requirements that the evidence be relevant, and be necessary to qualify or explain the already introduced evidence allegedly taken out of context."

In a model of judicial thoroughness, the D.C. Circuit panel then undertook an analysis of the statements on the tape Sucher had proffered in order to provide a fair counterweight to the statements that the government had admitted: "...Sucher's defense was that he innocently gave Kolbert the documents without any knowledge of illegality. Three of the four excluded statements would support an inference consistent with that defense. The second statement could have supported Sucher's assertion that he provided documents to

Kolbert out of a desire to cooperate with his fellow employee at DOE. The first and fourth statements would have supported an inference contrary to the government's contention that Sucher exhibited consciousness of his guilt. The possible contrary inference... is that Sucher gave documents innocently, and was afraid that Kolbert may have falsely told Maxwell that Sucher, as the source of the documents, was a knowing and willing participant in the illegal conspiracy.

"The excluded statements would have partially rebutted the government's use of the recordings, and were relevant to Sucher's defense. Since this was a criminal case Sucher had a constitutional right not to testify, and it was thus necessary for Sucher to rebut the government's inference with the excluded portions of these recordings... Under our analysis of Federal Rule of Evidence 106, Sucher should have been permitted to introduce these four portions of the recorded conversation with Peacock if considerations of 'fairness' justified contemporaneous admission and consideration."

(However, the appellate court concluded, following another analysis that is a model of thoroughness, that the judgment was not substantially swayed by the error, and affirmed the conviction.)

CHAPTER TWO
Article II – Judicial Notice

FRE 201(b) – Court Can Take Judicial Notice of Official Census Bureau Statistics

> **Rule 201. Judicial Notice of Adjudicative Facts**
> *(b) Kinds of Facts.* A judicially noticed fact must be one not subject to reasonable dispute in that it is either (1) generally known within the territorial jurisdiction of the trial court or (2) capable of accurate and ready determination by resort to sources whose accuracy cannot reasonably be questioned.
> *(c) When Discretionary.* A court may take judicial notice, whether requested or not.
> *(d) When Mandatory.* A court shall take judicial notice if requested by a party and supplied with the necessary information.

BARBER v. PONTE
772 F.2d 982 (1st Cir. 1985)

In his habeas corpus petition, James Barber argued that he was denied a constitutional right to an impartial jury because "young adults" were being systematically excluded from his Massachusetts state court jury venire. He had been charged with possessing marijuana, hypodermic needles and syringes while a prisoner at the Massachusetts Correctional Institution in Norfolk. His six-person jury convicted him of all the charges except marijuana possession. (Two members of the jury were under age 35.)

The U.S. District Court for the District of Massachusetts denied Barber relief. The First Circuit Court of Appeals granted certificate of probable cause. In its first decision, although the three-judge panel found Barber had made out a prima facie case that young adults were a "cognizable" or "distinctive" group in society, that the group was unfairly under-represented in jury venires generally, and that the under-representation was due to their systematic exclusion in the jury-selection process (these facts found mostly, in fact, by summary judicial notice), it remanded for updated data on the specific community Barber was tried in.

On rehearing *en banc* the First Circuit changed direction entirely. Taking judicial notice under Rule 201 of official statistics from the U.S. Bureau of the Census 1982-3 Statistical Abstract of the United States, the panel found too many disparities among 18-to-34-year-olds for them to be a distinctive or cognizable group. Census data revealed "meaningful contrasts in such social indicators as their marital and divorce rates, school enrollment and educational attainment, economic status, employment rate, criminality, experience in such matters as service in the armed forces in time of war or even in peacetime, mental health, attitude towards such important social issues as abortion, and participation in the political processes, and in the ownership of capital property. Such differences emphasize the inappropriateness of grouping potently dissimilar age categories..." There being no cognizable group to be under-represented, the habeas corpus petition was turned down.

FRE 201(b) – Judge's Unique Personal Knowledge of Fact Not Commonly Known Does Not Make Fact Admissible Under Judicial Notice

> **Rule 201. Judicial Notice of Adjudicative Facts**
> *(b) Kinds of Facts.* A judicially noticed fact must be one not subject to reasonable dispute in that it is either (1) generally known within the territorial jurisdiction of the trial court or (2) capable of accurate and ready determination by resort to sources whose accuracy cannot reasonably be questioned.

GRISWOLD v. COMMONWEALTH
453 S.E.2d 287, 19 Va. App. 477 (1995)

Norman Edward Griswold was convicted in Circuit Court for Richmond, Virginia, of driving under the influence of alcohol after having been previously convicted of the same offense.

Under Virginia law only prior offenses where the accused was represented by counsel may be used as "predicate" offenses. Griswold had been convicted in 1983 of driving under the influence, but had not been represented, and so the trial court barred use of that prior in the guilt phase of his current trial. He had been convicted again in 1985, but the warrant used as an exhibit in Griswold's trial to establish the 1985 conviction did not have the "attorney present" box checked, and contained illegible handwriting there. The warrant did indicate that Griswold had pled guilty "per p/a." The trial judge said this meant "a plea agreement. So he was represented."

Griswold appealed to the Virginia Court of Appeals, which reversed his conviction, saying that, in effect, the trial judge had taken judicial notice "that the Commonwealth Attorney's Office would not have entered into a plea agreement with an unrepresented defendant. Virginia's common law of evidence treats judicial notice in very much the same way as Federal Rule 201(b) does: judicial notice can be taken of facts which are either common knowledge or easily ascertainable by reference to reliable sources. The existence of a plea agreement as precluding a defendant being unrepresented was held to be neither of those: "The record contains no indication [of anything that] prohibits a prosecutor from entering into a plea agreement with an unrepresented defendant..." The appellate court held that, "Where the fact judicially noticed is not a fact universally regarded as established by common notoriety, it is irrelevant that the judge may have personal knowledge of such a practice."[1]

---

[1] But see, e.g., *United States v. Wiseman, infra* p. 203, where a trial judge in Massachusetts took judicial notice that "junk" is a "common synonym for heroin in New York and Boston."

CHAPTER THREE
Article III – Presumptions in Civil Actions and Proceedings

FRE 301 – In Absence of Evidence to the Contrary, Presumption of Official Regularity Requires That IRS Deficiency Notice Be Presumed Valid

> **Rule 301. Presumptions in General in Civil Actions and Proceedings**
> In all civil actions and proceedings not otherwise provided for by Act of Congress or by these rules, a presumption imposes on the party against whom it is directed the burden of going forward with evidence to rebut or meet the presumption, but does not shift to such party the burden of proof in the sense of the risk of nonpersuasion, which remains throughout the trial upon the party on whom it was originally cast.

UNITED STATES v. AHRENS
530 F.2d 781 (8th Cir. 1976)

The government sued Edward Ahrens to reduce to judgment an unpaid tax assessment of more than $152,000 for 1961. Ahrens was in Vietnam in June 1966 when the IRS statutory notice of deficiency was mailed to his Columbia, S.C. attorney, E.L. McGowan, to whom Ahrens had given a formal power of attorney some months earlier. McGowan wrote the Appellate Branch Office of the IRS regarding the June letter, asking that the matter "be held in abeyance" until Ahrens' return to the United States. Neither McGowan nor the IRS could produce the notice during discovery, and both Ahrens and the government moved for summary judgment. The district court granted Ahrens' motion and dismissed the case. The government appealed.

On appeal to the Eight Circuit Court of Appeals, two issues were presented regarding the operation of legal presumptions. The first concerned whether the notice had been mailed to Ahrens. The district court found that sufficient evidence existed to conclude that the IRS had mailed the notice to Ahrens. The appellate court found "as a matter of law" that the IRS established, through Post Office Form 3877, which recorded the mailing of the notice to Ahrens, that the form had been mailed. The court also held that the fact was also established through McGowan's letter and deposition testimony. "The government was not required to produce an affidavit of the IRS employee who completed the specific form in question." Completion of the postal form itself sets up a strong presumption that the mailing procedure had been complied with.

The second issue was probably the stickier of the two presumption issues: did the contents of the notice comply with statutory requirements? Because copies of the notice itself could not be produced, the district court held that the government "failed to sustain its burden of proving that a valid notice was sent." The Eighth Circuit panel reversed the grant of summary judgment in favor of Ahrens, and remanded for entry of summary judgment for the government. (Ahrens' only defense involved the sufficiency of the notice and its having been mailed.) The court said, "In our view, the presumption of official regularity controls the question of the validity of the notice of deficiency. The presumption of regularity supports the official acts of public officers and, in the absence of clear evidence to the contrary, courts presume that they have properly discharged their official duties.... A corollary to the general rule may be stated as follows:... All necessary prerequisites to the validity of official action are presumed to have been complied with, and... where the contrary is asserted it must be affirmatively shown....

"In the instant case it would be unreasonable to presume that the IRS employee who drafted the statutory notice failed to perform the ministerial function of properly recording the assessed amount and the taxable year involved. All other steps in the notification process were properly accomplished. In the absence of any rebuttal proof, we are bound to presume the validity of the contents of the statutory notice of deficiency."

Citing Rule 301 (albeit in a footnote) the court noted that the presumption of official regularity "shifted the burden of going forward with the evidence [of the notice's insufficiency or defect] to the taxpayer.... Since the taxpayer produced no evidence rebutting the presumption, the only permissible inference from the circumstances is that the notice of deficiency was valid. We hold that the district judge was required to draw that inference as a matter of law."

FRE 301 – Once Presumption of Receipt of Notice of Deadline for Filing Bankruptcy Claim Is Rebutted by Testimony of Non-Receipt, Presumption Retains No Probative Effect

> **Rule 301. Presumptions in General in Civil Actions and Proceedings**
> In all civil actions and proceedings not otherwise provided for by Act of Congress or by these rules, a presumption imposes on the party against whom it is directed the burden of going forward with evidence to rebut or meet the presumption, but does not shift to such party the burden of proof in the sense of the risk of nonpersuasion, which remains throughout the trial upon the party on whom it was originally cast.

IN RE THE YODER COMPANY
758 F.2d 1114 (6th Cir. 1985)

Mark S. Bratton had a product liability suit pending against The Yoder Company in a Michigan state court for the loss of four fingers, when Yoder in 1981 filed a petition for reorganization under Chapter 11 of the Bankruptcy Code in the United States District Court for the Northern District of Ohio. "Bratton's claim was listed as a 'contingent, unliquidated and disputed' claim in the amended schedule of assets and liabilities filed by Yoder. The Bankruptcy Court issued an order setting July 13, 1981 as the last date for creditors to file proofs of claim against Yoder (the 'bar date'). Bratton filed a proof of claim on March 15, 1982, about eight months after the bar date. Yoder applied to the Bankruptcy Court for an order expunging certain products liability claims, including Bratton's" which the court granted. Bratton insisted that he (and his law firm) had not received the requested notice of the "bar date," so should not have his claim dismissed. The Sixth Circuit Court of Appeals held in favor of Bratton's appeal, observing, "A creditor's knowledge that a reorganization of the debtor is taking place does not substitute for mailing notice of a bar date." The appellate panel found the Bankruptcy Court's unexplained finding that notice had been received, despite Bratton's and his lawyer's testimony of nonreceipt, was an abuse of discretion. The court held that "testimony of non-receipt, standing alone, would be sufficient to support a finding of non-receipt; such testimony is therefore sufficient to rebut the presumption of receipt."

The appellate court then engaged in a thoughtful review of the legislative history of Rule 301 and its common law sources as it tried to determine whether a "presumption, once rebutted, retains any effect" in establishing the fact contested – here the mailing of the notice of the bar date for claims. "A brief review of the history of this rule will aid in evaluating the Bankruptcy Court's reasoning. Before adoption of the Federal Rules of Evidence there were two major theories concerning the effect of a presumption once rebuttal evidence is admitted. Under the Thayer or 'bursting bubble' theory a presumption vanishes entirely once rebutted, and the question must be decided as any ordinary question of fact. Under a later theory, proposed by Morgan, a presumption shifts the burden of proving the nonexistence of the presumed fact to the opposing party.

"The version of Rule 301 that was proposed by the Advisory Committee, accepted by the Supreme Court, and submitted to Congress adopted the Morgan view. That rule, however, was not enacted by Congress. The Advisory Committee notes, on which the Bankruptcy Court relied, that reject the 'bursting bubble' theory pertain to the proposed rule, which was not enacted, and are thus of little help in interpreting the final rule.

"The House of Representatives adopted a rule espousing an intermediate view, which would allow a rebutted presumption to be considered evidence of the fact presumed. See H.R.Report No. 93-650, House Committee on the Judiciary, U.S.Code Cong. & Admin.News 1974, p. 7051. The Senate criticized the House rule on the ground that it made no sense to call a presumption evidence, and adopted the present language of Rule 301, which was adopted by the Conference Committee and enacted into law. See S.Report No. 93-1277, Senate Committee on the Judiciary; H.R. Report No.93-1597, Conference Committee, U.S.Code Cong. & Admin.News 1974, p.7051.

"Most commentators have concluded that Rule 301 as enacted embodies the Thayer or 'bursting bubble' approach. *See, e.g., 10 Moore's Federal Practice* §301.04[4.-1] (2d ed.); 1 *Weinstein's Evidence* 301-12; IX *Wigmore on Evidence* §2493h (Chadbourn rev. 1981). *Contra* 21 C. Wright & K. Graham, *Federal Practice and Procedure* §§ 5121, 5122, 5126. At least two other circuit courts have expressly agreed. *Reeves v. General Foods Corp.*, 682 F.2d 515, 522 n. 10 (5th Cir. 1982); *Legille v. Dann*, 544 F.2d 1, 6-7 (D.C.Cir.1976). The Thayer view is consistent with the language of Rule 301, which provides only that a presumption shifts 'the burden of going forward with evidence to rebut or meet the presumption.' Accordingly, we hold that a presumption under Rule 301 has no probative effect once rebutted. The Bankruptcy Court therefore erred in considering the presumption as evidence of receipt."

FRE 302 – Presumption in Diversity Wrongful Death Case as to Decedent's Exercise of Due Care Is Governed by State Law

> **Rule 302. Applicability of State Law in Civil Actions and Proceedings**
>
> In civil actions and proceedings, the effect of a presumption respecting a fact which is an element of a claim or defense as to which State law supplies the rule of decision is determined in accordance with State law.

MONGER v. CESSNA AIRCRAFT COMPANY
812 F.2d 402 (8th Cir. 1987)

Kevin and Anita Monger died when the Cessna 210-J aircraft Kevin Monger was piloting crashed on approach to Lee's Summit, Missouri. Their children filed a wrongful death suit against Cessna Aircraft Company under Missouri's statute. The suit was filed in federal district court for the Western District of Missouri because of diversity of citizenship, and alleged negligent design as well as strict liability, claiming undetected water in the fuel line caused the crash.

A three-week trial resulted in a verdict for Cessna, which contended Monger had run out of gas after failing to do a routine preflight inspection of the plane, including physically checking the fuel tank using a ladder. Evidence showed Monger had not used a ladder or physically checked the fuel level. Both plaintiff's and defendant's theories of the case were supported by some evidence, including expert testimony. Mongers appealed, arguing, among several theories, that the court erred in refusing to instruct the jury that Kevin Monger "was presumed to have exercised due care, in the absence of direct or persuasive circumstantial evidence that a proper pre-flight inspection was not performed."

The Eighth Circuit Court of Appeals affirmed, holding that under Rule 302, in a diversity case "the effect of presumptions is a substantive question, requiring application of state law." Under Missouri law, "slight circumstances" are all that is necessary to "overthrow" the presumption of due care. "In the present case, the district court concluded that the applicable [Missouri] law [under Rule 302] did not support a presumption of due care instruction because there was circumstantial evidence that Kevin Monger did not conduct a proper pre-flight inspection of the aircraft's fuel supply or for water in the fuel. We agree with the district court that circumstantial evidence of the decedent's negligence may be enough to deprive the plaintiff of an instruction on the presumption of due care... The testimony that Kevin Monger did not conduct a proper pre-flight inspection before leaving R & B Aircraft, and that he did not have a ladder with which to conduct a pre-flight inspection outside of the airport restaurant, support the inference that no such inspection occurred. This was direct and circumstantial evidence of Kevin's negligence in operating the plane. We thus hold that the district court did not err in refusing to instruct the jury on the presumption of due care, because there was sufficient 'contrary proof' to rebut any such presumption."

CHAPTER FOUR
Article IV – Relevancy and Its Limits

FRE 401 – Sufficiency of Relevance for Admissibility
Depends Upon Identification of Issue for Which Evidence Is Offered

> **Rule 401. Definition of "Relevant Evidence"**
> "Relevant evidence" means evidence having any tendency to make the existence of any fact that is of consequence to the determination of the action more probable or less probable than it would be without the evidence.

KNAPP v. STATE
79 N.E. 1076, 168 Ind. 153 (1907)

John Knapp tried to prove self-defense in his trial for first degree murder by testifying that he had reason to fear the deceased. He said he had heard from some unspecified people that the victim, the marshal of Hagerstown, had clubbed an old man while arresting him, and that the old man had died.[1]

On rebuttal the prosecution was permitted over objection to call the physician who had treated the old man in question. The doctor testified the old man had died of senility and alcoholism, with no physical signs of a beating present. Knapp contended that the sole fact in issue in his claim of self-defense was whether Knapp had heard the story, not whether it was true or false, so that it was irrelevant what had actually taken place. Upon his conviction, he renewed this argument on appeal.

The Indiana Supreme Court affirmed the admissibility of the doctor's testimony, holding that it was relevant to the issue of whether Knapp actually had heard the story he claimed to have heard. The testimony was not conclusive, but evidence is not required to be conclusive in order to be admissible. The court's explanation is memorable: "…Somewhere between the fact and the testimony there was a person who was not a truth speaker." Since Knapp couldn't (wouldn't?) identify his informant, the doctor's testimony "had a tendency to render his claim as to what he heard less probable…." This "tendency" to make a fact more or less "probable" is a direct antecedent of language found today in Rule 401, and is the sole threshold in determining logical relevance.

---

[1] This was not hearsay because Knapp was not offering the statement for its truth – see FRE 801(c).

FRE 401 – Prosecution May Not Use Accused's Failure to Call Witness to Suggest That Witness's Testimony Would Have Been Unfavorable

> **Rule 401. Definition of "Relevant Evidence"**
> "Relevant evidence" means evidence having any tendency to make the existence of any fact that is of consequence to the determination of the action more probable or less probable than it would be without the evidence.

STATE v. BREWER
505 A.2d 774 (Me. 1985)

Ricky Brewer admitted at his trial on charges of driving while intoxicated that he was intoxicated as alleged (his blood alcohol level was .21%). He testified, however, that he had not operated the motor vehicle, which was registered to his roommate, Andrew Pratt. Brewer said he and Pratt had been drinking together at a bar in Lewiston, that Pratt drove when they left together, and that when he awoke in the truck after the accident Pratt had left the scene. A Maine State Police trooper testified that when Pratt came to pick up Brewer, Pratt said that he had not used the truck that night but had gone to bed and left the truck keys on a table. Pratt was not called as a witness.

The case was tried without a jury. The Livermore Falls district judge hearing the case commented, "The court does have the right to infer, that if someone else was operating this car, as the defendant contends, then that someone, Mr. Pratt, is the party who would be his – Brewer's best alibi witness. He's not here today... obviously he's the witness who might clear him of this charge." The court then found Brewer guilty.

Brewer appealed and the verdict was affirmed by the Androscoggin County Superior Court. On appeal to the Supreme Judicial Court of Maine, Brewer's argument centered on the sufficiency of the evidence, specifically that the trial judge was in error when he drew an inference of guilt from Brewer's failure to call Pratt as a witness.

The Maine Supreme Court reversed the conviction. Under modern evidentiary rules, the mere calling of a witness does not amount to a party's "vouching" for the Witness's credibility.[2] The "missing-witness inference," that failure to call a witness who might corroborate a party's story can be treated as a fact of significance itself – "that the missing Witness's testimony would be unfavorable since otherwise the party would have called the witness and vouched for him" – is not justified under modern practice. It is especially unjustified when it is sought to be applied against an accused, who has no burden of producing evidence. "Since neither party vouches for any Witness's credibility, the failure of a party to call a witness cannot be treated as an evidentiary fact that permits any inference as to the content of the testimony of that witness." Any inference about Pratt's testimony would be highly speculative, and the fact of his absence must be, essentially, ignored.

---

[2] See FRE 607, under which a witness may be impeached by the party calling him. Maine's Rule 607 is identical to the Federal Rule.

FRE 401, 403 – To Be Relevant, Evidence Must Have Sufficient Probative Value to Overcome Likelihood of Misleading Jury

> **401. Definition of "Relevant Evidence"**
> "Relevant evidence" means evidence having any tendency to make the existence of any fact that is of consequence to the determination of the action more probable or less probable than it would be without the evidence.
>
> **Rule 403. Exclusion of Relevant Evidence on Grounds of Prejudice, Confusion, or Waste of Time**
> Although relevant, evidence may be excluded if its probative value is substantially outweighed by the danger of unfair prejudice, confusion of the issues, or misleading the jury, or by considerations of undue delay, waste of time, or needless presentation of cumulative evidence.

STATE v. KOTSIMPULOS
411 A.2d 79 (Me. 1980)

After experiencing "unexplained disappearances of meat," the Hannaford Brothers meat plant in South Portland, Maine was put under police surveillance. One morning Peter Kotsimpulos, a Hannaford employee, was twice observed entering the plant and returning to his car. He was arrested and found to have five pork tenderloins in his coat pocket, which corresponded to the amount of meat missing from the plant that morning. Kotsimpulos said he didn't know where the tenderloins had come from, but said he found them on his car floor and put them in his pocket thinking they were a package of meat he had bought somewhere.

At trial Kotsimpulos attempted to introduce testimony that a supervisor named Carver had threatened Kotsimpulos that he was going to make Kotsimpulos lose his job, to support the apparent defense theory that Carver had planted the meat in Kotsimpulos' car. The trial judge refused to allow the testimony under Maine Rules of Evidence 401 and 403, identical to the federal rules of the same number. Kotsimpulos was convicted by a jury, and appealed.

On appeal, the Maine Supreme Court upheld Kotsimpulos' conviction. As Carver was neither a party nor a witness, his alleged animosity toward Kotsimpulos was not relevant to any issue of his credibility. Carver had not participated in the surveillance or arrest of Kotsimpulos, and no other evidence remotely connected Carver to the meat found on Kotsimpulos' person. The appellate court held that "the probative value of the threat was too slight to warrant the risk of confusing the jury."

FRE 401 – For Nonoccurrence of Accidents at Same and Similar Locations to Be Admissible as Similar Happenings, Situations Must Be Sufficiently Similar

> **Rule 401. Definition of "Relevant Evidence"**
> "Relevant evidence" means evidence having any tendency to make the existence of any fact that is of consequence to the determination of the action more probable or less probable than it would be without the evidence.

HIGGINS v. HICKS CO.
756 F.2d 681 (8th Cir. 1985)

Two separate motorcycle accidents along a highway construction site on I-90 in South Dakota killed Steven Martinez and injured Mallard Teal. (Linda Higgins was Personal Representative for the estate of Martinez.) The Hicks Company had resurfaced the passing lane of eastbound I-90 leaving about a ¾-inch ridge up from the driving lane over a 5.4-mile stretch of highway. Both cyclists lost control of their bikes on the ridge.

Higgins and Teal sued Hicks and the State of South Dakota, alleging negligence in opening both eastbound lanes along that 5.4-mile distance without adequate warning signs. Defendants denied negligence and said Martinez and Teal were contributorily negligent, primarily in operating their motorcycles faster than was reasonable. The jury returned a verdict for defendants.

Plaintiffs appealed, arguing (among several grounds) that it was error for the trial court to admit evidence that no prior accidents had occurred along the segment in question or at other sites where similar lane differentials existed. To the extent notice was an issue, the Eighth Circuit held the evidence of the nonoccurrence of prior accidents was "relevant to the question of defendants' knowledge of the existence of any dangerous condition." The court stopped short of saying the absence of other accidents amounted to substantive evidence that the site was safe. Most jurisdictions will, however, admit evidence both of the occurrence of other accidents to show a dangerous condition and of the nonoccurrence of other accidents to show safe conditions, provided that sufficient similarity is shown between those situations and the case in question.

FRE 401, 403 – Relevance of Other Claims Made by Plaintiff Depends on Their Similarity to Current Claim

> **401. Definition of "Relevant Evidence"**
> "Relevant evidence" means evidence having any tendency to make the existence of any fact that is of consequence to the determination of the action more probable or less probable than it would be without the evidence.
>
> **Rule 403. Exclusion of Relevant Evidence on Grounds of Prejudice, Confusion, or Waste of Time**
> Although relevant, evidence may be excluded if its probative value is substantially outweighed by the danger of unfair prejudice, confusion of the issues, or misleading the jury, or by considerations of undue delay, waste of time, or needless presentation of cumulative evidence.

BUNION v. ALLSTATE INSURANCE CO.
502 F. Supp. 340 (E. D. Pa. 1980)

Levi Bunion filed a claim against Allstate for injuries he allegedly suffered to his chest, back, and internal organs in 1976 when his car was rear-ended by another vehicle. Allstate resisted, suggesting the claim was fraudulent. Allstate filed a motion *in limine*[3] asking to be allowed to present evidence at trial that Bunion had filed claims arising out of seven other accidents over the past nine years. Three were falls in his home in 1971, one was a rear-end collision in 1974, and three were apparently of an unspecified nature in 1972, 1977 and 1979, one of which may have involved a car accident.

In ruling on the motion, the trial court summarized the applicable law on the admissibility of other claims: they would be admissible if they were similar in nature and/or fraudulent. Here Allstate produced no direct proof of fraud, and the claims were not sufficiently similar to one another to set up a permissible inference of the "improbability of chance repetitions of similar accidents to the same person." In a pre-trial Memorandum and Order the court denied Allstate's motion and held evidence of the seven other claims inadmissible.

---
[3] That is, a motion made just before the start of trial. Motions *in limine* are more commonly used to request the exclusion of evidence, but as this case demonstrates, they can be also used to request permission to admit evidence.

FRE 401, 403 – For Similar Accidents Involving Same Product to Be Admissible They Must Implicate the Same Theory of Causation

> **401. Definition of "Relevant Evidence"**
>
> "Relevant evidence" means evidence having any tendency to make the existence of any fact that is of consequence to the determination of the action more probable or less probable than it would be without the evidence.
>
> **Rule 403. Exclusion of Relevant Evidence on Grounds of Prejudice, Confusion, or Waste of Time**
>
> Although relevant, evidence may be excluded if its probative value is substantially outweighed by the danger of unfair prejudice, confusion of the issues, or misleading the jury, or by considerations of undue delay, waste of time, or needless presentation of cumulative evidence.

PONDER v. WARREN TOOL CORP.
834 F.2d 1553 (10th Cir. 1987)

In December, 1979 a snow tire blew up as Wichita auto-body shop owner Bobby Ponder was trying to mount it using a Ken-Tool Bead Seater manufactured by Patch Rubber Co. and marketed by Warren Tool Corp. "The explosion propelled the tire upward and blew Ponder back several feet, virtually severing his hand from his arm." Ponder sued Patch and Warren Tool, claiming defects in the design and manufacture of the bead seater, failure to warn and negligence.

At trial Ponder attempted to introduce evidence of two other accidents involving tires exploding on mounting machines associated with Patch. The trial court ruled the other incidents were too dissimilar, and said they would be confusing, prejudicial and misleading. The jury found in favor of Patch and Warren Tool, and Ponder appealed, raising among several issues the matter of the other explosions.

The Tenth Circuit Court of Appeals found the incidents insufficiently similar too, upholding the trial court's ruling (although reversing on other grounds). "The claimed defect [here] was the failure of the bead seater to properly disengage," the appellate panel noted, while the tire explosions in the other incidents took place during tire inflation. Citing other cases and Weinstein's treatise, the court summarized the degree of similarity a plaintiff needs to prove: "If dangerousness is the issue [as it was in Ponder's case] a high degree of similarity will be essential... If the accident is offered to prove notice, a lack of exact similarity to conditions will not cause exclusion provided the accident was of a kind which should have served to warn the defendant." Here the tire explosions offered by Ponder were only "superficially" similar to the one that injured him, actually invoking different theories of causation and thus different bases for liability. "We find no error in the ruling that they were not substantially similar."

FRE 401, 403 – Evidence of Lack of Prior Claims Against Manufacturer of Product Is Admissible to Prove Both Lack of Defective Design and Lack of Notice

> **401. Definition of "Relevant Evidence"**
> "Relevant evidence" means evidence having any tendency to make the existence of any fact that is of consequence to the determination of the action more probable or less probable than it would be without the evidence.
>
> **Rule 403. Exclusion of Relevant Evidence on Grounds of Prejudice, Confusion, or Waste of Time**
> Although relevant, evidence may be excluded if its probative value is substantially outweighed by the danger of unfair prejudice, confusion of the issues, or misleading the jury, or by considerations of undue delay, waste of time, or needless presentation of cumulative evidence.

HINES v. JOY MANUFACTURING CO.
850 F.2d 1146 (6th Cir. 1988)

In an underground Peabody Coal Company mine in Kentucky on August 8, 1983, Carl Hines was pinned to the coal mine wall by the belt structure of a mobile bridge unit. He sustained crippling leg and hip injuries. He sued Joy Manufacturing Company, maker of the continuous miner machine that jackknifed, and Long-Airdox Company, maker of the attached continuous haulage system that Peabody yoked to the continuous miner. Hines' theories of liability were negligence, strict liability, breach of warranty and defective design and manufacture of the continuous miner and the continuous haulage system, also known as a mobile bridge unit.

Joy was granted summary judgment on the basis of a Kentucky statute that provides that the original manufacturer of a product is not liable for injuries the product causes if it has been modified; Joy's continuous miner was designed to be used with shuttle cars, and Joy appears to have played no role in the attachment of the continuous haulage system to its continuous miner. At trial Long-Airdox was permitted over Hines' objection to introduce evidence that with some 200 sets of similar equipment sold since the late 1950s, there had been no prior claims against Long-Airdox. The jury returned a verdict in favor of Long-Airdox. Hines appealed.

The Sixth Circuit Court of Appeals affirmed, holding that evidence of a lack of prior claims was admissible to show either the absence of a defective design or the defendant's lack of notice of any defect or both. The appellate court found no particular prejudice associated with the evidence of a lack of accidents the way evidence of another accident can sometimes "arouse the prejudice of a jury." No specific showing of unfair prejudice was made by Hines, so the trial court did not abuse its discretion in admitting the evidence.

FRE 401 – Nonprosecution of Insured for Arson Is Inadmissible in Action for Recovery of Insurance Proceeds

> **401. Definition of "Relevant Evidence"**
>
> "Relevant evidence" means evidence having any tendency to make the existence of any fact that is of consequence to the determination of the action more probable or less probable than it would be without the evidence.

KELLY'S AUTO PARTS, NO.1, INC. v. BOUGHTON
809 F.2d 1247 (6th Cir. 1987)

Three cases were consolidated for appeal when each presented a similar relevance issue nestled among a few others.

In the first, Kelly's Auto Parts was heavily damaged in a November 1982 fire. Its president and sole stockholder, Cynthia McCabe, had the business insured with Lloyd's of London (Barry Boughton was an underwriter) for $190,000. McCabe's claim on the policy for over $166,000 in losses was denied by Lloyd's, which claimed Kelly's had set or arranged the fire deliberately. Kelly's sued for breach of its policy. There was evidence presented at trial that the cause of the fire was arson, that gasoline (which McCabe said she did not store in the building) could be smelled in the building after the fire, that there were no signs of forced entry. At the time of the fire, the business, which was losing money and way behind in federal withholding taxes, was shut down pending a sale to Discount Tire for $125,000. The jury returned a verdict for the insurer. Kelly's appealed.

In the second, the Muskegon, Michigan home of Gene and Hazel Roberts was partially destroyed in a February 1982 fire. State Farm Fire and Casualty denied their claim, saying they had set the fire or hired it set by others. Two kids were seen running from the scene of the fire; the blaze was set in three different spots. Hazel Roberts was already living in Texas; when Gene Roberts left the house that day for Texas he did not drop a key off with a neighbor as was his custom. After the fire, both front doors of the house were found to be open and unlocked. No sign of forced entry was found. The Roberts said they had experienced threats of violence against them on several occasions, and had once reported a breaking and entering. The jury in this trial found for the Roberts for $65,690, and State Farm appealed.

In the third case consolidated in this appeal, the China Boy Restaurant in Allen Park, Michigan burned in May 1983. Yet Foo Wong, the owner, had insured the business for $432,500 with Travelers' Insurance Co., which denied Wong's claim, alleging Wong gave the arsonist a key. Wong had been in "extremely poor" financial condition before the fire, with total debts (including delinquent property and sales taxes) running to more than $300,000. The jury found for Travelers', and Wong appealed.

The common thread in the three cases is that in each case the owner whose premises burned was not prosecuted criminally for arson, and that fact became an issue in their trials. In *Kelly's,* the district court granted Lloyd's motion *in limine* to bar any evidence that no one connected with the auto parts business was ever charged with arson. In

Roberts the plaintiffs were allowed over State Farm's objection to introduce evidence that there was no physical evidence connecting Gene Roberts to the fire, and that he was not charged with arson, and Roberts' counsel made a fairly big deal out of the fact in opening statement and closing argument. In *Wong*, the owner's nonprosecution for arson was barred from evidence by pretrial order in response to Travelers' motion *in limine*.

On the consolidated appeal, the Sixth Circuit Court of Appeals affirmed *Kelly's* and *Wong* and reversed *Roberts* on the admissibility of the insured not having been criminally charged or prosecuted for arson. Citing a couple of Third Circuit cases and McCormick's treatise, the appellate panel held that just as a criminal acquittal is inadmissible in a civil proceeding arising out of the same facts, so is nonprosecution. The burden of persuasion is far higher in a criminal case, and nonprosecution may represent nothing so much as the prosecutor's opinion – and not necessarily that the insured is innocent, either. "Perhaps a decision had been reached that definitive proof, 'beyond a reasonable doubt' was lacking, or it is certainly possible that the county's investigative procedures had proven inconclusive or, in the alternative, were still underway."[4] Just as an acquittal does not necessarily reflect a judgment of innocence, nonprosecution is even less reliable as a barometer of factual innocence. "Of course," the court noted, "as a matter of consistency and fairness, the insurer may not admit evidence that criminal arson charges have been brought against the insured."

FRE 401, 403 – Insured's Willingness to Take Polygraph Examination Is Admissible in Suit Alleging Bad Faith Denial of Claim by Insurer

> **401. Definition of "Relevant Evidence"**
> "Relevant evidence" means evidence having any tendency to make the existence of any fact that is of consequence to the determination of the action more probable or less probable than it would be without the evidence.
>
> **Rule 403. Exclusion of Relevant Evidence on Grounds of Prejudice, Confusion, or Waste of Time**
> Although relevant, evidence may be excluded if its probative value is substantially outweighed by the danger of unfair prejudice, confusion of the issues, or misleading the jury, or by considerations of undue delay, waste of time, or needless presentation of cumulative evidence.

MURPHY v. CINCINNATI INSURANCE CO.
772 F.2d 273 (6th Cir. 1985)

Just before they closed on a deal to sell their Newport, Michigan home so they could move to Florida, the home of James and Rosemary Murphy burned down. In fact, an auctioneer had first arranged to remove their household furnishings and many antiques from the home the day of the fire, but had to reschedule. The fire

---
[4] Or perhaps the prosecutor's office was too overworked to bother with arson cases, or the assistant in charge of issuing warrants was having a bad day when the case was presented.

marshall concluded the fire was caused by arson; some 27 arson fires had occurred over a four-year period in the area of the Murphy home.

Cincinnati Insurance Co. refused to pay the Murphys' claim on the policy that covered the home and its contents, saying the Murphys were responsible for starting the fire. They sued on the policy, contending the company's denial was made in bad faith. The company argued Murphys' monthly obligation often exceeded their income, and the sale price on their house was some $14,000 less than the insurance value.

At trial James Murphy was permitted to testify that he had volunteered to Cincinnati's lawyer to take a polygraph examination to prove he wasn't involved in setting the fire. The jury found for Murphys on the policy, awarding them for $60,000 for the house, $30,000 for its contents, and $1,080 in living expenses. The district court then added nearly $17,000 in attorneys' fees because of the company's bad faith and "callous disregard for the rights of the plaintiffs." Cincinnati Insurance appealed.

The company argued that if polygraph results are inadmissible then so should be a willingness or unwillingness to undergo a polygraph examination. The Sixth Circuit Court of Appeals affirmed, saying the "logical link" between the two notions "is not, in fact, so evident. The threshold issue is whether plaintiff's willingness to submit to a polygraph examination is relevant. Fed.R.Evid. 401. Thus, admissibility turns on the relationship of the proffered evidence to other facts of the case, regardless of whether the results of polygraph tests are admissible. An insured's willingness to cooperate in an insurance company's investigation and request for a polygraph examination does not depend on the scientific acceptability which is necessary to support the admissibility of polygraph test results. Since James Murphy's willingness to submit to polygraph examination reflected upon his credibility and the defendant's motive in refusing the claim, the district court did not err in concluding that the evidence is relevant.

"Moreover, the district court permitted defendant wide latitude to present evidence to discount or discredit James Murphy's willingness to submit to a polygraph examination, thereby providing defendant a full opportunity to place the evidence in a balanced light. Accordingly, the district court did not abuse its discretion in finding, under Fed.R.Evid. 403, that any prejudice from the evidence did not substantially outweigh its probative value."

FRE 401, 403: Prejudice Inherent in Multiple Photographs of Injuries Is Not Substantially Greater Than Their Probative Value

> **401. Definition of "Relevant Evidence"**
>
> "Relevant evidence" means evidence having any tendency to make the existence of any fact that is of consequence to the determination of the action more probable or less probable than it would be without the evidence.
>
> **Rule 403. Exclusion of Relevant Evidence on Grounds of Prejudice, Confusion, or Waste of Time**
>
> Although relevant, evidence may be excluded if its probative value is substantially outweighed by the danger of unfair prejudice, confusion of the issues, or misleading the jury, or by considerations of undue delay, waste of time, or needless presentation of cumulative evidence.

PEOPLE v. MILLS
537 N.W.2d 909, 450 Mich. 61 (1995)

Cruising for crack and a fight, Vester Mills and his father-in-law, James Camilli, threw gasoline at 19-year-old Kristen Grauman and set her on fire. She survived severe burns to over 60 percent of her body and severe inhalation injuries. Separate juries convicted Mills and Camilli of assault with intent to commit murder. The defendants appealed.

The Michigan Court of Appeals reversed the convictions. It was error, the court said, for the trial judges to permit the prosecution to admit into evidence 17 photographic slides of the victim, taken over the course of eight months, at various stages of her medical and surgical treatment. Their probative value was "clearly outweighed" by the danger of unfair prejudice under Michigan Rule of Evidence 403, identical to the federal rule. The state appealed.

The Michigan Supreme Court reversed the Court of Appeals and reinstated the convictions, holding there were several distinct justifications for finding substantial probative value in the slides. The severity of the victim's injuries and the extent of her medical and surgical treatment helped to demonstrate the defendants' intent to kill; demonstrated a basis for expert medical opinions about the nature and extent of the burns; showed some splattering, suggesting that the gasoline was thrown on her, not merely spilled accidentally as defendants claimed; corroborated the victim's testimony about how the events of the night in question had unfolded; and demonstrated the victim's state of mind to allow the jury to evaluate defense cross-examination of the victim concerning inconsistent statements she had given investigators.

That the trial court viewed some 30 of the 150 slides available, carefully weighing matters of prejudice in deciding to admit only 17 of them, and excluding some because they looked "so painful," demonstrated that it had exercised its discretion carefully.

The Michigan Supreme Court noted that evidence that is damaging or even gruesome in its graphic depiction of injuries is not necessarily too prejudicial. There was little danger here of the jury giving "marginally probative evidence... undue or pre-emptive weight." What prejudicial danger there was (shock, emotional decision-making) could not be said to "substantially outweigh" the significant probative value of the slides.

FRE 401, 403, 702 – Probability Evidence Is Inadmissible When Based on Unproven Statistical Frequencies and When It Distorts Jury's Deliberative Function

> **401. Definition of "Relevant Evidence"**
> "Relevant evidence" means evidence having any tendency to make the existence of any fact that is of consequence to the determination of the action more probable or less probable than it would be without the evidence.
>
> **Rule 403. Exclusion of Relevant Evidence on Grounds of Prejudice, Confusion, or Waste of Time**
> Although relevant, evidence may be excluded if its probative value is substantially outweighed by the danger of unfair prejudice, confusion of the issues, or misleading the jury, or by considerations of undue delay, waste of time, or needless presentation of cumulative evidence.
>
> **Rule 702. Testimony by Experts**
> If scientific, technical, or other specialized knowledge will assist the trier of fact to understand the evidence or to determine a fact in issue, a witness qualified as an expert by knowledge, skill, experience, training, or education, may testify thereto in the form of an opinion or otherwise.

PEOPLE v. COLLINS
438 P.2d 33, 68 Cal.2d 319, 66 Cal. Rptr. 497 (1968)

The victim of a mugging/purse snatching in the San Pedro area of Los Angeles, and another witness, described a white woman, a little over five feet tall, medium build, wearing dark clothing, with dark blond hair done up in a ponytail, who ran out of an alley and got into a yellow car driven by a black man with a mustache and beard. Malcolm Ricardo Collins and his wife Janet Collins fit the description more-or-less (Malcolm sometimes wore a beard, sometimes did not) and were charged with second degree robbery. Neither witness could identify the Collinses with much certainty. Both Collinses testified and denied involvement or knowledge.

To fill in the blanks, the prosecutor called a mathematics professor to testify to the "product rule of probability": "The probability of the joint occurrence of a number of mutually independent events is equal to the product of the individual probabilities that each of the events will occur."

After assuming specified probabilities for each characteristic he identified (1 in 10 for a partly yellow automobile, 1 in 4 for a man with a mustache, 1 in 10 for a "girl with ponytail," 1 in 3 for a girl with blond hair, 1 in 10 for a "Negro man with beard" and 1 in 1000 for "interracial couple in car") the prosecutor multiplied them and declared to the jury "that there was but one chance in 12 million that any couple possessed the distinctive characteristics of the defendants," or, put another way, one chance in 12 million that some other "equally distinctive couple" committed the robbery. The Collinses were convicted by their jury after long deliberations and many ballots. Malcolm Collins appealed.

The California Supreme Court reversed the conviction. There had been no proof presented by the prosecution for the probabilities they had "assumed" for each characteristic identified by the witnesses, and the probabilities they invited the jury to multiply were associated with characteristics that were not sufficiently "independent" for the product rule to be validly applied to them: "e.g., Negroes with beards and men with mustaches obviously represent overlapping categories." Both of these defects were held to be "basic and pervasive," yielding "a wholly erroneous and exaggerated result... wild conjecture without demonstrated relevancy to the issues..." (The prosecution had argued it was using those calculations as "illustrative" only, and even invited jurors to come up with their own factors; the California Supreme Court rejected that defense of the technique employed.)

What gives this classic case its abiding significance for trial lawyers, however, is not merely the error of the particular numbers plugged into probability theory here. It is rather the court's observation that "the entire enterprise upon which the prosecution embarked, and which was directed to the objective of measuring the likelihood of a random couple possessing the characteristics allegedly distinguishing the robbers, was gravely misguided.... The prosecution's approach... could furnish the jury with absolutely no guidance in the crucial issue. *Of the admittedly few such couples, which, if any, was guilty of committing this robbery?*... No mathematical formula could ever establish beyond a reasonable doubt [even] that the prosecution's witnesses correctly observed and accurately described the distinctive features which were employed to link defendants to the crime. Conceivably, for example, the guilty couple might have included a light-skinned Negress with bleached hair rather than a Caucasian blonde; or the driver of the car might have been wearing a false beard as a disguise; or the prosecution's witnesses might simply have been unreliable."

The California court more than thirty years ago, then, was concerned that the false appearance of mathematical precision yielded by probability theory would distract a jury from its task of weighing the evidence and deciding if all reasonable doubt had been met, and in fact the 12-million-to-one odds generated by the multiplication formula don't even mean what they appear to mean. As the court explains in a very technical Appendix replete with mathematical proofs, "the prosecution's figures actually imply a likelihood of over 40 percent that the Collinses could be 'duplicated' by at least one other couple who might equally have committed the San Pedro robbery." To represent that such a process adequately addressed the question of reasonable doubt was "indefensible," even if done in good faith – in other words, out of an ignorance of the math probably shared by defense counsel and the jury.

In our scientifically sophisticated era of DNA evidence[5] purporting to establish facts by probabilities in the same stratospheric neighborhood, or beyond, as that in the *Collins* case, it is worth remembering the California Supreme Court's admonition that mathematical techniques in the proof of facts "must be critically examined" so as to avoid "distorting" the deliberative functions of the jury. Quite a number of courts have taken a wide variety of positions on probability evidence since *Collins*, but *Collins* remains the starting point in the discussion.

---

[5] See, e.g., two articles by Jonathan J. Koehler, "One in Millions, Billions, and Trillions: Lessons from *People v. Collins* (1968) for People v. [O.J.] Simpson" (1995), 47 Journal of Legal Education 214 (1997), and "On Conveying the Probative Value of DNA Evidence: Frequencies, Likelihood Ratios, and Error Rates," 67 Colorado Law Review 859 (1996).

FRE 403 – Danger of Unfair Prejudice from Identification of Predicate Crime Substantially Outweighs Evidence's Probative Value

> **Rule 403. Exclusion of Relevant Evidence on Grounds of Prejudice, Confusion, or Waste of Time**
>
> Although relevant, evidence may be excluded if its probative value is substantially outweighed by the danger of unfair prejudice, confusion of the issues, or misleading the jury, or by considerations of undue delay, waste of time, or needless presentation of cumulative evidence.

OLD CHIEF v. UNITED STATES
519 U.S. 172, 117 S. Ct. 644, 136 L. Ed. 2d 574 (1997)

A jury convicted Johnny Lynn Old Chief of several offenses arising out of a fracas involving a gunshot, including violation of a federal statute making it unlawful for a felon to possess a firearm. Old Chief had been convicted in 1988 of assault causing serious bodily injury.

Fearing that the similarity of the prior offense and the principal charged offense, assault with a dangerous weapon, would make it too difficult for the jury to hold the government to its burden of proof, beyond a reasonable doubt, defense counsel had offered a stipulation and proposed jury instruction that conceded only that Old Chief had previously "been convicted of a crime punishable by imprisonment for a term exceeding one year" (the language of the felon-in-possession statute) without mentioning the name or nature of the prior conviction. The government refused the stipulation, insisting on naming the offense, and the District Court ruled the government did not have to so stipulate. The Ninth Circuit Court of Appeals upheld the District Court's ruling, holding the government is able to prove a prior felony offense "through introduction of probative evidence." The Ninth Circuit said the district judge had not abused his discretion.

The U.S. Supreme Court in a 5-4 decision reversed the conviction, holding that the introduction of evidence about the name of the prior offense was unfairly prejudicial under Rule 403. Justice Souter wrote for the majority, "The term 'unfair prejudice,' as to a criminal defendant, speaks to the capacity of some concededly relevant evidence to lure the factfinder into declaring guilt on a ground different from proof specific to the offense charged." Souter then specifically identified the danger associated with the government's proof: unnecessarily allowing the jury to "generaliz[e] a defendant's earlier bad act into bad character and taking that as raising the odds that he did the later bad act now charged (or, worse, as calling for preventive conviction even if he should happen to be innocent momentarily)."

The Supreme Court adopted a contextual approach for making a Rule 403 analysis: evaluation of an item of evidence for prejudice and probative value should consider "any actually available substitute," taking into account "the offering party's need for evidentiary richness and narrative integrity." The court noted that the Advisory Committee Notes to several rules contemplate this approach.

In this case, all the government should have needed in order to prove the elements of the felon-in-possession charge was

38 Evidence Illustrated

possession, shown by the facts, and any old prior felony conviction, which was adequately established by defendant's proposed language. The probative value of that stipulation was equivalent to that of a full recitation of the precise charge Old Chief had previously been convicted of, without most of the attendant dangers of prejudice. Thus it was an abuse of the trial judge's discretion to admit the full record when an admission in more neutral terms was available. The Supreme Court noted, "[T]his will be the general rule when proof of convict status is at issue."

FRE 404(a)(1), 405(a) – Accused Alone Possesses Option of "Opening the Door" to Character Evidence

> **Rule 404. Character Evidence Not Admissible to Prove Conduct; Exceptions; Other Crimes**
> *(a) Character Evidence Generally.* Evidence of a person's character or a trait of character is not admissible for the purpose of proving action in conformity therewith on a particular occasion, except:
> *(1) Character of Accused.* Evidence of a pertinent trait of character offered by an accused, or by the prosecution to rebut the same;…
> **Rule 405. Methods of Proving Character**
> *(a) Reputation or Opinion.* In all cases in which evidence of character or a trait of character of a person is admissible, proof may be made by testimony as to reputation or by testimony in the form of an opinion. On cross-examination inquiry is allowable into relevant specific instances of conduct.

UNITED STATES v. GILLILAND
586 F.2d 1384 (10th Cir. 1978)

Roy Valentine Gilliland was arrested in 1978 near Guymon, Oklahoma while driving a vehicle stolen a few hours earlier in Dumas, Texas. He was charged with interstate transportation of a stolen car. His defense was that he had bought the car in a bar in Oklahoma from a man claiming to be a car salesman who owed Gilliland a gambling debt. The defense called Gilliland's stepson, Billy Tull, to testify that he was present at the transfer of title and observed the paperwork in the exchange.

On cross-examination the government attorney goaded Tull into agreeing that he didn't think Gilliland was the "kind of man" who would commit the crime charged. On the strength of that prosecution-induced character testimony alone, the trial court permitted the government to ask Tull[6] about convictions Gilliland had suffered for the same offense in 1942, 1950, and 1962. Gilliland's jury convicted him, and he appealed.

The Tenth Circuit Court of Appeals reversed Gilliland's conviction. The accused had not opened the door to character cross-examination: "Billy Tull was not a character witness.… The government may not turn him into a character witness by asking him

---

[6]Pursuant to FRE 405(a), last sentence.

what kind of man defendant was, and then use those questions to bootstrap[7] into the case evidence of defendant's prior convictions which it was prohibited from using in its case-in-chief."

The court also rejected, somewhat summarily but entirely correctly, the admissibility of Gilliland's prior acts of interstate car theft for non-character purposes under Rule 404(b).)

FRE 404(a)(2) – Exceptions to General Ban on Character Evidence May Be Invoked in Civil Case Involving Issue That Is Essentially Criminal in Nature

> **Rule 404. Character Evidence Not Admissible to Prove Conduct; Exceptions; Other Crimes**
>
> *(a) Character Evidence Generally.* Evidence of a person's character or a trait of character is not admissible for the purpose of proving action in conformity therewith on a particular occasion, except....
>
> *(1) Character of Accused.* Evidence of a pertinent trait of character offered by an accused, or by the prosecution to rebut the same; or, if evidence of a trait of character of the alleged victim of the crime is offered by an accused and admitted under Rule 404(a)(2), evidence of the same trait of character of the accused offered by the prosecution;
>
> *(2) Character of Victim.* Evidence of a pertinent trait of character of the victim of the crime offered by an accused, or by the prosecution to rebut the same, or evidence of a character trait of peacefulness of the victim offered by the prosecution in a homicide case to rebut evidence that the victim was the first aggressor;
>
> *(3) Character of Witness.* Evidence of the character of a witness, as provided in Rules 607, 608, and 609.

PERRIN v. ANDERSON
784 F.2d 1040 (10th Cir. 1986)

After Terry Kim Perrin's car rear-ended another car on an Oklahoma highway, he determined that no one was injured and walked to his home nearby. Two Oklahoma State Highway Patrolmen, Donnie Anderson and Roland Von Schriltz, went to Perrin's home to get some information about the accident. When they arrived Perrin was acting strangely. He refused to answer their knocks for twenty minutes and then yelled that the accident wasn't his fault. His moods seemed to be changing quickly. Von Schriltz, sensing a possibly dangerous situation developing, moved his hand slowly toward his gun in order, he said later, to secure its hammer with a leather thong. This seemed to set Perrin off and he slammed the door. It bounced open and a "fierce" fight broke out as Perrin attacked Trooper Anderson and Von Schriltz came to

---

[7]This example is one of many variations all known in the trade as "bootstrapping." Luring a defense witness who did not raise the issue of character into "opening the door" for other-acts cross-examination under FRE 405(a) is the most egregious.

Anderson's aid. The fight ended when Anderson shot and killed Perrin just as Anderson feared he was about to pass out from Perrin's repeated kicks to his face and chest. Anderson said he thought Perrin was going to kill him and Von Schriltz.

Deborah Kay Perrin, Terry Perrin's mother and the guardian of his son Chance, filed a civil rights lawsuit against the troopers on behalf of the son and Perrin's estate. At trial the defendants introduced evidence of Perrin's previous disturbed violent encounters with police in order to show Perrin was the first aggressor in his final encounter. The trial court admitted this testimony under Rule 404(a)(2). The jury verdict was for Troopers Anderson and Von Schriltz. Mrs. Perrin appealed.

The Tenth Circuit Court of Appeals affirmed, holding that although the exceptions to Rule 404(a)'s ban on character evidence by their "literal language" apply only to criminal defendants (there is no "accused" in a civil case), "when the central issue involved in a civil case is in nature criminal, the defendant may invoke the exceptions to Rule 404(a).... In a case of this kind the civil defendant, like the criminal defendant, stands in a position of great peril. A verdict against the defendants in this case would be tantamount to finding that they killed Perrin without cause... [and] warrants giving them the same opportunity to present a defense" that the rules afford a criminal defendant. "The self-defense claim raised in this case is not functionally different from a self-defense claim raised in a criminal case." Many jurisdictions are in accord, and more than a few disagree, holding to the literal language that limits the application of the exceptions to criminal cases.

(Despite holding that such character evidence must be presented in the form of reputation or opinion testimony under Rule 405(a), the appellate court in an odd and questionable twist then found this conduct evidence was admissible under Rule 406 as habit evidence.)

FRE 404(a)(2), 405(a) – Evidence of Victim's Character When Not an Essential Element of the Defense Must Be Proved by Reputation or Opinion Evidence

> **Rule 404. Character Evidence Not Admissible to Prove Conduct; Exceptions; Other Crimes**
>
> *(a) Character Evidence Generally.* Evidence of a person's character or a trait of character is not admissible for the purpose of proving action in conformity therewith on a particular occasion, except:
>
> ...
>
> *(2) Character of Victim.* Evidence of a pertinent trait of character of the victim of the crime offered by an accused, or by the prosecution to rebut the same, or evidence of a character trait of peacefulness of the victim offered by the prosecution in a homicide case to rebut evidence that the victim was the first aggressor....
>
> **Rule 405. Methods of Proving Character**
>
> *(a) Reputation or Opinion.* In all cases in which evidence of character or a trait of character of a person is admissible, proof may be made by testimony as to reputation or by testimony in the form of an opinion. On cross-examination, inquiry is allowable into relevant specific instances of conduct.
>
> *(b) Specific Instances of Conduct.* In cases in which character or a trait of character of a person is an essential element of a charge, claim, or defense, proof may also be made of specific instances of that person's conduct.

STATE v. BAZAN
561 P.2d 482, 90 N.M. 209 (1977)

Leroy Bazan was charged with assault with intent to commit a violent felony in connection with shooting in the direction of Sheriff's Officer Foster during a car chase. At trial Bazan proffered testimony about specific conduct of Officer Foster in an attempt to prove Foster was aggressive and reckless, asserting that those character traits of the officer were essential elements of his defense. The trial court excluded this evidence. A Bernalillo County District Court jury convicted Bazan of the charge, and he appealed.

The New Mexico Court of Appeals affirmed the verdict and the trial court's ruling on the character evidence offered. The defense had confused the whole matter of character evidence, it seems. First, because Bazan had not claimed self-defense, nor that Foster was the first aggressor, there was nothing to make any alleged aggressive or reckless character trait of Foster's "pertinent" to any aspect of the case under New Mexico's equivalent of Federal Rule 404(a)(2). Second, had it been relevant, such character trait could have been proven only through evidence of Foster's reputation or a witness's opinion of him, not through evidence of specific instances of Foster's conduct or behavior. Finally, the court said, correctly but without elaboration, that "Foster's asserted character traits were not essential elements of the defense in this case... and, thus, were not provable by specific acts of conduct."

FRE 404(a), 405(a), 610 – Religious Belief in Nonviolence Is Improper Way to Prove Defendant's Character and Inadmissible Bolstering of Credibility

> **Rule 404. Character Evidence Not Admissible to Prove Conduct; Exceptions; Other Crimes**
>
> *(a) Character Evidence Generally.* Evidence of a person's character or a trait of character is not admissible for the purpose of proving action in conformity therewith on a particular occasion, except:
>
> *(1) Character of Accused.* Evidence of a pertinent trait of character offered by an accused, or by the prosecution to rebut the same;...
>
> **Rule 405. Methods of Proving Character**
>
> *(a) Reputation or Opinion.* In all cases in which evidence of character or a trait of character of a person is admissible, proof may be made by testimony as to reputation or by testimony in the form of an opinion. On cross-examination, inquiry is allowable into relevant specific instances of conduct.
>
> **Rule 610. Religious Beliefs or Opinions**
>
> Evidence of the beliefs or opinions of a witness on matters of religion is not admissible for the purpose of showing that by reason of their nature the witness's credibility is impaired or enhanced.

GOVERNMENT OF VIRGIN ISLANDS v. PETERSEN
553 F.2d 324 (3d Cir. 1977)

After being ejected from a bar following a loud argument with other patrons, a young man returned to the bar, waited for the others to leave, and fired three shots into their car. Two men were killed.

Allan Petersen was arrested for the crimes and charged with murder. He produced several alibi witnesses who said he'd been home asleep the entire evening. The government produced three identification witnesses, the barmaid, the bar's proprietor, and a patron. A jury convicted Petersen of two counts of second degree murder.

He appealed on several grounds, including what he contended were a suggestive identification procedure and an improperly constituted jury panel. Petersen's appeal also raised a couple of intriguing evidentiary questions.

Petersen attempted to have one of his alibi witnesses, Rios, testify that he and Petersen were Rastafarians and as such rejected violence. The District Court of the Virgin Islands, Division of St. Croix, refused to allow this testimony. The Third Circuit Court of Appeals affirmed the trial court's ruling, saying that as to Rios's beliefs, the testimony could only have been designed to enhance his credibility, contrary to Rule 610. Petersen's appellate attorney claimed that as to Petersen's religious beliefs in nonviolence, "This was an inartful attempt to elicit an opinion as to defendant's peaceable character." The court looked beyond this characterization, however, and declared that the proposition that Rastafarians believe, on religious grounds, in nonviolence, that Petersen is a Rastafarian, and that therefore Petersen believes in nonviolence, was legally irrelevant: "A person may or may not act in accordance with a professed belief; it is the observation of the defendant's *behavior* over a length of time which is the recognized basis for both reputation and opinion [character] testimony."

FRE 404(a)(2), 405(a) – Limitations on Form Victim Character Evidence May Take Do Not Apply to Proof of Accused's State of Mind to Establish Self-Defense

> **Rule 404. Character Evidence Not Admissible to Prove Conduct; Exceptions; Other Crimes**
>
> *(a) Character Evidence Generally.* Evidence of a person's character or a trait of character is not admissible for the purpose of proving action in conformity therewith on a particular occasion, except:
>
> ...
>
> *(2) Character of Victim.* Evidence of a pertinent trait of character of the victim of the crime offered by an accused, or by the prosecution to rebut the same, or evidence of a character trait of peacefulness of the victim offered by the prosecution in a homicide case to rebut evidence that the victim was the first aggressor....
>
> **Rule 405. Methods of Proving Character**
>
> *(a) Reputation or Opinion.* In all cases in which evidence of character or a trait of character of a person is admissible, proof may be made by testimony as to reputation or by testimony in the form of an opinion. On cross-examination, inquiry is allowable into relevant specific instances of conduct.

STATE v. CARLSON
508 N.E.2d 999, 31 Ohio App. 3d 72 (1986)

Joe Thompson was shot in Cleveland's OxBow Saloon by the bartender, Richard Carlson. Thompson lived, but was in the hospital for a month and lost his spleen and a kidney. Carlson was charged with felonious assault.

Thompson and Carlson were the only people in the bar at the time of the shooting. Thompson said it was utterly without provocation. Carlson, who called police immediately after the shooting, said it was self-defense. He said Thompson "became upset" when Carlson told him it was closing time, and threw a beer can that hit Carlson in the head. When Thompson began to climb over the bar, Carlson said he pulled out his gun and told Thompson to stop where he was. Thompson told Carlson he'd have to kill him to stop him from killing Carlson, and Carlson shot him once in the chest.

The Ohio Common Pleas Court judge denied Carlson the opportunity to show that he feared Thompson because he knew of other violent acts committed by Thompson. Carlson was convicted, and sentenced to three to fifteen years in prison "with three years' actual incarceration on the gun specification." He appealed.

The Ohio Court of Appeals reversed. Although Thompson's violent character itself is not an essential element of self-defense (hence Rule 405(b) does not provide an avenue for the admission of specific conduct evidence), the court did not apply Rule 405(a) through Rule 404(a)(2) to the case either, because Carlson was not offering these specific instances of Thompson's conduct for the purpose of showing his violent character in order to prove "action in conformity therewith" on the night of the shooting. Carlson was trying to show his own state of mind, itself a theory of self-defense: he reasonably believed, right or wrong, that he needed to take the action he took to protect himself. Thus there should be no limitation as to reputation or opinion on Carlson's testimony about Thompson's prior conduct: "The court erred by excluding the appellant's testimony about prior violent acts of the victim that he, the appellant, was aware of at the time of the shooting. A defendant, when arguing self-defense, may testify about specific instances of the victim's prior conduct in order to establish the defendant's state of mind. These events are admissible in evidence, not because they establish something about the victim's character, but because they tend to show why the defendant believed the victim would kill or severely injure him. In the instant case, the court prevented the appellant from testifying that he had witnessed Thompson's violent behavior in several bars. This ruling resulted in the appellant's bare statement that he was afraid of the victim, being the only evidence of his state of mind reaching the jury."

FRE 404(b) – Drug Paraphernalia Is Admissible in Weapons Prosecution to Show Motive

> **Rule 404. Character Evidence Not Admissible to Prove Conduct; Exceptions; Other Crimes**
>
> *(a) Character Evidence Generally.* Evidence of a person's character or a trait of character is not admissible for the purpose of proving action in conformity therewith on a particular occasion....
>
> *(b) Other Crimes, Wrongs, or Acts.* Evidence of other crimes, wrongs, or acts is not admissible to prove the character of a person in order to show action in conformity therewith. It may, however, be admissible for other purposes, such as proof of motive, opportunity, intent, preparation, plan, knowledge, identity, or absence of mistake or accident, provided that upon request by the accused, the prosecution in a criminal case shall provide reasonable notice in advance of trial, or during trial if the court excuses pretrial notice on good cause shown, of the general nature of any such evidence it intends to introduce at trial.

UNITED STATES v. FULLER
887 F.2d 144 (8th Cir. 1989)

John Fuller, with three prior convictions for burglary and robbery, was arrested in possession of a sawed-off shotgun at his estranged wife's apartment. He was charged with possession of a firearm by a convicted felon and possession of an unregistered firearm. Fuller's wife testified for the defense that Fuller was at the apartment simply to visit his children. On cross-examination she said she didn't know about drug paraphernalia seized at the arrest under a valid warrant. The prosecution was then allowed in rebuttal to introduce into evidence the articles of drug paraphernalia found at her apartment. Fuller was convicted by a jury of both charges, and sentenced to concurrent prison terms of 15 and 10 years respectively. He appealed.

The Eighth Circuit Court of Appeals conceded that while "the record before us is unclear as to the basis for the admission of the [drug paraphernalia] evidence," there was no "abuse of discretion" in admitting it.

The court offered two possible bases for the legitimate admission of the drug paraphernalia: to impeach the testimony of Fuller's wife, and as motive evidence under Rule 404(b), "given the close and well-known connection between firearms and drugs. Firearms are known 'tools of the trade' of narcotics dealing because of the dangers inherent in that line of work."

The Eighth Circuit's "impeachment" theory will not stand up to much scrutiny, given that it was the government's cross-examination that first raised the question of the drug paraphernalia.[8] The "motive" theory under Rule 404(b), although amply supported by precedent from several circuits, is only a little less improbable. It seems unlikely that motive was much of an issue in Fuller's trial, as it is certainly not an element of the crimes charged. There seems to be a much greater likelihood that the evidence would have been seen by jurors as evidence simply of criminal propensity (forbidden by the Rule), especially because at trial the prosecution failed to clarify for the jury the exact Rule 404(b) issue it was offering this evidence for and how the two were connected.

FRE 404(b) – Prior Rapes Are Admissible to Prove Plan, Intent, Preparation, Motive Even if Accused Was Acquitted in Prior Case

> **Rule 404. Character Evidence Not Admissible to Prove Conduct; Exceptions; Other Crimes**
>
> *(b) Other Crimes, Wrongs, or Acts.* Evidence of other crimes, wrongs, or acts is not admissible to prove the character of a person in order to show action in conformity therewith. It may, however, be admissible for other purposes, such as proof of motive, opportunity, intent, preparation, plan, knowledge, identity, or absence of mistake or accident, provided that upon request by the accused, the prosecution in a criminal case shall provide reasonable notice in advance of trial, or during trial if the court excuses pretrial notice on good cause shown, of the general nature of any such evidence it intends to introduce at trial.

PEOPLE v. OLIPHANT
250 N.W.2d 443, 399 Mich. 472 (1976)

Charles Oliphant was convicted of forcible rape and gross indecency. The complainant was a college student who met Oliphant while window-shopping one evening in 1971 and agreed to go with him to a bar to talk. Later they drove around Lansing to various nightspots while the complainant asked to be taken back home. Finally, she testified,

---

[8] Another instance of "bootstrapping" that is usually disallowed, at least if objected to timely.

Oliphant drove to a secluded area and by means of threats forced her to engage in various sexual acts in the back seat of the car. She said he told her he had a gun and a knife and would "take care" of her if she didn't cooperate. Afterwards she said Oliphant allowed her to get dressed and drove her back to her dormitory, telling her she would never be able to prove rape if she prosecuted, and to be sure and get the car license number. Oliphant admitted having sex with the woman but claimed it was consensual; in fact he was in the East Lansing police station reporting that the woman had become angry after consensual sex when he told her she had an unpleasant body odor. He was asking for police advice when the woman's rape report came in. In support of Oliphant's claim of consensual sex, defense counsel emphasized the victim's admissions on cross-examination that she never saw a weapon, that Oliphant never struck her or tore her clothing, that she didn't try to escape while they were driving around Lansing, and that she didn't kick or bite defendant. The woman had noted that the inside door handle was missing from the passenger's side of Oliphant's vehicle.

The trial court permitted the prosecution to present rebuttal testimony of three other young women who said Oliphant had picked them up within a few months of the charged rape under roughly similar circumstances and raped them. Two said Oliphant had another man with him and one of them said the companion raped her as well; all three testified to similar topics of conversation (marijuana, white women dating black men) and similar threats. All said Oliphant was first friendly and then changed. Two said he forced them to dance naked first. One said he had raped her in her car. Two said he drove them home afterwards (the third said his car ran out of gas on the way); all three said he gave them back their clothes after the rape. One said he showed her his college identification.

One of the rebuttal witnesses never reported the rape. The other two filed complaints, and on each of those charges Oliphant was tried and acquitted. In these two trials no mention had been made of other allegations of rape against the defendant.

The "other acts" rule in effect in Michigan at the time was substantially similar to Rule 404(b) although in statutory form. (Michigan adopted Rule 404(b) in 1978, following the federal rule very closely.) The state urged the admissibility of testimony about the three other rapes to show Oliphant "had a sophisticated scheme, plan or system whereby... he would commit rape while orchestrating the circumstances so as to preclude his victims from proving their nonconsent."

The Michigan Supreme Court noted that the fact for which the other-rapes testimony was offered, namely the complainant's nonconsent, was "crucial," which made the other acts evidence more probative than prejudicial. (The trial judge gave extensive pre-testimony instructions[9] to the jury that they not conclude that Oliphant possessed a criminal character, and repeated the admonition in the jury charge.)

Oliphant's acquittal in the two prior cases also raised double jeopardy and collateral estoppel issues. The Michigan court rejected these claims, reasoning that the prior rapes were not being offered in this case to prove defendant's guilt but to establish his plan or system to make it appear that his victims had consented, which the court called "a totally distinct matter." The holding also illustrates the widely held principle that an acquittal is not usually an express finding of innocence,

---

[9] See FRE 105.

but rather of a failure by the prosecution to establish guilt beyond a reasonable doubt. (Many believe the O.J. Simpson verdict illustrates that point.)

Oliphant seems to be almost the poster child for proper use of other-acts evidence.

Without it the jury would be at a real disadvantage in properly assessing the behavior of the accused – as suggested by the two prior acquittals, in cases where the jury was given no information about his other conduct

---

FRE 404(b) – Other Crimes Evidence Is Admissible When Offered by Defendant to Prove Someone Else's Guilt of Crime Charged Even if Other Crimes Are Not Rigorously Similar to Crime Charged

> **Rule 404. Character Evidence Not Admissible to Prove Conduct; Exceptions; Other Crimes**
>
> *(a) Character Evidence Generally.* Evidence of a person's character or a trait of character is not admissible for the purpose of proving action in conformity therewith on a particular occasion....
>
> *(b) Other Crimes, Wrongs, or Acts.* Evidence of other crimes, wrongs, or acts is not admissible to prove the character of a person in order to show action in conformity therewith. It may, however, be admissible for other purposes, such as proof of motive, opportunity, intent, preparation, plan, knowledge, identity, or absence of mistake or accident, provided that upon request by the accused, the prosecution in a criminal case shall provide reasonable notice in advance of trial, or during trial if the court excuses pretrial notice on good cause shown, of the general nature of any such evidence it intends to introduce at trial.

STATE v. GARFOLE
388 A.2d 587, 76 N.J. 445 (1978)

On June 14, 1971 a man accosted a 16-year-old boy and a 15-year-old girl, held a gun to them, threatened both with death, and compelled the girl to perform oral sex on him. Raymond Garfole was charged with multiple felonies in connection with these events.

Garfole had originally also been indicted on charges in connection with five other "comparable episodes," four on earlier dates in 1971 and one in 1972. At the start of the trial involving the June 14 events, the prosecution moved to dismiss the charges involving the other 1971 incidents, "apparently because the witnesses in those incidents were either unable to identify the defendant or unwilling to undergo the experience of testifying..."

At trial, during defense cross-examination of a police witness, Garfole's attorney attempted to develop facts about the four other 1971 incidents. The defense theory was that they were sufficiently similar to the June 14 events to suggest the same person was responsible for all five episodes,[10] and that it was not Garfole inasmuch as he had an alibi for most of those dates.

The trial court sustained the prosecution's objection to this line of questioning. The

---
[10] Offered under the "identity" theory of the New Jersey version of FRE 404(b).

judge ruled that the defense could not offer other crimes evidence to show another's identity, and could only do so to offer a defense of alibi if the state had offered the other crimes evidence first to establish Garfole's identity as the offender in the crimes charged. Garfole was convicted following the jury trial, and appealed. The New Jersey Appellate Division affirmed on rather different grounds. The other crimes evidence was inadmissible, a majority ruled, because those crimes were insufficiently similar to the crimes charged to suggest that the same person (i.e., not Garfole) was responsible for all of them. The Appellate Division held that to be admissible on the question of identity, the other crimes evidence needed to bear the same "high degree of similarity" to the charged offenses that would be required of the state if it were offering the evidence against the accused.

The New Jersey Supreme Court reversed and declared both the trial court and the Appellate Division had misunderstood the other crimes evidence rule. The "exclusionary aspect" of the rule detected by the trial court is not based on the irrelevance of other crimes evidence to prove guilt, but rather on "its undue psychological effect with a jury against a defendant," that is, its tendency to encourage the jury to infer guilt based on criminal propensity, or character. Such a concern is not present when it is the defendant who offers the other crimes evidence to try to show someone else committed the charged acts.

And the "rigid standard of similarity" required when the prosecution offers other crimes evidence to prove the guilt of the accused is also a function of the prejudice inherent in similar crimes evidence; again, such a concern is not present when the accused offers the evidence to exculpate himself. "Simple relevance to guilt or innocence should suffice," held the court, especially because all the accused need prove to prevail is reasonable doubt.

FRE 404(b), 408 – Consent Decree in Earlier Action Is Admissible in Civil Case to Show Motive or Intent of Defendant, or Noncompliance With Decree

> **Rule 404. Character Evidence Not Admissible to Prove Conduct; Exceptions; Other Crimes**
>
> *(a) Character Evidence Generally.* Evidence of a person's character or a trait of character is not admissible for the purpose of proving action in conformity therewith on a particular occasion....
>
> *(b) Other Crimes, Wrongs, or Acts.* Evidence of other crimes, wrongs, or acts is not admissible to prove the character of a person in order to show action in conformity therewith. It may, however, be admissible for other purposes, such as proof of motive, opportunity, intent, preparation, plan, knowledge, identity, or absence of mistake or accident, provided that upon request by the accused, the prosecution in a criminal case shall provide reasonable notice in advance of trial, or during trial if the court excuses pretrial notice on good cause shown, of the general nature of any such evidence it intends to introduce at trial.
>
> **Rule 408. Compromise and Offers to Compromise**
>
> Evidence of (1) furnishing or offering or promising to furnish, or (2) accepting or offering or promising to accept, a valuable consideration in compromising or attempting to compromise a claim which was disputed as to either validity or amount, is not admissible to prove liability for or invalidity of the claim or its amount. Evidence of conduct or statements made in compromise negotiations is likewise not admissible. This rule does not require the exclusion of any evidence otherwise discoverable merely because it is presented in the course of compromise negotiations. This rule also does not require exclusion when the evidence is offered for another purpose, such as proving bias or prejudice of a witness, negativing a contention of undue delay, or proving an effort to obstruct a criminal investigation or prosecution.

<u>JOHNSON v. HUGO'S SKATEWAY</u>
949 F.2d 1338 (4th Cir. 1991)

James H. Johnson sued Hugo's Skateway, a Warrenton, Virginia roller rink, and a deputy sheriff, after he was arrested for refusing to leave the skating floor at the request of the owner. He claimed violations of federal and state civil rights and false arrest under state law.

At trial Johnson was permitted, over objection by Hugo's, to introduce evidence of a consent decree executed more than ten years earlier between Hugo's Skateway and the U.S. Department of Justice in an action filed by DOJ regarding equal access for black citizens to Hugo's facilities and services. The consent decree was "continuing in nature." Hugo's objection was based on Rules 408 and 404(b), as well as Rule 403. The district judge admitted the order to show noncompliance by Hugo's and to help Johnson prove Hugo's motive or intent to discriminate on the basis of his race. The jury returned a verdict for Johnson against Hugo's for $25,000 in compensatory damages and for $175,000 in punitive damages. Hugo's appealed.

The Fourth Circuit Court of Appeals affirmed the trial court's evidentiary rulings. On the Rule 408 issue concerning the consent decree, the court held that showing noncompliance by Hugo's with a continuing order of the court constituted a valid "other purpose" within the exception to the rule's ban on use of compromise settlements. Moreover, under Rule 404(b), the court held that admission of the order was not primarily to show a propensity on the part of Hugo's to discriminate against blacks,[10] but rather to show its motive and intent to do so as shown by the failure of Hugo's "to post signs or instruct employees concerning the skateway's pledge of equal access," as required by the decree.

FRE 404(b)- Evidence of Similar Acts Is Not Admissible to Prove Defendant's Plan Unless They Show More Than Mere Repetition of Charged Offense

> **Rule 404. Character Evidence Not Admissible to Prove Conduct; Exceptions; Other Crimes**
>
> *(a) Character Evidence Generally.* Evidence of a person's character or a trait of character is not admissible for the purpose of proving action in conformity therewith on a particular occasion....
>
> *(b) Other Crimes, Wrongs, or Acts.* Evidence of other crimes, wrongs, or acts is not admissible to prove the character of a person in order to show action in conformity therewith. It may, however, be admissible for other purposes, such as proof of motive, opportunity, intent, preparation, plan, knowledge, identity, or absence of mistake or accident, provided that upon request by the accused, the prosecution in a criminal case shall provide reasonable notice in advance of trial, or during trial if the court excuses pretrial notice on good cause shown, of the general nature of any such evidence it intends to introduce at trial.

UNITED STATES v. KREZDORN
639 F.2d 1327 (5th Cir. 1981)

Herman Krezdorn, a United States Immigration Inspector, was indicted on charges of forging the signature of another inspector on applications for border-crossing cards for five members of a Mexican family, the Ruizes, thereby shortening by several weeks the waiting period before the family could be issued the cards.

At his trial on the five counts of forging the applications, the government was permitted to introduce into evidence 32 additional forged applications that a handwriting expert linked to Krezdorn. The government's theory under Rule 404(b) was that the other forged applications showed a plan or scheme. After the court directed an acquittal on one count because of some documentational deficiencies, the jury convicted Krezdorn of the remaining four charges. Krezdorn appealed on the basis of the Rule 404(b) ruling. The Fifth Circuit Court of Appeals took a rather more careful look at the scheme or plan area of the rule than some courts are willing to do, and reversed Krezdorn's convictions, remanding for a new trial. The court noted first that "plan" was not an element of the charges against Krezdorn, the way it would be if the charge involved conspiracy. Therefore the existence of a plan or

---

[10] This is an interesting treatment of the notion of "propensity" (i.e., character) evidence – that a business entity might have character traits. Of course, here the business was relatively small, and we are probably talking about the character traits of a small handful of people, perhaps only the owner.

scheme would be admissible under Rule 404(b) only if it "logically raises an inference that the defendant was engaged in a larger, more comprehensive plan. The existence of a plan then tends to prove that the defendant committed the charged crime, since commission of that crime would lead to a completion of the overall plan."

Where most courts would be likely to perceive the existence of such a plan in 36 repetitions of the same conduct, to its credit the Fifth Circuit refused to take so superficial a position. Krezdorn was charged with four forgeries. The existence of 32 others is no evidence of a "a larger goal of which the four charged forgeries were only a part," merely that he did the same thing on numerous other occasions, "thus indicating Krezdorn's propensity to commit this crime," an impermissible purpose. (When courts use the word "propensity" they typically mean one's character.) Scheme evidence is admissible under Rule 404(b) when it is necessary to explain the "circumstances or setting" of the crime charged, when without the other acts evidence the jury would be unable to understand the charges in the present case.[11] In the absence of such necessity, the other acts evidence loses most of the probative value it would need to overcome the substantial prejudice carried by the information.

FRE 404(b) – Similarity of Other Crime to Present Charge Is Insufficient Basis for Admissibility

> **Rule 404. Character Evidence Not Admissible to Prove Conduct; Exceptions; Other Crimes**
>
> *(a) Character Evidence Generally.* Evidence of a person's character or a trait of character is not admissible for the purpose of proving action in conformity therewith on a particular occasion....
>
> *(b) Other Crimes, Wrongs, or Acts.* Evidence of other crimes, wrongs, or acts is not admissible to prove the character of a person in order to show action in conformity therewith. It may, however, be admissible for other purposes, such as proof of motive, opportunity, intent, preparation, plan, knowledge, identity, or absence of mistake or accident, provided that upon request by the accused, the prosecution in a criminal case shall provide reasonable notice in advance of trial, or during trial if the court excuses pretrial notice on good cause shown, of the general nature of any such evidence it intends to introduce at trial.

UNITED STATES v. BUCKHART
458 F.2d 201 (10th Cir. 1972)

William Earl Buckhart was charged with interstate transportation of a stolen motor vehicle under the federal Dyer Act. A 1961 Ford station wagon went missing from a used car lot in Ashland, Kentucky and Buckhart was arrested in it about six weeks later in Ellsworth County, Kansas. Buckhart claimed he had a receipt for the purchase of the car from the Kentucky lot from which it had gone missing, but couldn't find it. At trial the government

---

[11] See, e.g., *People v. Oliphant, supra* p. 46.

was allowed to introduce the testimony of FBI Special Agent John T. McMurrer in support of the admission of certified copies of prior Dyer Act convictions sustained by Buckhart, in Oregon in 1955 and in Mississippi in 1966. The trial court admitted these convictions under the common law theory that became a basis for Rule 404(b), that they showed knowledge or plan on the part of Buckhart to commit the crime currently charged.

The jury convicted Buckhart and he appealed, contending admission of the two previous Dyer Act convictions was erroneous.

The Tenth Circuit Court of Appeals reversed. Prior similar offenses do not automatically have relevance to motive, intent, knowledge, absence of mistake or common plan or scheme. They would be admissible only when there is a "clear and logical connection" between the prior offense and the charged offense. The court characterized the prior interstate car thefts Buckhart had committed as "remote and unconnected" to the one he was on trial for. Its only tendency here is to prejudice the jury against Buckhart: "An obvious truth is that once prior convictions are introduced the trial is, for all practical purposes, completed and the guilty outcome follows as a mere formality." (Which, of course is why the prosecution is usually so eager to admit other-acts evidence against the accused.)

FRE 405(a) – Specific Misconduct of Accused Is Proper Subject of Cross-Examination of Accused's Character Witness if Relevant to Character Witness's Testimony

> **Rule 405. Methods of Proving Character**
> *(a) Reputation or Opinion.* In all cases in which evidence of character or a trait of character of a person is admissible, proof may be made by testimony as to reputation or by testimony in the form of an opinion. On cross-examination, inquiry is allowable into relevant specific instances of conduct.

UNITED STATES v. BRIGHT
588 F.2d 504 (5th Cir. 1979)

Edgar Lee Whitten, a Mississippi lawyer, and Louin Ray Bright, his uncle and a former Chief Deputy Sheriff of Marshall County, Mississippi, were indicted for mail fraud. They were charged with trying (unsuccessfully) to obtain probate approval of a phony will of a cousin, J.B. Bright, naming them attorney and executor, respectively, and with using the mail service to notify relatives. Their two-week trial resulted in a guilty verdict.

On appeal, among several issues, Whitten claimed it had been error for the court to allow his character witness to be crossed-examined regarding some past official reprimands. Whitten had called an attorney to give character testimony on his behalf, that Whitten had a good reputation in his community for integrity and veracity. The court, over defense objection, allowed the government to ask[12] on cross-examination if the witness had heard that Whitten had been

---
[12] Admissible under FRE 404(a)(1) and 405(a).

reprimanded recently "by Judge Dick Thomas... for unprofessional conduct," as well as by the DeSoto County and State Bar Associations. (The witness, of course, said he was not aware of those reprimands.) Whitten contended such cross-examination was unfairly prejudicial to him.

The Fifth Circuit Court of Appeal sustained the convictions. Such cross-examination is expressly available when an accused offers good-character testimony. There are but two limitations: the misconduct inquired about must be relevant to the character testimony given (which it obviously was here); and the government must have "some good-faith factual basis for the incidents inquired about."[13] Here the government had letters of reprimand in its possession and showed them to the trial court and to Whitten's attorney, providing a factual basis for the question that was more than sufficient.

It is quite rare that relevant, factually established misconduct will not be ruled to be fair game in the cross-examination of a defense character witness. After all, the accused has all the options under Rule 404(a), and need not open that door if there are known skeletons lurking behind it. If attorney Edgar Lee Whitten has been publicly reprimanded for unprofessional conduct, he has some nerve calling a character witness to try to fool the jury about his integrity.

FRE 405(a) – Opinion Character Witnesses May Be Asked "Have You Heard?" Questions as Well as "Did You Know?" Questions on Cross-Examination

> **Rule 405. Methods of Proving Character**
> *(a) Reputation or Opinion.* In all cases in which evidence of character or a trait of character of a person is admissible, proof may be made by testimony as to reputation or by testimony in the form of an opinion. On cross-examination, inquiry is allowable into relevant specific instances of conduct.

SECURITIES AND EXCHANGE COMMISSION v. PETERS
978 F.2d 1162 (10th Cir. 1992)

The SEC brought a civil suit against Don S. Peters for insider trading, alleging that he supplied two individuals with information about a tender offer for stock in a company his partnership did some consulting work for, and those individuals then repaid debts to Peters amounting to $43,000 and $7,500. The jury returned with a verdict in favor of Peters. The SEC appealed, in part because the trial court had restricted the SEC's cross-examination of some of Peters' character witnesses regarding prior fraud lawsuits against Peters.

Peters served as his own character witness,[14] stating that in the 23 years he had worked at the bank, no one had made any claim against him "for having breached any confidence of any customer or of the bank."[15] He also called seven additional character

---

[13] The factual basis itself is ordinarily not admissible, however.

[14] No question was raised on appeal as to the propriety of applying a criminal exception (Rule 404(a)(1)) to a purported "civil" matter. SEC suits of this nature, which can lead to heavy financial penalties, are apparently considered in some quarters to be quasi-criminal for application of these rules.

[15] Hardly the "reputation" or "opinion" testimony called for by Rule 405(a), probably allowed under the "no harm, no foul" idea.

witnesses,[14] who stated (according to the Tenth Circuit Court of Appeals) "that, in their opinion, Peters' character was impeccable." The trial court, however, prevented the SEC from cross-examining Peters about an allegation that he passed confidential information after leaving the bank. It also barred the SEC from asking the opinion character witnesses if they had heard of a couple of lawsuits charging Peters with SEC Rule 10b-5 violations, and that a former client claimed Peters had told her he had inside information on a number of companies that he would use to her advantage. (The two suits were settled with no admission of wrongdoing.) The district court seems to have made much of the distinction between asking a witness "Did you know?" questions and "Have you heard?" questions.

The Tenth Circuit reversed the verdict, holding that Rule 405(a)'s provision for cross-examining a character witness regarding "relevant specific instances of conduct" all but obliterates the distinction between "Have you heard?" questions and "Did you know?" questions. Following the Advisory Committee comment, the court acknowledged that the distinction between the form of the cross-examination questions was "of slight if any practical significance," and that the Rule "eliminates" the distinction. "The allegations against Peters that the SEC wanted to explore on cross-examination potentially could bear on the witnesses' opinion of Peters and the SEC should have been permitted to explore that possibility. The fact that a party has previously been accused of fraud bears not just upon the party's reputation in the community. Such an accusation may bear also on the opinion witness's personal opinion of the party. Furthermore, such allegations may reflect upon the credibility and reliability of the opinion witness. If the witness has not heard of the allegations, the depth of his or her knowledge might be called into question. If the witness has heard of the allegations but nevertheless favorably appraises the party's character, the witness's objectivity might be called into question.

"In summary, cross-examination questions regarding allegations of prior misconduct could 'bear on [the Witness's] opinion' and thus... the district court should have permitted the inquiry.

"The district court stated that these opinion witnesses could not be questioned about matters as to which they lacked first-hand knowledge. Of course, the only way to find out whether these witnesses did have first-hand knowledge of the allegations against Peters would be through the very type of questions that the court refused to allow. Thus, the SEC was put in a catch-22 situation. In any event, it is well established that opinion witnesses may be asked 'have you heard' questions concerning rumors, allegations or events about which the witnesses may lack first-hand knowledge.

...

"Opinions are, after all, almost always based on more than first-hand experience. Opinions are formed from a complex mosaic that includes first-hand experiences, circumstantial inferences, and even hearsay rumors, anecdotes and opinions expressed by others. If a witness expresses a favorable opinion about a party on direct examination, the strength and reliability of that opinion may be tested on cross-examination on all the elements or components that contributed or may have contributed to the opinion."

FRE 405(b) – Civil Action Claiming Negligent Hiring or Retention of Employee Renders Employee's Character an Essential Element of Claim

> **Rule 405. Methods of Proving Character**
>
> *(a) Reputation or Opinion.* In all cases in which evidence of character or a trait of character of a person is admissible, proof may be made by testimony as to reputation or by testimony in the form of an opinion. On cross-examination, inquiry is allowable into relevant specific instances of conduct.
>
> *(b) Specific Instances of Conduct.* In cases in which character or a trait of character of a person is an essential element of a charge, claim, or defense, proof may also be made of specific instances of that person's conduct.

PANAS v. HARAKIS
529 A.2d 976, 129 N.H. 591 (1987)

John Harakis was employed as a security guard at a Manchester K-Mart. Early in the afternoon of January 30, 1983 he stopped Loukia and Nicholas Panas after they had gone from the department store to their car, and accused them of shoplifting some spark plugs. They denied it, saying the package of spark plugs in their car had been purchased at a different store a month earlier. Harakis said he saw Loukia Panas put them into her coat. The Panases said Harakis announced loudly when he stopped them, "You're under arrest." He denied it. They claimed he made Mrs. Panas return to the store with her hands raised, which Harakis denied. Although charges were filed against Loukia Panas and she was handcuffed and taken to jail in front of her children, Harakis disregarded a subpoena for the scheduled April 8 trial, and because no other K-Mart representative showed up the charges were dropped.

The Panases sued Harakis and K-Mart for false imprisonment, malicious prosecution, invasion of privacy, slander, loss of consortion, and negligent hiring, training, supervising and retention of Harakis. The Hillsborough County Superior Court granted the Panases' motion to admit into evidence the underlying facts and circumstances giving rise to Harakis's 1980 conviction for impersonating a police officer while accusing a K-Mart customer of shoplifting. (The court barred evidence of Harakis's conviction because it was later annulled; Panases were also barred from bringing up Harakis's 1976 conviction for attempted theft by deception because it was also annulled, although Panases claimed that Harakis's criminal record was annulled "either in whole or in part [only] after the plaintiffs had placed the defendants on notice of their claims.") The ten-day trial and three-day jury deliberations resulted in jury verdicts for Loukia Panas of $1,000,000 and for Nicholas Panas of $100,000. The trial court then set aside the damages awards as "manifestly exorbitant and unreasonable," and ordered a new trial limited to the damages amount. Panases and both defendants appealed.

The New Hampshire Supreme Court affirmed the liability verdict and the trial court's setting aside of the damages award. One key issue among many on appeal concerned the propriety of the trial court's rulings on admitting Harakis's convictions. New Hampshire's amendment statute, the court held, gave a court "little choice" about admitting evidence of annulled convictions.

However, the underlying facts may be fair game if they are relevant and otherwise admissible. The appellate panel focused on the allegation that "K-Mart had been negligent in hiring and supervising an employee who was untrustworthy and who displayed a negative characteristic of unjustifiably accusing K-Mart customers of shoplifting. Once Harakis' character had been called into question, [New Hampshire's] Rule 405(b) [nearly identical to the federal rule] enabled the plaintiffs to admit evidence of specific instances of conduct in which Harakis acted improperly. Certainly the 1980 incident, in which Harakis falsely represented himself as a police officer to a K-Mart customer, reflects on Harakis' character and improper job performance and was properly admissible into evidence."

(The court held that the facts underlying the theft conviction were less probative of poor job performance and were properly kept out of evidence.)

FRE 405(b) – Where Evidence of a Person's Character Is Admissible as an Essential Element of the Defense, the Specific Acts Offered to Prove Character Must Be Relevant to That Character

> **Rule 405. Methods of Proving Character**
>
> *(a) Reputation or Opinion.* In all cases in which evidence of character or a trait of character of a person is admissible, proof may be made by testimony as to reputation or by testimony in the form of an opinion. On cross-examination, inquiry is allowable into relevant specific instances of conduct.
>
> *(b) Specific Instances of Conduct.* In cases in which character or a trait of character of a person is an essential element of a charge, claim, or defense, proof may also be made of specific instances of that person's conduct.

STATE v. WOODSON
382 S.E.2d 519, 181 W.Va. 325 (1989)

Steven Simons was found beaten to death in hedges by the roadside in Weston, West Virginia. Eyewitnesses to a fight there connected a van to the body. The search for the van led police to Dewaine Woodson who, while police searched his van, blurted out that he had "kicked the fagot's ass." He was convicted by a jury in Lewis County Circuit Court of unlawful assault.

Woodson appealed to the Supreme Court of Appeals of West Virginia, citing (in addition to a *Miranda* statement suppression issue) the refusal of the Circuit Judge to allow him to introduce evidence of Simons' prior convictions. Although the appellate court reversed Woodson's conviction on the basis of the *Miranda* issue, it upheld the trial judge's handling of the issue surrounding the victim's convictions.

Woodson had tried to introduce evidence that Simons had been convicted twice for burglary in order to demonstrate that Simons was violent and that Woodson had been defending himself. West Virginia is one of a surprisingly sizeable number of states that hold that their state version of Rule 405(b) applies to self-defense claims: when an accused faces charges arising from violent conduct and cries self-defense, the character of the victim becomes an "essential element" of that defense theory.[16]

(West Virginia makes no distinction between the character of the victim itself being an issue and the state of mind of the accused regarding the victim's violent propensities being the real issue.[17])

The court then reached what it saw as the justification for excluding the burglary convictions: The convictions weren't relevant to a character trait of violence, as "the elements of that crime [burglary] do not involve violence to the person. Instead, they consist of a nighttime entry into a dwelling house or daytime breaking and entering of it with intent to commit a larceny or other felony. There was no evidence of a violent felony against a person which had been committed during the course of the burglary. Accordingly, the trial court properly excluded this evidence."

FRE 405(b) – Character Evidence Offered to Show Negligent Entrustment Must Be Relevant to Issue in Case and Must Be Fresh Enough to Be Probative of Current Conduct

> **Rule 405. Methods of Proving Character**
>
> *(a) Reputation or Opinion.* In all cases in which evidence of character or a trait of character of a person is admissible, proof may be made by testimony as to reputation or by testimony in the form of an opinion. On cross-examination, inquiry is allowable into relevant specific instances of conduct.
>
> *(b) Specific Instances of Conduct.* In cases in which character or a trait of character of a person is an essential element of a charge, claim, or defense, proof may also be made of specific instances of that person's conduct.

ROCKY MOUNTAIN HELICOPTERS, INC. v. BELL HELICOPTERS TEXTRON, INC.
805 F.2d 907 (10th Cir. 1986)

A helicopter engaged in logging operations near Darby, Montana crashed during landing in April 1979 killing the pilot and co-pilot. Rocky Mountain Helicopters, Inc. had bought the helicopter two years earlier from Bell Helicopters Textron, Inc. It was being used to carry logs attached to a long cable by a "choker." Rocky Mountain along with its insurance carrier, Southeastern Aviation (California), Inc. sued Bell, alleging that the crash was caused by "fatigue failure of the 'trunnion,'" the connection between the rotor blades and the mast. Bell argued Rocky Mountain's "reckless and inexperienced pilot… picked up a log that exceeded the external load weight limitation of the helicopter by 1660 pounds and then overreacted and lost control of the helicopter when he was forced to make an emergency release of the log near the landing site."

---

[16] See, by way of contrast, *State v. Carlson*, supra p. 44, an Ohio case holding that the victim's character is not an essential element of self-defense. The states are split on the question. The federal cases are clear that Rule 405(b) does not apply to self-defense. See, e.g., *United States v. Keiser*, infra p. 60.

[17] "Essential element" is conventionally taken to mean that a party must either present proof on the matter or automatically lose the case. That would mean Woodson, in order to warrant an instruction on self-defense, would have to establish not only that Simons provoked the fight, but also that Simons was by nature a violent guy. Surely the West Virginia court doesn't mean that.

Bell offered evidence at trial that tended to show Rocky Mountain's pilot, John Ball, was not ready to be a "left seat" (command) helicopter pilot, was regarded as "a little bit dangerous," had "overgrossed," i,e., picked up loads of logs too heavy for the helicopter, on at least four prior occasions that year, and that "mechanics, co-pilots and ground crews were unhappy about him." The district court excluded this evidence on a misapplication of a point of Texas law to the effect that negligent entrustment and respondent superior are mutually exclusive theories. (Here it is Bell raising the issue of negligent entrustment as an affirmative defense, not as a theory of recovery where we would ordinarily expect to encounter it.) The jury verdict found Rocky Mountain 45% negligent and Bell 55% negligent. (The report makes no mention of a damages figure.) Both parties appealed on a number of grounds, only one of which involves these evidentiary issues.

The Tenth Circuit Court of Appeals affirmed the exclusion of the evidence about John Ball's flying capabilities and tendencies on two separate grounds. The testimony about instances of overgrossing was rejected as unnecessary because Rocky Mountain agreed Ball was carrying a heavy load at the time of the crash. And testimony from Phil Massicotte, a chief pilot, about Ball's flying competence was properly excluded because it was old news – several months out of date by the time of the crash. "It was remote enough in time to lack relevance and raise concern about the possible prejudicial effect such evidence might have."

Although neither the trial court nor the appellate court cited Rule 405(b) by name, this case clearly illustrates limitations both on proper character evidence under the rule and on when character rises to the level of an "essential element" of a case. Ball's propensity for carrying loads that were dangerously unsafe was not regarded as "essential" here because Rocky Mountain did not contest the weight of the logs Ball was carrying when he crashed – i.e., Ball's "action in conformity" with his propensity.

FRE 405(b) – Child Custody Statute Invoking Moral Fitness of Competing Parties Renders Character an Essential Element of Both Parties' Cases

> **Rule 405. Methods of Proving Character**
>
> *(a) Reputation or Opinion.* In all cases in which evidence of character or a trait of character of a person is admissible, proof may be made by testimony as to reputation or by testimony in the form of an opinion. On cross-examination, inquiry is allowable into relevant specific instances of conduct.
>
> *(b) Specific Instances of Conduct.* In cases in which character or a trait of character of a person is an essential element of a charge, claim, or defense, proof may also be made of specific instances of that person's conduct.

MINTLE v. MINTLE
764 P.2d 255 (Wyo. 1988)

A major issue in the custody battle central to Robert and Teresa Rea Mintle's divorce trial after their ten-year marriage was whether Mrs. Mintle ever planned to "abscond" with their two daughters. Robert Mintle's lawyer was forbidden both to cross-examine Teresa Rea Mintle on the subject and to call a neighbor, Donna Boyd, to testify to what she knew about Mrs. Mintle's plan to take off to another state with the girls. When the divorce decree issued by the Natrona County, Wyoming District Court awarded custody to Teresa Rea Mintle and child support payments of $350 per month, Robert Mintle appealed.

The Wyoming Supreme Court held that a Wyoming statute that directed the trial court to "consider the relative competency of both parties" makes their moral character an issue:[18] "Thus, a party's fitness as a parent is a material fact that is of consequence to the determination of the custody question. Evidence that a custodial parent has taken children from a jurisdiction and thereby denied the other parent visitation can be grounds for modification of a custody decree.... In the same sense, evidence that a parent planned to abscond with children who are the subject of a pending custody battle, and thereby deny the other parent visitation, is relevant.... The trial court did not have to believe that wife planned to leave with the children in an effort to deny husband visitation, but husband's evidence on that issue was relevant.

"Testimony Donna Boyd might have given about wife's alleged plan was similarly relevant and should have been allowed by the trial court. Donna Boyd's conversations with wife about the alleged plan to leave with the children were also admissible as proof of a specific instance of wife's conduct offered to prove her lack of character as a competent custodial parent. In a divorce action involving custody of children, each party's fitness as a parent is an essential element of the claim involved. When a person's character is an essential element of the claim involved, proof of that character may be made by specific instances of conduct."

(The court then ruled the error harmless, saying that it was not likely the evidence if admitted would have changed the outcome.)

FRE 405(b) – Character of Victim Is Not an Essential Element of Self-Defense

> **Rule 405. Methods of Proving Character**
>
> *(a) Reputation or Opinion.* In all cases in which evidence of character or a trait of character of a person is admissible, proof may be made by testimony as to reputation or by testimony in the form of an opinion. On cross-examination, inquiry is allowable into relevant specific instances of conduct.
>
> *(b) Specific Instances of Conduct.* In cases in which character or a trait of character of a person is an essential element of a charge, claim, or defense, proof may also be made of specific instances of that person's conduct.

UNITED STATES v. KEISER
57 F.3d 847 (9th Cir. 1995)

Ronald Keiser, fearing that Victor Romero was going to shoot his brother, Randy Keiser, after a neighborhood altercation, fired a rifle into a group of people near Randy's pickup truck. A bullet struck Romero and paralyzed him from the waist down. Keiser was

---
[18] Many state custody statutes are even more direct in making the parents' moral character an essential element of their cases for custody.

convicted by a jury of assault resulting in serious bodily injury. Keiser testified he saw a companion of Romero's get a gun from his parked car and place it in the back of his pants as he approached the defendant's brother's truck. No such gun was ever found, and Romero's companion said it was beer he had retrieved.

Keiser's lawyer proffered testimony from his brother Randy concerning a verbal altercation with Romero outside the courtroom the previous day, on the issue (among several) of Romero's character, "indicative of his actions on the night in question." The district judge excluded the testimony and the Ninth Circuit Court of Appeals affirmed.

The defendant had the option of offering evidence of the victim's character under Rule 404(a)(2), but the form of such evidence would have been limited by Rule 405(a) to opinion and/or reputation testimony. Although Keiser had the option of placing Romero's character for violence "in issue" had he used reputation or opinion testimony, that did not make Romero's character for violence an "essential element" of Keiser's claim of self-defense under Rule 405(b) so as to enable Keiser to offer evidence of a specific act of Romero.

The court noted, "The relevant question should be: would proof, or failure of proof, of the character trait by itself actually satisfy an element of the charge, claim, or defense? If not, then character is not essential and evidence should be limited to opinion or reputation." As in nearly all[19] criminal cases, the court said the answer here is no. But in saying, "Even had Keiser proven that Romero is a violent person, the jury would still have been free to decide that Romero was not using or about to use unlawful force, or that the force Romero was using was not likely to cause death or great bodily harm, or that Keiser did not reasonably believe force was necessary, or that he used more force than appeared reasonably necessary," the court appears to forget a fundamental reality of evidence law: no single item of evidence is ever conclusive, dispositive by itself: juries are always free to credit or discount evidence, "essential" or not. The real question is, *must* the defense prove the victim to be generally violent in order to win? The answer, of course, is NO.

---

[19]Typical professorial hedge: in fact, the author, a veteran trial lawyer, Evidence professor and trial competition team advisor, has never encountered a contemporary adult crime or defense (except, in a few somewhat confused jurisdictions, entrapment) of which anyone's character trait is an essential element.

FRE 406, 404(b) – Evidence of Prior Conduct Is Admissible to Show Action in Conformity Therewith Only if Repeated Consistently Enough Times

> **Rule 406. Habit; Routine Practice**
> Evidence of the habit of a person or of the routine practice of an organization, whether corroborated or not and regardless of the presence of eyewitnesses, is relevant to prove that the conduct of the person or organization on a particular occasion was in conformity with the habit or routine practice.
>
> **Rule 404. Character Evidence Not Admissible to Prove Conduct; Exceptions; other Crimes**
> *(b) Other Crimes, Wrongs, or Acts.* Evidence of other crimes, wrongs, or acts is not admissible to prove the character of a person in order to show action in conformity therewith....

HALLORAN v. VIRGINIA CHEMICALS, INC.
361 N.E.2d 991, 41 N.Y.2d 386, 393 N.Y.S.2d 341 (1977)

While Frank Halloran, an automobile mechanic, was servicing the air-conditioning unit of a 1967 Chrysler, a can of Freon refrigerant exploded and seriously injured him. He sued the manufacturer, Virginia Chemicals, Inc.

At trial the judge prevented a witness from testifying that Halloran had on previous occasions used an immersion heating coil to accelerate the flow of the Freon into the system. Halloran had denied doing so on cross-examination; his testimony was that he put the can of Freon into a coffee can filled with warm tap water and carefully monitored its temperatures (90°-100°F.) to make sure it did not approach temperatures specified (130°F.) on warning labels.

The jury returned a verdict for Halloran, and Virginia Chemicals appealed. They argued that exclusion of the testimony about Halloran using the immersion heating coil was error.

The Court of Appeals of New York ruled that while evidence of past careless conduct is not admissible to prove action in conformity therewith,[20] evidence of "a consistent practice or method followed by a person" would be admissible as habit evidence to suggest the same thing. The court reversed the verdict and remanded for a new trial at which time Virginia Chemicals "must be able to show on voir dire, to the satisfaction of the Trial Judge, that [they] expect to prove a sufficient number of instances of the conduct in question" to establish a consistent habit.

---

[20] Consistent with the principles underlying FRE 404(b). New York does not have a 'code' of evidence rules – yet.

FRE 406 – Evidence of Habit Need Not Be Corroborated by Testimony That the Person Acted in Conformity With That Habit on the Occasion in Question

> **Rule 406. Habit; Routine Practice**
> Evidence of the habit of a person or of the routine practice of an organization, whether corroborated or not and regardless of the presence of eyewitnesses, is relevant to prove that the conduct of the person or organization on a particular occasion was in conformity with the habit or routine practice.

FRENCH v. SORANO
247 N.W.2d 182, 74 Wis.2d 460 (1976)

Arthur Harmann noticed a very damaged car parked in a lot near his Milwaukee apartment. When Harmann got close to it he could see paper money scattered about the front seat and floor of the car. He reached in, gathered it up, took it home to count it – it came to $2,020 – then went back, put the cash under the front seat, and notified police of his find.

Police contacted Mary Sorano, the widow of the car's previous owner, Sam Sorano; she had sold it two-and-a-half years earlier to an auto dealer. Thomas French was the current owner of the car. He sued for a declaratory judgment that he was entitled to the money as current owner of the car in which it was found, naming as defendants Harmann, Sorano, and the city of Milwaukee. Sorano maintained that her husband was in the habit of hiding money in the car, and that the cash Harmann found was money her husband had left behind in the car before he died five years before. She claimed it as the heir to her husband's estate. (The city disclaimed any interest in the money.)

At trial Mrs. Sorano tried to prove her deceased husband's habit of hiding money in the car a number of ways. She was allowed to testify that she often found money hidden in the car by her husband, but the court sustained an irrelevance objection to her testimony that he made a practice of carrying large sums of money on his person, and to her testimony that her husband's father, Frank Sorano, often hid money in his own car, too. Nor was her son, Gerald Sorano, allowed to testify that he had seen his father hide money in the car on a few occasions. The Milwaukee County Circuit Court entered a judgment declaring Harmann, the finder, to be the owner of the money. Mary Sorano appealed.

On appeal Harmann argued the exclusion of Gerald Sorano's testimony about seeing his father hiding money in the car was proper because there was no testimony offered that anyone had seen him hide the sum of money found by Harmann. The Supreme Court of Wisconsin disagreed, holding that the language of the state equivalent of Federal Rule 406 (Sec. 904.06(1), Stats.) did away with the old common law requirement for corroboration. Harmann argued the son's testimony recounted an insufficient number of observations of his father's practice for it to be admissible as "habit" evidence; the court, apparently unsure how many observations Gerald Sorano testified to, held, "This must be considered a question of sufficiency [weight?] and not admissibility." The court affirmed the trial court's judgment for the finder, Harmann, however, saying the error in excluding proper habit evidence was harmless in light of the near-impossibility of her establishing that her husband had hidden the money in the car.

"Appellant proceeded on the theory that the found money was placed in the car by her deceased husband. She sought to prove this fact by showing her husband had a habit of secreting money in the car and forgetting about it. There is absolutely no indication in the record that any evidence existed which could directly link appellant's husband with this found money. No evidence exists that appellant's husband ever secreted amounts as large as the amount in this case. Appellant testified that on occasion she found ten to twenty dollars in the glove compartment, fifty to two hundred dollars under the mat, or a few hundred dollars in the trunk.

"In addition, there is evidence which casts doubt upon the probability that this money was secreted by appellant's husband. After the husband died, Gerald Sorano used the car until it was sold almost three years later. The car was then owned for a short period of time by a car dealership and certainly could have been checked and cleaned for sale. The car was used by Mr. French for over two years, and the money was found over five and one-half years after the husband's death.

"The appellant, who bears the burden of proof of her contentions, was required to come forward with evidentiary facts which establish the ultimate facts. The degree of proof required must be such as will remove the ultimate facts to be found by the fact finder from the field of speculation and conjecture. Here, even if a habit of the husband had been conclusively established, it would be mere speculation that the found money was secreted by appellant's husband."

FRE 406 – Habit Evidence Must Be Sufficiently Distinctive and Specific to Distinguish It from Character Evidence

> **Rule 406. Habit; Routine Practice**
> Evidence of the habit of a person or of the routine practice of an organization, whether corroborated or not and regardless of the presence of eyewitnesses, is relevant to prove that the conduct of the person or organization on a particular occasion was in conformity with the habit or routine practice.

CHARMLEY v. LEWIS
729 P.2d 567, 302 Or. 324 (1986)

On "a dark and stormy night"[21] in November 1981, John R. Charmley was walking home from the grocery store in Portland. As he crossed North Ida Street at its T intersection with North Syracuse Street, he was struck and injured by a car driven by Ronald N. Lewis. At the trial of Charmley's personal injury lawsuit, Lewis testified that Charmley ran out from behind a parked car outside the unmarked crosswalk at the intersection. Charmley testified he had no recollection of the incident. There were no

---

[21] The appellate court's "hesitation" so to characterize the setting for this case must be noted, even if its reluctance is hardly shared by the author of this collection, who is delighted by the rare note of grace and levity.

other eyewitnesses to the collision. Charmley was permitted, however, to testify that it was his invariable habit to cross the intersection within the crosswalk: "when he crossed North Ida Street at the intersection, he always walked from the northwest corner to the northeast corner and then turned left and walked north about 20 feet along the sidewalk where he would enter the driveway to the store's parking lot. This route was within the unmarked crosswalk. Plaintiff testified that he never walked diagonally from the northwest corner to the driveway of the grocery store, and he never walked past the northwest corner to cross North Ida Street directly across from the driveway (and outside the unmarked crosswalk)." (If Charmley was within the crosswalk, albeit that it was unmarked, when he was hit by Lewis's vehicle, then he had the right of way.)

Five other witnesses corroborated Charmley's testimony about his habit of crossing that specific street in that particular manner. They "all testified that they had seen plaintiff cross straight across the street in the manner plaintiff described and never otherwise. The observations occurred on many occasions and at various times during the day and year, although most observations were made during the summer."

The jury verdict was in favor of the pedestrian Charmley (no damages figure is reported), and Lewis appealed on the sole issue of the habit evidence, contending it was admitted improperly because the situations the witnesses testified to did not include "rainy winter evenings."

Both the Oregon Court of Appeals and the Oregon Supreme Court affirmed the verdict. Although Oregon Rule 406 contains a provision not found in the text of the federal rule ("(2)...'habit' means a person's regular practice of meeting a particular kind of situation with a specific, distinctive type of conduct"), the added verbiage is exactly consistent with the McCormick passage that informs the federal rule. It was added to keep out "habits that everyone has, such as stopping at stop signs," and, like the federal rule, is meant to be more specific than a "habit of carefulness," which is more properly classified as character evidence. Charmley's habit of crossing North Ida Street in a specific way qualified: it was "ingrained," it was observed frequently, and it was described with painstaking specificity. Charmley was "confronted by a particular situation to which a variety of definable responses would be more or less equally reasonable." And the rule "does not necessitate an exact duplication of the climatic conditions" prevailing when Charmley was seen crossing the street all those times.

A dissenting justice thought the majority was too liberal in granting "habit" status to Charmley's pattern of crossing the street in his particular way.

FRE 406 – Evidence of Company's Routine Practice of Inserting Form in Mailings Is Admissible on Question Whether Party Received Form

> **Rule 406. Habit; Routine Practice**
> Evidence of the habit of a person or of the routine practice of an organization, whether corroborated or not and regardless of the presence of eyewitnesses, is relevant to prove that the conduct of the person or organization on a particular occasion was in conformity with the habit or routine practice.

PROGRESSIVE AMERICAN INSURANCE COMPANY v. KURTZ
518 So.2d 1339 (Fla. App. 1987)

An accident with an uninsured driver left George Kurtz with serious injuries. Progressive American Insurance Co. was Kurtz's automobile policy insurer. His coverage generally was $100,000/$300,000; at issue was the amount of "Uninsured Motorist" (UM) coverage he had. Kurtz thought it was $100,000/$300,000; the company claimed it was only $10,000/$20,000. Kurtz filed suit against the company in St. John's County Circuit Court, claiming the company failed to notify him in its renewal/premium notice of his UM options and failed to provide him the means of requesting higher UM coverages as required by Florida law. The insurer claimed it mailed a "Form 1258" to Kurtz with its October 27, 1982 renewal notice.

"The insurer established that it was the insurer's general and routine practice and procedure to insert a copy of its Form 1258 into each envelope containing a premium renewal notice mailed to each insured. However, the insurer presented no evidence that this practice was followed in the particular instance at issue." The trial court found for Kurtz, despite holding the company's "routine practice" evidence admissible under Florida's statutory version of Rule 406.[22] (It held the evidence insufficient to establish that the form was mailed on the particular instance in question.)

The Florida Fifth District Court of Appeal reversed, holding the "routine practice" evidence not only admissible but also sufficient to create a presumption that Kurtz received the form unless he specifically rebutted it. (Kurtz denied receiving that form with other mailings, but (likely inadvertently) failed to deny receiving the form with the October 27, 1982 notice.)

---
[22] Sec. 90.406, Fla.Stat.

FRE 407 – Subsequent Remedial Measures Are Admissible for Limited Purpose of Impeachment if Defense Witness Exaggerates Virtues of Product

> **Rule 407. Subsequent Remedial Measures**
> When, after an injury or harm allegedly caused by an event, measures are taken that, if taken previously, would have made the injury or harm less likely to occur, evidence of the subsequent measures is not admissible to prove negligence, culpable conduct, a defect in a product, a defect in a product's design, or a need for a warning or instruction. This rule does not require the exclusion of evidence of subsequent measures when offered for another purpose, such as proving ownership, control, or feasibility of precautionary measures, if controverted or impeachment.

MUZYKA v. REMINGTON ARMS CO. INC.
774 F.2d 1309 (5th Cir. 1985)

Dawn Muzyka was injured when her late husband's Remington rifle accidentally fired while her stepfather, who was helping her move, was checking it before packing it. Her complaint alleged the "two-position, bolt-lock safety" on the rifle was defectively designed and unreasonably dangerous in that it could be emptied only by taking the gun off safety position and working the bolt.

A few months after the accident Remington redesigned the model in question to permit working the bolt to unload the rifle without taking the safety off. Remington moved *in limine* to exclude evidence of the new design under Rule 407, and the trial court granted the motion.

The jury found for Remington. Muzyka appealed the denial of her motion for a new trial, contending Remington opened the door to use of the subsequent design change for impeachment purposes. The trial court had disallowed such use over Muzyka's repeated arguments that such impeachment was called for by Remington's defense posture.

The Fifth Circuit Court of Appeals quoted extensively from the record at trial, reasoning that in opening statements by Remington's counsel, in testimony by its experts, and in final argument, the safety of the rifle's design was extolled in unvarying superlatives: the Remington 700 was called "the most popular rifle in the whole world, the rifle against which other rifles are judged,... the best combination of safety and operation yet devised," "maybe the best production rifle ever designed in the world," a "9.8 or 9.9 [on a scale of one to ten]" where "nothing can be a ten," the "premier rifle in the country today," the standard against which all other rifle manufacturers measure their own products.

The court held that "in light of the posture of the defense, and the manner in which the evidence unfolded, especially in light of defense counsel's opening statement and closing argument, evidence of the design-change should have been permitted for purposes of impeachment." The verdict for defendant was vacated and the case remanded for a new trial.

It should be noted that it was not the mere denial of liability by Remington, nor even its entirely commonplace claim that its rifle was safe, that opened the door to use of its subsequent remedial measure for impeachment under Rule 407. Rather it was the extravagance of its claims for its gun, the extremeness of its defense, that did the defendant in. To permit such exaggerated claims to go unchallenged by evidence of the subsequent design change may well have misled the jury.

FRE 407 – Subsequent Remedial Measures Are Admissible to Show Feasibility of Precautionary Measures When Defense Witness Says Improvements Are Not Feasible

> **Rule 407. Subsequent Remedial Measures**
> When, after an injury or harm allegedly caused by an event, measures are taken that, if taken previously, would have made the injury or harm less likely to occur, evidence of the subsequent measures is not admissible to prove negligence, culpable conduct, a defect in a product, a defect in a product's design, or a need for a warning or instruction. This rule does not require the exclusion of evidence of subsequent measures when offered for another purpose, such as proving ownership, control, or feasibility of precautionary measures, if controverted or impeachment.

BOEING AIRPLANE CO. v. BROWN
291 F.2d 310 (9th Cir. 1961)

Air Force Major Albert Brown was killed when the B-52 he and his crew were delivering to the Air Force exploded and crashed over California in 1956. Brown's minor son was awarded $26,000 in a nonjury trial, and Boeing appealed.

Brown claimed Boeing was negligent for installing inherently defective components in an alternator turbine drive. During the fatal flight, the alternator drive's turbine wheel had gone into excessive overspeed and disintegrated. Pieces of the wheel penetrated a fuel tank causing the explosion and crash.

Brown presented expert testimony showing the alternator drive as designed was structurally inadequate, and that it would have been practicable to guard the wheel with one-tenth of an inch of steel armor-plating "instead of the 'fragile' aluminum shroud which was used," and to strengthen the parts to prevent failure. Boeing's expert testified that the parts as presently designed were sufficient, and that the weight involved in providing armor-plating would be prohibitive.

Brown was allowed to introduce evidence of changes Boeing made in the drive after the crash for the limited purpose of showing it would have been feasible and practicable to incorporate those features in the design of the drive. Boeing appealed on this issue, among several.

The Ninth Circuit Court of Appeals held that the District Court had not erred in receiving the evidence. The feasibility of designing a drive that would overcome the asserted defects had been controverted by Boeing when its expert said that changing the design would add too much weight to the plane. The common law bar against subsequent remedial measures (the predecessor to Rule 407) did not apply to the limited purpose of showing the feasibility of the plaintiff's proposed changes when the feasibility of such changes had been controverted by the defendant. Thus the admissibility of the subsequent remedial measure was, as always, to a large degree within the control of the defendant.

FRE 407 – Post-Accident Design Change by Non-Party Is Admissible on Question of Party's Negligence

> **Rule 407. Subsequent Remedial Measures**
> When, after an injury or harm allegedly caused by an event, measures are taken that, if taken previously, would have made the injury or harm less likely to occur, evidence of the subsequent measures is not admissible to prove negligence, culpable conduct, a defect in a product, a defect in a product's design, or a need for a warning or instruction. This rule does not require the exclusion of evidence of subsequent measures when offered for another purpose, such as proving ownership, control, or feasibility of precautionary measures, if controverted or impeachment.

HARTMAN v. OPELIKA MACHINE & WELDING COMPANY
414 So.2d 1105 (Fla. App. 1982)

Ida Jean Hartman worked at a Monsanto Textiles Company mill as a "drawtwist operator." She was injured when a machine manufactured by Opelika Machine & Welding Company broke and made her fall. "Her job was to take finished yarn from one drawtwist machine, put the spools of finished yarn onto the arms of a spin buggy, and move on to the next machine. The spin buggy had a rectangular base, and was mounted on four wheels so that it could be rolled by the operator along the plant floor from machine to machine. At each end of the spin buggy's rectangular base were stanchions to which were welded several projecting arms made of aluminum tubing, that served as handles for moving the buggy and to hold the bobbins of yarn. The accident occurred while [Hartman] was walking backwards pulling at the same time the top arm of the buggy with her right hand, when the arm handle broke off, thereby causing her to fall onto the concrete floor."

Hartman sued Opelika in Escambia County Circuit Court on theories of negligence, implied warranty, and strict liability. The trial court directed a verdict for Opelika on the strict liability count as to any manufacturing defect when all the evidence showed Monsanto supplied all the design specifications to Opelika for fabrication of the spin buggy. The jury found for Opelika on the negligence and implied warranty counts, and Hartman appealed.

At trial Opelika had offered evidence that after Hartman's accident, Monsanto had changed the design of the spin buggy by substituting "steel bars for the hollow aluminum tubing arms, and the welding of a bracket to each arm where it joined the stanchion." In her appeal to the Florida First District Court of Appeal Hartman argued that admitting this information was improper under Florida's equivalent of Rule 407.[23] The appellate court affirmed the trial court's handling of the evidence, because the rule

---
[23]Ordinarily, of course, it is the *plaintiff* trying to a offer such evidence and the *defendant* resisting its admission. What gives this case such an odd feel is that the d*efendant* is saying, in essence, "The Devil made me do it," and trying to show it was someone else's fault that the machine it manufactured came apart and caused an injury.

(and the policy underlying it) does not apply to a subsequent remedial measure taken by a non-party. Monsanto's design change was not offered against Monsanto, which was not a party to this suit, so nothing in the admission of such evidence would discourage Monsanto from continuing to improve upon its design. "This policy consideration is absent in a case… where imposition of liability is not sought against the person taking the remedial action."

(The court, however, reversed the directed verdict on the strict liability count: "Opelika was in the business of manufacturing and supplying products such as the spin buggy to independent customers, and we find no authority to suggest that Opelika's liability for a defectively welded part should be determined on different principles than for a manufacturer who places its product on the market for sale to the general public.")

FRE 408 – Expert's Report Prepared Expressly to Facilitate Settlement Is Not Admissible Under "Otherwise Discoverable" Clause

> **Rule 408. Compromise and Offers of Compromise**
>
> Evidence of (1) furnishing or offering or promising to furnish, or (2) accepting or offering or promising to accept, a valuable consideration in compromising or attempting to compromise a claim which was disputed as to either validity or amount, is not admissible to prove liability for or invalidity of the claim or its amount. Evidence of conduct or statements made in compromise negotiations is likewise not admissible. This rule does not require the exclusion of any evidence otherwise discoverable merely because it is presented in the course of compromise negotiations. This rule also does not require exclusion when the evidence is offered for another purpose, such as proving bias or prejudice of a witness, negativing a contention of undue delay, or proving an effort to obstruct a criminal investigation or prosecution.

RAMADA DEVELOPMENT CO. v. RAUCH
644 F. 2d 1097 (5th Cir. 1981)

In an attempt to settle a lawsuit arising out of Martin Rauch's refusal to authorize his lender to disburse the final payment of a motel construction contract for a building in Venice, Florida, Ramada Development company hired an architect to study the construction defects alleged by Rauch. The effort to settle was not successful, and at trial Rauch attempted to introduce the so-called Goldsmith Report in his case-in-chief. The district court judge for the Middle District of Florida excluded the report under Rule 408. Verdicts amounting to more than $500,000 were entered against Rauch, and he appealed on a variety of grounds.

In affirming the evidentiary ruling of the trial judge, the Fifth Circuit Court of Appeals considered the "otherwise discoverable" exception to Rule 408's ban on statements and conduct that occur during settlement negotiations. The court held that the Goldsmith Report was prepared to "function as a basis of settlement," and as such "would not have existed but for the negotiations." The exception invoked by Rauch in his appeal was intended to apply only to situations where bringing up information during compromise negotiations would "thwart discovery by making existing [evidence] unreachable." The Goldsmith Report would not have been unreachable, it would simply not have been prepared at all.

FRE 408 – Evidence of Settlement Negotiations Is Admissible on Question of Plaintiff's Failure to Mitigate Damages

> **Rule 408. Compromise and Offers to Compromise**
> Evidence of (1) furnishing or offering or promising to furnish, or (2) accepting or offering or promising to accept, a valuable consideration in compromising or attempting to compromise a claim which was disputed as to either validity or amount, is not admissible to prove liability for or invalidity of the claim or its amount. Evidence of conduct or statements made in compromise negotiations is likewise not admissible. This rule does not require the exclusion of any evidence otherwise discoverable merely because it is presented in the course of compromise negotiations. This rule also does not require exclusion when the evidence is offered for another purpose, such as proving bias or prejudice of a witness, negativing a contention of undue delay, or proving an effort to obstruct a criminal investigation or prosecution.

BHANDARI v. FIRST NATIONAL BANK OF COMMERCE
808 F.2d 1082 (5th Cir. 1987)

Jeetendra Bhandari, a citizen of India but a lawful permanent resident of the United States, applied for a bank credit card from First National Bank of Commerce. The bank denied the card because Bhandari was an alien and because of his short time at his current job. Although subsequent discussions between Bhandari, his attorney, and bank officials clarified Bhandari's status and produced an offer of a credit card, Bhandari demanded more, including attorneys' fees of $1,500 and the bank's explicit authorization for "Bhandari and his attorney to represent to various United States organizations and newspapers related to immigration and Indian affairs that First National's policy was changed due to their efforts." The bank, not surprisingly, refused. Bhandari filed suit alleging civil rights violations and violations of the federal Equal Credit Opportunity Act. The District Court for the Eastern District of Louisiana ruled that neither the civil rights act nor the credit act provided an alien a claim, but that the bank had violated the act by not fully disclosing all its reasons for denying Bhandari credit. He was awarded modest attorneys' fees of $1,500. Bhandari appealed, raising among several issues the fact that the trial court had permitted the bank to introduce evidence of the settlement negotiations.

The Fifth Circuit Court of Appeals reversed in part on questions of the applicability of the civil rights acts and the Equal Credit Opportunity Act, but affirmed the trial court's Rule 408 ruling. The court noted that the Rule excludes evidence of settlement negotiations when offered to prove liability (or its absence), but not for "another" purpose. Here it was properly offered and relevant to the question of mitigation of damages (which the appellate court seems to imply Bhandari failed to do).

FRE 408 – Letters Containing Offers to Settle Are Admissible for Purpose of Rebutting Testimony of Undue Delay

> **Rule 408. Compromise and Offers to Compromise**
>
> Evidence of (1) furnishing or offering or promising to furnish, or (2) accepting or offering or promising to accept, a valuable consideration in compromising or attempting to compromise a claim which was disputed as to either validity or amount, is not admissible to prove liability for or invalidity of the claim or its amount. Evidence of conduct or statements made in compromise negotiations is likewise not admissible. This rule does not require the exclusion of any evidence otherwise discoverable merely because it is presented in the course of compromise negotiations. This rule also does not require exclusion when the evidence is offered for another purpose, such as proving bias or prejudice of a witness, negativing a contention of undue delay, or proving an effort to obstruct a criminal investigation or prosecution.

FREIDUS v. FIRST NATIONAL BANK
928 F.2d 793 (8th Cir. 1991)

Ella Freidus sued the First National Bank of Council Bluffs, Iowa for breach of contract, claiming the bank had unreasonably withheld consent to allow her to sell farm land that she was purchasing on a land contract (contract for deed) from the bank. The bank imposed some conditions on the sale, which Freidus took as a refusal. Paragraph 16 of the land contract provided that Freidus had to obtain the bank's consent before selling, "which consent shall not be unreasonably withheld."

The parties exchanged a series of letters in August, 1989 in an effort to settle the lawsuit. Settlement fell through when Freidus' buyer, Danielski Farming and Harvesting, called off its purchase because of delays and changes. At trial the District Judge admitted into evidence two of the August letters exchanged between the parties. The jury found for the bank, finding no unreasonable withholding of consent.

Freidus appealed, citing Rule 408. The Eighth Circuit Court of Appeals affirmed the verdict, holding that the letters had not been admitted to prove "liability for or invalidity of a claim or its amount," which the rule forbids. The letters had been admitted properly, said the appellate court, to rebut testimony by Ella Freidus' husband and agent, Jacob Freidus, that the bank had never given any reasons for its requirement of the satisfaction of the conditions it imposed. "Left unrebutted, [Jacob Freidus' testimony] would have been devastating to the bank's position that it had not unduly delayed giving its consent."

FRE 408 – Third Party Settlements Are Ordinarily Inadmissible, But Are Admissible to Show Bias

> **Rule 408. Compromise and Offers to Compromise**
>
> Evidence of (1) furnishing or offering or promising to furnish, or (2) accepting or offering or promising to accept, a valuable consideration in compromising or attempting to compromise a claim which was disputed as to either validity or amount, is not admissible to prove liability for or invalidity of the claim or its amount. Evidence of conduct or statements made in compromise negotiations is likewise not admissible. This rule does not require the exclusion of any evidence otherwise discoverable merely because it is presented in the course of compromise negotiations. This rule also does not require exclusion when the evidence is offered for another purpose, such as proving bias or prejudice of a witness, negativing a contention of undue delay, or proving an effort to obstruct a criminal investigation or prosecution.

HUDSPETH v. COMMISSIONER OF INTERNAL REVENUE
914 F.2d 1207 (9th Cir. 1990)

A dispute between the owners of Husdpeth Pine, Inc., and the IRS concerned the valuation of harvested pine and fir for tax treatment for 1973, 1974 and 1975. To prepare for trial in tax court Hudspeth retained an expert, Gail Thomas, who submitted his report which based the timber's value on information generated in a dispute involving a different company, Pine Products Corporation. The IRS had settled its dispute with Pine Products.

The Commissioner moved to exclude the valuation data Thomas had generated based on Rule 408. The tax court agreed. The tax court's decision ultimately favored the Commissioner on the issue of timber valuation.

The Hudspeths appealed, asserting that Rule 408 does not apply to disputes to which they were not a party. They also contended that the data showed bias on the part of the Commissioner.

The Ninth Circuit Court of Appeals reversed the valuation decision. Admitting the prior settlement data with Pine Products in order to establish substantive value in this case would have undercut the basic policy behind Rule 408 because "settlements by the Commissioner would be inhibited if the Commissioner would have to review whether a settlement could be binding in subsequent cases." But given the similarities in the situations of both Pine Products and Hudspeth Pine, the disparities in the numbers arrived at by the IRS in the two cases should have been admitted on the issue of bias or prejudice of the Commissioner's valuation expert. Bias or prejudice of a witness is expressly excluded from Rule 408's bar on settlement information.

FRE 408 – Admissions Made During Civil Settlement Negotiations Are Fully Admissible in Criminal Case

> **Rule 408. Compromise and Offers to Compromise**
>
> Evidence of (1) furnishing or offering or promising to furnish, or (2) accepting or offering or promising to accept, a valuable consideration in compromising or attempting to compromise a claim which was disputed as to either validity or amount, is not admissible to prove liability for or invalidity of the claim or its amount. Evidence of conduct or statements made in compromise negotiations is likewise not admissible. This rule does not require the exclusion of any evidence otherwise discoverable merely because it is presented in the course of compromise negotiations. This rule also does not require exclusion when the evidence is offered for another purpose, such as proving bias or prejudice of a witness, negativing a contention of undue delay, or proving an effort to obstruct a criminal investigation or prosecution.

UNITED STATES v. GONZALEZ
748 F.2d 74 (2d Cir. 1984)

In connection with a scheme for fraudulently obtaining two five-million-dollar loans from banks in Spain and Portugal, Rufo Gonzalez was indicted on 13 counts of wire fraud and one count of mail fraud.

Over objection by Gonzalez's lawyer, based on Rule 408, the trial judge permitted David Frauman, an attorney for Banco Pinto, to testify that at a meeting in May 1982 that involved the bank's civil claims against Gonzalez arising from these loan transaction, Gonzalez conceded the note to Banco Pinto was a forgery and that he had used loan proceeds for commodity trading. The government also was permitted to offer into evidence a Confession of Judgment executed by Gonzalez in June 1982 admitting personal liability for the full amount of the debt to Banco Pinto.

The jury convicted Gonzalez on all counts and he appealed, in part on the Rule 408 issue raised at trial.

The Second Circuit Court of Appeals affirmed all but one of the convictions. The court ruled both the testimony about the earlier admissions and the Confession of Judgment to be admissible, not covered by Rule 408's exclusion: "In this criminal prosecution, Gonzalez's statements were admitted to establish that Gonzalez had committed a crime, and their relevance to that issue does not depend on an inference that Banco Pinto had a valid civil claim against Gonzalez. The evidence was offered for a purpose other than one for which Rule 408 requires exclusion."

The court went further still in its discussion of the admissibility in criminal cases of admissions made in the course of civil settlement discussions: the primary policy objective of Rule 408, "encouraging settlement, does not justify excluding probative and otherwise admissible evidence in criminal prosecutions. The public interest in the disclosure and prosecution of crime is surely greater than the public interest in the settlement of civil disputes."

FRE 409 – Admission of Testimony About Defendant's Offer to Pay Medical Expenses Is Reversible Error

> **Rule 409. Payment of Medical and Similar Expenses**
> Evidence of furnishing or offering or promising to pay medical, hospital, or similar expenses occasioned by an injury is not admissible to prove liability for the injury.

HOME INSURANCE COMPANY v. SPEARS
590 S.W.2d 71, 267 Ark. 704 (Ark. App. 1979)

While three local farmers were watching pollution tests being conducted on the creek below them, the iron bridge railings they were leaning on collapsed and they fell into the creek bed. The three, Bobby Jack Spears, Donald Jackson and Rex England, and their wives, sued Washington County for their personal injuries. The jury rendered verdicts of $30,000 for Spears and Jackson, $6,375 for England, $1,875 for Shirley Jean Jackson, and $750 for Shirley Jeanne Spears. The county's insurer, Home Insurance Company, appealed.

One prominent issue on appeal concerned testimony that was permitted over the county's objection, about an offer to pay medical expenses. Rex England testified that the county judge told him to bring him all the medical bills and "the insurance company would pay it."[24] The Arkansas Court of Appeals reversed, noting, "If there were doubt as to the purpose for which this evidence was offered, the record clearly indicates that appellee's purpose was to introduce evidence on the question of liability. The appellee admits that the testimony was 'simply to show the issue of liability.'" Hence the evidence was clearly barred by the Arkansas version of Rule 409, whose purpose is to encourage "humanitarian and benevolent instincts" free from the "hazard that assistance to an injured person might be taken as an admission of liability in a personal injury action."

---
[24]Rule 411 would surely render the reference inadmissible in any event.

FRE 410 – Disclosures by Accused Are Inadmissible Only if Made During Plea Discussion with Attorney

> **Rule 410. Inadmissibility of Pleas, Plea Discussions, and Related Statements**
>
> Except as otherwise provided in this rule, evidence of the following is not, in any civil or criminal proceeding, admissible against the defendant who made the plea or was a participant in the plea discussions:
>
> …
>
> (4) any statement made in the course of plea discussions with an attorney for the prosecuting authority which do not result in a plea of guilty or which result in a plea of guilty later withdrawn.

UNITED STATES v. ROBERTSON
582 F.2d 1356 (5th Cir. 1976)

Arrested on federal drug charges, Andrew Jackson Robertson and three others were given their Miranda warnings. Just before they were to be transported from the El Paso DEA office to the U.S. courthouse for arraignment before a magistrate, Robertson and William Butigan talked about their involvement in the crime with DEA agents in the parking lot. At trial those statements were admitted[25] over Robertson's objection under Rule 410 that the conversation constituted plea negotiations.

Robertson appealed his conviction to the Fifth Circuit Court of Appeals, which in an en banc opinion affirmed. A "detailed and careful review of the record" convinced the court that while Robertson may well have been sincere in stating he believed the context for his admissions was a plea negotiation, under all the circumstances he was both mistaken and unreasonably so. DEA Agent Pool said defendant Butigan first brought up the idea of telling agents "everything they wanted to know" if it might help get Butigan's wife and Robertson's female companion released uncharged. Pool and Agent Widener let them confer together, then both Butigan and Robertson gave an extensive, detailed statement admitting their own criminal activity. Agents Pool and Widener maintained they told Robertson and Butigan they had no authority to release the women or to make any promises to the men but that their co-operation would be noted to "Judicial Authorities," but Robertson testified he recalled no such disclaimers. Robertson seems to have been arguing that his co-defendant, Butigan, persuaded him to confess by representing that he, Butigan, had been promised by the agents that their co-operation would result in the release of the women.

The full panel of the Fifth Circuit was unconvinced that Robertson was reasonable in his belief that he was engaging in plea negotiations with individuals who had authority to bargain. "[S]urely not every discussion between an accused and agents for the government is a plea negotiation. Suppressing evidence of such negotiations serves the policy of insuring a free dialogue only when the accused and the government actually engage in plea negotiations." While the accused's state of mind is "critical," a "two-tiered" analysis or "wholistic" examination of the situation must be made which also takes

---

[25] See FRE 801(d)(2)(A) admitting party admissions over a hearsay objection.

into account the reasonableness of the defendant's objective belief. "A bargained confession, without more, is not a plea negotiation.... Robertson's expression of a subjective desire to negotiate a plea came after the fact."

FRE 410 – Statements Made Unconditionally or in Vague Hope of Benefits Are Fully Admissible

> **Rule 410. Inadmissibility of Pleas, Plea Discussions, and Related Statements**
>
> Except as otherwise provided in this rule, evidence of the following is not, in any civil or criminal proceeding, admissible against the defendant who made the plea or was a participant in the plea discussions:
>
> ...
>
> (4) any statement made in the course of plea discussions with an attorney for the prosecuting authority which do not result in a plea of guilty or which result in a plea of guilty later withdrawn.

UNITED STATES v. HARE
49 F.3d 447 (8th Cir. 1995)

When FBI agents arrived at the law office of Kevin Hare in Kansas City, Mo., to arrest him in connection with a scheme to defraud Ferrell T. Riley, the owner of an insurance agency, in a bogus attempt to get Riley a license through a phoney bribe set-up, Hare said he had been expecting them and showed them a written confession he had been preparing. In an interview that day with an Assistant U.S. Attorney, Hare spoke of his remorse and, with no talk of a plea or sentencing agreement on the table, admitted his participation in the criminal scheme. For the next several weeks Hare continued to co-operate in the investigation.

Two months after his arrest Hare and his federal public defender for the first time discussed possible plea and/or sentencing arrangements. An agreement was reached under which Hare would continue to cooperate in exchange for a reduction of charges to two lesser counts and a downward departure sentencing motion by the AUSA.

Two weeks later Hare was apprehended trying to flee to Canada, and he was indicted for six counts of wire fraud, three counts of money laundering, and criminal forfeiture. At trial Hare sought to have the district court suppress all statements he made to FBI agents and the AUSA under Rule 410. The trial court denied Hare's motion to suppress, and Hare was ultimately convicted of four counts of wire fraud and all three counts of money laundering. He was sentenced to 46 months in prison and fined $5250.

On appeal, the Eighth Circuit Court of Appeals affirmed the convictions, holding that Hare's statements were not protected by Rule 410. Any statements Hare made before formal plea and sentencing discussions began were not covered by Rule 410 no matter what Hare's subjective expectations were of the benefits his co-operation would gain him. Vague discussions not involving specifics of an offer did not make the statements plea negotiations. And the court held that statements Hare made after reaching a specific plea agreement were also not covered, because "statements made after the agreement had been reached cannot be said to have been made in the course of plea discussions."

It is not clear from the opinion how much use the government made of the statements Hare gave pursuant to the cooperation he undertook under the terms of the plea agreement once it was reached, but the Eighth Circuit's view of "plea discussions" covered by Rule 410 appears to be far narrower than would seem to be justified. The plea agreement called for continued cooperation, so Hare's statements were clearly being made to assure the availability of the reduced charges and downward sentencing departure motion, and ultimately these discussions did "not result in a plea of guilty." There is some support, however, in other cases for this ultra-narrow view of the scope of "plea discussions."

FRE 401, 410 – Testimony About Immunity Negotiations Is Admissible When Offered by Defendant

> **Rule 401. Definition of "Relevant Evidence"**
>
> "Relevant evidence" means evidence having any tendency to make the existence of any fact that is of consequence to the determination of the action more probable or less probable than it would be without the evidence.
>
> **Rule 410. Inadmissibility of Pleas, Plea Discussions, and Related Statements**
>
> Except as otherwise provided in this rule, evidence of the following is not, in any civil or criminal proceedings, admissible against the defendant who made the plea or was a participant in the plea discussions:
>
> (1) a plea of guilty which was later withdrawn;
>
> (2) a plea of nolo contendere;
>
> (3) any statement made in the course of any proceedings under Rule 11 of the Federal Rules of Criminal Procedure or comparable state procedure regarding either of the foregoing pleas; or
>
> (4) any statement made in the course of plea discussions with an attorney for the prosecuting authority which do not result in a plea of guilty or which result in a plea of guilty later withdrawn.
>
> However, such a statement is admissible (i) in any proceeding wherein another statement made in the course of the same plea or plea discussions has been introduced and the statement ought in fairness be considered contemporaneously with it, or (ii) in a criminal proceeding for perjury or false statement if the statement was made by the defendant under oath, on the record and in the presence of counsel.

<u>UNITED STATES v. BIAGGI</u>
909 F.2d 662 (2d Cir. 1990)

Former U.S. Congressman Mario Biaggi, his son Richard, his former law partner Bernard Ehrlich, former Bronx Borough President Stanley Simon, Peter Neglia, the former New York regional Administrator of the Small Business Administration, and John Mariotta, former C.E.O. of Wedtech, a defense contractor in the Bronx, were all convicted of a variety of charges, including bribery, stock fraud, extortion, filing false financial disclosures, and tax fraud. They received prison sentences of from two to eight years and fines of from $30,000 to $291,000. Substantial judgments of forfeiture were also entered against the six, in amounts ranging from $25,000 to $11,700,000 in the case of Mariotta.

Mariotta was prevented at trial from presenting evidence of immunity negotiations. He claimed he rejected an offer of immunity because he had no knowledge of Wedtech officers' wrongdoing. Thus the offer and its rejection (the government contended Mariotta simply was unable or unwilling to comply with the condition of the offer) were claimed to be relevant to Mariotta's "consciousness of innocence." The government argued the matter was irrelevant, or that Rule 410 kept it out of evidence.

On appeal to the Second Circuit Court of Appeals, John Mariotta won reversal of his convictions as to five of the many counts on which he had been tried. The appellate court noted that the government had been allowed to show evidence of Mariotta's consciousness of guilt, i.e., his wife's withdrawal of $3.5 million from a joint account shortly after co-operating witnesses pled guilty and her purchase of gold bars and other investments in her own name with the proceeds. Therefore it was especially relevant that Mariotta's rejection of immunity might show an innocent state of mind.

The government's argument that Rule 410 barred introduction of the immunity discussions was also rejected. The rule shields the defendant, not the government. Moreover, the Second Circuit seems to have had some doubts whether discussions involving immunity, as opposed to a plea agreement per se, whatever their probative force, were even governed by Rule 410.

FRE 411 – Evidence of Liability Insurance Is Admissible to Prove Ownership and Control

Rule 411. Liability Insurance
Evidence that a person was or was not insured against liability is not admissible upon the issue whether the person acted negligently or otherwise wrongfully. This rule does not require the exclusion of evidence of insurance against liability when offered for another purpose, such as proof of agency, ownership, or control, or bias or prejudice of a witness.

DOBBINS v. CRAIN BROTHERS, INC.
432 F. Supp. 1060 (W.D. Pa. 1976), aff'd in part, rev'd in part, 567 F.2d 559 (3d. Cir. 1977)

While in the process of "rounding" two barges (moving them manually by letting the river current shift their position) for his employer, the Pittsburgh and Lake Erie Railroad Co., stevedore Chester Dobbins slipped on the snow- and ice-covered deck of a barge that belonged to Crain Brothers. In Dobbins' suit, Crain Brothers contested, among several issues, their duty in light of their contention that the barge was effectively under P & LE's control. Following a verdict of $320,000 against Crain Brothers and P & LE, Crain Brothers moved for a new trial and for judgment n.o.v. One of the grounds advanced was that the court had erroneously permitted Dobbins to admit in evidence Crain Brothers' liability insurance policy on the barge Dobbins had slipped on.

The District Court denied the motions and noted that ownership and control had been "hotly contested" at trial. "The existence of insurance is some evidence of such ownership and control which may properly be considered by the jury under the exception clause to Rule 411..."

It is worth emphasizing that although Rule 411 does not contain the words "if controverted" as Rule 407 does,[26] the omission is not significant: courts treat Rule 411 as though those words were present to modify "proof of agency, ownership or control."

FRE 411 – Evidence of Liability Insurance Is Admissible to Impeach Witness Employed by Defendant's Insurer

> **Rule 411. Liability Insurance**
> Evidence that a person was or was not insured against liability is not admissible upon the issue whether the person acted negligently or otherwise wrongfully. This rule does not require the exclusion of evidence of insurance against liability when offered for another purpose, such as proof of agency, ownership, or control, or bias or prejudice of a witness.

CHARTER v. CHLEBORAD
551 F.2d 246 (8th Cir. 1977)

A highway flagman, Roger Charter, was hit by a truck and suffered serious injuries to both legs. Dr. William Chleborad, M.D., operated on Charter's legs. Complications developed and both Charter's legs had to be amputated above the knee. Charter sued Dr. Chleborad for malpractice, claiming the doctor's failure to use the requisite standard of care caused the post-surgical complications and the need for the amputations.

At trial Charter presented the testimony of Dr. Joseph Lichtor of Kansas City, Mo., an orthopedic surgeon, who supported Charter's theory of malpractice. The defense called attorney John Alder in rebuttal, who testified[27] that Dr. Lichtor's reputation for truthfulness was bad. Although Charter's attorney was permitted to elicit from Alder on cross-examination that Alder did some defense work in medical malpractice cases and that some of his defense clients were insurance companies, the district judge refused to permit inquiry that would have disclosed that Alder was employed by Dr. Chleborad's liability carrier.

The jury returned a verdict for the defendant and Charter appealed, claiming that he should have been allowed to impeach Alder for bias by showing his employment by defendant's insurer. The Eighth Circuit agreed, reversing the judgment and remanding for a new trial. Rule 411 excludes evidence of liability insurance only for the purpose of showing negligence or wrongful conduct. Establishing interest or bias of a defense witness is a very different purpose, fully admissible under this rule. And the appellate court failed to detect the threat of "any particular prejudice" under Rule 403 from the revelation that defendant was insured.

---
[26] See, e.g., *Boeing Airplane Co. v. Brown*, supra p. 68.
[27] Under FRE 608(a).

FRE 411 – References to Insurance Are Admissible to Account for Safety Inspections of Building

> **Rule 411. Liability Insurance**
>
> Evidence that a person was or was not insured against liability is not admissible upon the issue whether the person acted negligently or otherwise wrongfully. This rule does not require the exclusion of evidence of insurance against liability when offered for another purpose, such as proof of agency, ownership, or control, or bias or prejudice of a witness.

MORRISSEY v. WELSH CO.
821 F.2d 1294 (8th Cir. 1987)

A five-story brick wall of a St. Louis-area building just off I-55 owned by the Welsh Company collapsed during a thunderstorm. It fell on a car and crushed Jane Morrissey to death and injured two other occupants, Benedicte Monicat and Steven Crutcher. All three filed lawsuits against Welsh Co. and Albert D. Welsh, owner of the company, for negligent maintenance of the wall resulting in Morrissey's wrongful death and relatively minor injuries to Monicat and Crutcher. A jury verdict awarded Monicat $15,000 and Crutcher $3,000, $750,000 each in punitive damages, and Morrissey's parents $6,500,000.

One issue among many on Welsh's appeal to the Eighth Circuit Court of Appeals concerned references to Welsh's insurance coverage that were made at trial and the admission of letters and internal memoranda from the Home Insurance Company. Testimony from several witnesses depicted a turn-of-the-century building so ill-maintained that it had been falling apart for years, and Welsh had declined to spend $264,000 to repair it a few years earlier because the company planned to sell the building. An expert structural engineer testified that the thunderstorm's wind exerted about a quarter of the force on the wall that it should have been able to withstand. The appellate court ruled the several references to insurance "were not offered to prove that the Welsh Company acted negligently...[rather] to show the reason the safety inspections were made" that had already been testified to. "It is true, as the company argues, that the inspections could have been discussed without reference to insurance companies, but... not every reference to insurance constitutes reversible error." Similarly the court held that the admission of Home Insurance Company's internal documents discussing "the underwriting risk as to liability" was justified, and the admission of its letters to Welsh going to workers' compensation coverage issues was "not an abuse of discretion."

(The court did remand for a new trial as to damages and punitive damages alone.)

FRE 411 – Evidence of Lack of Malpractice Insurance Coverage for Treatment of Employees May Be Admissible to Prove Doctor's Motive in Failing to Treat Employee

> **Rule 411. Liability Insurance**
>
> Evidence that a person was or was not insured against liability is not admissible upon the issue whether the person acted negligently or otherwise wrongfully. This rule does not require the exclusion of evidence of insurance against liability when offered for another purpose, such as proof of agency, ownership, or control, or bias or prejudice of a witness.

MILLER v. SZELENYI
546 A.2d 1013 (Me. 1988)

Nurse's aide Therese Miller collapsed from an apparent heart attack at 6:40 a.m. on January 29, 1983 while on duty at Benda Hospital of the Pineland Center, a state facility for the mentally handicapped. While awaiting an ambulance to transport her to the Maine Medical Center where there were better emergency facilities, R.N. Darlene Turner started CPR and two other nurses were at the scene. Although she was not breathing on her own and had no detectable carotid pulse, Miller's pupils responded to light. At one point during the CPR, Miller took a few breaths on her own. One of the other nurses, Doris Babbidge, wheeled in a "crash cart" containing an electric heart defibrillator. Dr. Ernest Szelenyi, the doctor on-call, was awakened and arrived at the scene, but did not participate in the resuscitation nor authorize the use of the electric shock defibrillator. Although Dr. Szelenyi pronounced Mrs. Miller dead shortly after arriving, CPR continued and eventually the ambulance transported her to the Maine Medical Center. There she was defibrillated and briefly regained a heartbeat, but a while later she was pronounced dead.

Miller's husband and three adult daughters filed a medical malpractice lawsuit in Cumberland County Superior Court against Dr. Szelenyi and the Pineland Center's supervisor. Following an *in limine* ruling in their favor, plaintiffs offered testimony that Dr. Szelenyi refused to allow Mrs. Miller to be electrically defibrillated, or to do anything himself to assist in the effort to revive her, because, as he was alleged to have stated, his malpractice insurance did not cover his treatment of employees of the state facility.[28] Dr. Szelenyi denied saying that or "even thinking about insurance," and argued that the defibrillator was not used because Miller was dead "before she went down from the chair," apparently referring to the onset of the heart attack. The jury awarded George Miller a verdict of $260,000, finding Dr. Szelenyi grossly negligent by special verdict. Szelenyi appealed. (Miller appealed the trial court's dismissal of the supervisory defendants and of his §1983 civil rights claim.)

One of the main issues raised in Dr. Szelenyi's appeal concerned the references to insurance, which he contended violated Maine Rule of Evidence 411, comparable to the federal rule. The Supreme Judicial Court of Maine recognized that the rule's common law antecedents were "not absolute" in their general prohibition of testimony about insurance coverage or its lack, and that

---

[28] The statement itself was admissible under Rule 801(d)(2)(A) as a party admission.

when it is relevant to issues besides basic liability, evidence about insurance coverage can be admitted. "The trial court denied the motion *in limine* and admitted the evidence apparently on the theory that the evidence was admissible for another purpose other than liability in that it explained or provided a motive for Szelenyi's action or lack of action. The court instructed the jury that it could consider the evidence in order 'to understand the motivation of the parties,' but not to determine 'whether or not somebody is responsible because he might have insurance or might not have insurance.' At that time, the court had not bifurcated the case. Thus, the jury could properly consider this evidence in connection with the plaintiffs' section 1983 claims, for which they sought punitive damages. Whether punitive damages should be awarded depends largely on the defendant's motive... Accordingly, the trial court did not abuse its discretion by denying Szelenyi's motion *in limine*."

FRE 411, 103(c) – Good Faith Inquiry Mentioning Insurance Is Permissible on Jury Voir Dire to Ascertain Juror Bias Due to Media Accounts of "Medical Malpractice Crisis" or "Insurance Crisis"

> **Rule 411. Liability Insurance**
>
> Evidence that a person was or was not injured against liability is not admissible upon the issue whether the person acted negligently or otherwise wrongfully. This rule does not require the exclusion of evidence of insurance against liability when offered for another purpose, such as proof of agency, ownership, or control, or bias or prejudice of a witness.
>
> **Rule 103. Rulings on Evidence**
>
> ...
>
> *(c) Hearing of Jury.* In jury cases, proceedings shall be conducted, to the extent practicable, so as to prevent inadmissible evidence from being suggested to the jury by any means, such as making statements or offers of proof or asking questions in the hearing of the jury....

KOZLOWSKI v. RUSH
828 P.2d 854, 121 Idaho 825 (1992)

Stephanie Skiba suffered brain damage at birth, and her father, Piotr Skiba (along with Krzysztof Kozlowski, personal representative of her deceased mother, Zofia Skiba) sued Dr. Robert Rush, Bannock Regional Medical Center and Bannock County, alleging medical malpractice. Dr. Rush had had shoulder surgery two weeks earlier, and had to take his arm out of a sling to use the forceps required to deliver Stephanie, whom he did not detect would be an "extraordinarily large baby." Stephanie's shoulders were too big to come out after her head was delivered and she was born dusky or bluish and required "bagging" with oxygen. Not too long afterwards her hand tremors, facial palsy, "respiratory neurosis" and seizure led to a diagnosis of permanent, irreversible brain damage.

Prior to trial in Bannock County District Court the plaintiffs' lawyer sought to find out if any prospective jurors had been exposed to advertisements or articles in the media from insurance companies about the so-called "medical malpractice crisis" or "insurance crisis." The trial judge, apparently believing that all references to insurance are forbidden, refused to allow the voir dire questions. The verdict was for defendants. Skibas appealed.

The Idaho Supreme Court reversed. Noting that the rules of evidence do not, strictly speaking, apply to voir dire examination, but mindful of at least the policy underlying Rule 103(c), the court nonetheless noted that it is a legitimate purpose for counsel to try to excuse prospective jurors who have acquired a bias before they sit in judgment of a case. If, as is universally the case, "evidence of insurance [under Rule 411] is admissible if it tends to show bias on the part of a witness" despite its obvious tendency to prejudice jurors by revealing the fact of insurance coverage,[29] then the court should hardly ban voir dire questions to jurors that mention insurance for legitimate reasons, because "if anything, the prejudicial effect of the admission of evidence that a party is insured is greater than the prejudicial effect of allowing a party to mention insurance advertisements during voir dire. The comments of counsel are not evidence and juries are instructed as to that fact as a matter of course."

While other jurisdictions are split on the question, the Idaho court thought "the best resolution of the competing interests" is to permit the voir dire, subject to limitations, "upon a proper showing that members of the prospective jury panel may have been exposed to media accounts concerning allegations about the effect of jury awards on insurance costs," as opposed to a mere pretext.

"While we do not know whether the insurance companies involved here were among those who have advertised, we do note that any prohibition against comments regarding insurance would be a shield, not a sword. It would be manifestly unfair for insurance companies to use their substantial resources in order to persuade the public through the media that juries should not award or should award less in damages, while protesting that it would be too prejudicial to let the plaintiffs inquire of potential jurors whether the advertisements have biased them against plaintiff suits in general. The insurance companies have injected the issue of the effect of lawsuits on insurance into the public consciousness. Their purpose served by opening the door to the 'insurance crisis' debate, they cannot now expect to slam it shut in the face of plaintiffs who hope to discover the effect of the advertisements on the potential jurors in their case. If the tables were turned in this case, and the plaintiff's bar had launched a media campaign to increase jury awards in Bannock County by showing in graphic detail various personal injuries and the long term effect of same on the victims, we are convinced that the defendants in this case would demand the opportunity to determine whether any of the potential jurors had been biased against defendants in general by the exposure."

---

[29] See, e.g., *Charter v. Chleborad, supra* p. 80.

FRE 412 – Victim Is Entitled to Appeal Ruling Admitting Past Sexual History Evidence; Victim's General Reputation Is Inadmissible, But Defendant's Knowledge of Victim's Past Sexual Behavior Acquired Before Alleged Crime Is Relevant to Defendant's Intent

> **Rule 412. Sex Offense Cases; Relevance of Alleged Victim's Past Sexual Behavior or Alleged Sexual Predisposition**
>
> *(a) Evidence Generally Inadmissible.* The following evidence is not admissible in any civil or criminal proceeding involving alleged sexual misconduct except as provided in subdivisions (b) and (c):
>
> (1) Evidence offered to prove that any alleged victim engaged in other sexual behavior; and
>
> (2) Evidence offered to prove any alleged victim's sexual predisposition.
>
> *(b) Exceptions.*
>
> (1) In a criminal case, the following evidence is admissible, if otherwise admissible under these rules:
>
> (A) evidence of specific instances of sexual behavior by the alleged victim offered to prove that a person other than the accused was the source of semen, injury or other physical evidence;
>
> (B) evidence of specific instances of sexual behavior by the alleged victim with respect to the person accused of the sexual misconduct offered by the accused to prove consent or by the prosecution; and
>
> (C) evidence the exclusion of which would violate the constitutional rights of the defendant.
>
> (2) In a civil case, evidence offered to prove the sexual behavior or sexual predisposition of any alleged victim is admissible if it is otherwise admissible under these rules and its probative value substantially outweighs the danger of harm to any victim and of unfair prejudice to any party. Evidence of an alleged victim's reputation is admissible only if it has been placed in controversy by the alleged victim.
>
> *(c) Procedure to Determine Admissibility.*
>
> (1) A party intending to offer evidence under subdivision (b) must —
>
> (A) file a written motion at least 14 days before trial specifically describing the evidence and stating the purpose for which it is offered unless the court, for good cause, requires a different time for filing during trial; and
>
> (B) serve the motion on all parties and notify the alleged victim or, when appropriate, the alleged victim's guardian or representative.
>
> (2) Before admitting evidence under this rule the court must conduct a hearing in camera and afford the victim and parties a right to attend and be heard. The motion, related papers, and the record of the hearing must be sealed and remain under seal unless the court orders otherwise.

DOE v. UNITED STATES
666 F.2d 43 (4th Cir. 1981)

Donald Robert Black was charged with rape. He made a pre-trial motion to admit evidence concerning the past sexual behavior of the unnamed victim ("F. Doe") and to be permitted to cross-examine her about that information. The judge in the U.S. District Court for the Eastern District of Virginia granted the motion, and the victim appealed the rulings.

The Fourth Circuit Court of Appeals first overruled Black's objection that the court "lacks jurisdiction to entertain the victim's appeal." The court noted that Congress's purpose in enacting Rule 412, "to protect rape victims from the degrading and embarrassing disclosure of intimate details about their private lives," requires that there be for a victim the right to appeal an adverse ruling under Rule 412(b)(1)(C), "implicit as a necessary corollary of the rule's explicit protection" of the victim's privacy despite the absence of any reference to such a right to appeal. "The injustice to rape victims in delaying an appeal until conclusion of the criminal trial is manifest."

As to the substantive issues raised by Black's motion, the district court had granted him permission to admit "(1) evidence of the victim's 'general reputation in and around the Army post... where Mr. Black resided;

"(2) evidence of the victim's 'habit of calling out to the barracks to speak to various and sundry soldiers;'

"(3) evidence of the victim's 'habit of coming to the post to meet people and of her habit of being at the barracks at the snack bar;'

"(4) evidence from the victim's former landlord regarding 'his experience with her' alleged promiscuous behavior;

"(5) evidence of what a social worker learned of the victim;

"(6) telephone conversations that Black had with the victim;

"(7) evidence of the defendant's 'state of mind as a result of what he knew of her reputation... and what she had said to him.'"

He said all this evidence supported his defense of consent.

The appellate court ruled items (1) through (5) amounted to "essentially opinion or reputation evidence" that were not admissible under the "source of semen or injury" or "sexual behavior with the accused" exceptions to Rule 412. An accused does not have a constitutional entitlement "to present irrelevant evidence," and "reputation and opinion concerning a victim's past sexual behavior are not relevant indicators of the likelihood of her consent to a specific sexual act or of her veracity."

But the court ruled that items (6) and (7), the telephone conversation between Black and the victim and the evidence of Black's state of mind based on what he knew of the victim's reputation before the incident, were admissible. "Certainly, the victim's conversations with Black are relevant, and they are not the type of evidence that the rule excludes. Black's knowledge, acquired before the alleged crime, of the victim's past sexual behavior is relevant on the issue of Black's intent... Moreover, the rule does not exclude the production of the victim's letter or testimony of the men with whom Black talked if this evidence is introduced to corroborate the existence of the conversations and the letter."

The legislative history discloses that reputation and opinion evidence of the past sexual behavior of an alleged victim was excluded because Congress considered that this evidence was not relevant to the issues of the victim's consent or her veracity.... There is no indication, however, that this evidence was intended to be excluded when offered solely to show the accused's state of mind. Therefore, its admission is governed by the Rules of Evidence dealing with relevancy in general. Knowledge that Black acquired after the incident is irrelevant to this issue."

FRE 412 – Victim's Reputation as Prostitute Who Trades Sex for Drugs Is Not Relevant Where Consent Is Not Basis of Accused's Defense to Rape Charge

> **Rule 412. Sex Offense Cases; Relevance of Alleged Victim's Past Sexual Behavior or Alleged Sexual Predisposition**
>
> *(a) Evidence Generally Inadmissible.* The following evidence is not admissible in any civil or criminal proceeding involving alleged sexual misconduct except as provided in subdivisions (b) and (c):
>
> (1) Evidence offered to prove that any alleged victim engaged in other sexual behavior; and
>
> (2) Evidence offered to prove any alleged victim's sexual predisposition.
>
> *(b) Exceptions.*
>
> (1) In a criminal case, the following evidence is admissible, if otherwise admissible under these rules:
>
> (A) evidence of specific instances of sexual behavior by the alleged victim offered to prove that a person other than the accused was the source of semen, injury or other physical evidence;
>
> (B) evidence of specific instances of sexual behavior by the alleged victim with respect to the person accused of the sexual misconduct offered by the accused to prove consent or by the prosecution; and
>
> (C) evidence the exclusion of which would violate the constitutional rights of the defendant.
>
> (2) In a civil case, evidence offered to prove the sexual behavior or sexual predisposition of any alleged victim is admissible if it is otherwise admissible under these rules and its probative value substantially outweighs the danger of harm to any victim and of unfair prejudice to any party. Evidence of an alleged victim's reputation is admissible only if it has been placed in controversy by the alleged victim.
>
> *(c) Procedure to Determine Admissibility.*
>
> (1) A party intending to offer evidence under subdivision (b) must —
>
> (A) file a written motion at least 14 days before trial specifically describing the evidence and stating the purpose for which it is offered unless the court, for good cause, requires a different time for filing during trial; and
>
> (B) serve the motion on all parties and notify the alleged victim or, when appropriate, the alleged victim's guardian or representative.
>
> (2) Before admitting evidence under this rule the court must conduct a hearing in camera and afford the victim and parties a right to attend and be heard. The motion, related papers, and the record of the hearing must be sealed and remain under seal unless the court orders otherwise.

UNITED STATES v. SAUNDERS
943 F.2d 388 (4th Cir. 1991)

Patricia Duckett claimed Henry Saunders, while driving her to a friend's house after smoking crack cocaine with his friend "Tonka" Harris, drove into the woods near Fort Belvoir, Virginia and forced her to have sex with him twice. Saunders' version was that she offered to make him feel good in exchange for some of the crack, and had consensual oral sex with him in the car and consensual intercourse at his house. The jury convicted him of rape as charged. Saunders was sentenced as a career offender to 12 years in prison. He appealed to the Fourth Circuit Court of Appeals, contending among several arguments that the trial court had committed reversible error in excluding evidence under Rule 412 that Duckett was a "skeezer," i.e., a prostitute who trades sex for drugs. At the Rule 412(c) pre-trial hearing, "Saunders testified to his own prior sexual encounters with Duckett and to a conversation with Kenneth Smith one week prior to the alleged rape, in which Smith said that Duckett was a 'skeezer' and that Smith had had sex with Duckett in exchange for drugs. Smith confirmed that he had, in fact, had sex with Duckett, but he invoked the Fifth Amendment when asked if he had exchanged drugs for sex. The district court ruled that Saunders could testify to his own prior sexual relations with Duckett but that Smith could not testify to his experience with her." Saunders argued under *Doe,* supra p.100, that the evidence was relevant to his state of mind. The appellate court held that under Rule 412, "reputation and opinion evidence about a victim's past sexual behavior are never admissible, and evidence of specific prior acts is limited (to the extent constitutionally permitted) to directly probative evidence.... Rule 412 is an express limitation on the general rules of admissibility of evidence about the prior conduct of witnesses otherwise applicable."

Although the Fourth Circuit panel in this case was comfortable leaving the reputation/opinion testimony in the realm of Rule 412's apparent flat prohibition, it also noted that here Saunders' state of mind was not itself in issue. He and Duckett gave entirely contradictory accounts of the sexual event between them; this was not a case where the accused could have mistakenly thought the victim's sexual behavior amounted to consent. Saunders seems to have been offering the "skeezer" reputation testimony only to cast doubt on Duckett's credibility as his accuser, a purpose neither the Rule nor *Doe* permits. "Instead of contending that Duckett consented, Saunders testified that no sexual intercourse took place at this time and place. His state of mind that Duckett was a 'skeezer' is hardly relevant to that defense. Saunders did, however, provide an explanation for the presence of semen based on a consensual affair. He contended that he and Duckett had consensual sexual intercourse earlier in the evening at Saunders' house. For that reason Saunders could justify evidence of his own prior sexual conduct with Duckett under Rule 412(b)(2)."

The court's treatment of the Smith testimony is no less careful: "In this case, the district judge ruled that Saunders' testimony about his own past sexual relationship with Patricia Duckett was admissible under section (b)(2)(B), and that Smith's testimony, 'I had her [Patricia Duckett] home for three days,' was inadmissible because it was testimony of specific sexual behavior that did not come within one of the three exceptions of section (b). The only exception arguably applicable to Smith's testimony is that the evidence would be constitutionally required and thereby admissible under section (b)(1). The defendant has a constitutional right to present admissible evidence that is probative of his innocence by showing the government's failure to prove the offense charged, by establishing a defense, or by attacking the credibility or fair mindedness of a witness... We can discern no constitutional basis, however, that requires the admission of evidence about a three-day relationship between the victim and some third person."

FRE 412 – Victim's Prior Charges of Sexual Assault Against Family Members, Subsequently Withdrawn, Are Inadmissible in Rape Prosecution of Her Uncle

> **Rule 412. Sex Offense Cases; Relevance of Alleged Victim's Past Sexual Behavior or Alleged Sexual Predisposition**
>
> *(a) Evidence Generally Inadmissible.* The following evidence is not admissible in any civil or criminal proceeding involving alleged sexual misconduct except as provided in subdivisions (b) and (c):
> (1) Evidence offered to prove that any alleged victim engaged in other sexual behavior; and
> (2) Evidence offered to prove any alleged victim's sexual predisposition.
>
> *(b) Exceptions.*
> (1) In a criminal case, the following evidence is admissible, if otherwise admissible under these rules:
> (A) evidence of specific instances of sexual behavior by the alleged victim offered to prove that a person other than the accused was the source of semen, injury or other physical evidence;
> (B) evidence of specific instances of sexual behavior by the alleged victim with respect to the person accused of the sexual misconduct offered by the accused to prove consent or by the prosecution; and
> (C) evidence the exclusion of which would violate the constitutional rights of the defendant.
> (2) In a civil case, evidence offered to prove the sexual behavior or sexual predisposition of any alleged victim is admissible if it is otherwise admissible under these rules and its probative value substantially outweighs the danger of harm to any victim and of unfair prejudice to any party. Evidence of an alleged victim's reputation is admissible only if it has been placed in controversy by the alleged victim.
>
> *(c) Procedure to Determine Admissibility.*
> (1) A party intending to offer evidence under subdivision (b) must —
> (A) file a written motion at least 14 days before trial specifically describing the evidence and stating the purpose for which it is offered unless the court, for good cause, requires a different time for filing during trial; and
> (B) serve the motion on all parties and notify the alleged victim or, when appropriate, the alleged victim's guardian or representative.
> (2) Before admitting evidence under this rule the court must conduct a hearing in camera and afford the victim and parties a right to attend and be heard. The motion, related papers, and the record of the hearing must be sealed and remain under seal unless the court orders otherwise.

UNITED STATES v. CARDINAL
782 F.2d 34 (6th Cir. 1986)

Accused by his 13-year-old niece, Tammy Empen, of raping her while on a walk near her mother's home in the Keweenaw Bay Indian Reservation in Michigan's Upper Peninsula, Lawrence Cardinal, her 48-year-old uncle by marriage, moved to admit evidence that she had previously reported other instances of sexual assault against family members only to withdraw them later. Cardinal argued the evidence was important to impugn her credibility. The government contended "Empen's charges, made against Empen's stepfather and Cardinal, were true and were withdrawn because of fear of retaliation by Empen's mother." The trial court barred its admission under Rule 412. The jury convicted Cardinal of rape on an Indian reservation, and he appealed.

The Sixth Circuit Court of Appeals affirmed the conviction and held that exclusion of the prior charges was proper under Rule 412. Regardless of the credibility issues Cardinal wanted to raise with the information, the appellate court held the "basic policy" and "principal purpose" of the Rule ("to protect rape victims from the degrading and embarrassing disclosure of intimate details about their private lives") overrode Cardinal's contention. The district judge in the U.S. District Court for the Western District of Michigan, in holding "it's just the type of allegation that this young woman should be protected from" under Rule 412, "thus demonstrated a sensitivity to the policy supporting the rape-shield rule," the Sixth Circuit panel held. (No deeper or constitutional analysis of the ruling was indulged, and no Sixth Amendment issue appears to have been raised in Cardinal's appeal.)

FRE 412 – Woman's Prior Sexual History Is Admissible in Her Civil Suit for Transmission of Genital Herpes

> **Rule 412. Sex Offense Cases; Relevance of Alleged Victim's Past Sexual Behavior or Alleged Sexual Predisposition**
>
> *(a) Evidence Generally Inadmissible.* The following evidence is not admissible in any civil or criminal proceeding involving alleged sexual misconduct except as provided in subdivisions (b) and (c):
>
> (1) Evidence offered to prove that any alleged victim engaged in other sexual behavior; and
>
> (2) Evidence offered to prove any alleged victim's sexual predisposition.
>
> *(b) Exceptions.*
>
> (1) In a criminal case, the following evidence is admissible, if otherwise admissible under these rules:
>
> (A) evidence of specific instances of sexual behavior by the alleged victim offered to prove that a person other than the accused was the source of semen, injury or other physical evidence;
>
> (B) evidence of specific instances of sexual behavior by the alleged victim with respect to the person accused of the sexual misconduct offered by the accused to prove consent or by the prosecution; and
>
> (C) evidence the exclusion of which would violate the constitutional rights of the defendant.
>
> (2) In a civil case, evidence offered to prove the sexual behavior or sexual predisposition of any alleged victim is admissible if it is otherwise admissible under these rules and its probative value substantially outweighs the danger of harm to any victim and of unfair prejudice to any party. Evidence of an alleged victim's reputation is admissible only if it has been placed in controversy by the alleged victim.
>
> *(c) Procedure to Determine Admissibility.*
>
> (1) A party intending to offer evidence under subdivision (b) must —
>
> (A) file a written motion at least 14 days before trial specifically describing the evidence and stating the purpose for which it is offered unless the court, for good cause, requires a different time for filing during trial; and
>
> (B) serve the motion on all parties and notify the alleged victim or, when appropriate, the alleged victim's guardian or representative.
>
> (2) Before admitting evidence under this rule the court must conduct a hearing in camera and afford the victim and parties a right to attend and be heard. The motion, related papers, and the record of the hearing must be sealed and remain under seal unless the court orders otherwise.

JUDD v. RODMAN
105 F.3d 1339 (11th Cir. 1997)

After a sexual relationship with pro basketball star Dennis Rodman, Lisa Beth Judd developed symptoms of genital herpes. She filed a lawsuit against him "alleging several causes of action related to her contraction of genital herpes: tortious transmission of a sexual disease, battery, fraud, and intentional infliction of emotional distress," for which she sought actual and punitive damages and attorney's fees. Rodman belatedly filed a motion under Rule 412(c) to admit evidence of Judd's prior sexual behavior, and about her prior employment as a nude dancer and her breast augmentation surgery. The trial judge overruled Judd's cross-motion to exclude such evidence, holding that Rule 412 did not apply to this case. To avoid the sting of cross-examination about the topics, at trial Judd testified on direct examination about her sexual history and nude dancing jobs, and over her objection Rodman's counsel was permitted on cross-examination to raise the topic of her breast augmentation surgery. The jury returned a verdict for Rodman, and Judd appealed.

The Eleventh Circuit Court of Appeals "assumed without deciding" that Rule 412 applied to Judd's suit against Rodman, and held that Judd's prior sexual behavior was admissible: "A central issue of the case, however, is whether Judd contracted genital herpes from Rodman. Expert testimony revealed that the herpes virus can be dormant for long periods of time and the infected person can be asymptomatic. Consequently, evidence of prior sexual relationships and the type of protection used during sexual intercourse was highly relevant to Rodman's liability. The court did not abuse its discretion in admitting evidence of Judd's prior sexual history."

The court also held that Judd failed to show "that a substantial right was affected" by the admission of evidence of her prior employment as a nude dancer. The appellate court said, "The district court could have admitted evidence of Judd's nude dancing upon finding that the probative value substantially outweighed the prejudicial effect. The determination under such a balancing test is necessarily highly fact specific. Judd testified that she felt 'dirty' after she contracted herpes. The court determined that Judd's employment as a nude dancer before and after she contracted herpes was probative as to damages for emotional distress because it suggested an absence of change in her body image following the herpes infection. Thus, although we recognize the potentially prejudicial nature of the evidence of Judd's nude dancing, we find that, given the specific facts of this case and the considerable evidence of sexual history and predisposition which were appropriately admitted, the district court could have decided, within its discretion, that the probative value of the evidence substantially outweighed any prejudicial effect. Accordingly, we resolve that Judd has not shown that the court's admission of this evidence constituted reversible error."

(The court held that Judd had waived her right to appeal the issue about admission of evidence of her breast augmentation surgery under Rule 412 because her objections at pre-trial were based only on its irrelevance, not on Rule 412's provisions.)

FRE 413, 403 – Evidence of Prior Sexual Assaults Is Admissible Subject to Probative vs. Prejudicial Balancing

> **Rule 413. Evidence of Similar Crimes in Sexual Assault Cases**
> (a) In a criminal case in which the defendant is accused of an offense of sexual assault, evidence of the defendant's commission of another offense or offenses of sexual assault is admissible, and may be considered for its bearing on any matter to which it is relevant.
>
> **Rule 403. Exclusion of Relevant Evidence on Grounds of Prejudice, Confusion, or Waste of Time**
> Although relevant, evidence may be excluded if its probative value is substantially outweighed by the danger of unfair prejudice, confusion of the issues, or misleading the jury, or by considerations of undue delay, waste of time, or needless presentation of cumulative evidence.

UNITED STATES v. GUARDIA
135 F.3d 1326 (10th Cir. 1998)

Dr. David Guardia was accused by a New Mexico federal grand jury of two counts of sexual abuse in connection with gynecological exams he performed at Kirkland Air Force Base in the fall of 1995. Dr. Guardia moved *in limine* to exclude evidence of other sexual misconduct in cases involving four other women he had examined, which the government proffered under Rule 413. The district court found under Rule 403 that the risk of confusing the jury outweighed the probative value of the other sex crimes evidence, and granted Dr. Guardia's motion. The government appealed.

The Tenth Circuit Court of Appeals affirmed the ruling that excluded the other sexual misconduct evidence. The district court properly concluded that this evidence contained much that was too dissimilar to the charged behavior. In both charged incidents Dr. Guardia was alleged to have "engaged in direct clitoral contact that exceeded the bounds of medically appropriate examination techniques" and making a sexually suggestive comment ("I love my job") during one. In two of the "other acts" cases excessive, direct clitoral contact was alleged, and there was one complaint of a suggestive comment. But one witness said Dr. Guardia touched her breasts, not her pelvic area, one said he used a medical instrument, not his hands, and unlike the charged incidents, chaperons were present in the case of the examinations of two of the "Rule 413 witnesses."

The Tenth Circuit panel discussed the relationship between Rule 413 and Rule 404(b), a far more restricted allowance of other acts evidence. Because Rule 413 sex assault is rendered admissible "for its bearing on *any* matter to which it is relevant" (emphasis supplied), and it is conceded that criminal propensity is relevant,[30] other sex assault evidence is admissible on the issue of "propensity to commit the charged offense." Rule 404(b) evidence prohibits the use of other acts to prove propensity, so in sex crime prosecutions Rule 413 clearly "supersedes" Rule 404(b).

And the court held it is not correct to conclude that the rule's "is admissible" language means that it "creates an exception for itself to the Rule 403 balancing test." Several rules (e.g., 412, 609(a)) use the same "admissible" language and still are subject to Rule 403's precedence.

---
[30] Albeit ordinarily inadmissible when offered by the prosecution, see FRE 404(a).

Nor should a court automatically exclude all proffered evidence of other sex crimes as too prejudicial. "Rule 413 only has effect if we interpret it in a way that leaves open the possibility of admission."

FRE 414, 403 – Evidence of Similar Crimes in Child Molestation Prosecution Is Admissible Subject to Probative vs. Prejudicial Balancing

> **Rule 414. Evidence of Similar Crimes in Child Molestation Cases**
> (a) In a criminal case in which the defendant is accused of an offense of child molestation, evidence of the defendant's commission of another offense or offenses of child molestation is admissible, and may be considered for its bearing on any matter to which it is relevant.
>
> **Rule 403. Exclusion of Relevant Evidence on Grounds of Prejudice, Confusion, or Waste of Time**
> Although relevant, evidence may be excluded if its probative value is substantially outweighed by the danger of unfair prejudice, confusion of the issues, or misleading the jury, or by consideration of undue delay, waste of time, or needless presentation of cumulative evidence.

UNITED STATES v. SUMNER
119 F.3d 658 (8th Cir. 1997)

Stuart Lee Sumner, living with the mother of a young girl on the Red Lake Indian Reservation in Minnesota, was charged with touching the girl's genitals twice and having her touch his once. At trial the prosecution was permitted to present testimony of two prior sexual assaults on children, one of which was uncharged and one of which Sumner was convicted. The jury convicted Sumner of aggravated sexual abuse and abusive sexual contact, and he appealed.

The Eighth Circuit Court of Appeals first held that the trial court was in error in admitting the other assaults under Rule 404(b) as evidence of Sumner's intent, because Sumner had not raised a "general denial defense" nor a defense based on lack of intent, but rather relied on a specific denial that the criminal sexual touching had ever occurred.

The government had also proffered the evidence under Rule 414, but the trial court had held that the rule is unconstitutional because it allows "any kind of evidence to show propensity" without regard for a consideration of its prejudicial potential under Rule 403.

The Eighth Circuit panel held the balancing test of Rule 403 applies to Rule 414 evidence too.[31] The court held that Rule 414's "is admissible" language is no different from Rule 402's "is admissible" provision. It held that because Rule 403 applies to all other provisions in the rules that make evidence "admissible," "it is logical that Rule 403 applies to Rule 414 as well, and nothing in the language of Rule

---
[31] Interestingly, the government took this position too.

414 precludes the application of Rule 403." The court cited sponsoring statements by Representative Molinari and Senator Dole in the Congressional Record to the effect that although "the presumption is in favor of admission," Rule 414 is still subject to "the court's authority under Evidence Rule 403 to exclude evidence whose probative value is substantially outweighed by its prejudicial effect."

The appellate court reversed Sumner's convictions because the trial court had not undertaken a Rule 403 balancing analysis, and remanded for retrial.

FRE 414, 403 – In Deciding Whether Similar Crimes Evidence Is Admissible in Child Sex Offense Case, Court Must Apply Probative vs. Prejudicial Balancing Test So as to Allow Qualifying Evidence to Come in

> **Rule 414. Evidence of Similar Crimes in Child Molestation Cases**
> (a) In a criminal case in which the defendant is accused of an offense of child molestation, evidence of the defendant's commission of another offense or offenses of child molestation is admissible, and may be considered for its bearing on any matter to which it is relevant.
> (b) In a case in which the Government intends to offer evidence under this rule, the attorney for the Government shall disclose the evidence to the defendant, including statements of witnesses or a summary of the substance of any testimony that is expected to be offered, at least fifteen days before the scheduled date of trial or at such later time as the court may allow for good cause.
>
> **Rule 403. Exclusion of Relevant Evidence on Grounds of Prejudice, Confusion, or Waste of Time**
> Although relevant, evidence may be excluded if its probative value is substantially outweighed by the danger of unfair prejudice, confusion of the issues, or misleading the jury, or by considerations of undue delay, waste of time, or needless presentation of cumulative evidence.

UNITED STATES v. LeCOMPTE
131 F.3d 767 (8th Cir. 1997)

In the first trial of Leo LeCompte for sexual abuse of his wife's 11-year-old niece "C.D.," the government failed to give timely notice under Rule 414(b) of its intention to offer evidence of sex offenses committed by LeCompte eight years earlier against his first wife's niece "T.T.," but was permitted over objection to offer it under Rule 404(b). His conviction was overturned when the Eighth Circuit Court of Appeals ruled that the other sex crimes were not admissible under Rule 404(b).

LeCompte was recharged in the U.S. District Court for South Dakota, and when the government this time filed its Rule 414 notice in a timely fashion, LeCompte objected to the evidence via a motion *in limine* as substantially more prejudicial than probative. The district court agreed and ruled to exclude the evidence of LeCompte's earlier behavior with T.T. under Rule 403. The government appealed the pretrial evidentiary ruling.[33]

This time the Eighth Circuit reversed the exclusion of the evidence under Rule 414. It found the differences noted by the district court (whether or not siblings were present, whether he had played with the niece first) less significant than the "substantial similarity" between them, and found that the eight-year time lapse was not significant because LeCompte was in prison a portion of that, reducing his opportunities to molest other children.

The district court had found the major Rule 403 prejudicial impact of the other sex crimes testimony to lie in the "unique stigma" attached to child sex crimes, "on account of which LeCompte might be convicted not for the charged offense, but for his sexual abuse of T.T. This danger is one that all propensity evidence in such trials presents. It is for this reason that the evidence was previously excluded, and it is precisely such holdings that Congress intended to overrule.... On balance, then, we hold that the motion *in limine* should not have been granted."

....

---

[33]Under 18 U.S.C. § 3731, which provides in part:
"...An appeal by the United States shall lie to a court of appeals from a decision or order of a district court suppressing or excluding evidence... in a criminal proceeding, not made after the defendant has been put in jeopardy and before the verdict or finding on an indictment or information, if the United States attorney certifies to the district court that the appeal is not taken for purpose of delay and that the evidence is a substantial proof of a fact material in the proceeding..."

CHAPTER FIVE
Article V – Privileges

FRE 501, Fifth Amendment – Privilege Against Self-Incrimination Does Not Extend to Concern with Foreign Prosecution

> **U.S. Constitution, 5th Amendment...**
> No person... shall be compelled in any criminal case to be a witness against himself.
> **Rule 501. [PRIVILEGES] General Rule**
> Except as otherwise required by the Constitution of the United States or provided by Act of Congress or in rules prescribed by the Supreme Court pursuant to statutory authority, the privilege of a witness, person, government, State, or political subdivision thereof shall be governed by the principles of the common law as they may be interpreted by the courts of the United States in the light of reason and experience. However, in civil actions and proceedings, with respect to an element of a claim or defense as to which State law supplies the rule of decision, the privilege of a witness, person, government, State, or political subdivision thereof shall be determined in accordance with State law.

UNITED STATES v. BALSYS
524 U.S. 666, 118 S. Ct. 2218, 141 L. Ed. 2d 575(1998)

The Office of Special Investigations of the Criminal Division of the U.S. Department of Justice was created to find and deport suspected Nazi war criminals. One of it investigations focused on Woodhaven, N.Y. resident Aloyzas Balsys, a Lithuanian who came to the United States in 1961. An OSI administrative subpoena sought his testimony about his wartime activities between 1940 and 1944, a period during which Balsys, in his 1961 visa application, claimed he was living in hiding in Plateliai, Lithuania after serving for six years in the Lithuanian army. Balsys declined to answer OSI's questions under the Fifth Amendment right against self-incrimination. He cited his fear of prosecution by Israel, Lithuania and Germany. (The statute of limitations apparently prevented American prosecution for misrepresentation on his entry application.) The Federal district court granted OSI's petition to enforce the subpoena and ordered Balsys to testify, but on Balsys' appeal the Second Circuit Court of Appeals vacated the district court's order, holding that a legitimate fear of foreign prosecution alone can justify invoking the Fifth Amendment privilege. The government appealed.

The United States Supreme Court reversed, holding that the "any criminal case" language of the Amendment must be taken in its own context, which dictates that it was meant to apply only to domestic criminal prosecutions. Justice Souter, writing for the majority, said the Fifth Amendment's traditions do not, as Balsys argued, extend to all breaches of privacy. Besides, the settled rule "that a witness's silence may be used against him in a deportation or extradition proceeding... raises serious questions about the likely gain from recognizing fear of foreign prosecution."

FRE 104(a), 501 – Attorney-Client Privilege: Determination of Existence of Exception to Privilege for Communications in Furtherance of Illegal Conduct Is for Court to Make

> **Rule 104. Preliminary Questions**
> *(a) Questions of Admissibility Generally.* Preliminary questions concerning the qualification of a person to be a witness, the existence of a privilege, or the admissibility of evidence shall be determined by the court, subject to the provisions of subdivision (b). In making its determination it is not bound by the rules of evidence except those with respect to privileges.
>
> **Rule 501. [PRIVILEGES] General Rule**
> Except as otherwise required by the Constitution of the United States or provided by Act of Congress or in rules prescribed by the Supreme Court pursuant to statutory authority, the privilege of a witness, person, government, State, or political subdivision thereof shall be governed by the principles of the common law as they may be interpreted by the courts of the United States in the light of reason and experience. However, in civil actions and proceedings, with respect to an element of a claim or defense as to which State law supplies the rule of decision, the privilege of a witness, person, government, State, or political subdivision thereof shall be determined in accordance with State law.

UNITED STATES v. ZOLIN
491 U.S. 554, 109 S. Ct. 2619, 105 L. Ed. 2d 469 (1989)

The Internal Revenue Service sought production of 51 documents and two audio tapes from the clerk of the Los Angeles Superior Court, who held them in connection with a pending state lawsuit, for its investigation of the 1979-83 tax returns of L. Ron Hubbard, founder of the Church of Scientology. The Church and Mary Sue Hubbard opposed their production on the basis of the attorney-client privilege. The district court in which the IRS summons had issued held that absent independent evidence that the purpose of the communication was the furtherance of crime or fraud, the court was powerless to consider the contents of the documents and tapes. The Ninth Circuit Court of Appeals affirmed, and the IRS appealed.

Justice Blackmun, writing for the U.S. Supreme Court, vacated the judgment, rejecting a rigid independent-evidence approach and holding that the trial court may conduct an in camera inspection of allegedly privileged material to see if it is privileged or falls within an exception.

The Supreme Court observed that the attorney-client privilege, the oldest common law privilege, "must necessarily protect the confidences of wrongdoers," but that the policy reasons for it – the adversary system's need for candid communication between client and attorney – do not apply when legal counsel is sought concerning future wrongdoing.

Considering Rules 1101(c) and 104(a), the Supreme Court rejected a "Draconian" interpretation of them and held that courts may consider the contents of allegedly privileged material to determine if an exception takes the communication out of the privilege, just as they may consider the material's contents to determine the existence of the privilege itself. (And, of course, "disclosure of allegedly privileged materials to the district court for purposes of determining the merits of a claim of privilege does not have the legal effect of terminating the privilege.") The court recognized that this result is the opposite of that required by California's Rule 915(c), providing that "the presiding officer may not require disclosure of information claimed to be privileged ...in order to rule on the claim of privilege."

The Supreme Court crafted a "standard" of sorts to govern the trial court's use of in camera review of allegedly privileged material: The court shall first require the showing of a factual basis adequate to support a good faith belief by a reasonable person that in camera review may reveal evidence to establish the applicability of the crime-fraud exception to the privilege.

FRE 501 – Attorney-Client Privilege: Only Confidential Disclosures Are Protected

Rule 501. [PRIVILEGES] General Rule

Except as otherwise required by the Constitution of the United States or provided by Act of Congress or in rules prescribed by the Supreme Court pursuant to statutory authority, the privilege of a witness, person, government, State, or political subdivision thereof shall be governed by the principles of the common law as they may be interpreted by the courts of the United States in the light of reason and experience. However, in civil actions and proceedings, with respect to an element of a claim or defense as to which State law supplies the rule of decision, the privilege of a witness, person, government, State, or political subdivision thereof shall be determined in accordance with State law.

UNITED STATES v. OLOYEDE
982 F.2d 133 (4th Cir. 1992)

In connection with its investigation of a fraudulent immigration scheme, the U.S. Immigration and Naturalization Service searched the law offices of Clifford C. Cooper, who represented Nigerians and Ethiopians often referred to him by Oluwole Oloyede. Both Cooper and Oloyede were convicted of supplying false documents to aliens for citizenship applications.

Cooper appealed, contending that the evidence seized during the INS search of his office should have been suppressed because of the attorney-client privilege. The Fourth Circuit affirmed the convictions, noting the attorney-client privilege, as are all such privileges, is to be applied very narrowly. Because the communications between Cooper and his clients were intended to be used in the filing of citizenship applications, there was contemplated by all parties a voluntary disclosure to third parties of the information discussed, waiving the privilege. (The court declined to rule on the alternative government theory, the crime-fraud exception to the privilege.)

FRE 501 – Attorney-Client Privilege: Identity of Clients Is Protected if Disclosure Will Reveal Substance of Communication

> **Rule 501. [PRIVILEGES] General Rule**
> Except as otherwise required by the Constitution of the United States or provided by Act of Congress or in rules prescribed by the Supreme Court pursuant to statutory authority, the privilege of a witness, person, government, State, or political subdivision thereof shall be governed by the principles of the common law as they may be interpreted by the courts of the United States in the light of reason and experience. However, in civil actions and proceedings, with respect to an element of a claim or defense as to which State law supplies the rule of decision, the privilege of a witness, person, government, State, or political subdivision thereof shall be determined in accordance with State law.

UNITED STATES v. LIEBMAN
742 F.2d 807 (3d Cir. 1987)

Emanuel Liebman and his tax law firm evaluated real estate investments for clients, and advised the clients that their fees were tax-deductible legal expenses. The Internal Revenue Service contended the fees charged were brokerage charges which were not tax deductible. When an IRS summons demanded law firm records to help the agency identify firm clients who might have claimed a deduction for these fees, Liebman resisted, asserting the attorney-client privilege. The district court ordered production of the firm's clients' names, and Liebman and the firm appealed from the order.

Liebman argued that to disclose his firm's clients' identities would reveal protected confidential communications. Because the IRS summons demanded names of clients who had been advised these fees were tax-deductible, the Third Circuit Court of Appeals observed that "so much of the actual communication had already been established, that to disclose the client's name would disclose the essence of a confidential communication." The attorney-client privilege is not limited to consultations about crimes and torts: "Since the deductibility of a fee is a legal matter, it is a confidence ordinarily protected by attorney-client privilege." While disclosure of the fact of retaining a lawyer or obtaining a client is not ordinarily privileged, it is when to do so would reveal the essence of the confidence.

In reversing the order enforcing the IRS summons, the appellate court noted, "If appellants were required to identify their clients as requested, that identity, when combined with the substance of the communication as to deductibility that is already known, would provide all there is to know about a confidential communication between the taxpayer-client and the attorney."

FRE 501 – Attorney-Client Privilege: Disclosure of Identity of Third Party Who Paid Attorney Fee for Defendant Cannot Be Compelled Where Disclosure Would Reveal Purpose for Legal Consultation

> **Rule 501. [PRIVILEGES] General Rule**
> Except as otherwise required by the Constitution of the United States or provided by Act of Congress or in rules prescribed by the Supreme Court pursuant to statutory authority, the privilege of a witness, person, government, State, or political subdivision thereof shall be governed by the principles of the common law as they may be interpreted by the courts of the United States in the light of reason and experience. However, in civil actions and proceedings, with respect to an element of a claim or defense as to which State law supplies the rule of decision, the privilege of a witness, person, government, State, or political subdivision thereof shall be determined in accordance with State law.

IN RE GRAND JURY SUBPOENA
926 F.2d 1423 (5th Cir. 1991)

Jose Evaristo Reyes-Requena was arrested inside a house in Houston where some 160 kg. of cocaine were also found. He told DEA officers he had recently arrived in Texas from Matamoros, Mexico, and was guarding the house for someone he knew only as "Chapa," of whom he refused to give a physical description. "Despite Reyes-Requena's apparent indigence," he was represented at a preliminary hearing by an experienced criminal lawyer, Mike DeGeurin, who was immediately subpoenaed by a federal grand jury to produce records and information concerning the payment of Reyes-Requena's legal fees. DeGeurin moved to quash the subpoena, claiming the protection of the attorney-client privilege. The district court quashed the subpoena on Fifth- and Sixth-Amendment grounds, as well as those of privilege.

After Reyes-Requena was convicted of possession with intent to sell more than 5 kg. of cocaine and sentenced to 15 years in prison, the Government got another subpoena to compel DeGeurin to disclose the identity of the third party who paid Reyes-Requena's legal fees. After an in camera, ex parte showing that the third party was also a client of DeGeurin's in regard to the same matter for which Reyes-Requena was a client, the district court again quashed the subpoena. The Government appealed, contending that a client's identity and the payment of fees are "severable" from any confidential communication.

The Fifth Circuit Court of Appeals rejected that contention and held that here disclosure of the third-party client's identity and fee arrangements would "also reveal the confidential purpose for which he consulted an attorney," which the privilege was designed to protect. The matters were "connected inextricably with a privileged communication." The court rejected in this kind of situation the Government's apparent desire to "place chilling consequences on the very act of obtaining legal advice."

FRE 501 – Attorney-Client Privilege: Both Direct and Derivative Privilege Apply Only to Disclosures Made for Legal Representation

> **Rule 501. [PRIVILEGES] General Rule**
>
> Except as otherwise required by the Constitution of the United States or provided by Act of Congress or in rules prescribed by the Supreme Court pursuant to statutory authority, the privilege of a witness, person, government, State, or political subdivision thereof shall be governed by the principles of the common law as they may be interpreted by the courts of the United States in the light of reason and experience. However, in civil actions and proceedings, with respect to an element of a claim or defense as to which State law supplies the rule of decision, the privilege of a witness, person, government, State, or political subdivision thereof shall be determined in accordance with State law.

UNITED STATES v. TEDDER
801 F.2d 1437 (4th Cir. 1986)

David L. Tedder, a South Carolina attorney, was convicted of five counts of perjury in connection with a large-scale marijuana importation ring. Tedder was alleged to have been employed to launder drug proceeds through Bahamian bank accounts and to reinvest the proceeds in South Carolina real estate. The perjury occurred at a grand jury proceeding.

At trial an associate of Tedder's in his law firm, Judith Patterson, testified that Tedder told her he had perjured himself before the grand jury.[1] Tedder claimed the conversations were privileged *directly* because he was seeking legal advice and assistance from Patterson, and also that the conversations were *derivatively* privileged because "other members of the law firm at which they were both employed were providing [Tedder] with legal advice."

The Fourth Circuit Court of Appeals noted that the question of the applicability of the attorney-client privilege turned on "complex questions of fact": (1) Did Tedder seek to become Patterson's client? (2) Did Tedder seek Patterson's advice in her professional capacity? and (3) Did Tedder reasonably believe the communications would remain confidential? Adding to the ambiguity of the situation was the fact that Judith Patterson was the wife of Steven Patterson, the twin brother of Allen Patterson. Allen Patterson was alleged to be a principal in the drug smuggling operation, and had engaged in illegal drug transactions with Tedder in the early 1970's. The Fourth Circuit therefore closely examined the district court's factual findings to determine their reliability.

The district court had taken testimony from several witnesses, including Tedder, Judith Patterson, and the lawyer for Steven Patterson. Tedder occasionally would use Judith as a conduit for information to counsel for other co-defendants, and told her of his perjury right after it occurred, in part to assist Steven Patterson, who was under investigation. Judith Patterson said Tedder understood she was not his lawyer. "Significantly, Tedder shared with her information that he did not impart to those

---

[1] Admissible as a party admission under FRE 801(d)(2)(A) if the claim of privilege is rejected.

members of the firm actively engaged in his defense, and she on occasion discussed with him Allen and Steven's defense plans, although she did not participate professionally in their defense." Judith Patterson was primarily a negligence lawyer, and Tedder in fact sought no legal advice from her.

On this basis the Fourth Circuit concluded the district court had not erred in finding no *direct privilege* existed. And it was correct in rejecting the claims of *derivative* privilege because it found Judith Patterson did not by testifying disclose "information she obtained by virtue of her position at the firm representing Tedder," but rather merely the substance of personal conversations "apart from his legal defense."

FRE 501 – Attorney – Client Privilege: Communications Between Lawyer and Client Remain Privileged After Client's Death

> **Rule 501. [PRIVILEGES] General Rule**
>
> Except as otherwise required by the Constitution of the United States or provided by Act of Congress or in rules prescribed by the Supreme Court pursuant to statutory authority, the privilege of a witness, person, government, State, or political subdivision thereof shall be governed by the principles of the common law as they may be interpreted by the courts of the United States in the light of reason and experience. However, in civil actions and proceedings, with respect to an element of a claim or defense as to which State law supplies the rule of decision, the privilege of a witness, person, government, State, or political subdivision thereof shall be determined in accordance with State law.

SWIDLER & BERLIN v. UNITED STATES
524 U.S. 399, 118 S. Ct. 2081, 141 L. Ed. 2d 379 (1998)

Vincent W. Foster, Deputy White House Counsel, met in July 1993 with his own attorney, James Hamilton, of the Washington, D.C. firm Swidler & Berlin, to discuss the firing of employees of the White House Travel Office earlier that year and to discuss legal representation in connection with congressional or other investigations of the firings. During the two-hour meeting, Hamilton took three pages of handwritten notes, which he labeled "Privileged." Foster committed suicide ten days later.

At the request of the Independent Counsel, Kenneth Starr, a federal grand jury in December 1995 issued subpoenas to Hamilton and the law firm for the notes from the meeting and other matters. Swidler & Berlin filed a motion to quash the subpoena for the notes, contending they were privileged. The district court examined the notes *in camera* and concluded they were privileged.

On appeal by the Independent Counsel, the District of Columbia Circuit Court of Appeals reversed, holding that a balancing test, in which a court weighs the chilling effect of forced disclosure upon client communication against the "cost" of protecting communications after the client's death, must be applied before the posthumous invocation of the attorney-client privilege. A dissenting judge found no good reason to depart from the common-law rule that the privilege survived the client's death. Swidler & Berlin appealed.

The United States Supreme Court reversed and held that the notes were protected by the privilege. Justice Rehnquist, writing for the court, examined existing precedent to ascertain the status of the common law on the point, as Rule 501 requires, and found most state cases "presume the privilege survives [after the client's death], even if they do not so hold." The scholars and commentators are in accord. The burden is placed by the Rule on the Independent Counsel to show why "reason and experience" require a departure in this situation, or the carving out of an exception covering it. Starr contended "that in criminal proceedings, the interest in determining whether a crime has been committed should trump client confidentiality, particularly since the financial interests of the estate are not at stake."

But the Supreme Court found "weighty reasons" to recognize the continued existence of the privilege: "Knowing that communications will remain confidential even after death encourages the client to communicate fully and frankly with counsel. While the fear of disclosure, and the consequent withholding of information from counsel, may be reduced if disclosure is limited to posthumous disclosure in a criminal context, it seems unreasonable to assume that it vanishes altogether. Clients may be concerned about reputation, civil liability, or possible harm to friends or family. Posthumous disclosure of such communications may be as feared as disclosure during the client's lifetime." The privilege, held the court, serves broader interests than even the Fifth Amendment's protection against self-incrimination: "Many attorneys act as counselors on personal and family matters, where, in the course of obtaining the desired advice, confidences about family members or financial problems must be revealed in order to assure sound legal advice. The same is true of owners of small businesses who may regularly consult their attorneys about a variety of problems arising in the course of the business. These confidences may not come close to any sort of admission of criminal wrongdoing, but nonetheless be matters which the client would not wish divulged.... In the case at hand, it seems quite plausible that Foster, perhaps already contemplating suicide, may not have sought legal advice from Hamilton if he had not been assured the conversation was privileged."

In an intriguing footnote, the court noted that Hamilton conceded that "exceptional circumstances implicating a criminal defendant's constitutional rights might warrant breaching the privilege," but the court found no such "exceptional circumstances" here. (For example, a now-deceased client might have disclosed to his lawyer that he committed a crime for which another is wrongly accused or even being incarcerated.) Here, of course, it was the prosecution seeking the evidence.

Justices O'Connor, Scalia and Thomas dissented, arguing that both "a criminal defendant's right to exculpatory evidence or a compelling law enforcement need for information may, where the testimony is not available from other sources, override a client's posthumous interest in confidentiality," since "after death, the potential that disclosure will harm the client's interest has been greatly diminished, and the risk that the client will be held criminally liable has abated altogether."

FRE 501 – Attorney-Client Privilege: Intra-Corporate Communications to Corporate Counsel Are Protected

> **Rule 501. [PRIVILEGES] General Rule**
>
> Except as otherwise required by the Constitution of the United States or provided by Act of Congress or in rules prescribed by the Supreme Court pursuant to statutory authority, the privilege of a witness, person, government, State, or political subdivision thereof shall be governed by the principles of the common law as they may be interpreted by the courts of the United States in the light of reason and experience. However, in civil actions and proceedings, with respect to an element of a claim or defense as to which State law supplies the rule of decision, the privilege of a witness, person, government, State, or political subdivision thereof shall be determined in accordance with State law.

UPJOHN CO. v. UNITED STATES
449 U.S. 383, 101 S. Ct 677, 66 L. Ed. 2d 584 (1981)

After the pharmaceutical manufacturer Upjohn learned from auditors in January 1976 that a foreign subsidiary had bribed officials to earn government business, the company launched an internal investigation to learn how widespread the practice was. Company attorneys prepared a letter and a detailed questionnaire that sought information about any such payments and sent them to managers worldwide. Recipients were instructed to consult only with Upjohn employees who might provide useful information but otherwise to treat the investigation as highly confidential. Responses were sent directly to Upjohn General Counsel Gerard Thomas, who, with outside counsel, interviewed the managers and 33 other Upjohn employees and officers.

In March of that year Upjohn submitted a preliminary report on the matter to the Securities and Exchange Commission, copying the Internal Revenue Service. Soon the IRS issued a summons that demanded production of all documents generated by the investigation. Upjohn resisted, claiming the attorney-client privilege protected these documents from disclosure. The district court issued an order enforcing the summons, and Upjohn appealed.

The Sixth Circuit Court of Appeals applied the long-established "control group" test and ruled that the privilege was applicable only to senior management.

The United States Supreme Court reversed, per Justice Rehnquist, holding that the control group test "overlooks the fact that the privilege exists to protect not only the giving of professional advice to those who can act on it but also the giving of information to the lawyer to enable him to give sound and informed advice." The court addressed the concern of the appellate court that extending the privilege beyond the corporate control group "would entail severe burdens on discovery and create a broad 'zone of silence' over corporate affairs" when it observed, "The privilege only protects disclosure of communications; it does not protect disclosure of the underlying facts by those who communicated with the attorney." The court noted that Upjohn had given the IRS lists of all employees who had been interviewed and/or who had responded to the questionnaire.

The Supreme Court went to some length to make it clear that it was holding these specific communications privileged, not drafting a detailed set of rules governing the attorney-client privilege in the corporate setting.

FRE 501 – Spousal Privilege: Testifying Spouse Possesses Federal Privilege, Not Defendant Spouse

> **Rule 501. [PRIVILEGES] General Rule**
> Except as otherwise required by the Constitution of the United States or provided by Act of Congress or in rules prescribed by the Supreme Court pursuant to statutory authority, the privilege of a witness, person, government, State, or political subdivision thereof shall be governed by the principles of the common law as they may be interpreted by the courts of the United States in the light of reason and experience. However, in civil actions and proceedings, with respect to an element of a claim or defense as to which State law supplies the rule of decision, the privilege of a witness, person, government, State, or political subdivision thereof shall be determined in accordance with State law.

TRAMMEL v. UNITED STATES
445 U.S. 40, 100 S. Ct. 906, 63 L. Ed. 2d 186 (1980)

At Otis Trammel's trial on heroin importation and conspiracy charges, the jury heard detailed testimony from Elizabeth Ann Trammel, the defendant's wife. She was one of six unindicted co-conspirators in the case, and testified under a grant of immunity. Prior to trial Trammel had moved to sever his case from that of two other defendants, Edwin Lee Roberts and Joseph Freeman, or in the alternative to prevent his wife from testifying against him because of the long-established doctrine of spousal privilege. The District Judge denied both motions, and Trammel was ultimately convicted.

On appeal the Government conceded that Trammel's wife's testimony "constituted virtually its entire case against" him. The Supreme Court's most recent consideration of the spousal testimonial privilege had taken place in 1958 in *Hawkins v. United States*,[2] where they reaffirmed the centuries-old right of an accused to prevent his spouse from testifying against him.

In recasting the privilege here, the Supreme Court first considered the doctrine's origins in two principles repudiated in the law long ago and hardly lamented: (1) the disqualification of a criminal defendant from testifying in his own behalf, and (2) "the concept that husband and wife were one, and since the woman had no recognized legal existence, the husband was that one." The court read Rule 501 and its legislative history as enabling the federal courts to "develop rules of privilege on a case-by-case basis" as change is deemed necessary.

Noting that only 24 states still recognized the accused as the holder of the privilege (down from 31 just since the time of the *Hawkins* decision), Chief Justice

---
[2] 358 U.S. 74, 79 S. Ct. 136, 3 L. Ed. 2d 125.

Burger, writing for the court, cast the refashioning of the privilege in almost feminist terms: "Nowhere in the common-law world – indeed in any modern society – is a woman regarded as chattel or demeaned by denial of a separate legal identity and the dignity associated with recognition as a whole human being. Chip by chip, over the years those archaic notions have been cast aside so that '[n]o longer is the female destined solely for the home and the rearing of the family, and only the male for the marketplace and the world of ideas.'"[3]

The court held that the federal testimonial privilege belongs to the witness spouse: should she waive the privilege, as Elizabeth Trammel did here, her testimony is admissible. As for the concern expressed in *Hawkins* that permitting a willing spouse to testify against an accused mate "might alienate husband and wife, or further inflame existing domestic differences," the *Trammel* court offered what it gauged to be a more realistic assessment of the effect of relocating the privilege: If one spouse is willing to testify against another in a criminal trial, "their relationship is almost certainly in disrepair; there is probably little in the way of marital harmony for the privilege to preserve." (This conclusion may well underestimate the destructive impact on a marriage of government pressure on the uncharged spouse to testify against the incarcerated spouse.)

The court went out of its way to make clear that its ruling on the spousal testimonial privilege in no way undermines or affects the confidential marital communication privilege, which like the privileges associated with the priest-penitent, attorney-client, and physician-patient relationships, is "rooted in the imperative need for confidence and trust." Elizabeth Trammel had never been asked to testify as to confidential communications between herself and her husband that had not been not made in the presence of third parties.

---

[3] Justice Burger quoted a divorce case, *Stanton v. Stanton*, 421 U.S. 7, 14-15, 95 S. Ct. 1373, 1377- 78, 43 L. Ed. 2d 688 (1975), for that last irrelevant rhetorical flourish.

FRE 501 – Marital Communications Privilege: Privilege Is Not Available to Permanently Separated Couples

> **Rule 501. [PRIVILEGES] General Rule**
>
> Except as otherwise required by the Constitution of the United States or provided by Act of Congress or in rules prescribed by the Supreme Court pursuant to statutory authority, the privilege of a witness, person, government, State, or political subdivision thereof shall be governed by the principles of the common law as they may be interpreted by the courts of the United States in the light of reason and experience. However, in civil actions and proceedings, with respect to an element of a claim or defense as to which State law supplies the rule of decision, the privilege of a witness, person, government, State, or political subdivision thereof shall be determined in accordance with State law.

UNITED STATES v. BYRD
750 F.2d 585 (7th Cir. 1984)

Cornell Byrd's estranged wife testified at his arson and conspiracy trial that a few days after a Chicago food store was firebombed, Byrd had given her a piece of paper containing a list of food and liquor stores, telling her to tear it up and throw it in the toilet. Instead she called police, who found incriminating evidence against Byrd in an area of the basement that he continued to use. She testified he called her from jail a couple of weeks later and asked her to fly to Phoenix with another participant to collect a $12,000 payment for the arson Byrd was charged with; and two months later he instructed her to claim ignorance of the arson in response to a subpoena she had received.

Byrd objected to his wife's testimony, claiming the marital communications privilege. The district court admitted the testimony under the "joint participants" exception to the privilege. Upon his conviction and 10-year prison sentence Byrd appealed. The Seventh Circuit Court of Appeals affirmed the conviction and held that the wife's testimony was admissible because the spouses were permanently separated. The marital communications privilege "exists to insure that spouses generally... feel free to communicate their deepest feelings to each other without fear of eventual exposure in a court of law." It survives even marital difficulties (unlike the testimonial privilege[4]), having as its aim the protection of "the institution of marriage generally as a haven for confidential communications," rather than just the marital peace of the particular individuals involved. But the Seventh Circuit held that there is "little societal interest in protecting the confidential relationship of permanently separated couples." If the communication in question occurred after their separation it is admissible.

On the district court's ruling that the privilege didn't apply to this testimony because of the long-established "joint participants" exception, the appellate court found the exception inapplicable here, where Mrs. Byrd was "just the opposite" of a joint participant, working "with the police

---
[4] See *Trammel v. United States*, supra p. 106.

FRE 501 – Federal Privilege Is Now Recognized for Communications to Psychiatrists, Psychologists, Social Workers

> **Rule 501. [PRIVILEGES] General Rule**
>
> Except as otherwise required by the Constitution of the United States or provided by Act of Congress or in rules prescribed by the Supreme Court pursuant to statutory authority, the privilege of a witness, person, government, State, or political subdivision thereof shall be governed by the principles of the common law as they may be interpreted by the courts of the United States in the light of reason and experience. However, in civil actions and proceedings, with respect to an element of a claim or defense as to which State law supplies the rule of decision, the privilege of a witness, person, government, State, or political subdivision thereof shall be determined in accordance with State law.

JAFFEE v. REDMOND
518 U.S. 1, 116 S. Ct. 1923, 135 L. Ed. 2d 337 (1996)

Police officer Mary Lu Redmond of the Village of Hoffman Estates, Illinois responded to a report of a fight. After on-scene reports of a stabbing, Redmond said she saw several men running out of one of the buildings and Ricky Allen chasing another man with a butcher knife. Allen ignored Redmond's demands to drop the knife, and Redmond said she shot and killed Allen when she believed he was about to stab the man he was chasing.

The administrator of Allen's estate filed a federal civil rights action and state-law wrongful death claim against Redmond and the Village. When plaintiff learned that Redmond had attended some 50 counseling sessions with a licensed clinical social worker, Karen Beyer, she sought access to Beyer's notes to use when cross-examining Redmond. The district judge ordered disclosure of the notes, but neither Redmond nor Beyer complied. The judge instructed the jury that there was no legal justification for their refusal to turn over the notes, and that they could presume the contents of the notes would have been unfavorable to defendants. The jury awarded plaintiff $45,000 on the civil rights claims and $500,000 on the state wrongful death claim. Redmond appealed.

The Seventh Circuit Court of Appeals reversed and remanded, holding that the notes were protected by a federal privilege that covers psychotherapists which is recognized under Rule 501. The appellate court said federal decisions rejecting the privilege were mostly older decisions rendered before the contemporary "skyrocketing" of demand and need for counseling services, and that all 50 states have some form of this privilege. The Seventh Circuit also noted significantly that under Illinois law the psychotherapist-patient privilege extends to licensed social workers.

The United States Supreme Court, per Justice Stevens, emphasized the "reason and experience" clause in Rule 501 in affirming the Seventh Circuit's decision. Quoting its earlier spousal privilege decision in *Trammel*,[5] the court in a 7-2 decision held "the psychotherapist-patient privilege is 'rooted in the imperative need for confidence and trust'" in the relationship. "[T]he mere possibility of disclosure may impede development of the

---

[5]See *Trammel v. United States, supra* p. 106.

confidential relationship necessary for successful treatment." Absent the privilege, the court observed, the statements the other party will want disclosed at trial will probably not be made at all, rendering the "likely evidentiary benefit" of denying such a privilege "modest." A state privilege would be meaningless if it could be abrogated in an action in federal court, so federal recognition is both rational and necessary. Because "social workers provide a significant amount of mental health treatment," the federal privilege is extended to "confidential communications made to licensed social workers in the course of psychotherapy," which the court appears to be prepared to define quite broadly.

CHAPTER SIX
Article VI – Witnesses

FRE 601 – Child Is Presumed Competent to Testify Absent Showing of Disqualifying Fact

> **Rule 601. [WITNESSES] General Rule of Competency**
> Every person is competent to be a witness except as otherwise provided in these rules. However, in civil actions and proceedings, with respect to an element of a claim or defense as to which State law supplies the rule of decision, the competency of a witness shall be determined in accordance with State law.

STATE v. ROMAN
622 A.2d 96 (Me. 1993)

A Knox County, Maine, Superior Court jury found Jeffrey Roman guilty of gross sexual misconduct after listening to the testimony of the eight-year-old victim about what took place between Roman and herself while she was left alone with him in her parents' Rockland apartment.

On his appeal to the Supreme Judicial Court of Maine, Roman claimed the trial court committed reversible error in permitting the young victim to testify without first conducting a voir dire examination of her to ascertain whether she was a competent witness.

While Maine's equivalent of Federal Rule of Evidence 601 has a part (b) spelling out grounds for disqualifying a witness for lack of competency[1] that the federal rule lacks, Maine's part (a) makes the same presumption as the federal rule does that all witnesses are competent to testify. The Maine Supreme Court affirmed the conviction and upheld the trial court's allowance of the victim's testimony, saying, "Although the trial court held no competency hearing, it did have the opportunity to listen to and evaluate the competency of the victim during her testimony.... Contrary to Roman's contention, there is nothing in the record which would indicate that the victim was not competent to testify."

---

[1] Maine Rule of Evidence 601(b) provides: "(b) Disqualification of Witness. A person is disqualified to be a witness if the court finds that (1) the proposed witness is incapable of expressing himself concerning the matter so as to be understood by the judge and jury either directly or through interpretation by one who can understand him, (2) the proposed witness is incapable of understanding the duty of a witness to tell the truth, (3) the proposed witness lacked any reasonable ability to perceive the matter or (4) the proposed witness lacks any reasonable ability to remember the matter...."

FRE 601 – "Facilitated" Testimony Is Admissible if Trial Judge Is Satisfied Facilitator Is Not Influencing Witness; Testimony Challenging Validity of Facilitated Testimony Is Also Admissible

> **Rule 601. [WITNESSES] General Rule of Competency**
> Every person is competent to be a witness except as otherwise provided in these rules. However, in civil actions and proceedings, with respect to an element of a claim or defense as to which State law supplies the rule of decision, the competency of a witness shall be determined in accordance with State law.

STATE V. WARDEN
891 P.2d 1074, 257 Kan. 94 (1995)

Marc R. Warden was charged in Sedgwick County, Kansas district Court with indecent liberties with a child. The alleged victim, "JK," twelve years old at the time of trial, suffered from autism and profound mental retardation. Despite severely limited ability to communicate, JK was permitted to "testify" against Warden using a "facilitator" – where the witness uses a keyboard and a facilitator supports his wrist and arm and applies pressure to prevent selection of a key until the facilitator knows the witness is looking at all of the selections, as well as to prevent perseveration on the same key. Ward was convicted, and sentenced to three to ten years in prison. He appealed.

Despite a spotty history, some valid results have been achieved through facilitated communication, and in its consideration of Ward's appeal the Kansas Supreme Court conducted a relatively thorough review of the scientific literature about facilitated communication, as well as of the specifics surrounding JK's testimony in this case. At a pre-trial hearing on Warden's motion to exclude JK's testimony to be given with the aid of his facilitator, both Dr. Henry Marks, director of the department of psychology at Wichita's Institute of Logopedics, where JK lived and where Marc Warden worked, and Terese Conrad, a speech pathologist there – both with extensive training and research background in facilitated communication and both of whom had worked with JK – had testified that "JK was validly communicating through facilitated communication." Dr. Allen Schwartz disagreed.) The Kansas court noted, "Among the premises upon which facilitated communication is based is an assumption that the speaker is competent."

The Kansas Supreme Court affirmed Warden's conviction and upheld the use of facilitated communication. The *Frye*[2] test (general scientific acceptance) was held not to apply to facilitated communication since the real issue was simply "whether JK was communicating." The trial court was correct in letting the jury decide whether to credit

---

[2] *Frye v. United States,* 293 F. 1013 (D.C.Cir. 1923).

the resulting "testimony"[3] or not. And the trial court properly "permitted evidence challenging the validity of the facilitated communication process itself." (Warden denied the charges in court, but a co-worker at IOL and a police officer both testified to admissions he made about his contact with JK, which were more or less consistent with JK's "account" of it).

New York courts have considered the question of facilitated communication, and have reached mixed results based on differing levels of assurances of its reliability. *Matter of Luz P.*, 595 N.Y.S.2d 541, 189 A.D.2d 274 (1993), agreed with *Warden* that the essential question is not scientific reliability but, pragmatically, whether the interpreter or facilitator "effectively communicate with the witness and reliably convey the witness's answers to the court." Effectively, both decisions apply Rule 601's presumption of competence and leave it to the jury to decide issues of disqualification for themselves.

FRE 601 – State Law Barring Testimony Applies in Federal Civil Action

> **Rule 601. [WITNESSES] General Rule of Competency**
> Every person is competent to be a witness except as otherwise provided in these rules. However, in civil actions and proceedings, with respect to an element of a claim or defense as to which State law supplies the rule of decision, the competency of a witness shall be determined in accordance with State law. Civil Action

BRAND v. BRAND
811 F.2d 74 (2d Cir. 1986)

Some years after Anton Brand developed Parkinson's Disease following the death of his wife Maria in 1979, he began to transfer bank accounts, brokerage accounts (securities), and his house in Yaphank, New York to himself and his son Herbert Brand as joint tenants or with right of survivorship. Anton Brand died in July 1985. In November of that year, Herbert's brother, Robert Brand, who lived in Connecticut, filed a diversity lawsuit asking the court to impose a

---

[3] "JK testified at trial with Terese Conrad as his facilitator. JK used a yes/no board and also a Canon communicator to respond to questions. As with JK's statements before trial, Conrad did not wear headphones nor were other steps taken to insure she could not hear the questions. In fact, she heard all the questions asked at all times during the proceedings. When JK testified in court, he was not calm and was supported at the wrist.

"JK indicated that he knew who Warden was and that he saw the person who hurt him in the courtroom, but he pointed to 'no' when asked if he could point to the person who hurt him. Asked if Warden hurt him, JK typed ASS. Asked where he was when Warden hurt him, JK typed GAT FAW, and then he typed FUK when asked to keep trying. Asked if that meant 'fuck,' JK pointed to 'yes' twice. JK pointed to 'no' in response to questions whether Warden fucked his ear, mouth, or toes, and JK pointed to 'yes' three times when asked whether Warden fucked his butt. JK then pointed to 'no' in response to questions whether Warden fucked him with his nose, mouth, or a suppository. JK was asked if he knew what a penis was, and he pointed to 'yes.' Asked if Warden used his penis to fuck JK's butt, JK pointed to 'yes.' JK also indicated by pointing at 'yes' that the incident occurred in Wichita.

"Because testimony in the courtroom was traumatic for JK, cross-examination occurred in a room outside the presence of the jury, and the testimony was shown to the jury on closed-circuit television. JK typed that his mother's name was YTURBEE and his father's name was STEVE. Asked how many times he had been asked if somebody hurt him, JK typed RAT. When he was asked if Terese Conrad was always with him when he was asked about being hurt, JK typed AT SCHOOL, and when asked if Dr. Marks was always with him, JK typed AFTEN. Asked if he uses the communicator with people other than Conrad, JK responded SOME. Asked when his birthday is, JK typed WAS CIPL WEAKS. Asked if he had a sister, JK typed QWESTUN and then DUM. JK typed ASS when asked if Warden ever had to give him suppositories. Asked what city his mother lived in, JK typed T, and asked if he could tell where his mother lived, JK typed NO. JK's mother's last name is Yturbe, his father's first name is Steve, and JK had had a birthday three weeks earlier."

constructive trust on the accounts and real estate and to require an accounting by Herbert Brand, as well as damages.

A one-day bench trial resulted in a judgment for Robert Brand that imposed a constructive trust on the assets in question, worth something under $250,000. Herbert Brand's appeal contended that the trial court had placed too much weight on a letter he had written his brother some years earlier. The letter said the assets had been transferred to Herbert's name only as a convenience, and that he and their father both intended that the brothers should share the estate equally (just as Anton Brand's will had provided). Herbert Brand argued the letter was based on a misunderstanding and that he had a later conversation with their father in which the father had told Herbert that the assets including the house should all go to him. Herbert contended on appeal that the trial court should have given greater weight to his testimony that his father had later told him that he, Herbert, should have all the assets for himself.

Robert Brand's objection to that testimony was that New York's Dead Man's Statute[4] (precluding "an interested person from testifying as to his conversations with a decedent in an action against a person... who has derived his title or interest from, through or under" that decedent) barred Herbert from testifying about his alleged conversations with his father, in effect disqualifying him as a witness as to those matters under Rule 601. The judge sustained the objection, but took the testimony.

The Eighth Circuit Court of Appeals affirmed the trial court's imposition of the constructive trust, and as to the testimony of Herbert Brand, held that Rule 601 applied to the case: "Under Fed.R.Evid.601, New York's Dead Man's Statute applied to this diversity action. Previously we have recognized the application of the statute to diversity actions to impose a constructive trust.... [Herbert Brand's] trial counsel appeared to agree that the statute barred appellant's testimony. Although the court sustained [Robert Brand's] objection, the court nevertheless heard the testimony. This was a sensible way to handle the proffered testimony at a bench trial....

"Hence, the court took appellant's testimony into account and found that it deserved less weight than the evidence presented by appellee. Such assessments of credibility and weighing of evidence lie exclusively within the province of the trier of the facts and cannot be set aside by us unless clearly erroneous.... Therefore, whether appellant's testimony was properly or improperly considered, the court correctly concluded that the circumstances surrounding the transfer gave rise to an inference that appellant promised Anton to hold the property for his estate. The admission of appellant's testimony, even assuming it should have been barred by the Dead Man's Statute, surely was not prejudicial to appellant. After all it was appellant who offered it."

---

[4] N.Y.Civ.Prac.Law §4519 (McKinney Supp.1986).

FRE 602, 601 – Witness with Faulty Memory Is Not Incompetent to Testify If She Possesses General Recollection of Personal Knowledge

> **Rule 602. Lack of Personal Knowledge**
> A witness may not testify to a matter unless evidence is introduced sufficient to support a finding that the witness has personal knowledge of the matter. Evidence to prove personal knowledge may, but need not, consist of the witness's own testimony. This rule is subject to the provisions of Rule 703, relating to opinion testimony by expert witnesses.
>
> **Rule 601. General Rule of Competency**
> Every person is competent to be a witness except as otherwise provided in these rules. However, in civil actions and proceedings, with respect to an element of a claim or defense as to which State law supplies the rule of decision, the competency of a witness shall be determined in accordance with State law.

UNITED STATES v. PEYRO
786 F.2d 826 (8th Cir. 1986)

Debra Anton testified for the government against Jose Antonio Peyro in his trial on charges of conspiracy to distribute cocaine. Peyro's alleged boss, Jorge Lorente, was also indicted but died before trial. Anton testified to the relationship between Lorente and Steven Musick, who was arrested with 10½ kilograms of cocaine in California in December 1982. Musick said he dealt with someone named "Flaco," which was Peyro's nickname.

Anton admitted to having "some very substantial memory problems" and to being "emotionally unbalanced," and after testifying to certain events conceded on cross-examination, "I don't remember anything very well. There are, like, certain moments I know I remember, but nothing at all specific in any of it." The jury convicted Peyro, and he appealed.

The Eighth Circuit Court of Appeals affirmed, and specifically upheld the admissibility of Anton's testimony, memory problems and all. Rule 601 and 602 were satisfied, minimally if not optimally: "A competency determination, best made with the benefit of firsthand observation of the witness, is a matter of discretion with the trial judge. The appellate court will not interfere except where discretion is abused.... The trial court, upon defendant's objection, personally examined Anton outside the jury's ear, and determined that while she could not recall detail, 'she has a broad, general recollection.'... We have closely reviewed the record and cannot conclude that the trial court abused its discretion in refusing to strike Anton's testimony. In addition, we doubt that the ruling prejudiced Peyro's case, for Anton's recall and emotional problems were laid bare for the jury's consideration."

Rule 602 requires only personal knowledge on the part of the witness – not perfect recall, nor likely even good recall.

FRE 602 – Trial Court Has Discretion to Determine Whether Witness Was in Position to Observe Events He Proposes to Testify About, and to Exclude Testimony if Witness Could Not Have Observed Events in Question

> **Rule 602. Lack of Personal Knowledge**
> A witness may not testify to a matter unless evidence is introduced sufficient to support a finding that the witness has personal knowledge of the matter. Evidence to prove personal knowledge may, but need not, consist of the witness's own testimony. This rule is subject to the provisions of rule 703, relating to opinion testimony by expert witnesses.

McCRARY-EL v. SHAW
992 F.2d 809 (8th Cir. 1993)

While serving life plus 35 years in the administrative segregation wing (for the most violent and dangerous inmates) of the Farmington, Missouri federal prison for assault with intent to kill, arson and carrying a concealed weapon, Jerry McCrary-El got involved in a brief scuffle with corrections officers over whether a cell mate would be placed in his one-man cell. McCrary-El filed a §1983 suit against several prison employees claiming they used excessive force against him, that they picked him up and slammed him onto the cell's concrete floor and twisted his head and neck, causing him back, neck and shoulder injuries. The officers said McCrary-El initiated the confrontation by shoving the first officer who went through his door, and that they abided by established procedures when they restrained him and removed him from the cell.

At trial McCrary-El was not permitted to read to the jury the deposition of Antonio Jones, an inmate in the next cell. The trial judge ruled Jones' testimony did not satisfy the foundational requirements of Rule 602 in that Jones could not have seen the events he testified about. The jury found for the corrections officers, and McCrary-El appealed.

The Eighth Circuit Court of Appeals affirmed the verdict and upheld the trial court's exclusion of the Jones deposition. "The trial court heard Jones testify that there was a crack at the corner of his cell door that was about an inch and a half, through which he witnessed McCrary-El's assault. He also testified that he could see into the cell only until all the officers were inside. The trial court saw a diagram of the cell placement and heard Jones testify as to the space through which he could see, as well as to what he allegedly did see. After weighing the evidence, the trial court had the discretion to determine whether Jones qualified under Rule 602. Rule 602 excludes testimony concerning matters the witness did not observe or had no opportunity to observe.... We cannot say that the trial court abused its discretion in determining that no reasonable person could conclude that Jones was able to see anything of relevance. There was therefore no error in excluding his testimony."

FRE 602 – Hypnotically Induced Identification of Person Whom Witness Previously Knew Was Under Suspicion Is Inadmissible

> **Rule 602. Lack of Personal Knowledge**
> A witness may not testify to a matter unless evidence is introduced sufficient to support a finding that the witness has personal knowledge of the matter. Evidence to prove personal knowledge may, but need not, consist of the witness's own testimony. This rule is subject to the provisions of rule 703, relating to opinion testimony by expert witnesses.

UNITED STATES v. VALDEZ
722 F.2d 1196 (5th Cir. 1984)

After the owner of HEB Grocery Co. received an extortion letter threatening to poison food sold in his store if he didn't leave $125,000 at a remote location as directed, two Texas Rangers set up a surveillance blind at a roadside rest area nine miles from Eagle Pass. No one picked up the money, but among several people who crossed a fence into an adjacent pasture "to answer a call of nature" the Rangers noticed one man "walk between the drop site and their place of concealment, look in their direction, and then disappear into the brush in a direction opposite from the drop site. Neither officer considered this important to their investigation at the time, and neither could identify the man." Joe Corona Valdez's truck was one of many that stopped during the surveillance, identified later when license numbers recorded at the rest stop were checked.

As law enforcement officials expected, a second extortion letter was received some weeks later directing the money be left at a second drop site. This time FBI agents watched the site from airplanes, and although no one picked up the money this time either, Valdez's truck was seen parked behind an abandoned house near the spot.

Valdez was interviewed where he worked, at an HEB grocery store in Carrizo Springs, by Texas Ranger Jackson, who had been at the first surveillance site. When Valdez acted suspiciously, two more interviews of a possibly incriminating nature were conducted. "At none of the various interviews with Valdez did Ranger Jackson recall ever having seen Valdez before interviewing him at the HEB grocery. After the investigation had focused suspicion on Valdez, Jackson, [Ranger] Haralson, and FBI agent Curtis Hunt were hypnotized in an effort to refresh their memories. Immediately before undergoing hypnosis, Jackson reported recalling only that a green and white pickup had stopped at the first drop site; he remembered nothing of the truck's driver or his activities. At the trial, however, Jackson testified that, on March 1, when he and Haralson were in hiding at the rest area, he saw Valdez emerge from the pickup truck and sit on a bench in the rest area smoking a cigarette and looking around. Valdez entered the pasture, according to Jackson's testimony, and walked in the direction of the camouflaged hiding place until he came within forty feet of it. Jackson testified that Valdez then 'broke off to the right into the brush,' and surmised that Valdez must have detected the blind. Jackson said he later saw Valdez's truck leave the area. This testimony is consistent with statements Jackson had made during his hypnosis. Haralson never was able to identify Valdez. No one other than Jackson identified him as having approached the hiding place or the first drop site."

The jury convicted Valdez and he appealed, citing the government's use of Ranger Jackson's hypnotically enhanced recollections in his testimony.

The Fifth Circuit Court of Appeals reversed. The use made of hypnosis here raised serious questions about whether Ranger Jackson was testifying from remembered "personal knowledge" as required by Rule 602: "The use of hypnosis in criminal investigation is based on an implicit theory of memory: the brain stores all the information received by the body's senses, and forgetting is simply the inability to retrieve stored information. Hypnosis is a method of eliminating retrieval difficulties to give the hypnotized person access to the stored information. Many memory theorists believe, to the contrary, that what appears to be recall is actually a constructive process in which information received after an event is integrated by the mind into the memory representation of that event. According to this view, what appears to be a witness's recollection of the event itself may in fact be a composite made up of original recall, information learned from earlier and later events, suggestions received during hypnosis, and the witness's unconscious filling-in of missing details to make the story complete or logical or to fulfill the perceived desires of the hypnotist or someone else. Whether hypnosis actually improves memory remains an open question among scientists."

The Fifth Circuit panel declined to adopt a per se rule to exclude hypnotically refreshed testimony: "In the present case, we consider only one kind of post-hypnotic testimony: the identification of a person known by the witness to be under suspicion, whom the witness had nevertheless been unable to **identify** before being hypnotized. No **government witness could identify Valdez as** having been present at the Eagle Pass rest spot. More important, no one could testify that, if he were there, he had crossed the fence into the pasture where the drop site was located and where the law enforcement agents were lying in their camouflaged hiding place. When Jackson interviewed Valdez a few weeks later, he had no recollection of having seen Valdez before. After several interviews with Valdez, Jackson still could not identify him until undergoing hypnosis. At trial, there was not a word of corroboration of Jackson's post-hypnotic testimony. Valdez had been identified as the principal suspect before Jackson was hypnotized. In addition, Valdez had incurred Jackson's personal rancor. This enmity surfaced during hypnosis; immediately after his first reference to Valdez, Jackson said, 'The son of a bitch comes in the pasture... The son of a bitch is going to walk over us.' Under these circumstances, confabulation alone would provide the likely bridge: the person must have been Valdez.

"Moreover, the procedures employed during the hypnotic session were unduly suggestive. In every particular, they were at variance with the safeguards required in New Jersey and Oregon [discussed earlier in the opinion]. Several Texas Rangers, FBI agents, and an Assistant U.S. Attorney were present in addition to the hypnotist. Questions were directed to Jackson not only by the 'mental health professional' who hypnotized him, but also by an FBI agent. Both had evidently received information about the events being investigated before the session began. During the hypnotic session, additional questions were proposed orally by yet another FBI agent in the room. Only some of the agents present were videotaped; whether others may have unintentionally suggested 'recollections' cannot be determined. Because those present did not record their knowledge and beliefs relative to the investigation, we cannot examine what recollections could be attributable to their subtle cues. The most obviously suggestive question put to Jackson referred to the 'significant' green and white truck. An elaborate pre-induction discussion had already focused Jackson's attention on the truck, which Jackson presumably knew had been traced to Valdez.

"One authority has observed that inaccuracy in hypnotic recall increases with the number and detail of questions; the least-distorted recollections are provided by free narration. In all, nearly a hundred questions were put to Jackson. In addition, the confusion of true recollection and pseudomemory may be aggravated by the suggestion that post-hypnotic memory will be as vivid and detailed as hypnotic experience. This suggestion was also imparted to Jackson....

"We do not formulate a per se rule of inadmissibility for cases not involving personal identification. In a particular case, the evidence favoring admissibility might make the probative value of the testimony outweigh its prejudicial effect. If adequate procedural safeguards have been followed, corroborated post-hypnotic testimony might be admissible. However, when, as here, a hypnotized subject identifies for the first time a person he has reason to know is already under suspicion, the post-hypnotic testimony is inadmissible whatever procedural safeguards were used to attempt to sanitize the hypnotic session."

Inasmuch as several scenarios not involving Valdez's culpability could have accounted for his presence at the second site, the appellate panel found the admission of Ranger Jackson's testimony was reversible error.

FRE 603 – Accused Who Refuses to Swear or Affirm He Will Tell Truth Forfeits Right to Testify

> **Rule 603. Oath or Affirmation**
> Before testifying, every witness shall be required to declare that the witness will testify truthfully, by oath or affirmation administered in a form calculated to awaken the witness's conscience and impress the witness's mind with the duty to do so.

UNITED STATES v. FOWLER
605 F.2d 181 (5th Cir. 1979)

After not filing federal tax returns since 1953, gravestone dealer E.L. Fowler, "an apparent tax protester,"[5] was finally indicted for failure to file returns for 1971-75. He did not cooperate in the IRS investigation of his finances other than to provide partial records, so the government prosecution proceeded under the "bank deposits" method of proving its case. He was convicted of all counts charged, and appealed.

One issue on appeal concerned the trial court's refusal to allow Fowler to testify. Fowler refused to swear or affirm to tell the truth or to submit to cross-examination. The Fifth Circuit Court of Appeals affirmed his conviction, and approved the trial court's stance on Fowler's testimony: "At one point in their extended colloquy on the point, the judge offered to accept the simple

---

[5] The Fifth Circuit panel called him "a wheel that did not squeak."

statement, 'I state that I will tell the truth in my testimony.' Fowler was willing to do no more than laud himself in such remarks as, 'I am a truthful man,' and 'I would not tell a lie to stay out of jail.' Rule 603, Federal Rules of Evidence, is clear and simple: 'Before testifying, every witness shall be required to declare that he will testify truthfully, by oath or affirmation...' No witness has the right to testify but on penalty of perjury and subject to cross-examination. This contention is frivolous."

FRE 604 – Trial Judge Must Evaluate Accused's Need for Interpreter Outside Presence of Jury, and Must Provide One if Accused's Language Skills Effectively Prevent Him from Exercising Right to Testify

Rule 604. Interpreters
An interpreter is subject to the provisions of these rules relating to qualification as an expert and the administration of an oath or affirmation to make a true translation.

UNITED STATES v. MAYANS
17 F.3d 1174 (9th Cir. 1994)

Los Angeles police arrested Pablo Mayans as he drove up and down Otis Avenue near an apartment his family owned where several alleged members of a drug-trafficking ring had just been arrested hours earlier. The evidence against Mayans was mostly circumstantial, including other-acts evidence of three other drug deals he was allegedly involved in, admitted on the issue of Mayans' knowledge and intent.[6] Mayans' defense was that he was not involved in any drug conspiracy, and he needed to testify to provide exculpatory explanations for conduct the government portrayed as indicative of guilt.

Mayans, born in Cuba, had been in the U.S. since 1971. He had been provided with an interpreter throughout the trial, but at the point when he took the witness stand the judge withdrew the interpreter, saying, "Let's try it in English," that testimony takes "twice as long" when an interpreter must be used, and noted Mayans had been in the U.S. longer than he was in Cuba. Mayans' lawyer "objected, stating that appellant could not express himself in English. The judge responded by asking counsel repeatedly to 'try it.'... Counsel withdrew appellant as a witness, and asked for a sidebar. The court denied that request."

Following the government's rebuttal case, "defense counsel moved to reopen and to put Mayans on the stand, presumably without an interpreter this time. The court refused to reopen after rebuttal, and shortly thereafter explained again that appellant had been in the United States longer than in Cuba, and that appellant's brother, who had testified without an interpreter over defense objections, had had no trouble handling himself. Subsequently, the defense moved for a mistrial on the ground that defendants had been denied an interpreter. The court denied the motion."

Mayans was convicted of conspiracy to distribute and possession with intent to distribute cocaine. He appealed.

---

[6]Admitted under FRE 404(b). See, e.g., *United States v. Fuller, supra* p. 45, and *People v. Oliphant, supra* p. 46.

The right to an interpreter is initially statutory. The Ninth Circuit Court of Appeals considered Mayans' claim that the trial judge had violated both 28 U.S.C. §1827(d)(1)[7] and his constitutional right to testify. The court reversed Mayans' convictions, remanding for a new trial, noting it could not review the district judge's determination that Mayans did not need an interpreter, because he "never conclusively made that determination," instead withdrawing the interpreter rather summarily. Mayans' "counsel's statement to the court that appellant cannot express himself [in English][is] nowhere contradicted in the record. In the face of an uncontradicted statement that a defendant needs an interpreter, common sense dictates that a trial court must satisfy itself through personal observation that the defendant has no difficulty speaking English before the interpreter is withdrawn.

"Here, the trial judge was foreclosed from making any such observation, since his method was to test appellant's language skills by withdrawing the interpreter — and after this was done, appellant chose not to testify at all. However efficient the district court's method for gathering the relevant information may have been, it created obvious problems. If appellant's English was weak enough that an interpreter was necessary, this fact would not have emerged until after appellant had exhibited some confusion or miscomprehension on the stand. By that time, the damage sought to be avoided by the interpreter statute would already have been done. Equally troubling, appellant's miscomprehension might never have been recognized as such: he might have made damaging responses to questions he misunderstood, and those responses might have been taken to be accurate."

The appellate panel held that the trial court should have made a determination of Mayans' need for an interpreter out of the presence of the jury. The right to an interpreter also has constitutional roots, specifically in the Fifth Amendment's recognized right of an accused to testify, and here Mayans' exercise of those rights was violated.

FRE 605 – Trial Judge May Not Testify or Take Into Account His Own Testimony Based on His Personal Knowledge of Facts of Case

> **Rule 605. Competency of Judge as Witness**
> The judge presiding at the trial may not testify in that trial as a witness. No objection need be made in order to preserve the point.

FOX v. CITY OF WEST PALM BEACH
383 F.2d 189 (5th Cir. 1967)

The city of West Palm Beach in 1965 began pumping water from Lake Okeechobee into its catchment basin to increase its water supply. The catchment basin was adjacent to a

---

[7] Providing that the trial judge must provide the accused witness an interpreter if he or she "determines on [his or her] own motion or on the motion of a party that such party (including a defendant in a criminal case), or a witness who may present testimony... speaks only or primarily a language other than the English language... so as to inhibit such party's comprehension of the proceedings or communication with counsel or the presiding judicial officer, or so as to inhibit such witness' comprehension of questions and the presentation of such testimony."

large tract of land owned by Maurice Fox that shared a 2¾ mile-long boundary along the basin's undiked western boundary. Fox sued for an injunction and damages amounting to the costs of the litigation only, in the sum of $48,000, claiming the city's action interfered with his land's natural drainage.

The district judge denied Fox's request for injunctive relief and said Fox could have a jury trial on the issue of compensatory damages, which Fox had not sought. Fox appealed.

The Fifth Circuit Court of Appeals affirmed in part and reversed in part, and specifically held that the trial court acted improperly in one respect: "During the examination of the first witness court and counsel embarked upon a colloquy which took considerable time and covered many pages of the transcript. During this discussion the judge made frequent factual statements based upon his own experience with respect to lands in the area." In a footnote, the appellate court in this pre-Rules case quoted the trial court:

"As a matter of fact, I have litigated some of these things as a lawyer that you are litigating today.

"You are not entitled to have your land dried, I will say that, because your land was never dried, so far as I know. I flew over it forty years ago and it wasn't dry at all.

"The cost of making the changes here would be the cost of at least a billion dollars – at least a billion dollars to make this land dry and make sure that it will be dry.

"If you would go out there and drain that land or any other like land, the cost would be so atrocious that you could buy all the dry land in North Florida, practically, for what you are paying to drain a little of this land.

"I know. I had some of the land. I sold it. Let it go for taxes.

"We destroyed I guess 1,000 acres of pine in Dade county to get rid of it to make way for good subdivisions."

The court's holding amounts to a pre-Rule 605 holding that it was improper for the judge to testify and to take into account his own testimony the basis of which purported to be his own personal knowledge: "It is not at all unlikely that the appellant will be unable to support by evidence his claim for mandatory injunctive relief or for prohibitory injunctive relief, but he ought to be given the opportunity to try his case and submit his evidence free from the coloring of the personal knowledge of the judge."

FRE 605 – Judge's Interruption and Correction of Counsel on Point of Law Is Not Impermissible Judicial Testimony

> **Rule 605. Competency of Judge as Witness**
> The judge presiding at the trial may not testify in that trial as a witness. No objection need be made in order to preserve the point.

UNITED STATES v. MACEO
947 F.2d 1191 (5th Cir. 1991)

At the trial of four defendants involved in a complex, multi-national cocaine importation scheme, Idanael Martinez, a Colombian co-defendant, testified for the government about the events surrounding the frequent importing of large quantities (often hundreds of kilos) of the drug. When counsel for defendant John Cary tried to cross-examine Martinez about the terms of the witness's plea-bargain agreement, "in an attempt to show that the witness had a greater incentive to lie," the trial judge in the U.S. District Court for the Southern District of Texas interrupted and cut off the questioning, objecting "that counsel had misstated the law of plea bargains." Cary, Pedro Talamas and attorney Hiram Lee Bauman were convicted by the jury of conspiracy to import cocaine and conspiracy to possess cocaine with the intent to distribute it. Julio Maceo was convicted only of the second of the two charges. All appealed.

One of Carey's arguments to the Fifth Circuit Court of Appeals was that what the judge had done when he interrupted his lawyer's cross-examination of Martinez amounted to the judge giving his own testimony as a witness. The appeals court affirmed all the convictions, and specifically held that Rule 605 did not apply to this situation: "The judge did not impermissibly testify as to any fact issue when he told Cary's attorney he was misstating the law." (Cary also argued that the trial judge "accused his counsel of intentionally misstating the law, and therefore violated his right to effective assistance of counsel, his right to a trial by an impartial jury and his right to a fair trial. These overstated arguments also plainly lack merit.")

FRE 606(a) – Member of Grand Jury That Indicted Accused May Not Testify as Witness in Same Case

> **Rule 606. Competency of Juror as Witness**
> *(a) At the Trial.*
> A member of the jury may not testify as a witness before that jury in the trial of the case in which the juror is sitting. If the juror is called so to testify, the opposing party shall be afforded an opportunity to object out of the presence of the jury.

STATE v. AARON
692 P.2d 1336, 102 N.M. 187 (1984)

Titus Edwin Aaron, on trial in Bernalillo County District Court for multiple counts of fraud and writing bad checks, tried to call Patricia Kelan to testify, as an employee of one of the banks Aaron was charged with victimizing, that some of the bank officers who had testified against him were biased against him. The district judge barred Kelan's testimony under New Mexico's version of Rule 606(a) because she had served on the grand jury that indicted Aaron.

The jury convicted Aaron of 21 counts of fraud over $100 but less than $2,500 and five counts of issuing worthless checks, and he appealed. The New Mexico Court of Appeals affirmed. Rule 606(a), which renders jurors incompetent to testify, was held also to apply to grand jurors.

(In any event, when the trial court asked the defense for a good-faith basis for showing bias on the part of the bank witnesses, or for thinking Kelan had any personal knowledge of their bias, they were unable to show any such good-faith basis. And besides, "earlier three bank employees had testified and the defense did not seek to cross-examine to show bias... The allegations [of bias] were nothing more than speculation. He was attempting to engage in court-supervised discovery, which is not a function of... trial testimony.")

FRE 606(b) – Juror May Testify About Extraneous Prejudicial Information Concerning Accused's Prior Conviction That Was Brought to Jury's Attention During Deliberations

> **Rule 606. Competency of Juror As Witness**
> *(b) Inquiry Into Validity of Verdict or Indictment.*
> Upon an inquiry into the validity of a verdict or indictment, a juror may not testify as to any matter or statement occurring during the course of the jury's deliberations or to the effect of anything upon that or any other juror's mind or emotions as influencing the juror to assent to or dissent from the verdict or indictment or concerning the juror's mental processes in connection therewith, except that a juror may testify on the question whether extraneous prejudicial information was improperly brought to the jury's attention or whether any outside influence was improperly brought to bear upon any juror. Nor may a juror's affidavit or evidence of any statement by the juror concerning a matter about which the juror would be precluded from testifying be received for these purposes.

UNITED STATES v. SWINTON
75 F.3d 374 (8th Cir. 1996)

Real estate entrepreneur and contractor Bruce Raymond Swinton was charged with seven counts of causing misrepresentations to be made to federally regulated financial institutions, in connection with a scheme where he would persuade other people to buy houses on his behalf and take out loans in their own names to finance the purchases, falsely stating that they intended to reside in the homes. Swinton would then undertake to repay the loans. Swinton defaulted on the loans; "since the loans were all insured, the losses ultimately fell in the Department of Housing and Urban Development." There were also a dozen or so uncharged transactions of the same nature.

The jury in the U.S. District Court for the Eastern District of Arkansas convicted Swinton on all counts, and he was sentenced to 37 months' imprisonment followed by three years of supervised release.

On appeal to the Eighth Circuit Court of Appeals raising several issues, Swinton stated that after the trial a juror had contacted him, saying another juror told the jury during deliberations that Swinton had a criminal record. The trial judge had specifically prohibited the government from introducing evidence of Swinton's prior felony conviction.[8]

The appellate panel noted that although a juror is generally prohibited "from impeaching his or her own verdict," the exception recognized by Rule 606(b) is when the claim is made that "extraneous, prejudicial information" was brought to the jury's attention or that outside influence was brought to bear on any juror. The court agreed that "discussion of a prior conviction which was not introduced at trial fits the category" of extraneous, prejudicial information.

"The Government argues that if the jury improperly discussed defendant's prior conviction, such a discussion is not a matter of extrinsic evidence at all because it would have originated from within the jury room.

---
[8] See FRE 609. The nature of the conviction and the grounds for excluding it from evidence are not revealed in the report of the case.

The Government's position, basically, is that evidence coming form the jurors themselves is not 'extrinsic.'

"The question of when a juror is resorting to knowledge obtained outside the record presents some difficulties. Although jurors are expected to bring commonly known facts to bear in assessing the facts presented for their consideration, resort by a juror to anything other than common knowledge or record facts might be held to violate the right to confrontation....

"In this instance, we have an allegation that the jury considered a specific statement of fact that had not been admitted into evidence. We therefore conclude that the statement was 'extraneous prejudicial information' within the meaning of Rule 606(b)....

"The district court declined to investigate the purported statement any further because it incorrectly determined that any such testimony would be barred under Rule 606(b). Given the risk that the jury's discussion of a prior conviction may prejudice the defendant in a case where fraudulent intent is a key ingredient, we believe it is appropriate to remand to the district court to hold an evidentiary hearing....

"This circuit has established standards governing inquiries into juror misconduct. First, where juror misconduct exposes the jury to factual matters not in evidence, we presume prejudice and require the government to prove beyond a reasonable doubt that the inappropriate activity did not harm the defendant....

"Second, this circuit applies an objective test to assess whether the extraneous information would likely affect a typical juror when the government must overcome a presumption of prejudice.... The relevant considerations include (1) whether the extrinsic evidence was received by the jury and the manner in which it was received; (2) whether it was available to the jury for a lengthy period of time; (3) whether it was discussed and considered extensively by the jury; (4) whether it was introduced before a verdict was reached and, if so, at what point during the deliberations was it introduced; and (5) whether it was reasonably likely to affect the verdict, considering the strength of the government's case and whether it outweighed any possible prejudice caused by the extrinsic evidence." While rejecting Swinton's other appellate claims, the court remanded the case to the district court for "an evidentiary hearing as to potential juror misconduct" and to make a decision on a new trial based on its findings from that hearing.

FRE 606(b) – Trial Court Cannot Take Juror Testimony About Deliberations to Impeach Verdict

> **Rule 606. Competency of Juror as Witness**
> *(b) Inquiry Into Validity of Verdict or Indictment.*
>
> Upon an inquiry into the validity of a verdict or indictment, a juror may not testify as to any matter or statement occurring during the course of the jury's deliberations or to the effect of anything upon that or any other juror's mind or emotions as influencing the juror to assent to or dissent from the verdict or indictment or concerning the juror's mental processes in connection therewith, except that a juror may testify on the question whether extraneous prejudicial information was improperly brought to the jury's attention or whether any outside influence was improperly brought to bear upon any juror. Nor may a juror's affidavit or evidence of any statement by the juror concerning a matter about which the juror would be precluded from testifying be received for these purposes.

UNITED STATES v. STRAACH
987 F.2d 232 (5th Cir. 1993)

Dallas firearms dealer Gary Eugene Straach was caught selling firearms to nonresidents of Texas in "strawman transactions" in a federal sting operation. He was indicted on five counts of violating provisions of the Gun Control Act of 1968.[9] The sting was set up "after several Jamaican drug traffickers were apprehended in 1987 and 1988 and found to possess guns purchased from Shooting Sports," Straach's licensed gun shop.

A jury convicted Straach of two of the counts charged and acquitted him of the other three. He was sentenced to a year in prison followed by three years of supervised release. Although the jury was polled and all jurors indicated their agreement with the verdict, two jurors went to Straach's lawyer's office and signed affidavits saying they believed Straach to be innocent on all counts and that during deliberation they "repeatedly stated their belief that Straach was innocent."

"One of the two jurors who completed affidavits, stated that prior to reading the court's note telling them to continue deliberating, the jury had decided Straach was not guilty on counts two through five. According to this juror, the judge's note influenced the jury to reconsider the decision they had reached on counts two through five. Had the judge directed the jury to render their verdicts on counts two through five at the time the jury told the judge they were at an impasse, the only crime of which Straach might have been convicted was that listed in count one (conspiracy), a crime for which the judge had indicated he was unwilling to sentence defendant if defendant was acquitted on all other charges. The juror's affidavit also stated that some of the jurors wanted to convict Straach because they considered his behavior to be legal, but morally wrong; that on the first day of deliberations the jurors had agreed to 'compromise and trade off a guilty verdict on [count] five for a not guilty on [count] one;' and that on the last day of deliberations, the jurors agreed to another compromise, involving a guilty

---
[9] 18 U.S.C. §921 et. seq., especially §922(b)(3) and §924(a)(1).

verdict on counts two and five in exchange for a verdict of 'not guilty' on count one.'"

The district court denied Straach's motion for a mistrial, and he appealed that ruling as well as the verdict.

The Fifth Circuit Court of Appeals affirmed the verdict, and specifically held that under Rule 606(b) a juror's "testimony about the jury's internal deliberations cannot result in a mistrial." Only testimony about improper outside influences on jurors can be heard under the rule: "even a compromise verdict cannot be challenged later by a juror if a reasonable jury could have found that the conviction was supported by the evidence beyond a reasonable doubt.... Although testimony by jurors about 'objective jury misconduct' is admissible in some jurisdictions, it generally is not admissible in the federal courts.... Although two jurors came forward after the verdicts had been returned and recorded, stating that they had maintained throughout the jury's deliberations that defendant was not guilty on all counts, but had been pressured into compromising their verdicts on counts two and five, this 'pressure' cannot count as an outside influence....

"Defendant also claims that jurors considered the penalties that might be visited upon Straach if they found him guilty on various counts. However, there is no evidence that they learned about these penalties from outside sources and therefore the verdicts must stand. Finally, a jury verdict cannot be challenged as nonunanimous if the jurors agreed to the verdict when polled, unless some competent evidence is presented which does not involve delving into the jurors' actual deliberations."

FRE 607, 403 – Impeachment: Past Physical Abuse of Witness by Accused Is Admissible to Show Witness's Motive to Fabricate

> **Rule 607. Who May Impeach**
> The credibility of a witness may be attacked by any party, including the party calling the witness.
>
> **Rule 403. Exclusion of Relevant Evidence on Grounds of Prejudice, Confusion, or Waste of Time**
> Although relevant, evidence may be excluded it its probative value is substantially outweighed by the danger of unfair prejudice, confusion of the issues, or misleading the jury, or by considerations of undue delay, waste of time, or needless presentation of cumulative evidence.

UNITED STATES v. BRATTON
875 F.2d 439 (5th Cir.1989)

From her position as market coordinator for Diamond Shamrock Refining and Marketing Co. in San Antonio, Doris Bratton accomplished two unauthorized wire transfers amounting to more than $473,000 from Diamond Shamrock futures accounts to her husband's business. Doris and George Bratton were both indicted for wire fraud and receipt and possession of stolen property. Doris Bratton pled guilty, per a plea agreement, to two counts of wire fraud, but then testified that her husband had nothing to do with her fraudulent acts, and that she told him she had received an inheritance. The government was permitted over George Bratton's objection to impeach Doris Bratton by asking her on cross-examination about past instances of physical abuse she had suffered at her husband's hands. George Bratton was convicted by a jury of all six counts and sentenced to four years' imprisonment on each count, to be served concurrently.

Bratton appealed to the Fifth Circuit Court of Appeals, asserting the impeachment of his wife regarding his past physical abuse of her was too prejudicial under Rule 403. The court affirmed the convictions, noting a wealth of precedent to the effect that "cross-examination into any motivation or incentive a witness may have for falsifying his testimony must be permitted," subject only to the weighing of its probative value against its danger of unfair prejudice. The court noted that the trial judge had permitted testimony about Bratton's physical abuse of his wife and threats against her with a gun only as to incidents that occurred after both wire transfers were completed, and had barred impeachment concerning any such occurrences from before then. "This conduct on the part of Mr. Bratton could easily have affected the content of Mrs. Bratton's testimony by inducing her to testify falsely out of fear of her husband." The judge's instruction to the jury limiting their consideration of these events to the question of Doris Bratton's credibility was sufficient.

FRE 607 – Impeachment: Permissible Subjects of Cross-Examination of Eyewitness Include Quality of Witness's Eyesight

> **Rule 607. Who May Impeach**
> The credibility of a witness may be attacked by any party, including the party calling the witness.
> **Rule 611. (b) Scope of Cross-Examination.**
> Cross examination should be limited to the subject matter of the direct examination and matters affecting the credibility of the witness…

BATTLE v. UNITED STATES
345 F.2d 438 (D.C. Cir. 1965)

David Battle and Michael Davis were charged with robbery and assault with a dangerous weapon. The complaining witnesses were mugged at night and robbed. They identified Battle and Davis as their assailants.

The trial judge unaccountably refused defense counsel the opportunity to cross-examine one of the complaining witnesses about her eyesight. The jury convicted Battle and Davis of robbery and simple assault, and they were sentenced to four to twelve years' imprisonment.

On appeal to the District of Columbia Circuit Court of Appeals, the convictions were reversed. In addition to a procedural issue, the court cited the trial judge's error in restricting the impeachment of the complaining witness, because "identification at nighttime of the two men who attacked the complaining witnesses on the street was the principle issue." The capacity of any witness to observe that which he or she testifies about is always fair game for impeachment, by way of both cross-examination and, if necessary, the introduction of extrinsic evidence on the issue.

FRE 607 – Impeachment: For Witness's Narcotics Use to Be Admissible, Connection Must Be Established Between Drug Use and Subject of Testimony

> **Rule 607. Who May Impeach**
> The credibility of a witness may be attacked by any party, including the party calling the witness.

HENDERSON v. DeTELLA
97 F.3d 942 (7th Cir. 1996)

Ladell Henderson was charged in Illinois state court with breaking into the Chicago home of Mona Chavez and her uncle, shooting the uncle to death, and firing three bullets into Chavez's head for refusing to be Henderson's "lady." Somehow she survived the shooting, and a few hours later, when she regained consciousness, she identified Henderson as the shooter. Chavez repeated the identification at Henderson's trial.

The defense cross-examined Chavez, 16, about whether she had ever used "speed" in the presence of Henderson and Quintin Jones. She denied it. Later they tried to call Jones as a witness to testify that he had seen Chavez use drugs several times. The trial judge sustained the state's objection, refusing to allow Jones to testify to this effect, saying, "the only reason [you're] doing it is to dirty up the witness." The jury convicted Henderson of murder, attempted murder, conspiracy and home invasion, and sentenced him to life in prison. An Illinois appellate court affirmed all but the conspiracy convictions.

Henderson filed a federal petition for a writ of habeas corpus,[10] claiming several errors had been committed in his trial (including the admission of a partial confession). The petition claimed it had been reversible error for the trial judge to prevent Henderson's witness, Jones, from testifying about Chavez's drug use. The District Court for the Northern District of Illinois denied the petition, and Henderson appealed to the Seventh Circuit Court of Appeals.

Although the appellate court said, "the use of narcotics can, obviously, affect the ability of a witness to perceive, to recall, and to recount the events she has observed," the panel also noted that no effort was made by the defense to link any alleged drug use by Chavez to the time period surrounding the shooting. "It is thus not at all clear that the [Jones] testimony was probative of Chavez's ability to recognize and identify the individual who committed the offense. Absent a connection to Chavez's cognitive abilities, Jones' testimony would have served only to impeach her character, a purpose we have repeatedly deemed improper." The convictions were affirmed.

For Rule 607 purposes courts usually treat use of alcohol by witnesses the same way – admissible capacity impeachment only if a connection is established.[11]

---

[10] George E. DeTella is the warden of the Stateville Correctional Center and is thus the respondent in Henderson's petition.
[11] See *United States v. DiPaolo, infra* p. 137.

FRE 607 – Impeachment: Bias Is Relevant Enough That Denial of Right to Impeach Can Preclude Summary Judgment

> **Rule 607. Who May Impeach**
> The credibility of a witness may be attacked by any party, including the party calling the witness.

WILMINGTON TRUST CO. v. MANUFACTURERS LIFE INSURANCE CO.
624 F.2d 707 (5th Cir. 1980)

When Joseph D. Winsor was shot to death, Manufacturers Life Insurance Company disclaimed liability on its policy of life insurance, alleging that Winsor had made false statements in his application for the policy. Wilmington Trust, on behalf of policy beneficiaries, sued Manufactures for breach of contract.

The false statements concerned Winsor's having flown on non-scheduled aircraft within the preceding two years. There was no serious dispute that his denial on the application was false; the issue in dispute concerned the "materiality" of the misstatements to Manufacturers' decision to issue the policy. The company's underwriter, John L. Cummins, said the misrepresentation was material, but "emphasized, however, that actuarial evaluation of aviation risks is largely subjective, calling for case-by-case analysis."

Supported by Cummins' testimony, Manufacturers moved for summary judgment. Wilmington Trust argued that "their plan... was to impeach Cummins as biased in favor of his employer, the defendant." The District Court for the Southern District of Florida granted the insurer's motion, and plaintiffs appealed.

The Fifth Circuit Court of Appeals reversed "that portion of the judgment that summarily resolves whether Winsor's misstatement was 'material' under Florida law." The court held that "prospective impeachment of the movant's evidence, without more, can suffice to preclude summary judgment." Where the fact in dispute (here materiality) is within the exclusive knowledge of the party moving for summary judgment, where their supporting evidence is of necessity largely subjective, and where the moving party bears the burden of persuasion, denial of the opportunity to impeach amounts to reversible error. "The jury would be free to find that (Manufacturers') burden had not been met because of possible lack of credibility of [its] witness," exactly the sort of thing bias impeachment under Rule 607 is designed to elicit.

FRE 607 – Impeachment: Relationship Between Prosecution Witness and Investigating Officer Is Admissible

> **Rule 607. Who May Impeach**
> The credibility of a witness may be attacked by any party, including the party calling the witness.

UNITED STATES v. BUCHANAN
891 F.2d 1436 (10th Cir. 1989)

The trailer home of Jessie Ervin Buchanan's ex-wife's mother was firebombed and destroyed. John Omstead confessed to the firebombing, telling investigators he and Eric Elrod had been hired by Buchanan to burn the trailer. Buchanan was charged with manufacture and possession of an unregistered firearm and conspiracy. A first trial ended in a hung jury, and the second trial resulted in his conviction. Buchanan moved for a new trial, claiming the prosecution had failed to disclose information about a personal relationship between Buchanan's ex-wife, Gwen Whitten, and ATF Agent Doye Tilley. The District Court for the Eastern District of Oklahoma granted the motion, and the government appealed.

The Tenth Circuit Court of Appeals noted that defense counsel had filed, prior to trial, an extensive motion for the production of exculpatory material and of "any evidence which might be used for the impeachment of any witness for the prosecution at the time of trial" under *Brady v. Maryland*.[12] The government did not disclose that Whitten and Tilley had engaged in a romantic relationship that may have resulted in the birth of a child. While Whitten said she knew nothing about the fire, she did provide motive testimony about Buchanan's "rancorous relationship" with her mother, and thus her credibility was significant. The Tenth Circuit panel noted that Agent Tilley's relationship with Whitten could well have been used for impeachment via the exposure of "possible biases, prejudices, or ulterior motives" Whitten might have had to testify against Buchanan.

(The court reversed the District Court's order for a new trial, however, holding that a *Brady* evaluation of the effect of Whitten's testimony in establishing Buchanan's guilt showed "she was not a key witness to the government's case" given the other witnesses it produced. "The withheld evidence of the Tilley-Whitten relationship is not material under *Brady* because, as a matter of law, it does not raise a reasonable doubt as to Buchanan's guilt that did not otherwise exist." That did not prevent the court, however, from acknowledging the "dramatic effect" of such testimony had it been presented to a jury: "A jury cognizant of this [personal] relationship [between a witness and the government's investigator seated at counsel table throughout the trial] might have ignored admonitions that it was only relevant to Whitten's credibility and, out of sympathy or disdain, returned a verdict of not guilty." And, of course, it goes without saying that it might have concluded in good faith that Whitten was fabricating her testimony to please Tilley.)

---

[12] 373 U.S. 83, 83 S.Ct. 1194, 10 L.Ed.2d 215 (1963).

FRE 607, 401, 403 – Impeachment: Gang Membership Is Admissible to Show Bias of Defense Witness

> **Rule 607. Who May Impeach**
>
> The credibility of a witness may be attacked by any party, including the party calling the witness.
>
> **Rule 401. Definition of "Relevant Evidence"**
>
> "Relevant evidence" means evidence having any tendency to make the existence of any fact that is of consequence to the determination of the action more probable or less probable than it would be without the evidence.
>
> **Rule 403. Exclusion of Relevant Evidence on Grounds of Prejudice, Confusion, or Waste of Time**
>
> Although relevant, evidence may be excluded if its probative value is substantially outweighed by the danger of unfair prejudice, confusion of the issues, or misleading the jury, or by considerations of undue delay, waste of time, or needless presentation of cumulative evidence.

UNITED STATES v. ABEL
469 U.S. 45, 105 S. Ct. 465, 83 L.Ed.2d 450 (1984)

John Clyde Abel, Kurt Ehle, and Robert Mills were charged with a bank robbery in Bellflower, California. Ehle and Mills pled guilty, but Abel chose to go to trial. The government called Ehle, who testified to Abel's involvement. The defense called Mills, who testified that Ehle had told him in prison that Ehle planned to testify falsely against Abel.[13] The government was permitted to cross-examine Mills concerning a "secret prison organization" he and Abel belonged to that required members to lie for each other and to deny the existence of the organization itself. (The district court barred the government from identifying the organization as the "Aryan Brotherhood" because of the danger of undue prejudice.)

When Mills denied any knowledge of such an organization, the government was permitted to recall Ehle on rebuttal. Ehle testified to the membership of all three in a secret prison organization "whose tenets required its members to deny its existence and 'lie, cheat, steal [and] kill' to protect each other." Ehle denied telling Mills he would falsely implicate Abel: in light of the organization's rules and of how close Abel and Mills were, it would have been "suicide" to say such a thing.

Abel was convicted. He appealed, claiming Ehle's rebuttal testimony should have been excluded. A divided panel of the Ninth Circuit Court of Appeals reversed, saying the government may not convict an individual for his membership in an organization, and Ehle's testimony about Abel's belonging to the organization prejudiced him by association.

The United States Supreme Court, in a unanimous opinion written by Justice Rehnquist, reinstated Abel's convictions, holding that Ehle's testimony had sufficient probative value of Mills' bias regarding Abel to overcome any prejudicial danger. Although the court seemed a little surprised

---
[13] This was admissible under FRE 613(b).

that the Federal Rules of Evidence it had "promulgated" contained no rules specifically governing bias,[14] it was satisfied that witness bias was a proper subject for inquiry. And specifically the nature of the group, deceitful and murderous, was probative "not only on the fact of bias but also on the source and strength of Mills' bias."

FRE 607 – Impeachment: Witness's Mental Illness Is Admissible to Suggest Vendetta Against Accused

Rule 607. Who May Impeach
The credibility of a witness may be attacked by any party, including the party calling the witness.

Rule 608. Evidence of Character and Conduct of Witness
(b) Specific Instances of Conduct. Specific instances of the conduct of a witness, for the purpose of attacking or supporting the witness credibility, other than conviction of a crime as provided in rule 609, may not be proved by extrinsic evidence. They may, however, in the discretion of the court, if probative of truthfulness or untruthfulness, be inquired into on cross-examination of the witness (1) concerning the witness's character for truthfulness or untruthfulness, or (2) concerning the character for truthfulness or untruthfulness of another witness as to which character the witness being cross-examined has testified.

The giving of testimony, whether by an accused or by any other witness, does not operate as a waiver of the accused's or the witness's privilege against self-incrimination when examined with respect to matters which relate only to credibility.

UNITED STATES v. LINDSTROM
698 F.2d 1154 (11th Cir. 1983)

Legal secretary Joanne Lindstrom and her boss, Tampa trial attorney Dennis Slater, were charged with mail fraud and conspiracy in connection with their operation of a clinic called Bay Therapy. They were charged with inflating medical costs and defrauding insurance companies by sending patients to Bay Therapy for treatment they did not need or, often, even receive. The three-week trial heard testimony of 86 witnesses including the defendants who denied all charges. The jury found Slater and Lindstrom guilty of conspiracy and 17 substantive counts of mail fraud; Slater received concurrent sentences of five years' imprisonment (all but six months suspended), and Lindstrom was sentenced to three years' probation.

Both appealed their convictions to the Eleventh Circuit Court of Appeals, asserting that their right to impeach the government's key witness, was improperly limited. The key witness, never named in the opinion, succeeded a Rosamond Sloan, a licensed practical nurse, as operator of the clinic. She contacted authorities after about nine months of operating Bay Therapy, and this contact eventually led to state and federal investigations that produced the indictments.

---

[14]Compare, e.g., Virginia's Revised Proposed Rule 610: "IMPEACHMENT BY BIAS – A witness may be impeached by a showing that the witness is biased for or against a party. Extrinsic evidence of such bias may be admitted."

Lindstrom and Slater argued that the key witness "was carrying out a vendetta against them because she had not received a promised percentage of Bay Therapy when the business was sold." They claimed the vendetta was the result of "a continuing mental illness, for which she had been periodically treated and confined." She had a psychiatric history of several involuntary confinements, and events such as a suicide attempt, offering a patient $3,000 to murder her lover's wife, drug overdose, firing a shotgun through the window of her lover's house; she was diagnosed variously as schizophrenic, immature and manipulative, suicidal, homicidal and delusional. Many of these events and diagnoses occurred near the time she was gathering information for investigators in this case.

The district judge refused to let the defense "try this witness," and barred cross-examination questions about the murder contract, shotgun, and suicide attempt, and prevented them from entering hospital records into evidence that would have showed that the witness told hospital employees she attempted suicide to manipulate and punish her boyfriend.

The Eleventh Circuit panel reversed, calling the trial judge's ruling's here "an abuse of discretion" and "egregious." The disputed medical records suggested a history of psychiatric disorders, manifesting themselves in violent threats and manipulative and destructive conduct having specific relevance to the facts at issue…. The witness in question was the chief witness for the prosecution. She initiated and pursued the investigation of Bay Therapy. She was an insider to the fraud scheme, who testified in detail about the operation and about the activities of Slater and Lindstrom." The significance of a serious mental disorder goes beyond mere motive to lie, said the court: "A psychotic's veracity may be impaired by lack of capacity to observe, correlate or recollect actual events. A paranoid person may interpret a reality skewed by suspicions, antipathies or fantasies. A schizophrenic may have difficulty distinguishing fact from fantasy and may have his memory distorted by delusions, hallucinations and paranoid thinking. A paranoid schizophrenic, though he may appear normal and his judgment on matters outside his delusional system may remain intact, may harbor delusions of grandeur or persecution that grossly distort his reactions to events."

Thus the court's denial of the defense of an opportunity to question the witness fully and to use the hospital records was reversible error.

FRE 607 – Impeachment: Expert Witness May Be Asked About Fees Earned in Prior Cases

> **Rule 607. Who May Impeach**
> The credibility of a witness may be attacked by any party, including the party calling the witness.

COLLINS v. WAYNE CORP.
621 F.2d 777 (5th Cir. 1980)

Four injured survivors (of 11) and representatives of ten who died (of 19 total) sued Wayne Corp. in products liability. They claimed the bus they were riding in when it collided with a jackknifed cattle truck on a narrow New Mexico bridge was defectively designed and not crashworthy. The trailer of the cattle truck penetrated through the first four rows of the bus. At trial plaintiffs called Derwyn Severy, a nationally acknowledged expert on bus design. Wayne was permitted over their objection to cross-examine Severy about fees he had earned for testifying in other cases. He answered that plaintiffs were paying him $95 an hour, and that he had been testifying in accident cases for 20 years. Although the precise amount of his earnings was never established, a clear picture emerged of a professional expert witness who made a substantial six-figure income. The jury returned a "take nothing" verdict in favor of the defendant corporation. Plaintiffs appealed.

The Fifth Circuit Court of Appeals reiterated that cross-examination of a witness to reveal possible bias or interest is "entirely proper.... A pecuniary interest in the outcome of a case may, of course, bias a witness. A showing of a pattern of compensation in past cases raises an inference of the possibility that the witness has slanted his testimony in those cases so he would be hired to testify in future cases." Although the court in a footnote conceded Severy to be an "able, dedicated engineer... nonetheless, ability and dedication cannot insulate anyone from the suggestions of bias that a cross-examiner brings out when he plays his role in a trial."

FRE 607, Confrontation Clause – Impeachment: Denial of Opportunity to Cross-Examine Witness Concerning Bias Because of State's Dismissal of Charge Against Witness Violates Clause Subject to Harmless Error Analysis

> **U.S. Constitution, Sixth Amendment:**
> In all criminal prosecutions, the accused shall enjoy the right... to be confronted with the witness against him.
>
> **Rule 607. Who May Impeach**
> The credibility of a witness may be attacked by any party, including the party calling the witness.

DELAWARE v. VAN ARSDALL
475 U.S. 673, 106 S. Ct. 1431, 89 L.Ed.2d 674 (1986)

Separate state court juries acquitted Daniel Pregent and convicted Robert Van Arsdall in the New Year's Eve stabbing death of Doris Epps in Smyrna, Delaware. One prosecution witness, Robert Fleetwood, gave testimony favorable to Pregent and therefore damaging to Van Arsdall. It seemed from the testimony that by the time Epps was killed Van Arsdall and Pregent were the only two people in the apartment with her. Van Arsdall's attorney sought to cross-examine Fleetwood about his possible bias as a result of the state's dismissal of a criminal public-drunkenness charge. Out of the presence of the jury, Fleetwood denied that his testimony had been affected by the state dropping the charge in exchange for his assistance in the murder investigation The court then ruled that defense counsel could not cross-examine Fleetwood about the matter.[15]

The Delaware Supreme Court reversed Van Arsdall's conviction, holding that the denial of the opportunity for such bias cross-examination violated the Sixth Amendment's Confrontation Clause. The state appealed, continuing its argument that Fleetwood's testimony was merely cumulative and "unimportant."

The U.S. Supreme Court granted certiorari, and, per Justice Rehnquist writing for a majority of the court, held that Delaware's "per se error" holding was too broad, and that proper invocation of the Sixth Amendment requires an analysis of whether the error was harmless given the relative importance of the witness the defense was prevented from impeaching. (The court took pains, however, to note that this does not amount to an "outcome determinative" analysis: "The focus of the prejudice inquiry in determining whether the confrontation right has been violated must be on a particular witness, not on the outcome of the entire trial.") The case was remanded to the Delaware Supreme Court for the "harmless error" analysis called for. Justice Stevens dissented because he thought the Delaware ruling rested on adequate independent state grounds.

---

[15] The trial court's ruling was based on Delaware's equivalent of Rule 403, presumably in the belief that this line of questioning in light of Fleetwood's denial would be needlessly misleading.

FRE 607, 608(b) – Impeachment: Cross-Examination Concerning Past Alcohol Use Is Limited to Situations Where Alcohol Use May Have Affected Perception or Testimony; Extrinsic Evidence Is Impermissible to Impeach Witness

> **Rule 607. Who May Impeach**
> The credibility of a witness may be attacked by any party, including the party calling the witness.
>
> **Rule 608. Evidence of Character and Conduct of Witness**
> *(b) Specific Instances of Conduct.* Specific instances of the conduct of a witness, for the purpose of attacking or supporting the witness's credibility, other than conviction of a crime as provided in rule 609, may not be proved by extrinsic evidence. They may, however, in the discretion of the court, if probative of truthfulness or untruthfulness, be inquired into on cross-examination of the witness (1) concerning the witness's character for truthfulness or untruthfulness, or (2) concerning the character for truthfulness or untruthfulness of another witness as to which character the witness being cross-examined has testified.

UNITED STATES v. DiPAOLO
804 F.2d 225 (2d Cir. 1986)

Following an April 1984 Postal Service robbery that netted hijackers $221,000 in blank travelers' checks, Lucille Barone, a waitress who had became friendly with two Rochester, N.Y. police officers, told them she had information concerning the hijacking that involved her boyfriend, Nick DiPaolo, and his Hell's Angels friend, Edward Weather. When DiPaolo, Weather, and Paul "Dusty" Snyder got wind of Barone's discussions with police, they began threatening her and her family. Snyder allegedly raped Barone, and after she and her children were placed in protective custody, DiPaolo beat Lucille's sister-in-law, Joanne Barone, with a screwdriver.

A jury convicted DiPaolo, Weather and Snyder of conspiracy to intimidate witnesses and to prevent communication to law enforcement officers relating to the Postal Service robbery, and of using intimidation and physical force against Lucille and Joanne Barone. The heart of their appeal to the Second Circuit Court of Appeals lies in their attempts to impeach Joanne Barone using extrinsic evidence of her use of alcohol and of two prior instances of her conduct.

The district judge heard *in camera* testimony from Joanne Barone that she had had a drinking problem for two years, but that she had not been drinking on the day DiPaolo assaulted her, nor for the five months leading up to her testimony in court, although she had a "relapse" following the beating, for which she sought professional help two months later. The trial judge refused defense counsel's request to be permitted to cross-examine Joanne Barone regarding her use of alcohol, as they could produce no evidence to refute her contention that alcohol consumption had not affected her perception or testimony about the events in question. The Second Circuit affirmed this ruling, citing Wigmore, saying that because intemperance itself "does not involve the veracity trait" of moral character, alcohol use should not be admissible unless there was evidence to suggest "the witness was under the influence... either at the times she observed the events in dispute or at the time she was testifying."[16]

Defense counsel also sought to produce extrinsic evidence[17] to impeach Joanne Barone's credibility that she had once made an anonymous phone call to a brother-in-law saying some people were "in trouble" because she hadn't been invited to a family Christmas party, and that she had harassed two people unrelated to the case some months before her trial testimony. The trial judge permitted counsel to cross-examine Barone about the incidents, but not to produce extrinsic proof to rebut whatever she said. The Second Circuit affirmed this ruling as well, citing Rule 608(b). Counsel argued that the testimony was not covered by Rule 608(b) because it did not involve mere contradiction or reflection on credibility, but rather "would prove that her ability to perceive, record and recall... was impaired." The Second Circuit rejected that contention, saying "the incidents were unrelated in time and substance to the charges..." and had no probative value except to truthfulness.

FRE 608, 403 – Impeachment: Polygraph Results Are Inadmissible to Bolster Credibility

Rule 608. Evidence of Character and Conduct of Witness

(a) Opinion and Reputation Evidence of Character. The credibility of a witness may be attacked or supported by evidence in the form of opinion or reputation, but subject to these limitations: (1) the evidence may refer only to character for truthfulness or untruthfulness, and (2) evidence of truthful character is admissible only after the character of the witness for truthfulness has been attacked by opinion or reputation evidence or otherwise.

(b) Specific Instances of Conduct. Specific instances of the conduct of a witness, for the purpose of attacking or supporting the witness's credibility, other than conviction of crime as provided in Rule 609, may not be proved by extrinsic evidence. They may, however, in the discretion of the court, if probative of truthfulness or untruthfulness, be inquired into on cross-examination of the witness (1) concerning the witness's character for truthfulness or untruthfulness, or (2) concerning the character for truthfulness or untruthfulness of another witness as to which character the witness being cross-examined has testified.

Rule 403. Exclusion of Relevant Evidence on Grounds of Prejudice, Confusion, or Waste of Time

Although relevant, evidence may be excluded if its probative value is substantially outweighed by the danger of unfair prejudice, confusion of the issues, or misleading the jury, or by considerations of undue delay, waste of time, or needless presentation of cumulative evidence.

---

[16] See *Henderson v. DeTella*, supra p. 129.
[17] That is, evidence by means other than cross-examination of the witness herself, i.e., documents, other witnesses, etc.

BARNIER v. SZENTMIKLOSI
810 F.2d 594 (6th Cir. 1987)

Daniel and Marie Barnier, the parents of Timothy Barnier, got in the middle of things when Timothy was being arrested for driving under the influence in front of the Barnier residence in Milan, Michigan in the early morning of May 30, 1981. The elder Barniers were charged with criminal assault and battery; after several state court hearings the prosecution moved to dismiss the charges. The Barniers then filed a federal §1983 suit against police officers William Szentmiklosi and Peter Campbell, the City of Milan and the Milan Police Department, alleging deprivations of civil rights, due process and equal protection rights, and several state law claims for false arrest, malicious prosecution, assault and battery, malicious destruction of private property, and intentional infliction of emotional distress.

The trial court directed a verdict in favor of defendants on the §1983 claims, and the jury rendered a verdict in defendants' favor on all other counts except for a $5,500 verdict for Mrs. Barnier on the malicious prosecution claim. Both sides appealed on a variety of grounds. One seems well-suited to illustrate some polygraph issues.

At trial the Barniers' attorney had taken advantage of the trial court's allowance of references to the fact that both had taken lie detector tests, ostensibly on the issue of damages. After mentioning the polygraph test, both Barniers and the county prosecutor were asked pointed questions regarding the dismissal of the criminal charges against them after the tests were taken.

The Sixth Circuit Court of Appeals reversed the verdict in favor of Mrs. Barnier, holding these references to the polygraph more prejudicial than probative: They "clearly gave rise to the inference that the prosecutor dropped the charges because of the results of the lie detector test. More importantly, this testimony implied that the test demonstrated that the Barniers' story was true. Using evidence of a lie detector test in this manner with the effect of bolstering the Barniers' credibility was highly prejudicial, particularly since the entire case hinged on whether the jury believed the Barniers' version of the facts, and the burden cast was on plaintiff. The verdicts rendered for defendants on other claims of misconduct and wrongful activity arising out of the confrontation in controversy indicate that the version of events claimed by plaintiff and her family were not otherwise accepted by the jury."

Barniers' counsel had represented that he was offering this evidence on the issue of damages – presumably, how emotionally stressful the tests were to them. The Sixth Circuit panel rejected this claim out of hand: the Barniers had voluntarily submitted to the test at the suggestion of their own lawyers; defendants and their attorneys didn't even know the tests were being taken – indeed, the court said if the results had been unfavorable, "presumably [they] would not have been revealed." Given the general unreliability of polygraph results and their tendency to "over-impress" a jury, the Sixth Circuit held that polygraph references were inadmissible "for any purpose."

FRE 607, 608(b)- Impeachment: Psychiatric History of Delusions Is Admissible to Impeach Credibility of Witness; Failure to File Income Tax Returns Is Probative of Untruthfulness

> **Rule 607. Who May Impeach**
>
> The credibility of a witness may be attacked by any party, including the party calling the witness.
>
> **Rule 608. Evidence of Character and Conduct of Witness**
>
> *(b) Specific Instances of Conduct.* Specific instances of the conduct of a witness, for the purpose of attacking or supporting the witness's credibility, other than conviction of crime as provided in rule 609, may not be proved by extrinsic evidence. They may, however, in the discretion of the court, if probative of truthfulness or untruthfulness, be inquired into on cross-examination of the witness (1) concerning the witness's character for truthfulness or untruthfulness, or (2) concerning the character for truthfulness or untruthfulness of another witness as to which character the witness being cross-examined has testified.

CHNAPKOVA v. KOH
985 F.2d 79 (2d Cir. 1993)

Almost three years after having a facelift, Zdenka Chnapkova, a young model and aspiring actress, sued her plastic surgeon, Dr. Kong S. Koh for malpractice. She claimed several square-shaped scars on the side of her cheeks, in front of her ears, and across her forehead were the result of Koh's procedure. Dr. Koh claimed the temporal rhytidectomy he performed involved only a two-inch incision near the temple. The defense theory was that Chnapkova must have gone to another doctor after Koh's facelift for further surgery. She admitted to four previous plastic surgery procedures in Bratislava, London and New York (eyelids and nose).

Chnapkova filed a motion *in limine* to exclude psychiatric records from Roosevelt Hospital, New York, of her subsequent diagnosis of paranoid schizophrenia (delusional paranoia), and any testimony about her failure to file income tax returns for any of the eight years she had been in the United States after immigrating from Czechoslovakia. The district court agreed that both matters were irrelevant and too prejudicial, and ordered them excluded.

A jury returned a verdict in the amount of $150,000 in favor of Chnapkova, and Dr. Koh appealed.

The Second Circuit Court of Appeals reversed and remanded, ruling both evidentiary decisions of the district court were erroneous.

The court held first that there were two distinct grounds for viewing the psychiatric records as sufficiently relevant for admission. For impeachment purposes, the records were relevant because they would have provided "significant help to the jury in its efforts to evaluate the witness's ability to perceive or recall events or to testify accurately," and also because the records would have disclosed that Chnapokva did not mention any scarring nor, apparently, exhibit any significance scarring (except for a nose injury sustained, she told doctors, in a suicide

140 Evidence Illustrated

attempt) when she was seen at the hospital some 16 months after the Koh facelift.

And Chnapkova's failure to file tax returns for eight years, the court held, was no less "admissible on the issue of her truthfulness" under Rule 608(b) than a witness's false statement on a tax return, which is everywhere held to be "obviously" admissible on the question of credibility.

This case was especially dependent on the credibility of the plaintiff, the court held, and the trial court's exclusion of evidence going to questions of that credibility was an abuse of its discretion.

FRE 608(a) – Impeachment: Veracity Witness May Comment Only Generally on Witness's Truthfulness; May Not State He Doesn't Believe Witness's Testimony

> **Rule 608. Evidence of Character and Conduct of Witness**
> *(a) Opinion and Reputation Evidence of Character.* The credibility of a witness may be attacked or supported by evidence in the form of opinion or reputation, but subject to these limitations: (1) the evidence may refer only to character for truthfulness or untruthfulness, and (2) evidence of truthful character is admissible only after the character of the witness for truthfulness has been attacked by opinion or reputation evidence or otherwise.

UNITED STATES v. MALADY
960 F.2d 57 (8th Cir. 1992)

James Counts, a tavern owner in Piedmont, Missouri, ended up in possession of three stolen guns. Counts testified at the trial of Bobby Lee Malady on charges of being a felon in possession of a firearm that he bought the guns from Malady not knowing they were stolen.

Malady's counsel, trying to establish that Counts had a motive to fabricate his testimony against Malady, got the Piedmont sheriff to testify on cross-examination that Counts had a reputation in the community as a fence.[18] He also asked him if he believed Counts's statement that he did not know the guns were stolen. The district judge sustained the government's objection and barred the question. Malady was convicted and appealed.

The Eighth Circuit Court of Appeals affirmed the conviction, upholding the trial court's Rule 608(a) decision on the attempted impeachment. "Malady could have asked the sheriff for his general opinion of Counts's truthfulness," the court held, but asking a witness to state specifically that he does not believe another witness's testimony is improper.

---

[18] Not, strictly speaking, proper FRE 608(a) impeachment either, but allowed by the trial judge apparently under the ubiquitous, uncodified "no harm, no foul" theory.

FRE 608(b), 405(a) – Impeachment: Good Faith Basis in Fact Must Be Established Before Witness May Be Impeached with Questions About Accused's Misconduct

> **Rule 608. Evidence of Character and Conduct of Witness**
> *(b) Specific Instances of Conduct.* Specific instances of the conduct of a witness, for the purpose of attacking or supporting the witness's credibility, other than conviction of crime as provided in rule 609, may not be proved by extrinsic evidence. They may, however, in the discretion of the court, if probative of truthfulness or untruthfulness, be inquired into on cross-examination of the witness (1) concerning the witness's character for truthfulness or untruthfulness, or (2) concerning the character for truthfulness or untruthfulness of another witness as to which character the witness being cross-examined has testified.
>
> **Rule 405. Methods of Proving Character**
> *(a) Reputation or Opinion.* In all cases in which evidence of character or a trait of character of a person is admissible, proof may be made by testimony as to reputation or by testimony in the form of an opinion. On cross-examination, inquiry is allowable into relevant specific instances of conduct.

UNITED STATES v. DAVENPORT
753 F.2d 1460 (9th Cir. 1985)

Luwanda Sharif, an employee of Wells Fargo Bank, testified as an alibi witness on behalf of John Leonard Davenport that the day in August 1982 when San Francisco's Olympic Savings and Loan Bank was robbed, she was with Davenport at his apartment. On cross-examination over defense objection, Ms. Sharif was asked by the prosecuting attorney if she had told Mary Mabes, another Wells Fargo employee, that Davenport was thinking about robbing the Wells Fargo Bank and using her as a "passkey" to help him rob it. Sharif answered, "No." The district court denied Davenport's request for a mistrial, and a jury convicted him of the Olympic robbery. He appealed.

The Ninth Circuit Court of Appeals reversed the conviction because of the impropriety of the cross-examination. Its decision is curiously limited to the failure of the government to supply the court with a factual basis for the question: "The government... must have a good faith belief in the misconduct of the defendant which was the subject of the question. If mistrial is to be avoided, this good faith must be established to the satisfaction of the court, outside the presence of the jury, before the question is asked." The court regarded the question of Sharif as "arguably... probative of the witness's possible bias and self-interest, and her credibility was therefore an issue. *See* Fed. R. Evid. 608(b). If the witness denied the question, the jury could believe or disbelieve her answer."

What makes the court's limitation curious, however, is the failure of the court to address[19] the propriety, or potential for prejudice, of a question concerning the defendant's conduct, under Rules 404(a) or (b), despite conceding that a question of the accused's character may be indirectly involved: "Her denial would, however, leave uncontroverted the

---
[19] It may be a tad too convenient to blame this choice of issues on the alertness or competence of defense counsel's brief.

insinuation that the defendant had planned to engage in additional bank robberies. The prejudice to the defendant was, thus, created by the question itself rather than by the testimony given in response.... The danger in such a situation is that the prosecution will use the question to waft an unwarranted innuendo into the jury box, knowing that the witness's denial will only serve to defend her credibility, while leaving uncontradicted the reference to the defendant's prior bad conduct. *This danger of prosecutorial misconduct is especially acute where, as here, the insinuation is inadmissible propensity evidence...* (emphasis added)"[20] Despite quoting Wigmore on the underhandedness of "injuring by indirection a character which they are forbidden directly to attack in that way," the court disappoints by pretending this case turns on the mere absence of a factual basis for the questions.

FRE 609(a), 403 – Impeachment: Prior Conviction of Civil Non-Party Witness for Felony Drug Offense Can Be Sufficiently Probative of Untruthfulness

> **Rule 609. Impeachment by Evidence of Conviction of Crime**
> *(a) General Rule.* For the purpose of attacking the credibility of a witness,
> (1) evidence that a witness other than an accused has been convicted of a crime shall be admitted, subject to Rule 403, if the crime was punishable by death or imprisonment in excess of one year under the law under which the witness was convicted, and evidence that an accused has been convicted of such a crime shall be admitted if the court determines that the probative value of admitting this evidence outweighs its prejudicial effect to the accused; and
> (2) evidence that any witness has been convicted of a crime shall be admitted if it involved dishonesty or false statement, regardless of the punishment.
>
> **Rule 403. Exclusion of Relevant Evidence on Grounds of Prejudice, Confusion, or Waste of Time**
> Although relevant, evidence may be excluded if its probative value is substantially outweighed by the danger of unfair prejudice, confusion of the issues, or misleading the jury, or by considerations of undue delay, waste of time, or needless presentation of cumulative evidence.

RADTKE v. CESSNA AIRCRAFT CO.
707 F.2d 999 (8th Cir. 1983)

After a plane crash, several survivors sued Cessna Aircraft Co. in a products liability action. They claimed the pilot's seat had suddenly come unlatched during takeoff, causing the pilot to lose control of the plane. Cessna defended on the basis of pilot error. The only direct evidence that the pilot seat came unlatched and caused loss of control came from the pilot, Thomas Leonzi, through his videotaped deposition. Cessna was permitted over the objection of plaintiffs to introduce evidence of Leonzi's conviction within the past six years of a multi-count felony drug charge. The jury returned a verdict in favor of Cessna.

---

[20] After all, Sharif was an alibi witness – a fact witness – not a character witness.

On appeal to the Eighth Circuit Court of Appeals, Radtkes cited the failure of the trial court to make an explicit finding in the record that Leonzi's conviction was not substantially more prejudicial than probative of untruthfulness under Rule 403.[21] The appellate court noted the trial judge had considered the Rule 403 factors, and had excluded other criminal convictions the witness had sustained. "It is clear from the record that the court's ruling on admissibility... implied a balancing under Rule 403," the court said in affirming the verdict.

FRE 609(a)(1) – Impeachment: Cross-Examination of Accused Regarding Prior for Same Conduct as Current Charge Is Too Prejudicial

> **Rule 609. Impeachment by Evidence of Conviction of Crime**
> *(a) General Rule.* For the purposes of attacking the credibility of a witness,
> (1) evidence that a witness other than an accused has been convicted of a crime shall be admitted, subject to Rule 403, if the crime was punishable by death or imprisonment in excess of one year under the law under which the witness was convicted, and evidence that an accused has been convicted of such a crime shall be admitted if the court determines that the probative value of admitting this evidence outweighs its prejudicial effect to the accused; and
> (2) evidence that any witness has been convicted of a crime shall be admitted if it involved dishonesty or false statement, regardless of the punishment.

UNITED STATES v. SANDERS
964 F.2d 295 (4th Cir. 1992)

Carlos Sanders and Ricky Alston were indicted for assaulting Bobby Jenkins with intent to commit murder and for possession of a shank while all three were inmates at Lorton Reformatory in Virginia in 1989. Sanders testified that he acted in self-defense, and on cross-examination the government was permitted to bring up Sanders' 1988 convictions for the same offenses while imprisoned at the same federal facility (The trial judge ruled *in limine* that the government could not use a prior stabbing of which Sanders had been acquitted and an armed robbery for which his conviction had been reversed.) Sanders was convicted of both charges, and appealed.

The Fourth Circuit Court of Appeals reversed the assault conviction, observing, "Although evidence of the prior convictions may be thought somehow generally probative of Sanders' lack of credibility, they were [sic] extremely prejudicial since they involved the exact type of conduct for which Sanders was on trial." The jury is permitted under the rule to make the inference that guilt on prior charges somehow renders one less likely to tell the truth under oath – perhaps because one has thereby demonstrated a willingness to violate society's rules in a serious way. The jury is not permitted to conclude that guilt as to prior misconduct increases the

---

[21] The invocation of Rule 403 for the impeachment of non-accused witnesses was not express in Rule 609 at the time of this decision. The court, nonetheless, decided the case exactly as it would be decided and analyzed under the current version of Rule 609(a).

probability of guilt *per se* on the current charge, because that would involve the intermediate inference of criminal propensity, or bad character. "The jury," the court said, quoting another case, "can hardly avoid drawing the inference that the past conviction suggests probability that defendant committed the similar offense for which he is currently charged." (The Fourth Circuit held the erroneous use of the 1988 priors was harmless as to the weapon charge inasmuch as Sanders had admitted on the stand that he possessed the shank and used it to stab Jenkins in self-defense.)

(In the fashion typical of some intellectually lazy trial courts, the trial judge in the Eastern District of Virginia admitted the prior convictions on cross on both "intent and impeachment," implying a Rule 404(b) theory as well as a Rule 609 basis. The Fourth Circuit said what the prior conviction showed here was "only criminal disposition," i.e., bad character, not whether he acted with criminal intent on this occasion.)

FRE 609(a)(1) – Impeachment: Details Surrounding Prior Conviction Are Inadmissible for Impeachment of Witness

Rule 609. Impeachment by Evidence of Conviction of Crime
(a) General Rule. For the purpose of attacking the credibility of a witness,
(1) evidence that a witness other than an accused has been convicted of a crime shall be admitted, subject to Rule 403, if the crime was punishable by death or imprisonment in excess of one year under the law under which the witness was convicted, and evidence that an accused has been convicted of such a crime shall be admitted if the court determines that the probative value of admitting this evidence outweighs its prejudicial effect to the accused; and
(2) evidence that any witness has been convicted of a crime shall be admitted if it involved dishonesty or false statement, regardless of the punishment.

WILSON v. CITY OF CHICAGO
6 F.3d 1233 (7th Cir. 1993)

Andrew Wilson filed a civil rights lawsuit against five Chicago police officers and the city for torturing him to get him to confess to the murders of two other officers. He had been convicted of first degree murder in their deaths and sentenced to death, but the conviction was thrown out when the Illinois Supreme Court ruled his confession had been coerced. "Extensive contemporaneous medical and photographic evidence" corroborated Wilson's claim of having been "punched, kicked, smothered with a plastic bag, electrically shocked, and forced against a hot radiator throughout the day" of his arrest. Wilson was retried and again convicted, this time receiving a life sentence without possibility of parole, while his federal civil suit was pending.

When Wilson testified at the second trial of his lawsuit against the city and the officers (the first ended in a hung jury), the defense was permitted to cross-examine him not only regarding the fact of the murder conviction,[22] but also about the "sordid details" of the crimes themselves, including stealing a gun in a home invasion, helping a man who had been charged with murdering another Chicago policeman escape from jail, shooting one of the officers at close range at the base of his skull with the officer's own service revolver, and laughing about the killings. Photographs of the murder scene were also admitted into evidence. The defense claimed these details were necessary to support its theory that Wilson received his injuries during a scuffle with the slain officers.

The jury exonerated the officers and the city. Wilson appealed on a number of fascinating evidentiary grounds, including the Rule 609 impeachment.

Judge Richard Posner, writing for the Seventh Circuit Court of Appeals, reversed the verdict as to the police officer defendants, holding that it was improper to allow the jury to be "immersed" in the details of Wilson's crimes. The defense had turned the case into a trial of the plaintiff; "Of course, when the plaintiff in a case happens to be a murderer this turning of the tables has undoubted forensic appeal. But even a murderer has a right to be free from torture and the correlative right to present his claim of torture to a jury that has not been whipped into a frenzy of hatred." As to the defense's argument that Wilson might have been injured during the altercation that resulted in the shooting of the police officers – or that he might have faked his injuries to get his conviction vacated – the court said, "Neither ground was remotely plausible." (The scuffle in which the officers died was "decidedly one-sided," the court noted.) None of the details the government offered were relevant to the only fact of significance that a Rule 609 prior-convictions impeachment invokes: the likelihood that the witness will lie under oath in court.

---

[22]Perfectly ordinary under FRE 609(a)(1), if somewhat redundant, inasmuch as Wilson's theory of recovery was that they "tortured him *because* he was a cop killer."

FRE 609(a)(1) – Impeachment: Specific Details of Witness's Prior Conviction Are Admissible on Cross-Examination Only if Witness First Volunteers Details to Explain Away or Minimize His Guilt

> **Rule 609. Impeachment by Evidence of Conviction of Crime**
>
> *(a) General Rule.* For the purposes of attacking the credibility of a witness,
>
> (1) evidence that a witness other than an accused has been convicted of a crime shall be admitted, subject to Rule 403, if the crime was punishable by death or imprisonment in excess of one year under the law under which the witness was convicted, and evidence that an accused has been convicted of such a crime shall be admitted if the court determines that the probative value of admitting this evidence outweighs its prejudicial effect to the accused; and
>
> (2) evidence that any witness has been convicted of a crime shall be admitted if it involved dishonesty or false statement, regardless of the punishment.

UNITED STATES v. SWANSON
9 F.3d 1354 (8th Cir. 1993)

Wade Robert Swanson testified at his 1991 trial on charges of conspiracy to manufacture and distribute marijuana and of money laundering that Robert Miller and Brad Johnson coerced his participation in what the court called "one of the largest and most sophisticated indoor marijuana grow operations ever uncovered by enforcement officials in Minnesota." The jury convicted him and he appealed, contending that it was improper for the prosecution to have been allowed to ask questions on cross-examination about numerous specific details surrounding his 1987 conviction for a "felony menacing incident."[23]

The Eighth Circuit Court of Appeals acknowledged that generally such detailed questions are improper but said here Swanson had opened the door. He had not only testified in detail on direct examination about the circumstances surrounding the 1987 incident, he had also "conducted an in-court demonstration" of part of the incident, all aimed at "minimizing the impact of the evidence." The prosecution cross-examined him with details contained in police reports that directly contradicted his account.

---

[23] It is generally held proper to elicit from the witness being impeached only the name of the crime (e.g., "felonious assault"), the date, the location, and perhaps the sentence, although the four corners of Rule 609 contain no such restrictions.

FRE 609, 410 – Impeachment: Pleas of Nolo Contendere Are Not Inadmissible for Impeachment by Conviction

> **Rule 609. Impeachment by Evidence of Conviction of Crime**
> *(a) General Rule.* For the purpose of attacking the credibility of a witness, (1) evidence that a witness other than an accused has been convicted of a crime shall be admitted, subject to Rule 403, if the crime was punishable by death or imprisonment in excess of one year under the law under which the witness was convicted, and evidence that an accused has been convicted of such a crime shall be admitted if the court determines that the probative value of admitting this evidence outweighs its prejudicial effect to the accused.
>
> **Rule 410. Inadmissibility of Pleas, Plea Discussions, and Related Statements**
> Except as otherwise provided in this rule, evidence of the following is not, in any civil or criminal proceeding, admissible against the defendant who made the plea or was a participant in the plea discussions:
> (2) a plea of nolo contendere;...

UNITED STATES v. SONNY MITCHELL CENTER
934 F.2d 77 (5th Cir. 1991)

The government filed an *in rem* action to forfeit a San Antonio strip mall that undercover city police said was a haven for drug-trade activity in plain view day and night. Gaylon "Sonny" Mitchell and Pattie Mitchell filed claims of ownership. A jury rejected the Mitchells' claim that they were "innocent owners," and they appealed to the Fifth Circuit Court of Appeals.

The appeals court in a *per curiam* opinion affirmed the judgment of forfeiture. Much of the case turned on whether the jury believed Sonny Mitchell's testimony that he and Pattie Mitchell not only did not consent to the drug trafficking but also attempted to stop it. The government was allowed by the trial judge to impeach Sonny Mitchell with four prior felony drug convictions. Mitchell had pled nolo contendere in each of those cases and, on appeal, argued that no contest pleas were inadmissible. The Fifth Circuit rejected that argument, and noted that at one time the drafters of the Federal Rules of Evidence considered an exception to Rule 609 that would have excluded convictions based on pleas of nolo contendere, but deleted any such exception from the final draft. Based on this legislative history, the court held that the lack of any provision in Rule 609 having to do with no contest pleas meant they were as admissible as convictions by verdict or by guilty plea.

No consideration was given in this opinion to the danger of unfair prejudice because of the substantive similarity[24] of the past convictions to the issues in the forfeiture case itself, possibly because the matter was not raised at trial or on appeal.[25]

---

[24] See *United States v. Sanders, supra* p. 144.
[25] See FRE 103(a) and *People v. Dunham, supra* p. 4.

148 Evidence Illustrated

FRE 609(a)(2) – Impeachment: Prior Conviction for Crime of Dishonesty Is Admissible to Impeach Witness Without Regard to Conviction's Prejudicial Effect

> **Rule 609. Impeachment by Evidence of Conviction of Crime**
>
> *(a) General Rule.* For the purpose of attacking the credibility of a witness,
>
> (1) evidence that a witness other than an accused has been convicted of a crime shall be admitted, subject to Rule 403, if the crime was punishable by death or imprisonment in excess of one year under the law under which the witness was convicted, and evidence that an accused has been convicted of such a crime shall be admitted if the court determines that the probative value of admitting this evidence outweighs its prejudicial effect to the accused; and
>
> (2) evidence that any witness has been convicted of a crime shall be admitted if it involved dishonesty or false statement, regardless of the punishment.

UNITED STATES v. TONEY
615 F.2d 277 (5th Cir. 1980),

In his trial for mail fraud, James Finis Toney, Jr., elected not to testify in his own defense when the trial court decided under Rule 609(a)(2) that if he testified Toney could be impeached by reference to his 1977 mail fraud conviction. The jury convicted Toney and he appealed, claiming that the trial judge had read Rule 609(a)(2) too narrowly, and should have concluded the prior conviction was too prejudicial to be inquired into.

The Fifth Circuit Court of Appeals affirmed the conviction. The court said it was "established" that mail fraud is a crime involving dishonesty or false statement, and thus the crime falls within section (a)(2) of the Rule, not (a)(1) involving non-dishonesty felonies. The court held that section (a)(2) "contains no provision for excluding evidence of a crimen falsi on the ground of undue prejudice," and held Rule 403's "prejudice versus probative value weighing provision" inapplicable because of Rule 609 (a)(2)'s use of the phrase "shall be admitted." Citing the House Conference Committee Report regarding this Rule, the Fifth Circuit concluded that Congress had intended the courts to have no discretion at all in considering the admission of crimes of dishonesty to impeach a witness.

When prejudice is an issue – as in non-dishonesty felonies under Rule 609(a)(1) – one of the surest ways of having too much of it is when the accused's prior conviction is for the same crime as the one charged.[26] But under section (a)(2) the similarity of the accused's prior mail fraud conviction to the current mail fraud charge is irrelevant to the issue of its admissibility. A Rule 105(a) limiting instruction would be in order, instructing the jury to confine its consideration of the prior conviction to issues of credibility as a witness, not criminal propensity; whether such an instruction would be desirable is a matter of defense strategy.

---

[26] See, e.g., *United States v. Sanders, supra* p. 144.

FRE 609(a)(2) – Impeachment: Theft Misdemeanor Does Not Ordinarily Involve Dishonesty or False Statement

> **Rule 607. Who May Impeach**
> The credibility of a witness may be attacked by any party, including the party calling the witness.
> **Rule 609. Impeachment by Evidence of Conviction of Crime**
> *(a) General Rule.* For the purpose of attacking the credibility of a witness,
> (2) evidence that any witness has been convicted of a crime shall be admitted if it involved dishonesty or false statement, regardless of the punishment.

STATE v. ELLIS
303 N.W.2d 741, 208 Neb. 379 (1981)

John R. Ellis was charged with manslaughter in the death of Deborah Forycki, a college senior whose skeletal remains were found almost four years later inside an antique water wagon undergoing restoration in Elmwood, Nebraska.

At trial one of the state's many witnesses was a cellmate of Ellis after Ellis's arrest two years earlier for assaulting a young woman. The cellmate, Burns, testified that Ellis had told him he had taken people to a secluded place near Elmwood on a couple of occasions and that people there were stupid, "if you ever killed somebody and wanted to hide the body, that would be a really good place to do it, the police would never find it." Ellis was barred from attempting to impeach Burns with questions about Burns' prior conviction for petit larceny under Nebraska's statutory counterpart of Federal Rule 609. The jury convicted Ellis of manslaughter.

He appealed, citing a baker's dozen issues including the Rule 609 matter. The Nebraska Supreme Court affirmed and undertook a rather thoughtful response to the stereotypical notion that "to steal is to be dishonest; therefore larceny is a crime involving dishonesty." Citing Congressional Conference Committee Notes to Federal Rule 609, as well as a pair of 1976 cases from the Third and D.C. Circuits, the Nebraska court focused on the notion of "some element of deceitfulness, untruthfulness or falsification bearing on the [witness's] propensity to testify truthfully," which it concluded the ordinary, garden variety petit larceny does not possess.

While it was "conceivable" that a particular petit larceny might have been committed by means of deceit or false pretenses, the court noted the defense had made no showing that Burns' prior petit larceny was anything "other than ordinary stealing."

FRE 609(b) – Impeachment: To Determine if Witness's Conviction Is Too Old, Probationary Period Is Not "Confinement"

> **Rule 609. Impeachment by Evidence of Conviction of Crime**
>
> *(b) Time Limit.* Evidence of a conviction under this rule is not admissible if a period of more than ten years has elapsed since the date of the conviction or of the release of the witness from the confinement imposed for that conviction, whichever is the later date, unless the court determines, in the interests of justice, that the probative value of the conviction supported by specific facts and circumstances substantially outweighs its prejudicial effect. However, evidence of a conviction more than 10 years old as calculated therein, is not admissible unless the proponent gives to the adverse party sufficient advance written notice of intent to use such evidence to provide the adverse party with a fair opportunity to contest the use of such evidence.

UNITED STATES v. DANIEL
957 F.2d 162 (5th Cir. 1992)

Brothers Charles Daniel and Patrick Daniel, proprietors of a wholesale carpet business in Amarillo, Texas, bought a truckload of carpet for $17,000 from truck driver William Kunkle, who sold it to them instead of delivering it from the mill in Georgia to a destination in California. The Daniels were charged with possession of stolen goods from interstate shipment. They both claimed they didn't know the carpet was stolen, and that when they asked Kunkle directly, he denied it was stolen.

Kunkle testified that he had asked the Daniels if they were police officers, and had shown them the carpet's bills of lading. They denied this. He also said he had given a few hundred dollars of the cash he received from the Daniels to Daniels' employees so they would act faster to remove the carpet from his truck. He testified Charles Daniel had removed the plastic wrap and price tags from the carpet and said he was going to burn them.

The Daniels attempted to impeach Kunkle's testimony by bringing up a 1980 felony conviction for conspiracy, theft, burglary, and receiving stolen property, for which he had been fined and placed on three years' probation. The trial court sustained the government's objection to use of this past conviction under Rule 609(b) because it was older than the ten-year period by four days. The Daniels argued the period ought to be computed from the termination of the probationary period.

Upon their conviction by a jury, the Daniels appealed. The Fifth Circuit Court of Appeals affirmed, and held that probation is not "confinement." An earlier version of the rule had the ten-year period beginning at the termination of parole or probation, but it was amended to its current language in 1972, "foreclosing" the Daniels' argument.

FRE 607, 609(d) – Impeachment: Juvenile Offenses Are Admissible for Impeachment When Mandated by Confrontation Clause

Rule 607. Who May Impeach

The credibility of a witness may be attacked by any party, including the party calling the witness.

Rule 609. Impeachment by Evidence of Conviction of Crime

(a) General Rule. For the purpose of attacking the credibility of a witness,

(1) Evidence that a witness other than an accused has been convicted of a crime shall be admitted...

(d) Juvenile Adjudications. Evidence of juvenile adjudications is generally not admissible under this rule. The court may, however, in a criminal case allow evidence of a juvenile adjudication of a witness other than the accused if conviction of the offense would be admissible to attack the credibility of an adult and the court is satisfied that admission in evidence is necessary for a fair determination of the issue of guilt or innocence.

DAVIS v. ALASKA
415 U.S. 308, 94 S. Ct. 1105, 39 L. Ed. 2d 347 (1974)

Joshaway Davis was identified by 16-year-old Richard Green as one of two men Green had seen by a car near where a safe, stolen during an after-hours break-in at an Anchorage bar, was found. In the trunk of that car were paint chips and insulation particles that might have matched the stolen safe. Green said Davis asked if Green lived nearby and if his father was home; later he said he saw Davis with something like a crowbar in his hands. The safe had been pried open and over a thousand dollars had been removed.

Before trial in Alaska state court the prosecuting attorney requested an order barring the defense from making any reference to Richard Green's juvenile probationary status for two burglaries of his own. Defense counsel said he wished to use this information not for general impeachment of Green's character as a truthful person,[27] but rather to argue that Green acted from a motive to co-operate with his own probation officers in order to curry their favor, and/or to shift suspicion away from himself as the one who stole the safe. The trial court granted the prosecutor's motion under an Alaska statute and rule that make juvenile matters inadmissible in subsequent proceedings.

Davis was convicted of burglary and grand larceny. He appealed, claiming his right to confront the witness had been wrongly restricted. The Alaska Supreme Court affirmed and held that Davis's lawyer had been able to fully cross-examine Green.

The United States Supreme Court reversed. Because Davis had been prevented from inquiring about an adverse witness's past conviction, Justice Burger wrote, he had been denied a means to "afford the jury a basis to infer that the witness's character is such that he would be less likely than the average trustworthy citizen to be truthful in his testimony." And here the specific biases or ulterior motives of Green had been ruled off-limits to Davis at trial. The court reiterated that "exposure of a witness's

---
[27] See FRE 609.

152 Evidence Illustrated

motivation in testifying" is a fundamental function of cross-examination. "While counsel was permitted to ask Green *whether* he was biased, counsel was unable to make a record from which to argue *why* Green might have been biased...."

The Sixth Amendment right of cross-examination was held to be "vital" enough to override Alaska's policy interest in protecting the confidentiality of a juvenile's criminal record. It is this pre-rules case that accounts for the "however" clause in Rule 609(d).

FRE 610 – Impeachment: Statements of Religious Belief in Connection with Difficulty Attending Church Because of Medical Condition Are Not Inadmissible Bolstering of Credibility

> **Rule 610. Religious Beliefs or Opinions**
> Evidence of the beliefs or opinions of a witness on matters of religion is not admissible for the purpose of showing that by reason of their nature the witness's credibility is impaired or enhanced.

MAULDIN v. UPJOHN COMPANY
697 F.2d 644 (5th. Cir. 1983)

After suffering a serious hand injury while working on a lake barge in 1974, O.L. Mauldin was prescribed two Upjohn antibiotics, Lincocin and Cleocin. He began to experience "a tenacious bout of diarrhea." Ultimately Mauldin was hospitalized for more than two months and underwent several operations to deal with the ulcerative colitis that soon developed. He sued Upjohn in Louisiana state court for failure adequately to warn about the side effects of these drugs. Upjohn removed the suit to the federal court for the Eastern District of Louisiana, and the first trial ended in a mistrial. A second jury returned a verdict in favor of Mauldin for $570,000.

Upjohn appealed to the Fifth Circuit Court of Appeals on several grounds, the most substantial of which dealt with causation and the duty to warn. For our purposes we will confine the discussion to the final issue the court disposed of on its way to affirming the verdict.

Mauldin testified over objection to the hardships his present condition imposed upon his efforts to attend church and how important his practice of attending church was to him in light of his strong belief in "Almighty God." Upjohn argued on appeal that this testimony violated Rule 610's ban on statements of religious belief used to bolster witness credibility and was prejudicial. Noting that this argument "requires little discussion," the court held that the testimony was offered on an aspect of damages, not to bolster the witness's credibility.[28] It was therefore fully admissible, unaffected by Rule 610.

---

[28] See Rule 105's allowance of evidence that could be taken as relevant to two issues, one admissible and one inadmissible.

FRE 610 – Impeachment: Religious Affiliation of Witness Is Admissible to Extent Relevant to Show Witness's Bias, But Not to Undermine Credibility by Depicting Religious Extremism

> **Rule 610. Religious Beliefs or Opinions**
> Evidence of the beliefs or opinions of a witness on matters of religion is not admissible for the purpose of showing that by reason of their nature the witness's credibility is impaired or enhanced.

FIREMEN'S FUND INSURANCE COMPANY v. THIEN
63 F.3d 754 (8th Cir. 1995)

Charles Benedict was a passenger aboard a small plane owned by Mid-Plains Corp., an air courier business, when it crashed near Bentonville, Arkansas in September 1989. Benedict was an occasional employee of Mid-Plains, running errands and doing odd jobs for the company.

Benedict's parents and son filed a wrongful death lawsuit in Missouri state court against Mid-Plains, its director of operations, Michael Thien, and Richard Lund, who was acting as defendant ad litem for the pilot. Firemen's Fund, Mid-Plains' liability insurer, denied coverage to Thien and Lund under a fellow-employee exclusionary clause, and filed its own action in federal court for declaratory judgment against Lund and Thien under the clause. Factual issues concerned Benedict's employment status on the date of the accident and whether he was on the Mid-Plains airplane for business or for personal reasons. The jury found Benedict was an employee acting within the scope of his employment, and that consequently Firemen's Fund was not bound to indemnify Lund or Thien for any liability because of the crash that caused Benedict's death.

Benedicts, who had intervened as defendants, appealed, raising several evidentiary issues including whether the trial court had acted properly in excluding evidence of the religious beliefs of Benedict's widow, Martina, and his other son, Chris. They belonged to a small group called "Zion's Endeavor," led by Thien, that believed "participation in civil litigation is in violation of biblical law." This evidence was offered by Benedicts to impeach Martina's and Chris's unfavorable testimony.

The Eighth Circuit Court of Appeals affirmed. The jury had heard evidence of Chris and Martina's affiliation with Thien's group for purposes of suggesting their bias. Anything beyond that would violate Rule 610: "The reasons why Martina and Chris did not join the wrongful death action, and why Chad was late in joining, do not add to a showing of bias, and appear to us to be an attempt to undermine Martina's and Chris's credibility, and to prejudice the jury against them, by painting them as religious extremists...." It was not probative of any bias Chris and Martina might have had in favor of Thien. "We fail to see the relevance of this issue to the instant case, and we fail to see how showing that Martina and Chris had religious reasons to decide not to join the wrongful death action shows that they were biased witnesses in the insurance action."

FRE 611(a) – Trial Court Has Discretion to Allow Defense and Rebuttal Witnesses to Be Called Out of Order So Long as No Actual Prejudice to Either Party Results

> **Rule 611. Mode and Order of Interrogation and Presentation**
> *(a) Control by Court.* The court shall exercise reasonable control over the mode and order of interrogating witnesses and presenting evidence so as to (1) make the interrogation and presentation effective for the ascertainment of the truth, (2) avoid needless consumption of time, and (3) protect witnesses from harassment or undue embarrassment.

BERROYER v. HERTZ
672 F.2d 334 (3d Cir. 1981)

During a consultation about an impacted wisdom tooth, Dr. Sidney Hertz advised Patricia Berroyer that the tooth should be removed to avoid a purported 9% risk of developing cancer of the jaw. She agreed to the dental surgery, and later developed an infection in the area of the extraction, necessitating six or seven return visits for treatment. After she consulted another dentist, she filed suit against Dr. Hertz for dental malpractice. She alleged negligence in allowing the infection to develop and sought punitive damages for what she characterized as his "outrageous" conduct in fraudulently overstating the risk of cancer so as to induce her to consent to the extraction.

At some point during the plaintiff's case, the defendant's attorney asked permission to call his expert witness out of turn to accommodate his travel schedule. Berroyer did not object, and Dr. Shira testified that Dr. Hertz's treatment and advice were reasonable and appropriate. Dr. Shira also testified that if Berroyer had only been prescribed Wygesic, a very mild pain medication, her infection could not have been as serious as she maintained.

Plaintiff then sought to call a rebuttal witness, her pharmacist, to testify that her prescription wasn't for Wygesic at all, but rather for a much stronger pain-killer, Percodan. The defense objected both because the pharmacist's name hadn't appeared on the pretrial order witness list (although during trial apparently some notice had been given that he would be called) and because they said it was improper to call a rebuttal witness before the close of defendant's case. The trial judge overruled Dr. Hertz's objection and allowed the rebuttal testimony. The jury awarded $15,000 in compensatory damages and $25,000 in punitive damages, plus costs, attorney's fees and interest.

The Third Circuit Court of Appeals overturned the punitive damage award but affirmed the compensatory damages portion of the verdict, and held that under Rule 611(a) the trial court has ample discretion to allow a rebuttal witness to testify out of order. "Absent a showing of specific prejudice, we do not believe that an expert witness testifying in rebuttal should be entitled to any less accommodation than one testifying in a party's case-in-chief where, as here, the specific defense testimony to be rebutted is already in evidence." And defense counsel could hardly have been surprised by the calling of the pharmacist as a witness, as Berroyer's attorney identified him by name and occupation the day before he was called, during the discussion about the defense presenting Dr. Shira out of order.

FRE 611(b) – Court Has Discretion to Limit Cross-Examination Regarding Collateral Matter Not Shown to Have Likelihood of Connection to Case

> **Rule 611. Mode and Order of Interrogation and Presentation**
> *(a) Control by Court.* The court shall exercise reasonable control over the mode and order of interrogating witnesses and presenting evidence so as to (1) make the interrogation and presentation effective for the ascertainment of the truth, (2) avoid needless consumption of time, and (3) protect witnesses from harassment or undue embarrassment.
> *(b) Scope of Cross-Examination.* Cross-examination should be limited to the subject matter of the direct examination and matters affecting the credibility of the witness. The court may, in the exercise of discretion, permit inquiry into additional matters as if on direct examination.

BISHOP v. STATE
581 P.2d 45 (Okl. Cr. App. 1978)

Stephen Cletis Bishop was charged in Oklahoma County District Court with "taking indecent liberties" with his half-sister's six-year-old daughter while the mother was out on a date. The mother returned to her apartment at 1:30 a.m. to find the babysitter dismissed, the stereo playing loudly, and her daughter running naked, screaming, away from the bed Bishop was lying in. The room was a shambles and her daughter was hysterical, screaming, "He hurt me, he hurt me!" Her chest, arms and shoulders were bruised. The mother testified, "The area of her vagina was bloody, bruised. Her rectum was red and irritated." The forensic chemist for the Oklahoma City Police Department found semen on a sheet and blood on the victim's underwear. Bishop testified and denied everything. The jury convicted him, and he was sentenced to 20 years in prison.

One of the issues Bishop raised in his appeal to the Oklahoma Court of Criminal Appeals concerned the trial judge's refusal to let his lawyer try to suggest to the jury that the victim's mother was mistaken about what she said she had seen. He had wanted to cross-examine her about a sexual attack she herself had allegedly suffered as a child. When the trial court had asked what the point of this line of questioning was, Bishop's lawyer said, "It shows that she had a preconceived idea what might be happening. It goes to show her irrational behavior, her jumping to this conclusion this is what happened because she had suffered a similar almost identical situation." With no particular reason articulated, the trial judge found that the evidence wasn't "competent... Right now I don't see its admissibility."

This pre-rules case was decided by the appellate court largely on the basis of the wide discretion the trial court possesses in limiting the scope of cross-examination on matters of marginal or dubious relevance: "Certainly whether or not the victim's mother had suffered a similar attack when she was young is a collateral matter. And, while the permissible scope of cross-examination is broad, it nonetheless has its limits. These limits are determined in the first instance by the trial court, and... unless the defendant can show that the trial court

156 Evidence Illustrated

abused its discretion by unduly restricting the extent of cross-examination, no claim of error will lie.

"The defendant urges that whether the victim's mother suffered a similar attack could have affected her perceptions of what occurred on the night in question, and this is probably true in some subtle way. However, absent something more concrete than psychological theorizing, we are unable to conclude that the trial court abused its discretion in denying the defendant an opportunity to cross-examine the witness with regard to this obviously collateral matter."

FRE 611(b) – Trial Court Has Broad Discretion in Determining if Questions on Redirect Examination Are Permissible Despite Falling Outside Scope of Direct or Cross-Examination

> **Rule 611. Mode and Order of Interrogation and Presentation**
> *(a) Control by Court.* The court shall exercise reasonable control over the mode and order of interrogation witnesses and presenting evidence so as to (1) make the interrogation and presentation effective for the ascertainment of the truth, (2) avoid needless consumption of time, and (3) protect witnesses from harassment or undue embarrassment.
> *(b) Scope of Cross-Examination.* Cross-examination should be limited to the subject matter of the direct examination and matters affecting the credibility of the witness. The court may, in the exercise of discretion, permit inquiry into additional matters as if on direct examination.

UNITED STATES v. TAYLOR
599 F.2d 832 (8th Cir. 1979)

James Lee Taylor was tried on 11 charges of unregistered or unlicensed firearms that involved possession, transfer, conspiracy to deal, and receiving while under indictment for burglary. Much of the trial consisted of ATF agents testifying to transactions with an alleged accomplice or partner of Taylor's, Clifford Worley, who was observed going toward and away from Taylor's residence and getting in Taylor's car, and of Worley's testimony about his transaction with Taylor that produced all the weapons the agents bought from him.

On cross examination of Worley, Taylor's counsel attempted to show that Worley could have received the weapons from another individual, a man named Doniphan, rather than Taylor. The government was then permitted over defense objection to elicit Worley's testimony concerning several threats Taylor made against Worley to dissuade him from testifying. A jury convicted Taylor and he was sentenced to several concurrent terms of six years' imprisonment followed by five years' probation.

Taylor appealed. The Eighth Circuit Court of Appeals reversed the conviction as to five counts based on a close analysis of the search warrant that supported the entry of Taylor's residence and the seizure of weapons found there. It affirmed his conviction under the remaining six counts on several grounds raised, including that related to the redirect examination of Worley. Taylor contended that the government's questions on redirect went beyond the scope of both cross and direct examination,[29] because the threatening statements "had not been aired on either direct or cross-examination." The appellate court declined to consider whether the threats could be considered as "relating to credibility," or, as the government argued, whether the questions about Taylor's threats against Worley were in some way a "response" to the cross-examination about Doniphan. Instead, it ruled simply that the trial judge had not abused his discretion in allowing the redirect.

FRE 612 – Memory of Witness May Be Refreshed with Inadmissible Writing

> **Rule 612. Writing Used to Refresh Memory**
>
> Except as otherwise provided in criminal proceedings by section 3500 of title 18, United States Code, if a witness uses a writing to refresh memory for the purpose of testifying, either
>
> (1) while testifying, or
>
> (2) before testifying, if the court in its discretion determines it is necessary in the interests of justice, an adverse party is entitled to have the writing produced at the hearing, to inspect it, to cross-examine the witness thereon, and to introduce in evidence those portions which relate to the testimony of the witness. If it is claimed that the writing contains matters not related to the subject matter of the testimony the court shall examine the writing in camera, excise any portions not so related, and order delivery of the remainder to the party entitled thereto. Any portion withheld over objections shall be preserved and made available to the appellate court in the event of an appeal. If a writing is not produced or delivered pursuant to order under this rule, the court shall make any order justice requires, except that in criminal cases when the prosecution elects not to comply, the order shall be one striking the testimony or, if the court in its discretion determines that the interests of justice so require, declaring a mistrial.

WILSON v. STATE
639 S.W.2d 45, 277 Ark. 43 (1982)

James Wilson sold sawmill owner Clifford Dockins timber he didn't own. When Dockins discovered the ruse be demanded his money back. Wilson gave him two worthless checks for $100 and $15,000. After his arrest, Wilson escaped from the Izard County Jail with someone's expensive portable radio. A jury convicted him of two counts of theft by deception, one count of theft of property, and escape in the second degree. He was sentenced to 35 years' imprisonment as a habitual offender with four or more prior felony convictions.

He appealed on a number of grounds that the Arkansas Supreme Court ultimately held were without merit. One of them helps to illustrate the outer contours of Rule 612.

The trial court had permitted the sheriff to use a written version of an oral statement Wilson

---

[29] Note that Rule 611(b) purports to restrict the scope of cross examination but that no rule deals with the permissible scope of redirect examination. As with many matters of trial protocol, a long tradition and custom control the question, and here the tradition dictates that generally redirect is confined to the scope of cross examination – just as the scope of rebuttal evidence is generally confined to responding to the defense case just concluded.

had made after his arrest, to refresh the sheriff's memory about that statement so he could testify as to its contents. (The court ruled the written statement to be inadmissible because Wilson had never signed it. Wilson himself testified he had been given *Miranda* warnings and made the oral statement voluntarily.) It is not clear whether Wilson, acting pro se, timely objected to the use of the written version of his statement to refresh the sheriff's memory, but at any rate the state Supreme Court held that Arkansas's version of Rule 612, substantially identical to Federal Rule 612, allowed use of the writing to refresh his memory. The underlying admissibility of the writing itself is not a factor. Any thing – repeat any thing – may be used to refresh memory, subject of course to the strategic consideration that whatever is used must be shown to opposing counsel, who might well try to have it admitted.

FRE 612 – Writing Used to Refresh Recollection Need Not Have Been Prepared by or Even Previously Seen by Witness

Rule 612. Writing Used to Refresh Memory

Except as otherwise provided in criminal proceedings by section 3500 of title 18, United States Code, if a witness uses a writing to refresh memory for the purpose of testifying, either

(1) while testifying, or

(2) before testifying, if the court in its discretion determines it is necessary in the interests of justice, an adverse party is entitled to have the writing produced at the hearing, to inspect it, to cross-examine the witness thereon, and to introduce in evidence those portions which relate to the testimony of the witness. If it is claimed that the writing contains matters not related to the subject matter of the testimony the court shall examine the writing in camera, excise any portions not so related, and order delivery of the remainder to the party entitled thereto. Any portion withheld over objections shall be preserved and made available to the appellate court in the event of an appeal. If a writing is not produced or delivered pursuant to order under this rule, the court shall make any order justice requires, except that in criminal cases when the prosecution elects not to comply, the order shall be one striking the testimony or, if the court in its discretion determines that the interests of justice so require, declaring a mistrial.

R.A.B. v. STATE
399 So.2d 16 (Fla. App. 1981)

"R.A.B." was a juvenile in a delinquency proceeding arising out of a home break-in and theft of personal property. The youngster confessed in the offices of Mr. Paroti, the administrator of Boys Town, in the presence of Paroti and Detective Reese. R.A.B. had been in the temporary custody of Boys Town for eight months.

The trial court ruled R.A.B.'s interrogation was non-custodial and thus he was not legally entitled to *Miranda* warnings, and it admitted his confession. The judge, however, had also held that Paroti could not testify that Detective Reese advised R.A.B. of those *Miranda* rights because that would involve inadmissible hearsay, and that the prosecution could not try to refresh Paroti's memory with a *Miranda* card, because all Paroti said he remembered was that Detective Reese read to R.A.B. from a card. The rulings effectively prevented the state from proving that *Miranda* warnings had been given in the first place. R.A.B. was adjudged a delinquent, and appealed.

The Florida Third District Court of Appeals affirmed in part and reversed in part. The appellate court upheld the admissibility of the confession without the need of *Miranda* warnings, but noted both that an advice of rights by a police officer to a suspect is not hearsay (there is no "truth of the matter asserted" for which it is being offered[30]) and, curiously enough in a footnote, that a "writing used to refresh recollection need not be one which was made by or [even] previously seen by a witness," because it is not itself being offered into evidence. (The court scolded the State of Florida for not having cross-appealed on the question, as Florida procedural rules allow.)

---

[30]See Rule 801(c).

160 Evidence Illustrated

FRE 612, 501 – Use of Interview Summaries to Refresh Witness Recollection Amounts to Waiver of Attorney-Client and Work Product Privileges, Entitling Adverse Party to Inspect Them

> **Rule 612. Writing Used to Refresh Memory**
>
> Except as otherwise provided in criminal proceedings by section 3500 of title 18, United States Code, if a witness uses a writing to refresh memory for the purpose of testifying, either
>
> (1) while testifying, or
>
> (2) before testifying, if the court in its discretion determines it is necessary in the interests of justice, an adverse party is entitled to have the writing produced at the hearing, to inspect it, to cross-examine the witness thereon, and to introduce in evidence those portions which relate to the testimony of the witness. If it is claimed that the writing contains matters not related to the subject matter of the testimony the court shall examine the writing in camera, excise any portions not so related, and order delivery of the remainder to the party entitled thereto. Any portion withheld over objections shall be preserved and made available to the appellate court in the event of an appeal. If a writing is not produced or delivered pursuant to order under this rule, the court shall make any order justice requires, except that in criminal cases when the prosecution elects not to comply, the order shall be one striking the testimony or, if the court in its discretion determines that the interests of justice so require, declaring a mistrial.
>
> **Rule 501. [PRIVILEGES] General Rule**
>
> Except as otherwise required by the Constitution of the United States or provided by Act of Congress or in rules prescribed by the Supreme Court pursuant to statutory authority, the privilege of a witness, person, government, State, or political subdivision thereof shall be governed by the principles of the common law as they may be interpreted by the courts of the United States in the light of reason and experience. However, in civil actions and proceedings, with respect to an element of a claim or defense as to which State law supplies the rule of decision, the privilege of a witness, person, government, State, or political subdivision thereof shall be determined in accordance with State law.

SAMARITAN HEALTH SERVICES, INC. v. SUPERIOR COURT
690 P.2d 154, 142 Ariz. 435 (1984)

In anticipation of a lawsuit as a result of "events surrounding the birth" of Shereese Jones at Maryvale Samaritan Hospital in Phoenix, Samaritan Health Services in-house counsel Cathy Milam interviewed a number of hospital employees. She prepared written summaries of the interviews, including her "impressions and thought processes as well as factual matters." The child's parents, Gwendolyn and Ronald Jones, eventually did file a medical malpractice action against Samaritan in Maricopa County Superior Court. In the course of preparing for their depositions, four Samaritan employees were permitted to review Milam's summaries of their interviews. Jones than served Milam with a subpoena duces tecum requiring Milam to produce for their inspection, under Arizona's counterpart to Federal Rule 612, the interview summaries that the employees had used to refresh their recollection. Samaritan's objection to the subpoena's requirement to produce the summaries was overruled by the Superior Court judge, and Samaritan filed a "special action" in the Arizona Court of Appeals to resolve the issue conclusively before trial.

Samaritan argued that Rule 612's inspection requirement should not be taken to override the attorney-client and work-product privileges. Jones contended that no exemption existed in the rule's requirement. Because the Arizona rule is nearly identical to the federal rule, the appellate court undertook an extensive review of the "ambiguous" legislative history of Federal Rule 612 with respect to privileged documents used to refresh memory. "While Rule 612 does not explicitly refer to privileged matters, Congress could have employed language comparable to 26(b)(1), Federal Rules of Civil Procedure, which restricted discovery to 'any matter not privileged.' Congress, however, did not explicitly circumscribe the exercise of discretion by courts when ordering the disclosure of privileged information" when it is used to refresh a witness's memory.

"The rule was intended to allow opposing counsel the opportunity on cross-examination to search out discrepancies between a writing used to refresh recollection and the witness's direct testimony. Without access to the materials that the witnesses used for review, opposing counsel cannot inquire into the extent to which a witness's testimony has been shaded by counsel's presentation of the factual background. The logic... is sound and we hold that by using the interview summaries to refresh the recollections of its employees, Samaritan waived, except as qualified hereafter, the attorney-client and work product privileges that initially attached to the interview summaries."

The Arizona Court of Appeals then ordered the trial court to conduct an in camera examination of the summaries to protect from disclosure "those items that could not have had an influence on the witnesses." The court observed, "It is quite possible that everything in the statements is subject to production and that under the criteria we have laid out that the petitioner will agree that that is the case. The trial court may wish to facilitate the *in camera* inspection by requesting the petitioner to furnish a memorandum highlighting the matters it believes remain protected."

FRE 613 – Impeachment: Evasive, Equivocal Testimony Is Sufficiently Inconsistent with Prior Statement to Allow Statement's Use to Impeach Witness

> **Rule 613. Prior Statements of Witnesses**
>
> *(a) Examining Witness Concerning Prior Statement.* In examining a witness concerning a prior statement made by the witness, whether written or not, the statement need not be shown nor its contents disclosed to the witness at that time, but on request the same shall be shown or disclosed to opposing counsel.
>
> *(b) Extrinsic Evidence of Prior Inconsistent Statement of Witness.* Extrinsic evidence of a prior inconsistent statement by a witness is not admissible unless the witness is afforded an opportunity to explain or deny the same and the opposite party is afforded an opportunity to interrogate the witness thereon, or the interests of justice otherwise require. This provision does not apply to admissions of a party-opponent as defined in rule 801(d)(2).

PEOPLE v. PETERSEN
23 Cal. App. 3d 883, 100 Cal. Rptr. 590 (1972)

When Oakland Police Department trainee Arthur Roth's attention was directed during a driveway conversation with Frederick Connolly to the garage of the multiple-building apartment complex in Berkeley where they both lived, he found some 36 sticks of dynamite in a wooden drawer on a shelf in plain sight in the rear of the garage. Eventually Terrence M. Petersen, also a resident of the complex, was charged with possession of an explosive in or near a public building.

At trial in Alameda County Superior Court, Connolly gave vague and evasive testimony about a conversation he had had with Petersen two or three weeks before Roth discovered the dynamite, allowing that Petersen "threw in something about dynamite or explosives or something in a joking manner." He said, however, that he didn't recall Petersen saying it was his dynamite in the garage. When the prosecutor asked Connolly foundational questions about the earlier conversation in order to introduce extrinsic evidence of it under the California counterpart to Federal Rule 613(b),[31] Connolly said his recollection of that earlier conversation with Petersen was "vague" and "very limited" (although he had signed a statement at the Berkeley Police Department the day after Roth discovered the dynamite that was relatively firm its recall of Petersen's statements, and was shown this statement at trial). "Under both direct and cross-examination, he changed and rechanged his account of the conversation, successively testifying that he could not recall whether it was appellant or someone else who had mentioned dynamite, nor whether appellant had said anything at all at the time; next, that appellant had in fact 'mentioned something... explosives or dynamite' during the conversation; again that he (Connolly) could not 'specifically' remember who had mentioned dynamite, nor 'any mention about where any explosives or dynamite was being kept'; and, finally, that he did not 'know' whether appellant had told him that he (appellant) had dynamite in the garage."

The prosecutor was then permitted to recall Arthur Roth to testify to Connolly's prior inconsistent statements. "Roth gave this

---
[31] California Evidence Code Sections 1235 and 770.

testimony when recalled to the stand: On September 23, after the dynamite had been found in the garage and Connolly had seen it, Connolly said in Roth's presence 'Jesus Christ, he wasn't kidding,' that [t]his is Terry's [appellant's] shit,' and that 'he [Connolly] had asked Terry and Terry said it was his.' Over an objection by defense counsel, Roth was also permitted to testify to a second conversation with Connolly, at the latter's apartment on the night of September 23, in which Connolly said that he (Connolly) 'was informed that it [the dynamite] was there and that he... asked Terry,... and that Terry said that it was his and that he was going to remove it from the garage.... He said he'd get rid of it.'"

The prosecutor also was permitted to introduce, through the testimony of Berkeley P.D. Inspector Bergfeld, Connolly's signed statement of September 24:

"About 2 or 3 weeks ago I had occasion to talk to Terry Petersen [appellant] in the vicinity of my apartment. During our conversation Terry said jokingly that he had a box of dynamite in the garage, after which we laughed and nothing more was said.

"On 9-23-69 Arthur arrived at my place. He and I were standing outside when a friend named Tom arrived. While all three of us were standing in the driveway in front of the garage admiring a new motorcycle one of us mentioned something about fire or explosives. I then ventured the thought that there may be some explosives in the garage. With this comment Tom went into the garage and took a dresser drawer from the second shelf. He showed Arthur and I the contents, which all three of us recognized as dynamite. I then said 'Jesus Christ, he wasn't kidding.' Arthur then took the drawer containing the dynamite and put it in his jeep.

"S/ Frederick M. Connolly"

The jury convicted Petersen, and he appealed. One of the many issues he raised concerned the admissibility of Connolly's prior statements, which Petersen's appellate counsel characterized as "inadmissible hearsay." The real issue, of course, was whether Connolly's evasions and "apparent lapse of memory" during his in-court testimony were sufficiently different from his prior statements to render those prior statements "inconsistent" for purposes of admitting them for impeachment.

The California Court of Appeal, First District, affirmed Petersen's conviction and upheld the Superior Court's handling of the prior inconsistent statements. It held that Connolly's testimony about Petersen's statements[32] "was typically evasive and equivocal, and he (Connolly) was shown to have been a reluctant witness from the outset. Moreover, his 'apparent lapse of memory' was not total: despite contradictions in his testimony on the subject, he admitted at some points that he remembered appellant saying 'something' about dynamite... For these reasons, the trial court was entitled to doubt the genuineness of his claimed memory lapse, and his evasive answers – as to appellant – were fairly deemed to have been 'implied denials' of the latter's declarations linking him (appellant) to the dynamite. Connolly's trial testimony to that point was consequently – and materially – 'inconsistent' with his prior statements to Bergfeld and Roth."

While this decision is consistent with legions of Rule 613 holdings, the student of evidence is always entitled to be somewhat skeptical about the efficacy of the distinction between using the out-of-court statements of Connolly substantively, that is for their truth, which the rules do not permit, and using them as permitted only for impeachment

---

[32] To the extent Connolly's in-court testimony or out-of-court statements quoted Petersen, Petersen's statements themselves are admissible as party admissions. See FRE 801(d)(2)(A).

of his in-court testimony, which didn't amount to very much.

If a limiting instruction is sought, will a jury be able to consider Connolly's words about Petersen's dynamite only to question Connolly's in-court testimony, or will they tend to take it into account when assessing Petersen's guilt?

FRE 613, 801(d)(2)(B) – Impeachment: Silence of Accused Is Not Prior Inconsistent Statement nor Admission by Silence

> **Rule 613. Prior Statements of Witnesses**
> *(a) Examining Witness Concerning Prior Statement.* In examining a witness concerning a prior statement made by the witness, whether written or not, the statement need not be shown nor its contents disclosed to the witness at that time, but on request the same shall be shown or disclosed to opposing counsel.
>
> **Rule 801. Definitions.**
> *(d) Statements Which are Not Hearsay.* A statement is not hearsay if (2) The statement is offered against a party and is (B) a statement of which the party has manifested an adoption or belief in its truth,[…]

DOYLE v. OHIO
426 U.S. 610, 96 S. Ct. 2240, 49 L. Ed. 2d 91 (1976)

The state's witnesses, chief among them William Bonnell, a long-time criminal who was working with narcotics investigators to gain more lenient treatment following his own latest criminal arrest, depicted a "routine marijuana transaction." Jefferson Doyle and Richard Wood were arrested within minutes after Bonnell allegedly bought some ten pounds of it from them.

Doyle and Wood testified to a far different encounter with Bonnell. It was Bonnell who sold the marijuana to them, they said, and Doyle had changed his mind about the quantity, wanting one or two pounds instead of the agreed upon ten. Bonnell got angry at the change of plan, threw $1,320 into Doyle's car, and took the ten pounds of grass back to his own car and took off. Doyle and Wood were arrested as they tried to chase down Bonnell "to find out what the $1,320 was all about."

Over defense objection the prosecutor was allowed to cross examine Wood with repeated references to Wood's failure to put forth that explanation upon being arrested by the narcotics agent: "I assume you told him all about what happened to you?" and "If that is all you had to do with this and you are innocent, when Mr. Beamer [the officer] arrived on the scene why didn't you tell him?" and other references to Wood's silence. Defendants were convicted, and appealed.

The State contended that necessity often compels use of post-arrest silence against an accused who fabricates a story "to fit within the seams of the State's case as it was developed," because little else is available to refute such an exculpatory story. The State of Ohio said it was not attempting to use Wood's reticence as a substantive admission, as evidence of guilt, but rather for impeachment purposes, "to present to the jury all information relevant to the truth of petitioners' exculpatory story."

The United States Supreme Court reversed, holding that "the *Miranda*[33] decision compels rejection of the State's position.... Silence in the wake of these [*Miranda*] warnings may be nothing more than the arrestee's exercise of these... rights." Even impeachment use of an accused's silence, said the court, "violated the Due Process Clause of the Fourteenth Amendment." So an accused's failure to account for his actions post-arrest is neither an admission by silence nor a prior inconsistent (non)statement usable to impeach him.

FRE 613(b) – Impeachment: Witness Need Not Be Cross-Examined About All Details of Prior Inconsistent Statement Before Extrinsic Evidence of Same Is Admissible

> **Rule 613. Prior Statements of Witnesses**
>
> *(b) Extrinsic Evidence of Prior Inconsistent Statement of Witness.* Extrinsic evidence of a prior inconsistent statement by a witness is not admissible unless the witness is afforded an opportunity to explain or deny the same and the opposite party is afforded an opportunity to interrogate the witness thereon, or the interests of justice otherwise require. The provision does not apply to admissions of a party-opponent as defined in rule 801(d)(2).

UNITED STATES v. McLAUGHLIN
663 F.2d 949 (9th Cir. 1981)

The principal witness against William E. McLaughlin in his trial on charges of filing false federal tax returns for 1975, accountant Howard Weitz, testified under a grant of immunity that he had advised McLaughlin, a residential framing contractor in Orange County, California, "that it was necessary to withhold federal taxes from the amounts sent to carpenters by second checks" (a bonus paid above union scale for carpenters of higher skill levels). McLaughlin's defense to the charges was that in 1973 Weitz had advised him that federal taxes did not have to be withheld from the "second checks" because the carpenters were independent contractors, not employees.

McLaughlin sought to testify about allegedly inconsistent statements made by Weitz at a 1977 meeting with McLaughlin's attorney. The government objected that the foundational requirements of Rule 613(b) had not been satisfied, and the district court sustained the objection: "because of the nature of the questions asked without any indication of time, place, persons present or other identifying material, Weitz ... was not given a fair opportunity to deny or explain his alleged prior inconsistent statements, and the opposite party was not afforded an opportunity to interrogate him thereon as required by Federal Rule of Evidence 613(b) before extrinsic evidence of such claimed statements is admissible."

The jury convicted McLaughlin of eight counts of making and subscribing a false

---
[33] *Miranda v. Arizona*, 384 U.S. 436, 86 S. Ct. 1602, 16 L. Ed. 2d 694 (1966).

federal tax return and was sentenced to one year's imprisonment and a $5,000 fine on each count, the prison sentences to run concurrently. He appealed, raising the Rule 613(b) issue among several.

The Ninth Circuit Court of Appeals reversed McLaughlin's convictions, holding the trial court's concern with Rule 613(b)'s "opportunity to explain or deny" language was "misplaced." Citing the Advisory Committee Notes, the appellate court said the rule contains no requirement for a set sequence of events: "On cross-examination, Weitz denied making the statement in question at the 1977 meeting. On direct examination McLaughlin should have been permitted to testify as to his version of the meeting. The government would have been free to re-call Weitz as a witness and give him an additional 'opportunity to explain or deny' the statement attributed to him. Rule 613(b) requires no more."

Because Weitz, a government witness, testified before McLaughlin did, and was asked if he had stated to McLaughlin's attorney at the 1977 meeting that in 1973 he had advised McLaughlin that the carpenters were independent contractors, the customary impeachment protocol was observed – that the witness to be impeached with extrinsic evidence should be asked about the matter first so that if he admits the matter there is no need for the extrinsic proof of it. The records show that the meeting in question was adequately described to Weitz," the court said, laying a perfectly adequate (not necessarily optimal) foundation for McLaughlin's testimony about Weitz's prior inconsistent statement.

FRE 614(b) – Interrogation of Witnesses by Trial Judge Must Be Fair, Impartial

> **Rule 614. Calling and Interrogation of Witnesses by Court**
>
> *(a) Calling by Court.* The court may, on its own motion or at the suggestion of a party, call witnesses, and all parties are entitled to cross-examine witnesses thus called.
>
> *(b) Interrogation by Court.* The court may interrogate witnesses, whether called by itself or by a party.
>
> *(c) Objections.* Objections to the calling of witnesses by the court or to interrogation by it may be made at the time or at the next available opportunity when the jury is not present.

UNITED STATES v. HICKMAN
592 F.2d 931 (6th Cir. 1979)

Police in Louisville, Kentucky searched the apartment of Darryl Hickman and Fred Head on the strength of a search warrant. They found a shotgun, a pistol, and about four pounds of marijuana. Hickman and Head were arrested soon after the search as they returned to their apartment. Trial of this "non-complex, routine case" took a day; both defendants were convicted of being felons in possession of the guns, and Head was also found guilty of possession of a small amount of marijuana he was said to have dropped on the ground just before he was arrested. The jury could not agree on a verdict on charges of possession with intent to distribute against the two.

The convictions were reversed, however, because of the repeated intervention of the trial judge, who took on the role of a "surrogate prosecutor." The Sixth Circuit held that while the trial judge may intervene for legitimate reasons (e.g., to "clarify what is going on" in a long, complicated trial, to clarify if counsel are not doing their job, to "deal with a difficult witness," and to "clear up inadvertent witness confusion") the court must avoid the appearance of partiality or advocacy. The court quoted two substantial exchanges from the trial transcript in which the judge conducted his own rehabilitation of a government chemist, John Stokes, who had testified to expert identification of the marijuana, including a "brilliant redirect examination" after what might have otherwise been an effective defense cross examination. "We are convinced that judged as a whole, the conduct of the trial judge must have left the jury with a strong impression of the judge's belief of the defendant's [sic] probable guilt such that it was unable to freely perform its function of independent fact finder."

Empirical studies[34] have confirmed the great influence judges' attitudes can have on juries' decisions, notwithstanding the subtlety of their manifestation and even the lack of deliberate intent on the part of the judges to communicate their attitudes toward the defendant to the jury.

FRE 615 – Right to Sequester Witnesses Does Not Apply to Law Enforcement Officer in Charge of Investigation of Case

> **Rule 615. Exclusion of Witnesses**
> At the request of a party the court shall order witnesses excluded so that they cannot hear the testimony of other witnesses, and it may make the order of its own motion. This rule does not authorize exclusion of (1) a party who is a natural person, or (2) an officer or employee of a party which is not a natural person designated as its representative by its attorney, or (3) a person whose presence is shown by a party to be essential to the presentation of the party's cause.

BURKE v. STATE
484 A.2d 490 (Del. 1984)

Following a Pagan Motorcycle Club swap meet and party, Paul R. Hamilton, Paul Morris and James T. Burke went to the apartment of a young woman who had briefly attended the festivities. They kicked in the door, ripped her clothes off, and raped her, "burned her hair with cigarettes, violated her with an empty beer bottle, and committed other gross personal abuses," then left with her clothes. Despite the recantation of a friend of the victim, the victim's refusal to testify, an initial mistrial, and then the friend's claimed loss of memory following a car crash that left her in a coma for several days, a second trial resulted in convictions of all three defendants of rape in

---

[34] See, e.g., Robert Rosenthal, "Note: The Appearance of Justice: Judges' Verbal and Nonverbal Behavior in Criminal Jury Trials," 38 Stan. L. Rev. 89 (1985).

the first degree and conspiracy in the second degree. All received life sentences. They appealed on a variety of fascinating grounds, one of which involved the trial court's refusal to sequester the state's chief investigating officer. Delaware's Rule of Evidence 615 is similar to Federal Rule 615 (except that the Delaware rule says the court "may" sequester a witness upon request of a party), and the Delaware Supreme Court held that the refusal to sequester was proper under exception (2) because the state's chief investigating officer "is an officer of the state, a party which is not a natural person." This holding is entirely consistent with federal cases holding on the same issue.[35]

FRE 615 – Unintentional Violation of Sequestration Order Should Not Result in Exclusion of Defense Witnesses Unless Necessary to Preserve Integrity of Trial

> **Rule 615. Exclusion of Witnesses**
> At the request of a party the court shall order witnesses excluded so that they cannot hear the testimony of other witnesses, and it may make the order of its own motion. This rule does not authorize exclusion of (1) a party who is a natural person, or (2) an officer or employee of a party which is not a natural person designated as its representative by its attorney, or (3) a person whose presence is shown by a party to be essential to the presentation of the party's cause.

STATE v. BURDGE
664 P.2d 1073, 295 Or. 1 (1983)

Counsel for Emery Monroe Burdge in his trial for selling a pound of marijuana to an undercover operative did not learn what telephone number Burdge was alleged to have provided the agent to talk to him at night until they were cross examining him. The number, 367-4815, turned out to be Burdge's estranged wife's home number. She was present in the courtroom during the operative's testimony, and because Burdge had not intended to call her as a witness, her name was not on the defense witness list. When Burdge's lawyer attempted to call her as a witness, the prosecution objected in part because the parties had stipulated to the sequestration of witnesses under Oregon's version of Rule 615. The trial court refused to allow her to testify that Burdge didn't live in the residence served by that number and that during the period the undercover operative said he called it and spoke to Burdge, she never received any such calls. Without that evidence, the jury convicted Burdge, and he appealed.

The Oregon Supreme Court reversed the conviction. "We hold that a violation of an exclusion order is not, of itself, sufficient to disqualify a defense witness in a criminal case, and that the trial court cannot exclude the testimony based upon this ground alone.... [We] hold that exclusion of a witness in a criminal case is too grave a sanction where the violation of the order was not intentional and not procured by a connivance of counsel or for some improper motive. We think

---
[35]See, e.g., *United States v. Payan*, 992 F.2d 1387 (5th Cir. 1993).

this represents a practical and sensitive accommodation between a criminal defendant's right to present witnesses in his behalf and the court's need to control the trial proceedings. "Refusal to allow defense witnesses to testify for violation of an exclusion order should be imposed only when necessary to preserve the 'integrity of the fact-finding process' and requires that the competing interests be closely examined.... The witness in the instant case was being called to impeach the testimony of the operative. The particular testimony to be impeached dealt with a telephone number which had not been previously provided to the defense and, therefore, it could not have been anticipated that it would become necessary to call this impeachment witness."

CHAPTER SEVEN
Article VII – Opinion and Expert Testimony

FRE 701 – Lay Witness May Give Estimate of Speed of Vehicle

> **Rule 701. Opinion Testimony by Lay Witnesses**
> If the witness is not testifying as an expert, the witness's testimony in the form of opinions or inferences is limited to those opinions or inferences which are (a) rationally based on the perception of the witness, and (b) helpful to a clear understanding of the witness's testimony or the determination of a fact in issue, and (c) not based on scientific, technical or other specialized knowledge within the scope of Rule 702.

SMITH v. PRAEGITZER
749 P.2d 1012, 113 Idaho 887 (1988)

As Richard Smith was jogging one August morning along Miller Avenue in Burley, Idaho, he noticed Joyce Praegitzer's car on 24th Street approaching the Miller intersection. He thought the car's distance from the intersection was sufficient for him to make it across 24th, but when he looked back the car seemed to be accelerating and veering toward him. He was struck and seriously injured. Praegitzer said she never saw Smith because the sun was in her eyes (despite a weather report that the sky had broken, heavy cloud cover that day). In the trial of Smith's lawsuit against her for negligence, Praegitzer was permitted to testify that she estimated she was driving 20 to 25 miles per hour at the time of the accident. A jury special verdict found each party to be 50 percent at fault. Smith moved for judgment notwithstanding the verdict, and the trial court granted it, finding Praegitzer one hundred percent at fault. The court and also granted a motion for a new trial on the issue of damages alone. Praegitzer appealed.

The Court of Appeals of Idaho reversed the granting of the judgment n.o.v., holding that drawing every reasonable inference in the light most favorable to the non-moving party compelled the conclusion that there was some substantial evidence to support the jury's verdict. Smith contended on appeal that Praegitzer lacked sufficient direct knowledge of her speed to be able to say she was going 20-25 mph, but the court called her testimony "a mixture of direct evidence and acceptable inference," and said flatly, "A lay witness' opinion or inference as to speed is admissible" under the Idaho counterpart to Federal Rule 701.

FRE 701 – Witness May Be Asked if Accused Was Defending Himself When He Attacked Victim

> **Rule 701. Opinion Testimony by Lay Witnesses**
> If the witness is not testifying as an expert, the witness's testimony in the form of opinions or inferences is limited to those opinions or inferences which are (a) rationally based on the perception of the witness, and (b) helpful to a clear understanding of the witness's testimony or the determination of a fact in issue, and (c) not based on scientific, technical or other specialized knowledge within the scope of Rule 702.

STATE v. SALAZAR
289 N.W.2d 753 (Minn. 1980)

George Richard Edward Salazar was charged with assault with a deadly weapon in connection with a screwdriver stabbing. During his state district court trial the prosecutor was permitted to ask a key eyewitness whether Salazar was protecting himself from any kind of attack by the victim, over a defense objection that the question sought to elicit an impermissible legal opinion on self-defense. Salazar was convicted and sentenced to a "maximum indeterminate term of 5 years in prison." He appealed on the opinion-testimony issue (and an interesting if fruitless Sixth Amendment issue about the absence of the victim at trial).

The Minnesota Supreme Court affirmed Salazar's conviction. The point of the question was not to elicit an impermissible legal opinion, but merely a lay opinion based on his observation – "whether the witness saw the victim do anything which prompted defendant to stab him." Implicit in the holding and its invocation of Rule 701, substantially the same in Minnesota as in the federal rules, is the notion that such testimony from a non-expert witness is a permissible subject for opinion testimony.

FRE 701 – Lay Opinion Testimony Identifying Subject in Photograph is Admissible if Witness is in Position to Make More Accurate Identification Than Jury

> **Rule 701. Opinion Testimony by Lay Witnesses**
> If the witness is not testifying as an expert, the witness's testimony in the form of opinions or inferences is limited to those opinions or inferences which are (a) rationally based on the perception of the witness, and (b) helpful to a clear understanding of the witness's testimony or the determination of a fact in issued, and (c) not based on scientific, technical or other specialized knowledge within the scope of Rule 702.

UNITED STATES v. ROBINSON
804 F.2d 280 (4th Cir. 1986)

At the bank robbery trial of Leon Robinson, his brother Sylvester was permitted to testify for the prosecution that the individual shown in bank surveillance tapes at the Citizens Savings and Loan of Laurel, Maryland was Leon. Leon Robinson was convicted by a jury, and he appealed on this and other grounds.

The Fourth Circuit Court of Appeals affirmed. Sylvester Robinson's "testimony was based upon his perceptions from viewing the photographs and from his perceptions of and close association with his brother over the years. Although the defendant's appearance may not have physically changed from the time of the bank surveillance photograph until the time of trial, the individual in the photograph was wearing a hat and dark glasses, and the testimony of Sylvester Robinson could be helpful to the jury on the issue of fact of whether the appellant was the person shown in the bank surveillance photograph. A lay witness may give an opinion concerning the identity of a person depicted in a surveillance photograph if there is some basis for concluding that the witness is more likely to correctly identify the defendant from the photograph than is the jury."

And although Leon Robinson argued that his brother's identification of him was based on the brother's awareness of Leon's prior armed robberies, thus precluding effective cross-examination of the brother on the point, the court found the record adequately supported the identification based on simple recognition.

FRE 701 – Intoxication Is Proper Subject of Lay Opinion Testimony

> **Rule 701. Opinion Testimony by Lay Witnesses**
> If the witness is not testifying as an expert, the witness's testimony in the form of opinions or inferences is limited to those opinions or inferences which are (a) rationally based on the perception of the witness, and (b) helpful to a clear understanding of the witness's testimony or the determination of a fact in issue, and (c) not based on scientific, technical or other specialized knowledge within the scope of Rule 702.

LOOF v. SANDERS
686 P.2d 1205 (Alaska 1984)

Frank Loof was hired one night over beers at the Breakers Bar in Kodiak as a "skiff man" by Frank Ahsoak, the skipper of the boat "Cape Cheerful" owned by Warren Sanders. While climbing aboard a short time later, Loof fell off the dock ladder and sustained (unspecified) injuries requiring hospitalization for 11 days and from which by the time of trial he faced only a 50/50 likelihood of full recovery. He sued Sanders, arguing three theories of liability: Ahsoak's negligence; unseaworthiness of the boat; and "maintenance and cure for injuries sustained in service of the ship." Sanders' answer and defense were based on Loof's alleged intoxication, and the jury returned a verdict finding Loof's injuries were attributable solely to his intoxication.

At trial Kodiak police officer Douglas Kniss, who had answered the call along with fire department paramedics, testified that his "impression" was that Loof was intoxicated. The Supreme Court of Alaska in affirming the verdict held the testimony admissible: the subject, intoxication, is one long recognized to be a proper subject for lay opinion testimony; the "impression" he related was the equivalent of an opinion; and as to the foundation required by Alaska's Rule 701 (the same as the Federal Rule), "It is undisputed that Kniss arrived at the scene of Loof's accident shortly after Loof had been pulled from the water, and that Kniss had an opportunity to examine Loof, albeit cursorily, at that time. In these circumstances, we conclude that Kniss' testimony was admissible. The weight of Kniss' testimony regarding Loof's state of sobriety was for the jury."

FRE 701 – Non-Expert Opinion Is Admissible Regarding Likely Injury from Accused's Knife

> **Rule 701. Opinion Testimony by Lay Witnesses**
> If the witness is not testifying as an expert, the witness's testimony in the form of opinions or inferences is limited to those opinions or inferences which are (a) rationally based on the perception of the witness and, (b) helpful to a clear understanding of the witness's testimony or the determination of a fact in issue, and (c) not based on scientific, technical or other specialized knowledge within the scope of Rule 702.

LEWIS v. STATE
416 A.2d 208 (Del. 1980)

Two Wilmington, Delaware police officers responding to a burglary call found Ray Lynn Lewis removing articles from a closet in the home he had broken into. He was ordered to raise his hands, but instead lashed out at the officers with a knife. At Lewis's Superior Court trial, Officer Stevens was permitted over defense objection to testify that had he not resisted Lewis's knife attacks he would have been seriously injured. The jury convicted Lewis of several felonies, including attempted murder.

On Lewis's appeal, his conviction was affirmed by the Delaware Supreme Court. Lewis argued that the degree of injury the officer might have sustained, if any, required expert testimony and also embraced an ultimate issue to be decided by the jury. Applying a Delaware evidence rule identical to Federal Rule 701, the appellate court observed, "the probable physical injury resulting from an assault with a knife is not a matter beyond the comprehension of non-experts." The jury had been instructed to decide the relative merits of the trial testimony for themselves, without relying too much on the opinion of others.

FRE 701 – Author of Notation "Mentally Unbalanced" on Witness's Probation File Must Be Present for Conclusion to Be Admissible Lay Opinion

> **Rule 701. Opinion Testimony by Lay Witnesses**
> If the witness is not testifying as an expert, the witness's testimony in the form of opinions or inferences is limited to those opinions or inferences which are (a) rationally based on the perception of the witness and, (b) helpful to a clear understanding of the witness's testimony or the determination of a fact in issue, and (c) not based on scientific, technical or other specialized knowledge within the scope of Rule 702.

UNITED STATES v. ANTHONY
944 F.2d 780 (10th Cir. 1991)

Mark Joel Anthony was convicted with several others in U.S. District Court for the Northern District of Oklahoma of conspiring to distribute more than 50 grams of a cocaine-base substance. A key witness against Anthony was Willie Junior Louis, who testified "that during his absence from his apartment in March, 1989, at a time when he left his apartment in charge of his girlfriend, the defendants, or at least most of them, 'moved' into his apartment, and for the ensuing five or six weeks conducted a 'crack cocaine' business out of his apartment. He described how the defendants, including Anthony, would cut up rock cocaine with a razor blade, sell it to customers who came to the apartment, and give it to 'runners,' often juveniles, who would then sell it to passing motorists outside the apartment. Louis further testified that these 'runners' would later return with monies received from the sales made." Other witnesses "tended to corroborate" Louis's testimony.

Louis admitted on direct examination that he had been convicted in federal court for interstate transportation of a stolen motor vehicle and that at the time of the raid on his apartment that led to his testimony against Anthony and the others, Louis was on probation for a state marijuana charge. When Louis's probation officer, Ronny Goins, was called as a defense witness (in April 1989 he had seen no evidence of drug activity during a visit to Louis's apartment) the defendants tried to offer into evidence the notation on Louis's probation file that Louis was "mentally unbalanced." Goins said he hadn't written the words.

On appeal Anthony argued that refusing to admit the file notation was one basis for reversing his conviction. The Tenth Circuit Court of Appeals disagreed, observing that while Rule 701 permits a lay witness to testify as to the general sanity or insanity of another person, a foundational requirement is that the witness must establish "an acquaintance of such intimacy and duration" that his rational perception of the other's mental state is both accurate and helpful to a jury. In affirming the conviction, the appellate court said, "Whoever made this notation was presumably not an expert. However, Fed.R.Evid. 701 permits a lay witness to express an opinion if, *inter alia,* it is 'rationally based on the perception of the witness.' So if the author of the notation had been present at trial, he would not have been allowed to give his opinion until it had first been shown that such opinion was 'rationally based on [his] perception.' Such being the case, it would have been a bit incongruous to admit the notation, with no basis therefor, when the author was not present at trial."

FRE 701 – Admissible Lay Opinion Testimony May Be Based on Review of Business Records or on Industry Experience

> **Rule 701. Opinion Testimony by Lay Witnesses**
>
> If the witness is not testifying as an expert, the witness's testimony in the form of opinions or inferences is limited to those opinions or inferences which are (a) rationally based on the perception of the witness, and (b) helpful to a clear understanding of the witness's testimony or the determination of a fact in issue, and (c) not based on scientific, technical or other specialized knowledge within the scope of Rule 702.

BURLINGTON NORTHERN RAILROAD CO. v. STATE OF NEBRASKA
802 F.2d 994 (8th Cir. 1986)

Burlington Northern Railroad Company filed suit to challenge the constitutionality of a 1983 Nebraska statute that required the last car on any train over 1,000 feet long to be a manned caboose. The state justified the requirement because of safety concerns: prevention of right-of-way fires, spotting or even preventing accidents occurring toward the rear sections of long trains, and spotting defective equipment and other mechanical problems missed by the locomotive crew that might cause a derailment. Although the trial court found that the increasing use of mechanical means of detection of these problems "significantly reduces the role played by caboose crews," the crews' supplemental roles rendered the caboose law's safety effect "not slight, dubious, problematic or illusory," so that the railroad's Commerce Clause challenge did not prevail. Burlington Northern appealed.

The lone evidentiary issue raised on appeal concerned the district court's refusal to hear testimony in the form of lay opinion from four executives of other railroads that had been operating without cabooses for some years. They would have testified that in their experience, and based on a review of industry accident reports, "trains with cabooses were no safer than cabooseless trains." The trial court allowed their lay opinion only to the extent it was based on personal experience.

The Eighth Circuit Court of Appeals reversed and remanded on this issue. The requirement that lay opinions be "rationally based on perception" is satisfied by "personal knowledge or perception acquired through review of records prepared in the ordinary course of business, or perception based on industry experience." Here, the court held, "the railroad executives' testimony, based on knowledge derived from supervising railroad operations, years of experience in the industry, and review of employee accident reports prepared in the ordinary course of business, satisfies the foundation requirements for lay opinion testimony. The fact that some knowledge was gained from employee accident reports does not in this case, render the testimony hearsay."

(This may be as close as a court has ever come to declaring that Rule 703 (despite its language) applies more-or-less to non-expert opinion testimony too.)

FRE 702 – Expert Testimony Must Be Helpful to Trier of Fact to Be Admissible

> **Rule 702. Testimony by Experts.**
> If scientific, technical, or other specialized knowledge will assist the trier of fact to understand the evidence or to determine a fact in issue, a witness qualified as an expert by knowledge, skill, experience, training, or education, may testify thereto in the form of an opinion or otherwise, if (1) the testimony is based upon sufficient facts or data, (2) the testimony is the product of reliable principles and methods, and (3) the witness has applied the principles and methods reliably to the facts of the case.

UNITED STATES v. AMARAL
488 F.2d 1148 (9th Cir. 1973)

Manuel Amaral and Douglas Nordfelt, Amaral's alleged accomplice in a bank robbery, were tried separately and convicted. Amaral had proffered expert testimony impugning the accuracy and the reliability of eyewitness testimony generally, although not impeaching any particular witness. The trial court refused to allow defendant's expert to testify.

Amaral appealed to the Ninth Circuit Court of Appeals, which affirmed his conviction. Applying a pre-rules standard that has been largely incorporated into Rule 702's "if [it] will assist the trier of fact" provision, the court said, following Wigmore, that the test is whether the testimony would give the jury "appreciable help." The trial court was within its broad discretion in determining that the jury did not need help in evaluating the reliability of eyewitness testimony, given the full opportunity the defense had to cross examine the witnesses and to uncover any deficiencies in their perception or recollections. This was particularly true in light of the danger of prejudice inherent in the "aura of special reliability and trustworthiness" associated with scientific or expert testimony.

Amaral illustrates the typical approach of courts to the question of admissibility of expert testimony regarding the general reliability of eyewitness testimony.

RE 702 – Police Officer's Expert Testimony Interpreting Records of Drug Transactions Is Admissible Because Helpful

> **Rule 702. Testimony by Experts**
> If scientific, technical, or other specialized knowledge will assist the trier of fact to understand the evidence or to determine a fact in issue, a witness qualified as an expert by knowledge, skill, experience, training, or education, may testify thereto in the form of an opinion or otherwise, if (1) the testimony is based upon sufficient facts or data, (2) the testimony is the product of reliable principles and methods, and (3) the witness has applied the principles and methods reliably to the facts of the case.

UNITED STATES v. de SOTO
885 F.2d 354 (7th Cir. 1989)

Over a two-year period, undercover FBI Agent Gregorio Rodriguez made cocaine buys from Mrs. Fanny Altamirano, who was supplied by people who employed her as a housekeeper. In October, 1986 a task force made several arrests, including Gustavo Chaverra Cardona, his wife Ruth Urrego Chaverra, and her sister Maria Urrego de Soto. A jury found them guilty of conspiring to distribute cocaine and of possession of cocaine with intent to distribute. They appealed their convictions to the Seventh Circuit Court of Appeals.

A principal ground of the appeal concerned expert testimony admitted by the trial judge. Lieutenant Dailey, a member of the task force that watched de Soto's apartment, was permitted to testify that as an expert he recognized documents seized at the de Soto residence, despite their never using words like "cocaine," "drugs," or "heroin," as records of drug transactions. The appellate court affirmed, noting that the records were "quite obscure," that Lt. Dailey's training and experience made his expert interpretation "helpful" to the jury, and that he restricted his testimony on this issue to an interpretation of the records themselves, never trying to "link these documents to the defendants on trial."

FRE 702 – Expert Opinion Testimony May Be Based on Skill and Experience Alone Without Training or Education

> **Rule 702. Testimony by Experts**
> If scientific, technical, or other specialized knowledge will assist the trier of fact to understand the evidence or to determine a fact in issue, a witness qualified as an expert by knowledge, skill, experience, training, or education, may testify thereto in the form of an opinion or otherwise, if (1) the testimony is based upon sufficient facts or data, (2) the testimony is the product of reliable principles and methods, and (3) the witness has applied the principles and methods reliably to the facts of the case.

UNITED STATES v. 77,819.10 ACRES OF LAND MORE OR LESS
647 F.2d 104 (10th Cir. 1981)

The United States condemned two successive "evacuation estates" over most of a ranch in Socorro and Catron counties owned by Jay and Imogene Taylor, about a fourth of which was on land leased from the state of New Mexico. The government needed to evacuate people from time to time in connection with the Athena H Missile project at the White Sands Missile Range. The taking in question here, that is the length of time the evacuation lasted, was 13 months. The dispute, as always in a condemnation case, was over the value of the taking, the damages owed the Taylors for the evacuation period. The commission that was appointed pursuant to Fed. Rules Civ. Pro. Rule 71A(h) awarded the Taylors $33,375 and New Mexico $4,237.25. The government appealed on a number of issues, including whether the Taylors' expert witness, Charles Crowder, gave testimony that was too speculative. He testified, based on his experience, that if he were going to lease the Taylor ranch he would discount the rent by at least 50% to adjust for the taking.

On appeal the United States reiterated its objection to the court's allowance of Crowder's testimony because it was "too speculative," by which it meant that he was not an expert appraiser. The Tenth Court Circuit Court of Appeals cited his experience and skill: "Crowder testified that he had very successfully participated in sales of over 3 million acres of ranch property in New Mexico, either individually or corporately and always as a principal. He never used an appraiser; rather, he valued the land himself. In addition, Crowder stated that he was familiar with the Taylor ranch from past business experience and because he had a ranch nearby.... It is permissible for an expert witness to arrive at his opinion in a way that any man of intelligence would have arrived at a valuation of the property for ordinary business purposes."

The appellate court held that the commission's reliance on Crowder's testimony was "justified and proper."

FRE 702 – "General Acceptance" Test for Scientific Evidence Is Replaced by Responsibility of Trial Judge to Ensure Reliability of Scientific Methods and Procedures Generating Proposed Evidence

> **Rule 702. Testimony by Experts.**
> If scientific, technical, or other specialized knowledge will assist the trier of fact to understand the evidence or to determine a fact in issue, a witness qualified as an expert by knowledge, skill, experience, training, or education, may testify thereto in the form of an opinion or otherwise, if (1) the testimony is based upon sufficient facts or data, (2) the testimony is the product of reliable principles and methods, and (3) the witness has applied the principles and methods reliably to the facts of the case.

DAUBERT v. MERRELL DOW PHARMACEUTICALS, INC.
509 U.S. 579, 113 S. Ct. 2786, 125 L.Ed.2d 469 (1993)

The parents and guardians of Jason Daubert and Eric Schuller sued Merrell Dow in California state court,[1] claiming the children's serious birth defects were caused by Bendectin, a prescription anti-nausea drug taken by their mothers during pregnancy. Merrell Dow removed the case to federal district court on the basis of diversity of citizenship.

Following "extensive discovery," Merrell Dow moved for summary judgment, saying it would not be possible for plaintiffs to produce any admissible evidence that Bendectin causes birth defects in human beings. Merrell Dow produced an affidavit from an expert on the risks of exposure to chemicals, Dr. Steven H. Lamm, who stated that he reviewed some 30 published studies

---
[1] William Daubert is Jason's father. The case is styled, " William DAUBERT, et. ux., etc., et. al.,..."

involving 130,000 patients and found no link between Bendectin and malformations in human fetuses.

Plaintiffs responded to the motion and affidavit with testimony from eight of their own impressively credentialed experts. On the basis of animal studies, pharmacological studies of the chemical structure of Bendectin (showing similarities with other substances known to cause birth defects) and "reanalysis" of the previously published studies, they all concluded Bendectin can cause birth defects.

The district judge granted Merrell Dow's motion for summary judgment, rejecting plaintiffs' expert testimony. The court held that their evidence would be inadmissible because plaintiffs had not established sufficiently that it had gained general acceptance in its scientific field under the long dominant standard of *Frye v. United States*.[2]

Daubert appealed, and the Ninth Circuit Court of Appeals affirmed, holding that plaintiffs' expert testimony was based on a methodology that diverges too much from procedures accepted by recognized authorities. The fact that the reanalyses of published data had not been published nor subjected to peer review was "particularly problematic."

The United States Supreme Court granted certiorari. The central question the court focused on was "the continuing authority" of the 1923 *Frye* standard of general acceptance after the 1975 adoption of the Federal Rule of Evidence. Justice Blackmun's majority opinion held Rule 702 "supersedes" *Frye,* and the Rule's lack of any "general acceptance" language means *Frye's* "austere standard" of general acceptance "should not be applied in federal trials," at least not alone. The summary judgment in favor of Merrell Dow was set aside.

Yet "the trial judge must ensure that any and all scientific testimony or evidence admitted is not only relevant, but reliable.... Proposed testimony must be supported by appropriate validation – i.e., 'good grounds,' based on what is known." The court offered several bases[3] for federal trial judges to assess the soundness of any scientific evidence or testimony offered: (1) whether the theory or technique employed can be or has been tested; (2) whether it has been subjected to peer review and publication; (3) its known or potential rate of error and "the existence and maintenance of standards controlling the technique's operation;" and (4) its general acceptance (relegated to but one factor among many). "The inquiry envisioned by Rule 702 is, we emphasize, a flexible one," focusing "solely on principles and methodology, not on the conclusions that they generate," noted the court. Courts must be mindful of Rule 703's requirement that if an expert bases his/her opinion "on otherwise inadmissible hearsay,"[4] it must be "of a type reasonably relied upon by experts" in that field, as well as of Rule 706's grant of authority to a trial court to call its own expert, and of Rule 403's restriction on evidence that is too prejudicial.

To the concerns of the defendant and various *amici* that erosion of the *Frye* test "will result in a 'free-for-all' in which befuddled juries are confounded by absurd and irrational pseudoscientific assertions," also known as "junk science," the court reiterated its confidence in the jury system

---

[2] 293 F. 1013 (D.C. Cir. 1923).
[3] Under the rubric of "general observations," not a "definitive checklist or test."
[4] The actual words in the rule do not confine the principle's applicability to hearsay alone, but to evidence inadmissible on any ground. Hearsay is only the most popular basis.

and the adversary system: "Vigorous cross-examination, presentation of contrary evidence, and careful instruction on the burden of proof are the traditional and appropriate means of attacking shaky but admissible evidence."

A partial dissent by Chief Justice Rehnquist worried that the hundreds of federal district judges would not be able to apply the majority's "general observations" very well.

FRE 703 – Expert Testimony Based on Inadmissible Hearsay Is Admissible if the Expert's Reliance on the Hearsay Is Reasonable and Customary

Rule 703. Bases of Opinion Testimony by Experts

The facts or data in the particular case upon which an expert bases an opinion or inference may be those perceived by or made known to the expert at or before the hearing. If of a type reasonably relied upon by experts in the particular field in forming opinions or inferences upon the subject, the facts or data need not be admissible in evidence, in order for the opinion or inference to be admitted. Facts or data that are otherwise inadmissible shall not be disclosed to the jury by the proponent of the opinion or inference unless the court determines that their probative value in assisting the jury to evaluate the expert's opinion substantially outweighs their prejudicial effect.

STATE v. HENZE
356 N.W.2d 538 (Iowa 1984)

After his arrest in November 1982 for operating a motor vehicle while intoxicated, James Roger Henze was examined by Dr. Michael Berstler at a hospital emergency room so it could be determined whether in his condition Henze could tolerate confinement in jail overnight. The doctor, who had never seen Henze before, concluded he could.

At his trial Henze offered Dr. Berstler as an expert witness to testify that his appearance and behavior on the night of his arrest could be explained without the conclusion that he was intoxicated. Dr. Berstler prepared for this testimony by reviewing medical records prepared by his associates in a medical clinic, who had treated Henze several times before his arrest and who had made repeated diagnoses of anxiety neurosis and depression. The records showed long-term use of Valium.

The prosecuting attorney objected to the doctor's use of Henze's medical records inasmuch as they were hearsay, and the trial judge sustained the objection, permitting Dr. Berstler to give testimony based only on his personal observations of Henze the night he was arrested. (On that basis alone, Dr. Berstler testified he was unable to come to an opinion on whether Henze was intoxicated.) Henze was convicted, and appealed.

The Iowa Supreme Court reversed the conviction. The medical records were themselves hearsay (out-of-court statements used to show the truth of their contents, i.e., Henze's prior condition). But Dr. Berstler's reliance on them was permitted by Iowa's Rule of Evidence 703, substantially identical to the federal rule. Henze's records were "facts or data of a type reasonably relied upon by doctors in forming opinions" and thus Dr. Berstler should have been allowed to testify based on those records. A dissent found a defense offer of proof inadequate to establish reasonable reliance.

FRE 703 – Charts Summarizing Expert's Economic Damages Testimony Are Admissible

> **Rule 703. Bases of Opinion Testimony by Experts**
>
> The facts or data in the particular case upon which an expert bases an opinion or inference may be those perceived by or made known to the expert at or before the hearing. If of a type reasonably relied upon by experts in the particular field in forming opinions or inferences upon the subject, the facts or data need not be admissible in evidence, in order for the opinion or inference to be admitted. Facts or data that are otherwise inadmissible shall not be disclosed to the jury by the proponent of the opinion or inference unless the court determines that their probative value in assisting the jury to evaluate the expert's opinion substantially outweighs their prejudicial effect.

CARTER v. WIESE CORPORATION
360 N.W.2d 122 (Iowa App. 1984)

A ladder fell on Thomas Carter, an employee of Kinney Truck Lines, while he was unloading steel bars from his truck at the Wiese Corporations's plant. He suffered recurrent neck, shoulder and arm pain, was off work about five weeks, and 18 months after returning to work, Carter quit citing continuing health problems, although it was disputed whether in fact he quit Kinney because he was unhappy with a work assignment. After surgery on a protruded disc, Carter was still in pain but expected to improve over time. He was working as a mechanic at the time of trial.

Carter's economist witness, Wayne E. Newkirk, testified as to the value of the household activities Carter could not perform "to the date of trial and for plaintiff's future life expectancy." His testimony was based on reports he reviewed outside of court, and he said it was not unusual to rely on this type of information. At the conclusion of his testimony some charts were admitted into evidence that summarized the testimony he had given. Wiese's objection to Newkirk's testimony and the charts was that they were "speculative" and "without foundation." The jury awarded Carter $117,500 and Wiese appealed.

The Court of Appeals of Iowa, applying Iowa's replica of Federal Rule 703, affirmed, finding Newkirk's reliance on outside data to be proper, and held that admitting the charts "to aid the jury in understanding the opinion," based similarly on outside data, was perfectly valid under the Rule.

FRE 704 – Opinion on Ultimate Issue Is Admissible if Helpful and Otherwise Qualified

> **Rule 704. Opinion on Ultimate Issue**
>
> (a) Except as provided in subdivision (b), testimony in the form of an opinion or inference otherwise admissible is not objectionable because it embraces an ultimate issue to be decided by the trier of fact.
>
> (b) No expert witness testifying with respect to the mental state or condition of a defendant in a criminal case may state an opinion or inference as to whether the defendant did or did not have the mental state or condition constituting an element of the crime charged or of a defense thereto. Such ultimate issues are matters for the trier of fact alone.

REDMAN v. FORD MOTOR COMPANY
170 S.E.2d 207 (S.C. 1969)

Eight days after Edward B. Redman bought a new 1958 Ford one of its rear wheels came loose and the left rear axle shaft became disengaged, causing a rollover accident that killed Redman and destroyed the car. His administrator, L.B. Redman, sued Ford in Darlington County Common Pleas Court for wrongful death, pain and suffering and other damages, alleging a failure of due care in manufacturing the car.

At trial, over defense objection Redman introduced the deposition testimony of V.D. Ackerman, an engineer and mechanic with more than 50 years' experience in automotive mechanics. Ackerman said no type of accident could result in an axle disconnecting the way Redman's car was found, and that if the axle were engaged according to specifications, "the only methods by which… [it] could be disengaged would be to use the hydraulic press or an acetylene torch." A Ford expert contradicted Ackerman's conclusion, testifying that the impact of a highway crash could knock out a rear axle. The jury returned verdicts in favor of Redman (although the amounts are not disclosed in the opinion) and Ford appealed.

Ford asked the South Carolina Supreme Court to reverse the verdicts because, it claimed, Ackerman was not qualified, his testimony was too speculative, and it contained "conclusions as to the very issue to be decided by the jury, and, therefore, invaded the province of the jury."

The state appellate court, in affirming the trial court in this pre-Rules case, took a very modern position on this "ultimate issue" question, saying, "There is no invasion of the province of the jury, for the jury retains its power and duty to judge both the credibility of the witness and the weight to be given to his opinion," and that admission of this ultimate-issue opinion testimony was not an abuse of discretion.

FRE 705 – Expert Must Be Permitted to Disclose Basis for Opinion That Defendant Accused of Murder Is Schizophrenic

> **Rule 705. Disclosure of Facts or Data Underlying Expert Opinion**
> The expert may testify in terms of opinion or inference and give reasons therefor without first testifying to the underlying facts or data, unless the court requires otherwise. The expert may in any event be required to disclose the underlying facts or data on cross-examination.

STATE v. ALLISON
298 S.E.2d 365, 307 N.C. 411 (1983)

Johnny Allison, 37 years old with a long history of mental problems, lived with his parents and received weekly injections from a mental health clinic. He stabbed his mother to death one night in December 1980, stabbed his brother and father, and burned down the house. He confessed, and was convicted of two counts of assault with a deadly weapon with intent to kill inflicting serious bodily injury, second degree murder, and wilfully and wantonly setting fire to a dwelling house. He was sentenced to various lesser prison terms concurrent with his 25-to-30-year sentence for the murder count. He appealed to the North Carolina Court of Appeals, which affirmed. He then appealed further to the Supreme Court of North Carolina.

Allison's two psychiatrists, Dr. James Groce and Dr. Harris L. Evans, testified that they believed Allison couldn't distinguish right from wrong the night of the stabbings and the arson. Dr. Groce had seen Allison two days after the killing and was allowed to testify to his eventual diagnosis of chronic undifferentiated schizophrenia. But when Allison's attorney asked him what Allison had told him that led to his diagnosis, the court sustained the prosecution's objection. (On voir dire, Dr. Groce told of a defendant who heard voices every day, heard his family plotting against him and heard killers they had hired practicing their shooting while waiting for him to come out of the house. Dr. Groce said hearing this from Allison assisted him in forming his opinion.)

The state supreme court reversed and held it was error to refuse to allow the expert to explain the basis for his opinion under North Carolina's provision comparable to Federal Rule 705. The rule "appears to assume that at some point during the direct examination the expert will disclose the basis of his opinion: the statute merely provides that the expert need not give the basis first," said the court.[5] Without a full disclosure of the basis, the jury is given an empty "trust-me" conclusion. "The jury apparently was not persuaded by either doctor's opinion as to defendant's sanity because it found defendant guilty of the crimes for which he was tried. Given that Allison's defense rested on these two doctors' testimony, the level of credibility the jury gave each doctor's opinion was crucial. It follows, therefore, that the basis of each opinion, evidence which would have gone to the credibility and coherence of each expert's opinion, was important as well.

"In its opinion, the Court of Appeals wrote that the testimony of Dr. Groce which the jury heard was sufficient to demonstrate to it that he had spent 'considerable time working with the defendant and had a deep and broad basis

---

[5] Cf., Advisory Committee Notes to Rule 705 assuming admissibility of the "underlying facts or data."

for his opinion as to the defendant's legal sanity.' This statement essentially points out how limited the information was that the jury was allowed to hear: it heard only enough evidence to determine that the doctor had a basis. Specifically, the jury was told the *types* of facts or data the doctor used in reaching his opinion; it did not hear, however, what all the *data* or *facts* themselves were."

FRE 705 – If Expert Witness Declines to Disclose Underlying Facts or Data, Court May Exclude Expert's Opinion Testimony

Rule 705. Disclosure of Facts or Data Underlying Expert Opinion
The expert may testify in terms of opinion or inference and give reasons therefor without first testifying to the underlying facts or data, unless the court requires otherwise. The expert may in any event be required to disclose the underlying facts or data on cross-examination.

FOREHEAD v. GALVIN
371 N.W.2d 271, 220 Neb. 578 (1985)

James P. Forehead's car ran a stop sign on 120th street in Omaha and collided with Frank Galvin's vehicle on Maple street. Forehead sued Galvin to recover for his injuries, claiming Galvin was speeding and thus failed to stop in time when he should have been able to do so. Forehead's contention apparently was that if Galvin had not been speeding the collision would not have occurred, even with Forehead ignoring the sign.

At trial in state district court, Forehead attempted to have his accident reconstruction expert, Dr. John E. Baerwald, testify that in his opinion Galvin's car was traveling at 59 miles per hour at the time of the collision. The trial judge sustained the defense objection to this testimony when Dr. Baerwald failed to disclose to the court the facts upon which this conclusion was based. The jury returned a verdict for defendant Galvin. Forehead appealed.

The Nebraska Supreme Court affirmed the verdict. Although the trial court "by precise order declined to receive the opinion into evidence until the facts were disclosed," such disclosure never happened. "While appellant's counsel laboriously asked of the witness the factors that he considered in arriving at an opinion as to the speed of the Galvin vehicle, he failed to ask of the witness the facts upon which the calculations were based." The rule was never complied with.

This appears to have been either an inept examination of the witness or an inept witness. Most accident reconstructionists are all too happy to fill blackboards with endless equations and calculations; perhaps this witness left his notes back at the office, or based his testimony on a computer program he didn't understand.

FRE 706 – Appointment of an Expert Witness by Court Is Ordinarily Discretionary

> **Rule 706. Court Appointed Experts**
>
> *(a) Appointment.* The court may on its own motion or on the motion of any party enter an order to show cause why expert witnesses should not be appointed, and may request the parties to submit nominations. The court may appoint any expert witnesses agreed upon by the parties, and may appoint expert witnesses of its own selection. An expert witness shall not be appointed by the court unless the witness consents to act. A witness so appointed shall be informed of the witness's duties by the court in writing, a copy of which shall be filed with the clerk, or at a conference in which the parties shall have opportunity to participate. A witness so appointed shall advise the parties of the witness's findings, if any; the witness's deposition may be taken by any party; and the witness may be called to testify by the court or any party. The witness shall be subject to cross-examination by each party, including a party calling the witness.
>
> *(c) Disclosure of Appointment.* In the exercise of its discretion, the court may authorize disclosure to the jury of the fact that the court appointed the expert witness.
>
> *(d) Parties' Experts of Own Selection.* Nothing in this rule limits the parties in calling expert witnesses of their own selection.

STATE v. ARCHAMBEAU
333 N.W.2d 807 (S.D. 1983)

Louis Archambeau was charged with aggravated assault in connection with rifle-fire that concluded an escalating father-son argument after an all-night drinking party at a mobile home in Vermillion. Archambeau's adult son Kenneth was struck in the abdomen with a bullet. According to both Archambeaus the gun discharged accidentally during a struggle for its possession; other witnesses thought the shooting was rather more deliberate, albeit the rifle was pointed at the ground in Kenneth's direction. (Other gunfire occurred that morning, besides the shot that struck Kenneth Archambeau.)

Two weeks before trial Archambeau moved to have the court appoint a "bullisitics [sic] and fingerprint expert" to attempt to refute the anticipated testimony of Dr. Ilya Zeldes of the South Dakota Division of Criminal Investigation. The defense had received Dr. Zeldes' reports a few days earlier. The trial judge in Clay County Circuit Court denied the motion, but assured Archambeau's lawyer he would be able to interview Dr. Zeldes and inspect all the state's evidence.

Archambeau was convicted and sentenced to seven years' imprisonment. He appealed on several grounds, including the trial judge's refusal to appoint an expert for his benefit, under South Dakota's statutory evidence rule on the subject.[6]

The Supreme Court of South Dakota affirmed Archambeau's conviction. In

---

[6]Although S.D. Comp. Laws Ann. §19-15-9-17 is structured quite differently from FRE 706, its discretionary language follows the spirit of the Federal Rule: The court may appoint an expert "whenever... issues arise upon which the court deems expert evidence is desirable..."

upholding the trial court's discretion, the appellate court observed, "Although there may be cases in which it is essential that an expert be appointed for a criminal defendant, as, for example, when the physical evidence material to the defendant's guilt is of such a nature that a lay person cannot determine whether it is in the nature of contraband,… we do not view this as such a case.

"…At the hearing on the motion, defendant gave as reasons for wanting a ballistics expert the desire to refute, if possible, Dr. Zeldes' testimony and the desire to have the victim's shirt examined for powder residue.

"At trial, Dr. Zeldes testified that he had tested the rifle for fingerprints and that the several partial finger or palm prints on the rifle had insufficient individual characteristics for identification purposes. He also testified that he had found no powder residue on Kenneth Archambeau's shirt.

"In view of the foregoing, we cannot say that the trial court's refusal to appoint an expert constituted an abuse of discretion. Defendant's motion lacked the specificity contemplated by the guidelines we set forth [in an earlier case]. Moreover, the evidence introduced at trial made it highly unlikely that any expert appointed on behalf of defendant would have reached any conclusions regarding the fingerprints or gunpowder residue that would have been different from Dr. Zeldes' findings."

While it is somewhat remarkable that a court would anticipate what an appointed expert would or would not discover or conclude, the South Dakota Supreme Court's refusal to second-guess the trial court on the matter is not remarkable at all.

CHAPTER EIGHT
Article VIII – Hearsay

FRE 801(a) – Hearsay Definition: For Nonverbal Conduct to Be Hearsay, It Must Be Intended to Be An Assertion by "Declarant"

> **Rule 801. Definitions**
> The following definitions apply under this article:
> *(a) Statement.* A "statement" is (1) an oral or written assertion or (2) nonverbal conduct of a person, if it is intended by the person as an assertion.
> *(b) Declarant.* A "declarant" is a person who makes a statement.
> *(c) Hearsay.* "Hearsay" is a statement, other than one made by the declarant while testifying at the trial or hearing, offered in evidence to prove the truth of the matter asserted.

IN RE DEPENDENCY OF PENELOPE B.
709 P.2d 1185, 104 Wash.2d 643 (1985)

A caseworker for the Washington State Department of Social and Health Services filed a dependency petition alleging that the father of six-year-old Penelope B. asked her to perform oral sex with him and that her mother was unable to protect her. At the court hearing in Spokane County Superior Court, Juvenile Division, some 15 witnesses testified, but at its conclusion the court issued a Memorandum Decision dismissing the petition because it was "based entirely upon hearsay evidence of statements made by a five year old child," who did not herself testify. The state appealed the dismissal.

A fair amount of the testimony concerned Penelope B.'s conduct and demeanor during "play therapy." A therapist testified that when Penelope was playing with an anatomically correct doll, she spontaneously pushed the doll to within a foot or two of another therapist's face and, while holding the doll's penis, said "something like either 'put this in your mouth' or 'suck me.'" Other witnesses testified that she showed "precocious knowledge of explicit sexual matters and certain private names for male and female genitalia..."

The Supreme Court of Washington reversed the trial court's dismissal and remanded, holding that Penelope's actions were nonassertive nonverbal conduct and that her utterances were nonassertive verbal conduct. "If tulips bloom, they are not making assertions that it is spring; but the testimony of a witness that tulips were observed to be blooming may be offered as circumstantial evidence of spring. If a dog limps, it is not thereby making an assertion and the testimony of a witness that the dog was observed to be limping may be offered as circumstantial evidence that the dog was injured."

The test under Washington's hearsay definition, identical to that in the Federal Rule, is whether the child <u>intended</u> by her conduct or her utterances to be making some sort of statement about her father's treatment of her. As with the crying of an infant, the court found no such intent. "Other examples of nonassertive conduct by the child, as testified to by others, included the following: Penelope's moods fluctuating between openness and evasiveness; her uncomfortableness in handling the anatomically correct dolls and not wanting to undress the male doll; her fearfulness and anxiety in different contexts; her defensiveness when asked about 'her secret'; her barricading herself behind furniture or stuffed toys when talked to; and when, at not seeing her father someplace where she had expected to see him, her fear that he was in jail. None of this was hearsay testimony and it was admissible."

FRE 801(c) – Hearsay Definition: Statement Is Not Hearsay When Offered as Circumstantial Evidence of State of Mind

> **Rule 801. Definitions**
> The following definitions apply under this article:
> *(c) Hearsay.* "Hearsay" is a statement, other than one made by the declarant while testifying at the trial or hearing, offered in evidence to prove the truth of the matter asserted.

UNITED STATES v. EMMONS
24 F.3d 1210 (10th Cir. 1994)

At Roger Emmons' trial on charges related to growing marijuana, the government sought to admit into evidence a hand-drawn map found in Emmons' kitchen during the execution of a search warrant. Kansas Bureau of Investigation Special Agent Atteberry testified that the map "corresponded to the configuration of the marijuana patches" he and several Wichita police detectives had seen earlier at the farm of Emmons' friend Jack Rivard.

The map (or "sketch" or "drawing" as the court variously refers to it) "marks out 13 different locations identified by letters, each with a number as well. There was also a key in the corner of the map, showing a star as the symbol for 'lime' (there were six locations so marked on the map itself) and a '+' as the symbol for urea (shown at one location)." Lime and other cultivation items were found on Emmons' farm.

Emmons objected to the map as hearsay. It was admitted into evidence, and the Tenth Circuit affirmed its admission, as non-hearsay: the map was not offered for the truth of the matter asserted therein ("that marijuana was indeed growing on Roger's property"). Instead, the court said, it was "plainly admissible for the non-hearsay purpose of demonstrating that [Emmons] had knowledge of the location and quantity of the marijuana plants and of the efforts to treat the ground for their cultivation."

The map is treated as an out-of-court statement, which the court translates as, "Marijuana is growing on Emmons' property." The translation was based on the correspondence between the patterns shown on the map and the configuration of the marijuana plants actually found, as well as the key.

It is unclear exactly who the declarant is in this case – that is, who drew the map. If it was Rivard or anyone other than Emmons, its being in Emmons' possession, regardless of "the truth of the matter" it asserts, should shed some light on the extent of his knowledge and participation in the enterprise. If it was Emmons who drew it, the map would also have been admissible as a party admission under Rule 801(d)(2)(A), and thus would have been fully admissible for the truth of its contents.

FRE 801(c), 801(d)(2)(A),(B) – Hearsay Definition: Statements to Party Are Admissible as Warnings; Consequent Statement by Party Is Admissible as Party Admission Despite Lack of Personal Knowledge

> **Rule 801. Definitions**
> The following definitions apply under this article:
> *(c) Hearsay.* "Hearsay" is a statement, other than one made by the declarant while testifying at the trial or hearing, offered in evidence to prove the truth of the matter asserted.
> *(d) Statements Which Are Not Hearsay.* A statement is not hearsay if
> *(2) Admission by Party-Opponent.* The statement is offered against a party and is (A) the party's own statement in either an individual or a representative capacity or (B) a statement of which the party has manifested an adoption or belief in its truth.[...]

SMEDRA v. STANEK
187 F.2d 892 (10th Cir. 1951)

Zig Smedra underwent spinal surgery in a Denver hospital. Twice in the following year, sizable pieces of surgical dressings were removed from the site of the operation, and Smedra sued Doctors William Stanek and Foster Matchett for malpractice.

At trial Smedra was not allowed to introduce evidence that the surgeons had been warned that the post-surgical sponge count was "off," nor that Dr. Stanek said to a colleague afterwards that he had been delayed because the sponge count didn't come out right after Smedra's operation. The trial judge ruled both accounts inadmissible hearsay. The verdict was in favor of the doctors. Smedra appealed.

The Tenth Circuit Court of Appeals reversed, holding that this evidence should have been admitted.

The testimony about the statements made to the doctor was a "warning," not hearsay (i.e., not offered for the truth of the contents of the statement, rather for its effect on the listener), relevant instead to show "in light of this warning the doctors [failed to] exercise due care."

And the testimony about Dr. Stanek's statement was ruled a party admission whether or not it was proven independently that Dr. Stanek actually had personal knowledge of the sponge count – the premise is that a party will make such a statement only if "constrained to do so by the force of the evidence. The source from which a knowledge of the facts is derived is a circumstance for the jury to consider, in estimating the value of the evidence, but that is all."

FRE 801(c) – Hearsay Definition: Act of Voting Is Verbal Act, Not Offered for Truth of Any Assertion

> **Rule 801. Definitions.**
> *(c) Hearsay.* "Hearsay" is a statement, other than one made by the declarant while testifying at the trial or hearing, offered in evidence to prove the truth of the matter asserted.

LOCAL 512, WAREHOUSE & OFFICE WORKERS UNION v. NATIONAL LABOR RELATIONS BOARD
795 F.2d 705 (9th Cir. 1986)

In August 1981, employees of Felbro, Inc. elected Local 512 as their bargaining agent. Felbro, of South Gate, California manufactured wire and tubular displays. After the election, a series of disputes arose, one of which concerned the timing of three events: (1) an offer by Felbro; (2) the union's ratification vote accepting it; and (3) the employer's purported repudiation of the offer.

An NLRB Administrative Law Judge found that after several meetings between Felbro's attorney and Local 512's agent, an agreement was reached on November 16, 1981, subject only to ratification by Local 512 members employed by Felbro. The ALJ found that at a January 5 union meeting the employees ratified the agreement, and that this occurred before Felbro sent the union agent a mailgram revoking its offer. Felbro was found to have failed to execute a valid collective bargaining agreement.

Felbro objected to the testimony of two union officials about the results of the secret ballot conducted at the January 5 meeting, saying testimony about the contents of the ballots amounted to hearsay. (The ballots themselves were apparently destroyed after the meeting and so were not able to be offered into evidence.) The ALJ admitted the testimony.

The Ninth Circuit Court of Appeals held that the testimony about the ratification vote was admissible. Such testimony was not hearsay because "we are not concerned with the 'truth' of any matter expressed by the individual casting a ballot," rather what mattered was that the election was held and its outcome; "the casting of a vote is a verbal act, in which the statement itself has legal effect." Its significance is that it occurred.

FRE 801(c), 801(d)(2)(E) – Hearsay Definition: Statements Are Not Hearsay When Offered for Their Independent Significance to the Crime Charged or to the Establishment of a Conspiracy

> **Rule 801. Definitions.**
> The following definitions apply under this article:...
> ***(c) Hearsay.*** "Hearsay" is a statement, other than one made by the declarant while testifying at the trial or hearing, offered in evidence to prove the truth of the matter asserted.
> ***(d) Statements Which Are Not Hearsay.*** A statement is not hearsay if
> *(2) Admission by Party-Opponent.* The statement is offered against a party and is... (E) a statement by a coconspirator of a party during the course and in furtherance of the conspiracy...

UNITED STATES v. ALOSA
14 F.3d 693 (1st Cir. 1994)

Pasquale and Lisa Alosa were convicted of growing a substantial marijuana garden in the basement of their home in New Hampshire. Over the defendants' hearsay objection, the trial court admitted two sets of ledgers, found inside the kitchen stove and in the living room of the Alosa home. The ledgers contained entries of transactions with amounts and customer names. Handwriting experts tied the ledger to Lisa Alosa and a Robb Hamilton, and a DEA agent gave expert opinion testimony that the ledger recorded drug transactions.

The First Circuit Court of Appeals undertook a three-step analysis of the hearsay claim. First, the ledgers were "real evidence" on a par with "drugs, scales and guns" that go to establish the nature of the activity going on at the premises. No "truth of the matter asserted" concerns surround their relevance to the charge. The substantive details oaf any specific entry were unimportant.

Second, because most of the evidence implicated only Pasquale Alosa, the existence of the ledgers partly in Lisa Alosa's handwriting helped to establish the existence of the conspiracy, entirely independently of the truth of the individual statements in the ledgers, which was "beside the point."

The significance of the ledgers was not the contents of the statements they contained, but rather their existence. They can then be seen as verbal acts – or as *verbal parts of the acts* involved in conducting a drug manufacturing and selling enterprise.

Finally, when the government reserved the right to offer specific ledger entries for their truth in proving the extent of the conspiracy the court found that Rule 801(d)(2)(E) was satisfied – the entries were statements made by coconspirators in furtherance of the conspiracy. There was ample independent evidence of the conspiracy – including Lisa Alosa's presence as a resident of a home in which "pervasive drug production and dealing" was going on.

FRE 801(d)(1)(A), 613 – Feigned Loss of Memory by Witness Renders Prior Statements "Inconsistent"

> **Rule 801.**
> *(d) Statements Which Are Not Hearsay.* A statement is not hearsay if
> *(1) Prior Statement by Witness.* The declarant testifies at the trial or hearing and is subject to cross-examination concerning the statement, and the statement is (A) inconsistent with the declarant's testimony, and was given under oath subject to the penalty of perjury at a trial, hearing, or other proceeding, or in a deposition...
>
> **Rule 613. Prior Statements of Witnesses**
> *(a) Examining Witness Concerning Prior Statement.* In examining a witness concerning a prior statement made by the witness, whether written or not, the statement need not be shown nor its contents disclosed to the witness at that time, but on request the same shall be shown or disclosed to opposing counsel.
>
> *(b) Extrinsic Evidence of Prior Inconsistent Statement of Witness.* Extrinsic evidence of a prior inconsistent statement by a witness is not admissible unless the witness is afforded an opportunity to explain or deny the same and the opposite party is afforded an opportunity to interrogate the witness thereon, or the interests of justice otherwise require. This provision does not apply to admissions of a party-opponent as defined in rule 801(d)(2).

VAN HATTAN v. STATE
666 P.2d 1047 (Alaska App. 1983)

Alaska State Troopers arrested Richard Van Hattan at his Fairbanks home after his wife called them to report he had attempted to rape his 17-year-old stepdaughter, "T.M.W." The stepdaughter testified before the grand jury that Van Hattan came into her bedroom, groped her under her robe, left when she fought him off, but returned soon, put her on her bed and climbed on top of her. She said she screamed and bit Van Hattan, who stopped only when her mother came into the room. Adrianna Van Hattan gave similar testimony before the grand jury. Both had given statements to troopers the night of the attack that were consistent with their later grand jury testimony.

At the start of Van Hattan's trial on charges of attempted first degree sexual assault Mrs. Van Hattan and T.M.W. said they did not want to proceed with the prosecution and would refuse to testify. "At the state's request, depositions of both T.M.W. and Mrs. Van Hattan were taken; both witnesses responded to questions concerning the specifics of Van Hattan's assault either by claiming an inability to remember or by expressly refusing to answer."

Trial then began and after the two troopers who had arrested Van Hattan testified, T.M.W. was sworn and testified only to preliminary matters before again claiming she was "unable to recall most details." The prosecution then played to the jury a recording of her grand jury testimony. Sergeant Murphy then testified to the statements T.M.W. had made when he interviewed her at the residence. The trial judge admitted the grand jury recording under Alaska's Rule 801(d)(1)(A) and allowed Sergeant Murphy's testimony about her unsworn statement under Alaska Rule 613, both very similar to their federal counterparts.[1] Van Hattan was convicted, and sentenced to 10 years in prison (eight suspended on condition of five years' post-release probation).

On appeal, Van Hattan contended T.M.W.'s trial testimony was not testimony at all, and could not be considered to be inconsistent with the earlier statements. The Alaska Court of Appeals affirmed, choosing to adopt a "broad" view of inconsistency, thus following Wigmore, McCormick, Weinstein and most federal circuits. "Intentional" or feigned memory loss can well be considered inconsistent with prior sworn or unsworn statements for purposes of the respective rules. However, "genuine forgetfulness or loss of memory may not justify a finding of inconsistency" in all situations.

FRE 801(d)(1)(B) – Prior Consistent Statements of Witness Is Admissible Only if Made Before Motive to Fabricate Arose

> **Rule 801. Definitions.**
> *(d) Statements Which Are Not Hearsay.* A statement is not hearsay if
> *(1) Prior Statement by Witness.* The declarant testifies at the trial or hearing and is subject to cross-examination concerning the statement, and the statement is...
> (B) consistent with the declarant's testimony and is offered to rebut an express or implied charge against the declarant of recent fabrication or improper influence or motive...

TOME v. UNITED STATES
513 U.S. 150, 115 S. Ct. 696, 130 L. Ed. 2d 574 (1995)

Matthew Wayne Tome was convicted of the sexual abuse of his four-year-old daughter while she was in Tome's custody. The government claimed she disclosed the crime while spending vacation visitation with her mother. The defense theory was that the allegations were fabricated in the context of an ongoing custody dispute so that the mother could gain custody of their daughter.

The daughter testified at trial. Not yet seven years old by then, she gave testimony consisting of mostly "one- and two-word answers to a series of leading questions."[2] Cross examination of the little girl on the substance of the charges, coming a day after a meeting between the prosecutor and the witness, was difficult and inconclusive. "Reluctant at many points to answer," the child often waited nearly a full minute to answer a question and toward the end "seemed to be losing concentration."

To rebut the implicit charge of recent fabrication of the child's story, that it was motivated by a desire to live with her mother, the

---

[1] Most practitioners, of necessity pragmatic souls, will maintain that it hardly ever matters whether a prior inconsistent statement comes in *for its truth* under Rule 801(d)(1)(A) or *merely for impeachment* under Rule 613. (Their point is that if the jury hears the words it will be very difficult for them to restrict their consideration of the words to questions of credibility and not think of the words substantively.) However, *Van Hattan* is a tailor-made illustration that the difference can sometimes be very significant: often in domestic assault cases the victim recants her accusation, and without prior statements that are admissible *for their truth,* the prosecution is not able to prove a prima facie case.
[2] Permitted under the "as necessary" clause of FRE 611(c).

government then was permitted by the trial judge under Rule 801(d)(1)(B) to call six witnesses (the child's baby sitter, social worker, mother, and three pediatricians) who all recounted detailed statements the child had made about the sexual contact. Defense counsel objected, arguing that the statements made by the child that the six witnesses testified about had all been made *after* the child's motive to fabricate arose, and therefore could not "rebut a... charge against the declarant of recent fabrication."

The trial court and Tenth Circuit Court of Appeals had rejected as "too broad" any blanket "pre-motive" requirement for the admissibility of the statements, saying that was but one factor to be weighed in assessing the relevance of such testimony.

But the Supreme Court by a 5-4 vote reversed the conviction, returning to the common law rule that a prior consistent statement, to be admissible, must have been made before the motive to fabricate arose. The court noted the clear difference embodied in the Rule between "rebutting an alleged motive" to fabricate and generally "bolstering the veracity of the story told." The court explained, "A consistent statement [with the declarant's in-court testimony] that predates the motive is a square rebuttal of the charge that the testimony was contrived as a consequence of that motive." The court held that Rule 801(d)(1)(B) was meant to apply much more narrowly than as an aid to the jury's general assessment of the truthfulness of the in-court testimony.

FRE 801(d)(1)(C) – Out-of-Court Identification Is Admissible Only if Declarant Testifies at Trial

> **Rule 801. Definitions**
> The following definitions apply under this article:
> *(c) Hearsay.* "Hearsay" is a statement, other than one made by the declarant while testifying at the trial or hearing, offered in evidence to prove the truth of the matter asserted.
> *(d) Statements Which Are Not Hearsay.* A statement is not hearsay if
> *(1) Prior Statement by Witness.* The declarant testifies at the trial or hearing and is subject to cross-examination concerning the statement, and the statement is... (c) one of identification of a person made after perceiving the person...

STATE v. BARELA
643 P.2d 287, 97 N.M. 723 (1982)

Before the elderly victim of a Christmas Eve stabbing died four days later, he recovered enough to see visitors. The detective in charge of the case went to his hospital room and showed him a photo array. The victim identified Frankie Barela, who was by then a prime suspect. The victim was sick at the time of the stabbing. Either because the prosecutor didn't think the State could prove that the stabbing caused the death, or because they didn't think it was in fact the cause of the victim's death, Barela was charged with aggravated battery.

At trial in Otero County District Court the detective was allowed to testify to the hospital room identification of Barela by the victim. The jury convicted Barela and he was sentenced as a habitual offender. He appealed.

The Court of Appeals of New Mexico reversed, noting that the out-of-court identification did not comply with the requirement of New Mexico's Rule 801(d)(1)(C) (substantially identical to the federal rule of the same number) that the declarant must testify at the trial or hearing for his identification hearsay statement to be admitted.

(The appellate court also rejected the state's arguments that the identification was a "dying declaration"[3] because the victim was not shown to believe his death was imminent; that it fell under New Mexico's "statement of recent perception"[4] exception because it was made in response to a law enforcement officer's question for purposes of litigation; and that it fell within New Mexico's "catch-all" hearsay exception[5] because the circumstances surrounding the identification did not suggest reliability as strongly as those surrounding statements fitting within most hearsay exceptions.)

FRE 801(d)(2)(A)- Accused's Holdup Note Is Party Admission and as Such Is Substantive Evidence of Note's Contents

> **Rule 801. Definitions**
> The following definitions apply under this article:
> *(c) Hearsay.* "Hearsay" is a statement, other than one made by the declarant while testifying at the trial or hearing, offered in evidence to prove the truth of the matter asserted.
> *(d) Statements Which Are Not Hearsay.* A statement is not hearsay if
> *(2) Admission by Party-Opponent.* The statement is offered against a party and is (A) the party's own statement in either an individual or a representative capacity or (B) a statement of which the party has manifested an adoption or belief in its truth. [...]

BEAMON v. STATE
286 N.W.2d 592, 93 Wis.2d 215 (1980)

Nola Lee Beamon was charged with armed robbery, alleged to have robbed a Gimbels store in downtown Milwaukee of $5100 armed with a bottle of nitroglycerine. After Beamon's arrest the bottle was never found.

Beamon had passed a note to Lori Spredeman, a clerk in the cashier's office. The note was also read by Mary Pye, another Gimbels Employee. The note was never found either; Spredeman was allowed to testify that it said Beamon had a bottle of nitroglycerine and she would blow up the store if she wasn't given the money. At the close of proofs, Beamon moved to dismiss the armed robbery charge because there was no evidence of the "dangerous weapon" as required by Wisconsin statute. The trial judge denied the motion, and the jury convicted Beamon.

On appeal Beamon renewed her contention that her conviction "should be overturned because the state failed to produce any evidence demonstrating that she was armed with a dangerous weapon during the course of the robbery." The Wisconsin Supreme Court

---
[3] See FRE 804(b)(2).
[4] Rejected by the U.S. Congress, see proposed (deleted) FRE 804 (b)(2).
[5] See FRE 807.

affirmed, holding that the cashier's testimony about Beamon's note – which claimed the bottle contained nitroglycerine, and which threatened to blow up the store with it – was substantive evidence, being a party admission. "Its nature is not affected by the fact that the assertion by defendant was not made on the witness stand."

Note again that, as with the other party admission cases, the Wisconsin court is not saying the "admission" in the note is *binding,* or in any way *conclusive* proof that the bottle Beamon waved around actually did contain nitroglycerine. The holding is simply that the note is *some* evidence that it did, as capable of being contradicted, impeached, denied, or rebutted as any other piece of testimony, as much entitled to credit or disbelief as any other evidence. "This evidence is sufficient to have led a rational trier of fact to find that the defendant committed the robbery while armed with a dangerous weapon."

FRE 801(d)(2)(A),(C) – Admission in Pleadings in Another Case Is Not "Judicial Admission" in Current Case, But Is Admissible (and Rebuttable) as Party Admission

> **Rule 801. Definitions**
> The following definitions apply under this article:
> *(c) Hearsay.* "Hearsay" is a statement, other than one made by the declarant while testifying t the trial or hearing, offered in evidence to prove the truth of the matter asserted.
> *(d) Statements Which Are Not Hearsay.* A statement is not hearsay if
> *(2) Admissions by Party-Opponent.* The statement is offered against a party and is (A) the party's own statement in either an individual or a representative capacity or (B) a statement of which the party has manifested an adoption or belief in its truth, or (C) a statement by a person authorized by the party to make a statement concerning the subject…

CAMERON COUNTY v. VELASQUEZ
668 S.W.2d 776 (Tex. App. 1984)

After fooling around for 15 to 20 minutes on top of the pilot house of the 60-foot shrimp boat, *Kerry Dancer,* Jose Velasquez either dove or fell off, severely injuring his spine. The boat had run aground a month earlier on a sandbar just off Andy Bowie Park in Cameron County, Texas. Velasquez sued Cameron County under the Texas Tort Claims Act, alleging that the County had operated the park negligently by allowing the partially sunken boat to remain on its premises and by failing to remove it or to warn the public about its dangers. The County defended by contending that Velasquez's own negligence caused his injuries and that, in any event, the State of Texas, not the County, owned the site where the boat was stuck. The jury rendered a verdict that held that the County was 70% negligent and Velasquez 30%, which reduced his damages to $1,085,000. The County appealed. The Court of Appeals of Texas reversed and adjudged that Velasquez "take nothing by his suit."

A principal issue at trial had been who owned or controlled the place where the *Kerry*

Dancer was stuck in the sand. After Velasquez was injured, the County had filed suit against the owners of the *Kerry Dancer* for an injunction to force them to remove the boat from "the waters of Cameron County" and from "the beach of Andy Bowie Park." Velasquez filed a motion for rehearing, arguing that those words in the other suit constituted a "judicial admission," which would make it binding on the County in this action.

The appellate court, in an extensive discussion quoting McCormick, Wigmore and other authorities and cases, held the pleadings in the other suit were admissible as party admissions, but were not binding or conclusive as judicial admissions. To be judicial admissions, the statements would have to have been made in the pleadings of *this* case. These statements, although fully admissible against the County, were also fully susceptible of being denied, impeached, rebutted, contradicted, disavowed, or qualified. "They are merely some evidence," said the court, quoting another case, "and they are not conclusive upon the admitter. The weight to be given such admissions is decided by the trier of fact." The motion for rehearing was denied.

FRE 801(d)(2)(A) – Evidence of Speaker's Identity as Party May Be Circumstantial to Render Admissible Words Heard by Witness Who Cannot Identify Speaker

> **Rule 801. Definitions**
> The following definitions apply under this article:
> *(c) Hearsay.* "Hearsay" is a statement, other than one made by the declarant while testifying at the trial or hearing, offered in evidence to prove the truth of the matter asserted.
> *(d) Statements Which Are Not Hearsay.* A statement is not hearsay if
> *(2) Admission by Party-Opponent.* The statement is offered against a party and is (A) the party's own statement in either an individual or a representative capacity…

STATE v. MANICCIA
355 N.W.2d 256 (Iowa App. 1984)

Jon Michael Maniccia was charged with delivery of cocaine. An informant, Steve Norman, and undercover police officer McPherren went to Maniccia's home to buy cocaine. Conflicting testimony had either Maniccia going to the basement followed by the informant, or Maniccia refusing to go to the basement and the informant going himself to get cocaine. The informant was wired with a microphone and transmitter and was being monitored from two locations. At trial a Department of Criminal Investigations agent, Roger Timco, was permitted to testify about what he heard while monitoring the radio receiver. He said he heard "an unidentified male" say, "What do you want?" followed by the informant, Norman, responding, "A quarter, I guess." After some "hushed conversation or whispering," the unidentified male said, "You get the money from him, and take him to the basement." Later the same voice said,

"You can cut it with no problem," according to agent Timco. The defense had moved to exclude this testimony because of agent Timco's inability to identify the declarant.

The jury convicted Maniccia, and he appealed. The Court of Appeals of Iowa reversed on other grounds (see below) but agreed with the trial court's ruling on the unidentified admission issue. Ample corroboration existed that the voice talking to informant Norman belonged to Maniccia: "Officer McPherren, who was in the defendant's home when the statements were made, testified as to the persons present and their activities. While McPherren did not hear the statements testified to by agent Timco, his testimony regarding the persons present, as well as the defendant's actions during the transaction, does circumstantially corroborate Timco's testimony."

...

One of two grounds for reversal[6] amounts to a useful "heads up" to the future trial lawyer regarding hearsay practice. At trial the prosecution was allowed to have Officer McPherren testify as to what the informant *told* him that Maniccia *said* to him (to the effect that he didn't want to hand the cocaine directly to McPherren).[7] The prosecution argued that Norman's out-of-court statement about Maniccia's statement was not being offered for the truth of the matter(s) asserted, but was "introduced to explain subsequent conduct" of Officer McPherren. As the Iowa Court of Appeals correctly perceived, this explanation was nonsense. Officer McPherren's "conduct as an undercover police officer in this transaction could easily be explained without resorting to the use of the statements admitted here." There was no other rational use for the statements except to "prove the defendant's involvement... in this alleged cocaine transaction." Criminal defense counsel especially must remain vigilant for pretext offerings of such rank hearsay.

FRE 801(d)(2)(B) – Reliance on Deposition in Legal Proceedings Amounts to Adopting It for Admissibility as Adoptive Admission

> **Rule 801.**
> *(d) Statements Which Are Not Hearsay.* A statement is not hearsay if
> *(2) Admission by Party-Opponent.* The statement is offered against a party and is...
> (B) a statement of which the party has manifested an adoption or belief in its truth...

SAUDI ARABIAN AIRLINES CORPORATION v. DUNN
438 So.2d 116 (Fla. App. 1983)

Hazza Saud Al-Faqeer, driving his cousin's car to a grocery store in October 1979, lost control of it in a Jacksonville intersection. The car went airborne and landed on top of Thomas Dunn's car, causing Dunn severe head injuries. Al-Faqeer was in the U.S. as an

---

[6] The other was that because the state had erased a tape recording of the transaction, allegedly because it was unintelligible from static, the jury should have been instructed to make an inference adverse to the state and favorable to Maniccia.

[7] A party admission within inadmissible hearsay – see Rule 805, which requires *both* hearsay components to be admissible independently.

employee of Saudi Arabian Airlines to learn English and to go to technical training school. Dunn sued Al-Faqeer and his cousin, Abdullah Ali Shihry. When Dunn's attorney took Al-Faqeer's deposition two months later and learned why Al-Faqeer was in this country, the complaint was eventually amended to add Saudi Arabian Airlines under respondeat superior. Saudi Arabian filed a "motion to abate for lack of jurisdiction," citing Al-Faqeer's deposition for factual support of the proposition that he was not acting within the course and scope of his employment at the time of the accident. When the motion was denied, Saudi Arabian appealed. The Florida First District Court of Appeal turned Saudi Arabian down, and the case went to trial.

At trial, after Al-Faqeer was fired by the airline and returned to Saudi Arabia, Dunn was permitted over defense objection to introduce parts of Al-Faqeer's deposition into evidence. The jury awarded Dunn $325,000 damages against all defendants. The airline appealed, reiterating its objection, among several issues, to Dunn's use of the deposition because it was not a party to the suit at the time it was given.

The Court of Appeal affirmed the verdict and held the deposition admissible as an adoptive admission under the Florida Evidence Code.[8] Saudi manifested its adoption or belief in its truth when, in its interlocutory appeal, it "relied on Al-Faqeer's deposition testimony as support for its position that Al-Faqeer was not acting in the course and scope of his employment," and again later when it "asserted it as a basis for its motion for summary judgment."

Of course, "adopting" the deposition's contents only gets it into evidence; it is not "legally binding" on Saudi, and the company remains free to disavow it, rebut it, impeach it, and characterize its contents to the jury as unreliable, unbelievable, and so forth.

FRE 801(d)(2)(B) – Words Spoken to Party Are Admissible as Adoptive Admission if Sufficient Facts Are Introduced for Jury to Conclude Party Heard, Understood, and Acceded to Statement

---

Rule 801. Definitions
The following definitions apply under this article:
(c) Hearsay. "Hearsay" is a statement, other than one made by the declarant while testifying at the trial or hearing, offered in evidence to prove the truth of the matter asserted.
(d) Statements Which Are Not Hearsay. A statement is not hearsay if
(2) Admission by Party-Opponent. The statement is offered against a party and is
(A) the party's own statement in either an individual or a representative capacity or
(B) a statement of which the party has manifested an adoption or belief in its truth. [...]

---

[8] As several states continue to do and as was the case at common law, Florida's Evidence Code makes party admissions of all varieties admissible as *exceptions* to the ban on hearsay, not as *"non-hearsay"* the way the Federal Rules do (Fla.Stat.Ann. 90.803(18)(A)-(E)). Party admissions are, after all, out-of-court statements offered for their truth; to categorize them as "non-hearsay" only because they come in for reasons that are thought to be different from the reasons underlying most of the Rule 803 and 804 exceptions seems needless sophistry. It is certainly an academic's distinction not a practitioner's. It also ignores the wide variety of reasons for the other exceptions, not all of which trade primarily in reliability.

UNITED STATES v. MONKS
774 F.2d 945 (9th Cir. 1985)

Gary Holt and Charles Monks arrived at the home of convicted bank robber James White's mother. Monks told White they had just robbed a branch of Arizona's Union Bank. White testified that Holt brought in some clothing and asked White to destroy it, and that he also brought in a bag of money that Monks divided into two shares. When White went to the FBI, and Monks and Holt were arrested, a jail officer heard Monks tell Holt the only thing he had to worry about was being photographed by the bank camera. At the joint trial of Holt and Monks, the two statements by Monks were admitted into evidence, as direct admissions against Monks[9] and as adoptive admissions against Holt. Both appealed their convictions on a variety of grounds.

Holt contended that when he and Monks were in White's bedroom, and Monks said they'd just robbed a bank, he was too "plastered" to be able to understand and acquiesce in Monks' statement. However, the Ninth Circuit Court of Appeals panel noted that "Holt was able to comment on how easy the robbery was, participate in the discussion about the police pulling over the wrong car, bring in a bag of clothes and tell White to bury it or burn it, and shave off his mustache. It is therefore doubtful that he could do all of these things and yet not be able to hear Monks' statement or deny it" if he were innocent, as one would expect an innocent man to do.

As to Holt's silence in response to Monks' comment about the bank camera at the jail, Holt argued that his silence reflected mere prudence inasmuch as the conversation was taking place in a holding cell where other prisoners and jail personnel could overhear anything he said. The appellate court, however, said that since Monks' words could be heard by anyone in the vicinity, "it is more reasonable to expect Holt to make some exculpatory response, rather than do nothing and give the other inmates reason to believe he was acquiescing in Monks' comments. A jury reasonably could conclude that Holt acquiesced in Monks' comments. The district court did not abuse its discretion in allowing Monks' comments to come in as adoptive admissions."

(Monks did not testify at trial. Holt also argued that when Monks' statements came in, he was thus denied his Sixth Amendment right to confront Monks about the statements attributed to him. The court held that since Holt "adopted" Monks' statement, a recognized hearsay exception was implicated, taking the matter out of the Clause[10] since Monks was "unavailable" and the statement was "reliable" in that Monks had personal knowledge of the matter and the remarks were made within two weeks of the robbery.)

---

[9] Under FRE 801(d)(2)(A).
[10] See also *White v. Illinois, infra* p. 212.

FRE 801(d)(2)(B) – Accused's Nod in Acknowledgment of Characterization by Another Renders Characterization Admissible as Adoptive Admission

> **Rule 801. Definitions**
> The following definitions apply under this article:
> *(c) Hearsay.* "Hearsay" is a statement, other than one made by the declarant while testifying at the trial or hearing, offered in evidence to prove the truth of the matter asserted.
> *(d) Statements Which Are Not Hearsay.* A statement is not hearsay if
> *(2) Admission by Party-Opponent.* The statement is offered against a party and is (A) the party's own statement in either an individual or a representative capacity or (B) a statement of which the party has manifested an adoption or belief in its truth. [...]

UNITED STATES v. WISEMAN
814 F.2d 826 (1st Cir. 1987)

An ostensible drug buy was set up by Drug Enforcement Agent Reginald Tillery operating undercover. Tillery had already scored heroin several times from Melvin Smith and Otis Glenn when Smith brought Paul Wiseman to a Dorchester, Massachusetts restaurant to meet with Tillery. Smith introduced Wiseman to Tillery by saying, in substance, "This here is Mac. He was brought up from the City to help distribute the junk on the street because business has been so good." Wiseman nodded at the introduction. When Smith and Wiseman were arrested the next day, Wiseman was found to have 27 packets of heroin in his underwear, packaged the same way and with the same degree of purity as heroin found on Smith.

At Wiseman's bench trial on charges of possession and conspiracy to possess with intent to distribute heroin, Agent Tillery was permitted to testify over the defense's hearsay objection to Smith's characterization of Wiseman when he introduced him to the agent, and to say that Wiseman nodded "in silent acknowledgment of the introduction." Wiseman attempted to argue that he didn't understand English or that he didn't understand the word "junk" to mean heroin, but the district judge took Wiseman's nod, his voluntary appearance at the scene of a drug deal twice in two days, and the fact (judicially noticed[11]) that "junk" is a "common synonym for heroin in New York and Boston" as ample support for the finding that Wiseman knew what Smith was saying and agreed with it. "Under these circumstances it would have been natural for an innocent person to object to the characterization of why he was there. The defendant failed to do that...."

Wiseman was convicted, and he appealed, in part on the hearsay/adoptive admission issue. The First Circuit Court of Appeals affirmed on all counts, and in Wiseman's argument that he might not have been sufficiently familiar with the terminology employed by Smith for Smith's remark to be a true adoptive admission, the appellate court found "no merit:... From other evidence, the [district] court was well aware appellant could understand English; the fact that, when searched, he was carrying 27 packets of heroin was evidence, if any were needed, that he was no stranger to street jargon."

As always with party admissions, it should be noted that Wiseman was free to dispute the court's finding for admissibility purposes that he understood Smith's words and acknowledged them with his nod.

---
[11] See FRE 201.

FRE 801(d)(2)(C) – Doctor's Statement About Patient to Specialist Authorized by Patient Who Sought Referral Is Admissible as Party-Authorized Admission

> **Rule 801. Definitions**
> The following definitions apply under this article:
> *(c) Hearsay.* "Hearsay" is a statement, other than one made by the declarant while testifying at the trial or hearing, offered in evidence to prove the truth of the matter asserted.
> *(d) Statements Which Are Not Hearsay.* A statement is not hearsay if
> *(2) Admission by Party-Opponent.* The statement is offered against a party and is...
> (C) a statement by a person authorized by the party to make a statement concerning the subject...

COVINGTON v. SAWYER
458 N.E.2d 465, 9 Ohio App. 3d 40 (1983)

Virginia Price's slow-moving car was struck from behind by a Coca-Cola truck being driven by Kevin Sawyer. Although relatively slight damage was inflicted on Price's car ($200 to $300) in this August 1978 accident, her Franklin County Common Pleas Court lawsuit against Sawyer and Coca-Cola claimed substantial damages in that the accident was alleged to have caused her pre-existing breast cancer to spread. (She died of cancer in 1981 and her executrix, Donna M. Covington, pursued the suit on behalf of her estate.)

Price's general practitioner, Dr. John Stephens, detected her cancer in late 1972 and referred her to a surgeon, Dr. Francis Barnes, for a biopsy, which was finally done in January 1974. Both doctors diagnosed early cancer of the breast ducts and recommended a mastectomy. Price, resistant to the idea, asked Barnes to refer her to Dr. George Crile, a breast cancer specialist at the Cleveland Clinic. Dr. Crile agreed with the diagnosis and with the recommendation for a mastectomy. Price refused. By June 1979, 10 months after the accident, when Price was admitted to the hospital, the cancer had spread to her bones, causing spontaneous fractures. A major question at trial (apparently bypassing a more fundamental issue as to causation[12]) was *when* the cancer had spread from the breast's duct system to surrounding breast tissue or into the lymphatic system.

Dr. Barnes testified that in March 1978, five months before the accident, Dr. Stephens told him that "Price had a rather sizable breast mass and the cancer had spread to the axilla or armpit...indicating the cancer had spread from the breast to the lymphatics." (Stephens testified at trial he did not think the cancer had spread before the accident.)

The jury awarded Price's estate $1,052, "substantially less" than the amount sought, and Covington appealed, raising the issue of Dr. Stephens' out-of-court statement among several. The Ohio Court of Appeals, Franklin County, affirmed. The court said Dr. Stephens was "implicitly authorized" to discuss Price's case with Dr. Barnes by the 1972 referral, and Barnes' testimony recounting Stephens' statement was offered against Price as an authorized statement, or admission.

---
[12] See, e.g., *Daubert v. Merrell Dow Pharmaceuticals, Inc.*, supra p. 179.

"A patient whose general practitioner refers her to a specialist for diagnosis and interpretation of specific symptoms, particularly at the patient's own request, authorizes her doctor to discuss her symptoms with the specialist. If we were to decide that Dr. Stephens was not authorized by Price to discuss Price's case with the specialist to whom she had been referred, a general practitioner would have no reason to refer a case to a specialist and would be prohibited from using the specialist's more specific training and knowledge. We would also be denying a rather obvious inference that virtually every patient with a potential serious disorder expects that his or her referring doctor will discuss the diagnosis and treatment with a specialist to whom the patient has been referred. Thus, since Dr. Stephens was authorized by Price to make statements to Dr. Barnes regarding the subject of Price's cancer, Dr. Barnes' testimony repeating Dr. Stephens statement" was admissible under Ohio's equivalent of Federal Rule 801(d)(2)(C) as an authorized admission.

FRE 801(d)(2)(D) – For Statement of Purported Agent to Be Admissible Against Principal as Agent-Admission, the Agency Relationship Must Be Established by More Than Conduct of Purported Agent Alone

> **Rule 801. Definitions**
> The following definitions apply under this article:
> *(c) Hearsay.* "Hearsay" is a statement, other than one made by the declarant while testifying at the trial or hearing, offered in evidence to prove the truth of the matter asserted.
> *(d) Statements Which Are Not Hearsay.* A statement is not hearsay if
> *(2) Admission by Party-Opponent.* The statement is offered against a party and is …
> (D) a statement by the party's agent or servant concerning a matter within the scope of the agency or employment, made during the existence of the relationship. […]

PRZERADSKI v. REXNORD, INC.
326 N.W.2d 541, 119 Mich. App. 500 (1982)

Robert and Connie Przeradski were remodeling their home in 1972. While cleaning a Rexnord cement mixer, Connie Przeradski fell and her long hair became entangled in a moving winch. Neither she nor her husband could disengage her from it nor shut off the machine before she was killed. Robert filed a wrongful death action against Rexnord based on product liability, alleging Rexnord breached express and implied warranties, manufactured an inherently dangerous product, and was grossly negligent.

To establish that Rexnord was negligent in not providing adequate warnings, Robert Przeradski tried to testify himself that he was told by employees of a retail store that carried Rexnord products that an owner's manual for the cement mixer was unavailable. Rexnord objected to their out-of-court statements as hearsay, and the trial court sustained the objection. Ultimately the jury returned a verdict of no cause of action, and Przeradski appealed, on that ground among several.

The Michigan Court of Appeals affirmed the verdict, and on the issue of the store employees' statements the court noted that Przeradski "had not established an agency relationship" between Rexnord and the retail outlet. "The apparent authority of an agent to speak on behalf of a principal may not be established by the acts and conduct of the agent alone." Nor, apparently, may agency be presumed merely from obvious appearances, for purposes of the agent-admission rule. (Michigan's rule is substantially identical to its federal counterpart.)

FRE 801(d)(2)(D) – Internal Corporate Memorandum Between Party's Employees Is Admissible Against Corporate Party as Agent – Admission Even if Self-Serving

> **Rule 801. Definitions**
> The following definitions apply under this article:
> *(c) Hearsay.* "Hearsay" is a statement, other than one made by the declarant while testifying at the trial or hearing, offered in evidence to prove the truth of the matter asserted.
> *(d) Statements Which Are Not Hearsay.* A statement is not hearsay if
> *(2) Admission by Party-Opponent.* The statement is offered against a party and is ...
> (D) a statement by the party's agent or servant concerning a matter within the scope of the agency or employment, made during the existence of the relationship...

SCIENTIFIC APPLICATIONS, INC. v. DELKAMP
303 N.W.2d 71 (N.D. 1981)

After Darryl Delkamp attended a demonstration of "Spraylock," a catalytic coating product applied with a spray gun attached to two tanks, he became a dealer and went into business as Capitol Homefoamers Inc., entering into contracts to spray-seal several homes and agricultural buildings. He experienced difficulties with clogging and impurities in the resin product, and when Spraylock's distributor, Scientific Applications, Inc., sued him in state district court for nonpayment of his account, Delkamp countersued for damages, lost profits and promotional expenses. A jury returned a verdict slightly in excess of $100,000 in favor of Delkamp, and the trial judge ordered a $65,000 reduction in the verdict. Both parties appealed.

Among many questions involving the North Dakota Commercial Code, one interesting evidentiary issue was raised by Scientific. Delkamp offered into evidence a memorandum written by Scientific's Minneapolis Division Manager, Jim Young, to another corporate employee, Gary Lappe, whose title is unspecified. Young's memo details many faults with the Spraylock product, process and equipment and recommends that the company "take back all equipment and all material on hand at actual cost and credit dealers account." Scientific had objected to the memo as hearsay, prejudicial and self-serving.

The North Dakota Supreme Court affirmed the lower court judgment on all counts. Specifically the court noted that Scientific responded to Delkamp's requests for admissions by confirming that both Young and Lappe were corporate employees at the time the memo was written,[13] and therefore the state

---
[13]Cf., *Przeradski v. Rexnord, Inc.,* supra p. 205.

rule equivalent of Federal Rule 801(d)(2)(D) was satisfied. The memo was damaging to Scientific, but hardly prejudicial in the sense of misleading the jury.[14] And finally, the court said "Declarations are admissible even though they are self-serving... Scientific had an opportunity to explain it... could have introduced evidence concerning the reliability of the memo."

FRE 801(d)(2)(D) – Statement by Government Agent Cannot Be Party/Agent-Admission in Criminal Prosecution

> **Rule 801. Definitions.**
> *(d) Statements Which Are Not Hearsay.* A statement is not hearsay if
> *(2) Admission by Party-Opponent.* The statement is offered against a party and is...
> (D) a statement by the party's agent or servant concerning a matter within the scope of the agency or employment, made during the existence of the relationship...

UNITED STATES v. SANTOS
372 F.2d 177 (2d Cir. 1967)

After a trial that ended in a hung jury, Armando Santos was tried a second time for assaulting a federal narcotics officer with a deadly weapon. Santos offered in evidence a sworn affidavit by narcotics agent Edward Dower that someone else, not Santos, had committed the assault. The defense theory was that the affidavit was admissible as an admission against the government. The trial court excluded the affidavit. Following his conviction Santos appealed.

The Second Circuit Court of Appeals observed that "if the defense had adopted different trial tactics" Dower's affidavit would have been admissible to impeach his trial testimony as a prior inconsistent statement.

But in a criminal trial, there can be no party admission by a government agent: "When the Government prosecutes, it prosecutes on behalf of all the people of the United States; therefore all persons, whether law enforcement agents, government investigators, complaining prosecuting witnesses, or the like, who testify on behalf of the prosecution and who, because of an employment relation or other personal interest in the outcome of the prosecution, may happen to be inseparably connected with the government side of the adversary process, stand in relation to the United States and in relation to the defendant no differently from persons unconnected with... the prosecution." Therefore, the statements are not admissible substantively, i.e., as "evidence of the fact," in criminal prosecutions, although the Second Circuit went out of its way to note that the affidavit would have been admissible against the government as a substantive admission in a civil case.

In affirming Santos' conviction, the appellate court noted that the government and its agents "are supposedly uninterested personally in the outcome of the trial." To counteract "the seeming unfairness" of allowing a defendant's statements to be admissible as party admissions but not so for a government agent's statements, the court noted Congress has enacted a statutory provision requiring the government to turn

---
[14] See Rule 403.

over to the defense any statements its witnesses have given that are inconsistent with their trial testimony so the defense may impeach them.

Despite criticism of this holding, *Santos* remains good law today, having survived the enactment of Rule 801(d)(2)(D).[15]

FRE 801(d)(2)(D) – Agent-Admission by Government Department Is Admissible in Civil Case

> **Rule 801. Definitions**
> *(d) Statements Which Are Not Hearsay.* A statement is not hearsay if
> *(2) Admission by Party-Opponent.* The statement is offered against a party and is...
> (D) a statement by the party's agent or servant concerning a matter within the scope of the agency or employment, made during the existence of the relationship...

BURKEY v. ELLIS
483 F. Supp. 897 (N.D. Ala. 1979)

Olivia Burkey, as administratrix for the estate of Earle Montgomery, deceased, sought an injunction against the Soil Conservation Service of the U.S. Department of Agriculture, to prevent SCS from proceeding with a stream modification and channelization project that involved eight miles of Blue-Eye Creek in Talledega County, Alabama. It included a stretch running through lands owned by Montgomery.

SCS omitted from its Revised Environmental Impact Statement information generated by the Corps of Engineers about downstream flooding that was contrary to its own conclusions. The Corps had written, in a letter in 1971 in connection with a mall project on another river, that such channelization causes water velocity to increase and thus accelerates erosion and downstream flooding. The district court held that "when facts contrary to the conclusions advanced by SCS are known to them or its sister agencies of the government, it is necessary to disclose them in an EIS...."

The court dealt with the central party admission issue obliquely, and in a footnote at that. It appears the Corps of Engineers letter was offered by the plaintiffs, satisfying the "offered against the party" provision. Considering the requirement embodied in part D of the rule, the court characterized the statements in the Corps' letter an "inconsistent statements of an agent of the same principal, i.e., the U.S. Government.... Preparation of an EIS and consultation regarding similar matters are certainly within the scope of authority of the Corps of Engineers.... If SCS feels it can refute or explain away facts that are contrary to its conclusions, then it is free to do so...."

Of course, the observed "inconsistency" of the Corps' letter with the SCS Environmental Impact Statement is not itself a *sine qua non* of admissibility; relevance is all that is necessary as a content test of a party admission. Here relevance is supplied by that inconsistency as well as by the substance of the letter's conclusions.[16]

---

[15] See *Burkey v. Ellis, infra* p. 208, holding that there can be an agent-admission admissible against the government in civil cases.
[16] See *United States v. Santos, supra* p. 207, holding there can be no party admission by the government in criminal cases.

FRE 801(d)(2)(E) – Agreement to Conceal Crime Does Not Extend Life of Conspiracy for Purpose of "During the Course" Clause

> **Rule 801.**
> *(d) Statements Which Are Not Hearsay.* A statement is not hearsay if...
> *(2) Admission by Party-Opponent.* The statement is offered against a party and is...
> (E) a statement by a coconspirator of a party during the course and in furtherance of the conspiracy. The contents of the statement shall be considered but are not alone sufficient to establish... the existence of the conspiracy and the participation therein of the declarant and the party against whom the statement is offered under subdivision (E).

STATE v. YSLAS
676 P.2d 1118, 139 Ariz. 60 (1984)

Henry Tona Garcia and Art Pain were driving around Tucson one night in August 1981 looking for a lawnmower to steal. At the El Dorado bar around 1:30 a.m. they were joined by Joseph Louis Yslas and someone called "Gaby." Yslas told them where they might find a lawnmower and a house to burglarize too. They drove to the home of an elderly woman, Gregoria Pesqueria. Yslas and Pain took bolt cutters they had brought along and went in. Garcia left with Gaby and when he came back alone, Pain asked where he had been, and told Garcia, "He hit her." After a night of loading Pesqueria's personal property in the car trunk and trying to retrieve everything that might have their fingerprints on it, Pain was confronted by Garcia's sister, Rosemary Perez, and told her Yslas had "hit her" with a "fierro," apparently referring to the bolt-cutters. Early that morning Mrs. Pesqueria was found dead of a skull fracture. Sometime later Yslas, Garcia and Pain were arrested, and the bloody bolt-cutters were surrendered by Garcia.

At the Pima County Superior Court jury trial of Yslas on charges of first-degree murder, second-degree burglary, and theft of property, the Pain statements to Perez and Garcia were admitted into evidence over defense objection as party admissions attributable to Yslas through the co-conspirator rule. Yslas was convicted on all charges and sentenced to prison.

He appealed the conviction, contending that the Pain statements should not have been admitted as co-conspirator admissions. The Arizona Supreme Court reversed, holding that the statement to Perez was not made during the course of any conspiracy because the final act of the conspiracy seemed to be the division of the property, and when Perez confronted Pain later, all they were doing was "unplanned-for 'cover-up' activity which was not part of the original conspiracy."

As to the Pain statement to Garcia, the Arizona court looked at the "usual rule" for determining whether the statement was made during the course of the conspiracy, and determined that the object of the conspiracy, if any, was to steal stuff: "Garcia and Pain initially had only planned on stealing a lawnmower and only if they happened to find one within easy reach. It is unclear that after meeting appellant they had any specific plans for what they would steal when they reached the victim's house. Granting that there was a plan to steal anything of value that was found, it is unlikely, and there is no evidence that the criminals' plans originally went so far as to formulate the methods of escape, disposal of the fruits of the crime, and/or concealment of the crime." (Of course, under that view, the conspiracy did not extend to the act of murder at all, and Yslas would have been acting alone, so Pain's statement to Garcia wouldn't have had anything to do with the "original" conspiracy.)

(The state Supreme Court offered possibly gratuitous instruction to the trial court for the retrial of the case: Pain's statement to Garcia, given Pain's agitation and breathlessness, should be admitted as an excited utterance under Arizona's Rule 803(2).)

FRE 801(d)(2)(E) – "In Furtherance" Requirement for Admissibility of Co-Conspirator Admission Is Separate and Distinct from "During the Course" Requirement

> **Rule 801.**
> *(d) Statements Which Are Not Hearsay.* A statement is not hearsay if...
> *(2) Admission by Party-Opponent.* The statement is offered against a party and is... (E) a statement by a coconspirator of a party during the course and in furtherance of the conspiracy. The contents of the statement shall be considered but are not alone sufficient to establish... the existence of the conspiracy and the participation therein of the declarant and the party against whom the statement is offered under subdivision (E).

WILLIAMSON v. STATE
692 P.2d 965 (Alaska App. 1984)

When they left the Hallea Lodge on Halloween night, 1981, Ronald Williamson shot and killed John Dunkin, either while fending off a homosexual rape or in an attempted robbery, depending on whose testimony is credited. Afterwards Williamson and his friend Otis Orth drove the body to a remote location and mutilated it "almost beyond recognition," then hid Dunkin's car and his valuables separately. Williamson was charged with robbery, second degree murder and tampering with physical evidence. A jury in Anchorage District Court convicted him of manslaughter and the evidence tampering charge.

He appealed to the Court of Appeals of Alaska. One issue he raised concerned testimony about a statement Orth made in another bar while Williamson and Dunkin were gone. Patricia Lynn Boyles had been allowed to testify that at about 1:30 a.m., at Huppies Roadhouse in Wasilla, she asked Orth where Williamson was, and he replied, "He went out to roll a queer who had a lot of money." The trial judge admitted the statement as a co-conspirator admission under Alaska Rule of Evidence 801(d)(2)(E), which follows the requirements of the corresponding federal rule.

The state Court of Appeals deliberately chose to forego an analysis of whether there was in fact any conspiracy in existence. "Even assuming that the existence of a conspiracy between Williamson and Orth had been independently established by a preponderance of the evidence,... it is difficult to conceive how Orth could be found to be advancing the purpose of the joint undertaking by casually divulging it to witnesses." This is an important *separate* requirement from the mere continuing existence of the conspiracy at the time the statement is made – and a requirement the prosecution is often tempted to slight.

(The state on appeal conceded the error, arguing instead that its admission was harmless error. The appellate court noted how the hearsay statement directly undermined Williamson's "assertion of an innocent motive," and held the error grounds for reversal.)

FRE 801(d)(2)(E) – Telephone Call Recruiting Additional Participant Is Admissible as Co-Conspirator Admission if Other Evidence Is Adequate to Establish Prior Conspiracy; Post-Arrest Statement Is Inadmissible Because Conspiracy Terminated.

> **Rule 801.**
> *(c) Hearsay.* "Hearsay" is a statement, other than one made by the declarant while testifying at the trial or hearing, offered in evidence to prove the truth of the matter asserted.
> *(d) Statements Which Are Not Hearsay.* A statement is not hearsay if
> *(2) Admission by Party-Opponent.* The statement is offered against a party and is (E) a statement by a coconspirator of a party during the course and in furtherance of the conspiracy.

BERGERON v. STATE
271 N.W.2d 386, 85 Wis.2d 595 (1978)

Marvin Boguskie was shot to death with a 12-gauge shotgun in his Green Bay backyard. He was the stepfather of co-defendant Terry Neeley, who wanted to kill Boguskie because of mistreatment of his mother. Neeley and Walter Bergeron were charged with asking John Schroeder to find someone to do the job; Schroeder allegedly hired Mark Moes to do it for $1,000, with Schroeder getting a $100 finder's fee. All four were charged with first degree murder as co-conspirators.

At Bergeron's trial, he testified to the plan to kill Boguskie. He said he told Neeley that he wouldn't do the murder but would find someone who would. He claimed he withdrew from the conspiracy before it achieved the murder, in that after Moes was unable to shoot Boguskie as he left work on December 29, 1975, because there were too many people around, at a December 30 meeting all murder plans were called off, according to testimony of both Bergeron and Neeley. (Boguskie was shot the evening of December 30.)

During the State's case-in-chief, Schroeder testified over the defense's objection to his telephone conversation with Moes in which he offered the thousand dollar if Moes would kill Boguskie. This was considered a key fact in establishing the existence of the conspiracy. The trial judge found the statements were co-conspirator admissions. Bergeron was found guilty by the jury and sentenced to life in prison. He appealed.

The Wisconsin Supreme Court affirmed. Bergeron argued that no conspiracy existed until a meeting the day after Schroeder's phone call to Moes, so the phone call was not during the course of the conspiracy as required by Wisconsin's counterpart to Federal Rule 801(d)(2)(E). The appellate court, however, found adequate evidence that the conspiracy as to Neeley, Bergeron and Schroeder began before Moes was contacted.

"A conspiracy commences with an agreement between 2 or more persons to direct their conduct toward the realization of a criminal objective and each member of the conspiracy must individually and consciously intend the realization of the particular criminal venture," the court pronounced, then recited all the facts going to the existence of a conspiracy to kill Boguskie well before the Schroeder call to Moes. "Conspiracies usually develop in successive stages when essential parties are recruited to fulfill the illegal scheme."

The trial court had also admitted into evidence a post-arrest statement given by Neeley (the full contents of which are unspecified). The Wisconsin Supreme Court held that this statement was not made in furtherance of the conspiracy as required, but that its admission into evidence was harmless error because it was "not factually prejudicial to the defendant as the statement was consistent with the defendant's withdrawal defense," and Neeley confirmed the incriminating portions with his in-court testimony.

Sixth Amendment – Confrontation Clause: Hearsay Is Fully Admissible Under Traditional Exceptions Against Criminal Defendant

> **U.S. Constitution, Sixth Amendment:**
> In all criminal prosecutions, the accused shall enjoy the right… to be confronted with the witnesses against him.
>
> **Rule 803. Hearsay Exceptions; Availability of Declarant Immaterial**
> The following are not excluded by the hearsay rule, even though the declarant is available as a witness:
>
> *(2) Excited Utterance.* A statement relating to a startling event or condition made while the declarant was under the stress of excitement caused by the event or condition.
>
> *(4) Statements for Purposes of Medical Diagnosis or Treatment.* Statements made for purposes of medical diagnosis or treatment and describing medical history, or past or present symptoms, pain, or sensations, or the inception or general character of the cause or external source thereof insofar as reasonably pertinent to diagnosis or treatment.

WHITE v. ILLINOIS
502 U.S. 346, 112 S.Ct. 736, 116 L. Ed. 2d 848 (1992)

Randall White was convicted by a jury of a number of charges related to a sexual assault upon a four-year-old girl. The victim was not technically unavailable but did not testify at trial. Her mother, her babysitter, an investigating officer, a doctor and an emergency room nurse all recounted the victim's statements describing the crime, which was permitted by the trial court under state law hearsay exceptions for spontaneous declarations[17] and for statements made in the course of obtaining medical treatment.[18]

White appealed, arguing that admission of the child's out-of-court statements against him violated the Confrontation Clause of the constitution.

---
[17] Cf. FRE 803(2).
[18] Cf. FRE 803(4).

The Supreme Court affirmed. It followed a line of recent cases that hold that the purposes of the Confrontation Clause of the Sixth Amendment are fully served by the safeguards present in the traditional, well established hearsay exceptions. Hearsay falling within an established exception is thus admissible in criminal cases against the defendant. The Court also clarified a few recent cases by holding here that the declarant need not be shown to be legally unavailable[19] if the hearsay exceptions invoked do not require unavailability.

(The United States, as *amicus,* urged the court to adopt the narrowest of interpretations of the Confrontation Clause, and to hold that its purpose was only to prevent trial by *ex parte* affidavits, common in 16th and 17th century England. The court formally rejected this interpretation.)

FRE 803(1) – Hearsay Exception: Present Sense Impression Is Admissible Even if Declarant Is Not Identified

Rule 803. Hearsay Exceptions; Availability of Declarant Immaterial
The following are not excluded by the hearsay rule, even though the declarant is available as a witness:
(1) Present Sense Impression. A statement describing or explaining an event or condition made while the declarant was perceiving the event or condition, or immediately thereafter.

FIRST STATE BANK OF DENTON v. MARYLAND CASUALTY CO.
918 F.2d 38 (5th Cir. 1990)

The Mills residence, insured by the Maryland Casualty Insurance Company, was completely destroyed by fire. The policy provided that in the event of total loss, J.T. Mills would receive $133,000, the face amount of the policy. After inspecting the site, the insurance company concluded that the fire was set intentionally and refused to make payment on the policy. Mills sued to recover on the policy, but died before trial. The First State Bank of Denton continued the claim as executor.

At trial, the insurance company introduced evidence that showed that the house was unoccupied for several weeks prior to the fire, but a neighbor had seen a light in the home a few hours before the fire. The insurance company also introduced the testimony of a witness who testified that, right before the fire started, he had seen a pickup truck leaving the road that provided access to the Mills home. Only Mills and his wife had a key to the house, and Mills owned a pickup truck.

The insurance company concluded its case by introducing evidence that showed Mills was not at his new home at the time the fire started. About 15 minutes after the fire began, a police dispatcher attempted to contact Mills at his new residence to notify him of the fire. The dispatcher testified that when she called for Mills, an unidentified person answered, left the phone, and then returned reporting that Mills was not at home. The plaintiff

---
[19] Cf. FRE 804(a),(b).

objected, arguing these statements were inadmissible hearsay. The trial court admitted the statements over the objection.

After a jury verdict for Maryland Casualty, the plaintiff appealed, contending again that the contents of the phone call were inadmissible hearsay. The Fifth Circuit Court of Appeals affirmed the verdict, citing Rule 803(1) in support of the admissibility of the statements. The court noted, "The statements were made virtually on the heels of the discovery that Mills was not at home." The court concluded that the "substantial contemporaneity of [the] event and statement negate the likelihood of deliberate or conscious misrepresentation."

The failure of the defense to ascertain the identity of the declarant was not fatal – or even significant – to the applicability of the present sense impression hearsay exception.

FRE 803(1) – Hearsay Exception: Statement Made Several Minutes After Event Is Too Late for Admissibility as Present Sense Impression

> **Rule 803. Hearsay Exceptions; Availability of Declarant Immaterial**
> The following are not excluded by the hearsay rule, even though the declarant is available as a witness:
> *(1) Present Sense Impression.* A statement describing or explaining an event or condition made while the declarant was perceiving the event or condition, or immediately thereafter.

HEWITT v. GRAND TRUNK WESTERN RAILROAD CO.
333 N.W.2d 264, 123 Mich. App. 309 (1983)

David Hewitt, 55 years old, married 35 years, in good spirits, was hit by a train and killed as it crossed Fifth Street in downtown Royal Oak, Michigan in January 1972. His widow, Dorothy, sued Grand Trunk Western Railroad Co. claiming a metal band that had secured a load of wooden crates on a flat car toward the rear of the train had broken when the crates shifted. The band, Hewitt contended, stuck out from the side of the train and knocked her husband into the train. Grand Trunk defended on a theory of suicide.

The deposition of one teenage witness was admitted. He couldn't tell whether Hewitt jumped into the train or was hit by it, "as Mr. Hewitt was already in motion and was being struck by the caboose by the time he looked over." Another young eyewitness in a statement to a police officer who arrived to investigate the accident said, essentially, that Hewitt had jumped into the side of the train. The officer made notes and then later used the notes to prepare an accident report incorporating the substance of the statement. By the time of trial, the officer testified, "he had absolutely no recollection of the interview with the witness," although he identified the notes as his own. Grand Trunk offered the accident report under a variety of hearsay exceptions, including Michigan's Rule 803(1), identical to the federal rule. The trial judge in Oakland County Circuit

Court admitted the report.[20] After a two-week trial the jury by special verdict found Grand Trunk's negligence was not the proximate cause of Hewitt's fatal injuries. Dorothy Hewitt's appeal focused exclusively on the accident report, which she contended was inadmissible hearsay.

The Michigan Court of Appeals reversed and remanded for a new trial. The statements of the boy to the officer "were not made while the witnesses saw Mr. Hewitt being struck by the train or even 'immediately thereafter.' While the record is not clear, it is apparent that at least several, and possibly as many as 30, minutes passed before the officer took the witnesses' statements. Moreover, the reporting officer could in no way corroborate the truth of the witnesses' statements since he was not present at the scene of the accident until after the fact. While our conclusion in this regard could perhaps be viewed as imposing an unduly restrictive interpretation of the phrase 'immediately thereafter,' a more expansive interpretation would only serve to further blur the distinction between the 'present sense impression' exception and the 'excited utterance' exception which we have concluded, as discussed below, is also inapplicable. The purpose and intent of subrule 803(1) can be served most effectively by limiting the scope of that exception to statements made while describing the event or condition or instantly thereafter."

(The appellate court also found the statement inadmissible under Michigan's excited utterance exception, Rule 803(2), because the police officer could not recall "anything remarkable about [the declarant's] demeanor" to satisfy the "stress of excitement" requirement. And the court found the recorded recollection exception, Rule 803(5), inapplicable because it should have been offered with the officer's notes themselves. The court noted, in any event, that because the report was hearsay within hearsay under Rule 805, each portion of the combined statement had to be admissible separately, and the boy's words to the officer did not qualify.)

---

[20]The student of evidence, whether a law student or an experienced practitioner, will be justifiably frustrated (but should hardly be shocked) by the inexactitude of the trial judge's ruling: "...[the witnesses' statements] were made within a reasonable length of time in this particular matter and I think it comes within the exception to the hearsay rule and I think the officer's, the way he recorded the particular matter, would not allow me to strike or not allow it into evidence at this time." Perhaps this was an opportunity for Hewitt's counsel to seek a brief time-out to argue against each specific exception with the particularity it demanded. Or perhaps that would not have helped.

FRE 803(1) – Hearsay Exception: Unverifiable Statement by Absent Declarant Claiming Murder Victim Was Seen After Alleged Date of Murder Is Too Unreliable for Admissibility

> **Rule 803. Hearsay Exceptions; Availability of Declarant Immaterial**
> The following are not excluded by the hearsay rule, even though the declarant is available as a witness:
> (1) *Present Sense Impression.* A statement describing or explaining an event or condition made while the declarant was perceiving the event or condition, or immediately thereafter.

STATE v. CASE
676 P.2d 241, 100 N.M. 714 (1984)

*Lack of Due Diligence by defense counsel.

Carl Case was convicted by a jury of first degree murder and first degree criminal sexual penetration. Witnesses testified that on New Year's Day 1980, they heard Case, Curtis Worley, and Joseph Brown planning to force Nancy Mitchell to have sex, and saw them striking her, undressing her, sexually assaulting her, and then dressing her again after Case struck her with an object that might have been a pipe. They dragged her away and abandoned her. On January 3 the three were overheard discussing her rape and murder. Mitchell's body, her skull fractured, was discovered near the Six-Mile Dam area of the Pecos River in Eddy County, New Mexico some weeks later. Case was sentenced to life imprisonment, and he appealed.

One issue Case raised before the New Mexico Supreme Court concerned the admissibility of testimony the defense had offered by Tammie Simmons. She said that, around January 6, her friend Michelle Kent had said, "There goes Nancy Mitchell," and that Simmons turned but did not see her. The trial court had sustained the prosecution's objection and excluded the statement because it was not reliable enough to be a present sense impression, as claimed by the defense.

The state Supreme Court affirmed, noting that, although the statement was apparently made while the declarant was observing whatever she thought she saw, there were too many other indications of unreliability: "the statement of identification was made by a declarant whose whereabouts were unknown at the time the statement was offered into evidence. Furthermore, there were no identifying details in the statement. The record indicates that this identification was based on the absent declarant's brief glimpse of the person she believed to be Nancy Mitchell. By the time Simmons looked up in response to Kent's declaration, the person was no longer visible. Therefore, Simmons was unable to verify that Nancy Mitchell was in the passing car.... The trial court may consider whether the absent declarant's observation could be verified by the witness who heard the declaration. In order for the trial court to assess the value of the testimony in a situation where a statement made under questionable circumstances is offered, the witness offering the statement must be capable of being thoroughly cross-examined. Here there was no possible way to cross-examine Simmons because she did not see what Kent saw. Given the questionable nature of Kent's statement, we find that the trial court did not abuse its discretion by excluding Simmons' testimony. Absent a clear abuse of that discretion, reversal is not appropriate."

FRE 803(2) – Hearsay Exception: Witness's Testimony That Declarant Was Visibly Shaken upon Learning His Tax Liability Was Far Greater Than Expected Is Adequate Foundation for Excited Utterance

> **Rule 803. Hearsay Exception; Availability of Declarant Immaterial**
> The following are not excluded by the hearsay rule, even though the declarant is available as a witness:
>
> *(2) Excited Utterance.* A statement relating to a startling event or condition made while the declarant was under the stress of excitement caused by the event or condition.

LEWIN v. MILLER WAGNER & CO., LTD.
725 P.2d 736, 151 Ariz. 29 (1986)

Burton J. Lewin sold his wholesale plumbing-supply business, Pioneer Plumbing Supply Co., in 1979 to Amfac Distribution, Inc., in a tax-free exchange for Amfac stock. Later that year he sold half his Amfac shares to Goldman Sachs & Company and received almost $1,260,000 over four months in two tax years. Early in 1980 Lewin began meeting with Carl Dornan, the head of the tax department of the accounting firm, Miller Wagner & Co. Ltd., he had engaged to provide services for his plumbing business and personal financial affairs. He wanted to see if there was some way to structure the sale of the rest of his Amfac shares to minimize his tax liability in 1980. "Lewin attempted to communicate his goal of paying no more than $32,000 in taxes for 1980,... the amount that was being withheld from his earnings that year." Dornan recommended a cash sale followed by a mix of charitable gifts, stock option straddles and oil and gas investments. When Lewin sold his Amfac shares that spring, he received almost $1,300,000, bringing his 1980 capital gains from the two sales to more than $2,430,000. Two days before the April 15 filing deadline, Lewin learned that his tax liability would be more than $300,000 more than the $32,000 he had withheld.

Lewin and his wife, Jackie, sued Miller Wagner and its principals and Dornan, alleging malpractice in that they failed to render proper advice. Miller Wagner counterclaimed for unpaid fees. The jury's verdict was for the Lewins for $200,000, and for Miller Wagner on the counterclaim for $4,450. Lewin was also awarded almost $62,000 in attorney's fees. The accountants appealed.

A major issue on the appeal concerned testimony by Harry Cavanagh, Lewin's longtime friend and attorney. When Lewin left Dornan's office on April 13, he went right to Cavanagh's office in the same building. Cavanagh was permitted over a defense objection *in limine* to testify that Lewin, appearing "ashen and disturbed," told him that Dornan had admitted forgetting the alternative minimum tax, and that the news about his huge unexpected tax liability had caught Lewin "totally off guard."[21]

The Arizona Court of Appeals affirmed in part and reversed in part, but it upheld the trial court's decision on the admissibility of Cavanagh's testimony as an excited utterance on Lewin's part. Lewin seemed adequately "excited," the statement about Dornan's admission related to the startling event, and Lewin had no time to fabricate the story. "Cavanagh saw Lewin immediately and noted his distressed state of mind. This evidence satisfies the excited utterance exception."

FRE 803(2) – Hearsay Exception: Excited Utterance Identification Made Weeks After Assault Is Still Admissible

> **Rule 803. Hearsay Exceptions; Availability of Declarant Immaterial**
> The following are not excluded by the hearsay rule, even though the declarant is available as a witness:
> (2) Excited Utterance. A statement relating to a startling event or condition made while the declarant was under the stress of excitement caused by the event or condition.

UNITED STATES v. NAPIER
518 F.2d 316 (9th Cir. 1975)

Jimmy Lee Napier was convicted of transporting a stolen car across state lines and of interstate kidnapping. The woman he was charged with kidnapping, Mrs. Caruso, was found unconscious with severe head injuries. Hospitalized for seven weeks, she had two brain surgeries and suffered brain damage that left her memory intact but severely restricted her ability to communicate orally.

Over defense objection Caruso's sister, Eileen Moore, was permitted under Rule 803(2), excited utterances, to testify that a week after Caruso returned home from the hospital, Moore showed her a newspaper article containing Napier's picture. Without reading the article, Caruso became distraught, and she pointed to the picture and said clearly, "He killed me, he killed me." Other strong crime-scene evidence linked Napier to Caruso's kidnapping and beating as well.

On Napier's appeal to the Ninth Circuit Court of Appeals, appellate counsel argued that Caruso's statement referred to the assault, and that the assault therefore must be the "startling event" of which Rule 803(2) speaks. The statement could not have been made "under the stress of excitement" of the assault, but only of seeing the photograph.

The Ninth Circuit rejected that argument and affirmed the conviction. It held that just seeing the photograph in the newspaper was sufficiently startling to Caruso to ensure the reliability of her statement that identified the defendant as her assailant.

An alternative analysis favored by some courts has it that seeing the photograph *revived* the "stress of excitement" of the assault

---

[21] Lewin could have testified himself, of course, to Dornan's admission under Rule 801(d)(2)(A). But imagine how much more believable the information is coming in this way, even though now it is hearsay within hearsay, confirming the admission, because this way we have a third party depicting Lewin saying it happened right after the moment he heard the admission, not weeks or months later when the jury might conclude Lewin had had time to think about it and make it up.

itself. Either way, all the authorities (the court cites McCormick and quotes Wigmore) seem to place their trust in the spontaneity of the declaration, rather than in its strict referent.

FRE 803(2) – Hearsay Exception: Excited Utterance Is Reliable Although Declarant Is Unidentified

> **Rule 803. Hearsay Exceptions; Availability of Declarant Immaterial**
> The following are not excluded by the hearsay rule, even though the declarant is available as a witness:
> *(2) Excited Utterance.* A statement relating to a startling event or condition made while the declarant was under the stress of excitement caused by the event or condition.

COLE v. TANSY
926 F.2d 955 (10th Cir. 1991)

Dawson Cole was convicted in a New Mexico state court of attempted armed robbery. At trial, Officer Hamner testified that while she was working near the Last Chance Package Store in Roswell, New Mexico, in July 1985, a car pulled up in front of her. The driver told Hamner that she had just seen a man leave that store with a gun in his hand. The driver also gave a brief description of the man, his motorcycle, and part of the motorcycle's license-tag number. Officer Hamner also testified that the driver was excited, talking fast, and pointing around. The officer remembered seeing a person matching the driver's description just a few minutes earlier. Meanwhile, Officer Hamner received a dispatch that an armed robbery had taken place at the Last Chance Package Store. Without getting the driver's name, Officer Hamner immediately proceeded to the scene of the crime. The State agreed it had not attempted to identify the out-of-court declarant.

Cole, arguing that the hearsay statements of the unidentified witness were inadmissible, petitioned the United States District Court for the district of New Mexico for a writ of habeas corpus. The writ was denied, and Cole appealed. The Tenth Circuit Court of Appeals affirmed, holding the statements were an excited utterance.

The State offered the driver's statement for its truth – especially as to Cole's possession of the gun – so the statement was hearsay. The Tenth Circuit agreed with the District Court and the New Mexico court that the declarant's description of Cole outside the store with a gun in his hand was an excited utterance. The event seen and reported was certainly startling; the declarant's manner suggested she was under the stress of excitement caused by the event; and the statement describing the man with the gun outside a store amply related to the startling event.

Without going into much detail, the Tenth Circuit also concluded the statement was reliable. Although the context for this conclusion was a Sixth Amendment confrontation issue,[22] it also bears on the admissibility of the excited utterance. Courts have barred admission – or seem to have at least reserved the right to bar admission – to excited utterance hearsay that didn't seem as

---
[22] See *White v. Illinois, supra* p. 212.

reliable as it should have been. But mere declarant unavailability is not the sole litmus test to be applied, as this case illustrates. Reliability – or perhaps the absence of factors suggesting unreliability – seems to have been satisfied here by the urgency of the declarant's message to the officer and the officer's need to act on it quickly, as well as by the message's point-by-point confirmation by subsequent events.

The court also concluded – unfortunately, in only summary fashion – that no unreliability was suggested by the apparent presence of "conscious reflection" in the declarant's decision to tell the officer what she had seen, nor in her recollection of a partial license-plate number. This holding is entirely consistent with the traditions of Rule 803(2), which do not require rigorous spontaneity so much as simply the influence of excitement.

FRE 803(3) - Hearsay Exception: Statement of Plan Is Admissible as State of Mind, Relevant to Prove Conduct as Consequence of Plan

> **Rule 803. Hearsay Exceptions; Availability of Declarant Immaterial**
> The following are not excluded by the hearsay rule, even though the declarant is available as a witness:
> *(3) Then Existing Mental, Emotional, or Physical Condition.* A statement of the declarant's then existing state of mind, emotion, sensation, or physical condition(such as intent, plan, motive, design, mental feeling, pain, and bodily health), but not including a statement of memory or belief to prove the fact remembered or believed unless it relates to the execution, revocation, identification, or terms of declarant's will.

MUTUAL LIFE INSURANCE CO. v. HILLMON
145 U.S. 285, 12 S. Ct. 909, 36 L. Ed. 706 (1892)

Sallie Hillmon sued Mutual and two other insurance companies on life insurance policies issued a year and a half earlier on the life of her husband, John. Mutual denied that John Hillmon was dead and claimed he was in hiding after concocting a scheme where the dead body of a companion, Frederick Adolph Walters, was falsely represented to be that of John Hillmon.

At trial there was considerable contradictory evidence, including autopsy photographs, testimony and exhibits, as to whether the dead body had been Hillmon's or somebody else's, perhaps Walters'. Hillmon and John Brown had been traveling from Wichita through southern Kansas, looking for a suitable site for a cattle ranch. A couple of weeks out, Hillmon was said to have been accidentally shot and killed at a camp at Crooked Creek. Brown was said to have arranged for an inquest and burial at a nearby town.

Mutual introduced testimony that the body was Walters', not Hillmon's. Walter had left Fort Madison, Iowa, a year earlier and wrote occasional letters back home to his family.

Mutual tried unsuccessfully to admit into evidence testimony about a letter[23] Walters wrote his sister, dated a couple of weeks before Hillmon's supposed death. The

---

[23] See FRE 1002 and 1004(1), and *Neville Construction Co. v. Cook Paint and Varnish Co., infra* p. 327, regarding the admissibility of *testimony about* a writing instead of the writing itself. Here Walters' sister had lost the original letter.

letter said Walters "expect[ed] to leave Wichita... March the 5th with a certain Mr. Hillmon... for Colorado, or parts unknown to me." (Walters was never again heard from.) Plaintiff's hearsay objection to the letter's contents was sustained, and the jury returned a verdict in favor of Mrs. Hillmon. Mutual appealed.

The United States Supreme Court held Walters' letter was a trustworthy statement of his intention to go away with Hillmon, "which made it more probable both that he did go and that he went with Hillmon, than if there had been no proof of such intention." The court quoted an earlier case for authority that "Wherever the bodily or mental feelings of an individual are material to be proved, the usual expressions of such feelings are... competent evidence. Those expressions are the natural reflexes of what it might be impossible to show by other testimony."

Hillmon is widely credited as a principal theoretical antecedent of Rule 803(3).

FRE 803(3) – Hearsay Exception: Declarant's Statement About Threats by Accused Is Admissible to Show Declarant's Fear, Unlikelihood of Accused's Version of Events

> **Rule 803. Hearsay Exception; Availability of Declarant Immaterial**
> The following are not excluded by the hearsay rule, even though the declarant is available as a witness:
> *(3) Then Existing Mental, Emotional, or Physical Condition.* A statement of the declarant's then existing state of mind, emotion, sensation, or physical condition (such as intent, plan, motive, design, mental feeling, pain, and bodily health), but not including a statement of memory or belief to prove the fact remembered or believed unless it relates to the execution, revocation, identification, or terms of declarant's will.

STATE v. AUBLE
754 P.2d 935 (Utah 1988)

Claudette Auble was shot twice with a high-powered rifle, once in the face from between 18 and 24 inches away and once in the back of the head from one inch away. Jerry Auble, her husband, claimed it was an unintentional shooting, that when he stepped out of the shower one morning after the couple had been arguing, his wife was holding his hunting rifle, coming at him with it and goading him to kill himself with it as he had threatened to do. The gun went off accidentally as they struggled, he said, and again after he managed to cock the lever-action rifle so he could shoot himself after he got the gun away from her. Jerry Auble was charged in Weber County District Court with his wife's murder.

The trial court initially denied a prosecution motion *in limine* to admit testimony that Jerry Auble had earlier threatened to kill his wife, but said that ruling would be reconsidered if Jerry Auble raised a self-defense argument. After Auble's testimony about the struggle, the trial court "determined that Jerry's testimony could be the predicate for a self-defense claim," and changed its ruling. The prosecution on rebuttal then called John Marsh, a longtime friend of the victim, who testified that Jerry Auble had on occasion threatened to kill himself if his wife left him, but that once recently he threatened to kill her if she moved out to an apartment she had found.[24] The jury convicted Jerry Auble of second degree murder, and he appealed.

The Utah Supreme Court affirmed the conviction, upholding the admissibility of Claudette Auble's statement of her husband's threat. In finding her hearsay statement admissible under the state-of-mind exception (as well as not excessively prejudicial under Rule 403), the court noted, "Claudette's state of mind was put directly into issue by Jerry's testimony, and the hearsay statement was highly probative on that issue. Based on that statement, the jury could reasonably have found that Claudette feared her husband might kill or seriously injure her and, therefore, she would not have confronted him aggressively and attempted to force a loaded gun upon him in the midst of a heated argument. The witness who testified about the hearsay threat was a long-time acquaintance of Claudette's, and there was no evidence to suggest that his testimony was unreliable. Thus, the evidence had significant probative value..."

FRE 803(3) – Hearsay Exception: Statement That Declarant Had "Heard Voices" Described Past Sensation, So Was Inadmissible Under Exception for Then-Existing State of Mind

> **Rule 803. Hearsay Exceptions; Availability of Declarant Immaterial**
> The following are not excluded by the hearsay rule, even though the declarant is available as a witness:
> *(3) Then Existing Mental, Emotional, or Physical Condition.* A statement of the declarant's then existing state of mind, emotion, sensation, or physical condition (such as intent, plan, motive, design, mental feeling, pain, and bodily health), but not including a statement of memory or belief to prove the fact remembered or believed unless it relates to the execution, revocation, identification, or terms of declarant's will.

<u>**STATE v. NYE**</u>

551 A.2d 844 (Me. 1988)

Richard Larry Nye was convicted of 10 counts of varying degrees of criminal sexual conduct, all involving contact with his stepdaughter over three years' time when the girl was between 3½ and 6 years old. Nye denied he ever abused the girl, and claimed it was her natural father who had done so. He appealed the convictions.

The Supreme Judicial Court of Maine affirmed the convictions on six counts and vacated convictions as to four counts, and remanded for entry of judgments of acquittal

---

[24] The trial court's treatment of this threat shows a fairly typical confusion in the use of state-of-mind hearsay. The judge cautioned the jury when the threat came in that they should not consider Claudette's statement for its truth, but only on the question of her state-of-mind – fear of her husband and of his intentions with the rifle – at the time she was killed. But of course, if she really was afraid of her husband, and that is why the statement is being offered, the prosecution needs her to have been telling the truth to John Marsh. If she was making it up, presumably she would not actually have been afraid. Therefore the statement needs to be admissible "for the truth of the matter asserted," and the applicable hearsay exception, here Rule 803(3), allows it to come in for its truth. (The jury does not appear to have let the distinction bother it.)

222 Evidence Illustrated

on those. On the way to reaching that conclusion, however, the appellate court considered and affirmed the trial court's denial of admission to an out-of-court statement Nye had sought to introduce. To cast doubt on the little girl's accusations, Nye proffered testimony that the victim had told her mother that she had "heard voices." Nye offered the hearsay statement under the exception for a declarant's then existing state of mind or mental feeling, under Maine Rule 803(3), the equivalent of the same federal rule. The court held the statement "described a past sensation,... not a contemporaneous statement of the declarant's then existing state of mind or mental feeling."

FRE 803(3) – Hearsay Exception: Statement of Belief About Past Event Is Disqualified from Admissibility as State of Mind

> **Rule 803. Hearsay Exceptions; Availability of Declarant Immaterial**
> The following are not excluded by the hearsay rule, even though the declarant is available as a witness:
>
> *(3) Then Existing Mental, Emotional, or Physical Condition.* A statement of the declarant's then existing state of mind, emotion, sensation, or physical condition (such as intent, plan, motive, design, mental feeling, pain, and bodily health), but not including a statement of memory or belief to prove the fact remembered or believed unless it relates to the execution, revocation, identification, or terms of declarant's will.

PEOPLE v. CARLSON
712 P.2d 1018 (Colo. 1986)

A Greeley, Colorado building owned by Ione Jacobs burned down in February, 1980. Beverly Carlson leased space in the building for her store where she dealt in genealogical books and supplies, other rare and used books, and Scottish imports; her business was having serious financial difficulties at the time of the fire. Carlson had a fire insurance policy from Commercial Union for $40,000, less a loss-payable clause in favor of the Small Business Administration for their $25,000 security interest in Carlson's equipment, furniture, inventory and accounts receivable. Forensic evidence at the scene suggested an arson fire – Lieutenant Dan Alexander of the Greeley Fire Department "observed charred patterns on the tile beneath the store's carpeting [that were]... similar to those associated with fires ignited by a flammable liquid." This evidence conflicted with Carlson's account of returning to her locked store to retrieve documents she needed for a meeting she was in the middle of at the Dial Finance Company, and noticing smoke coming from the inside of a closet. Eventually she was charged with first degree arson.

At trial one of the prosecution witnesses was the claims manager of Commercial Union, Mr. Gardner. He was asked what decision the insurance company had made about paying Carlson's claim, and testified, "We denied it." When he was asked why, the defense objected that the insurer's reason was irrelevant. The trial judge overruled the objection, and Gardner stated, "Based on our evaluation of the evidence we had, and on the advice of our attorney we felt a provable arson defense." The court then instructed the jury that the claims adjuster's testimony was admitted not "as proof of the fact that arson occurred, but only to show the corporate state of mind, if you will, in their refusing to guarantee coverage on the policy." Carlson was convicted and sentenced to eight years' probation and ordered to make restitution of more than $14,000.

She appealed to the Colorado Court of Appeals, which reversed, holding that the reason for the denial of the insurance claim was irrelevant and prejudicial. The prosecution petitioned for state Supreme Court relief.

The Colorado Supreme Court upheld the Court of Appeals' reversal of Carlson's conviction. After an analysis of the relevancy dimensions of the questions, the court agreed that "the insurance company's state of mind was of no consequence to the resolution of the arson charge." In a significant footnote, the court said the testimony of the claims manager was actually a hearsay "statement of belief about a past event," excluded under the final clause of Colorado's version of Rule 803(3). "To permit statements of memory [or belief] to come in under the state of mind exception would result, for all practical purposes, in the abolition of the exclusionary rules pertaining to hearsay evidence."

FRE 803(4) – Hearsay Exception: Statement for Purposes of Medical Diagnosis or Treatment Applies to Patient's Statement to Doctor, Not to Doctor's Statement to Patient

> **Rule 803. Hearsay Exceptions; Availability of Declarant Immaterial**
> The following are not excluded by the hearsay rule, even though the declarant is available as a witness:
>
> *(4) Statements for Purposes of Medical Diagnosis or Treatment.* Statements made for purposes of medical diagnosis or treatment and describing medical history, or past or present symptoms, pain, or sensations, or the inception or general character of the cause or external source thereof insofar as reasonably pertinent to diagnosis or treatment.

BULTHUIS v. REXALL CORPORATION
789 F.2d 1315 (9th Cir. 1985)

After Elizabeth Bulthuis' mother had three miscarriages she may have been given Diethylstilbestrol (DES) to prevent further miscarriages. She then gave birth to Elizabeth, who as an adult some 30 years later developed cervical cancer that may or may not have been caused by her mother's having taken DES. Bulthuis sued Rexall Corp., Upjohn Co., Merck & Co., Inc., E.R. Squibb & Sons, Eli Lily & Co., Warner-Lambert Co., Abbott Laboratories, and White Laboratories, Inc., under negligence, strict liability and breach of warranty theories.

The U.S. District Court for the Central District of California granted the defendants summary judgment, holding there was no credible, admissible evidence developed during discovery that suggested Bulthuis' mother ever took DES during her pregnancy with the plaintiff. The Ninth Circuit Court of Appeals reversed, holding the trial court should have considered the affidavits of two doctors who treated Elizabeth Bulthuis because under Rule 705 enough factual basis was set forth in the depositions to defeat summary judgment.

But along the way to that result, the appellate court considered whether the district court should have taken into account plaintiff's mother's deposition testimony that in 1952 her attending doctor told her she was being given "Stilbestrol," a shortened name for DES. Bulthuis argued it was admissible under Rule 803(4) as a statement of medical diagnosis or treatment. The Ninth Circuit panel said, "Rule 803(4) applies only to statements made by the patient to the doctor, not the reverse."

(The court also noted the testimony of the doctor's out-of-court statement was inadmissible under the residual exception because it was "plainly self-serving" with no guarantees of trustworthiness.)

FRE 803(4) – Hearsay Exception: Mother's Relating of Child's Statement to Doctor Qualifies for Admission as Statement for Medical Diagnosis and Treatment

> **Rule 803. Hearsay Exceptions; Availability of Declarant Immaterial**
>
> The following are not excluded by the hearsay rule, even though the declarant is available as a witness:
>
> *(4) Statements for Purposes of Medical Diagnosis or Treatment.* Statements made for purposes of medical diagnosis or treatment and describing medical history, or past or present symptoms, pain, or sensations, or the inception or general character of the cause or external source thereof insofar as reasonably pertinent to diagnosis or treatment.

STATE v. JUSTINIANO
740 P.2d 872, 48 Wash. App. 572 (1987)

Four-year old "Jane Doe" was unable to express much as a witness in the courtroom in which her mother's live-in boyfriend, David Justiniano, was being tried for taking indecent liberties with her. The state was permitted over defense objection to admit into evidence the testimony of Dr. Susan Reimer, the child's pediatrician, as to what Jane's mother told her about what Jane had said to her at home about the incident.[25] When Jane's mother was bathing her in the shower and washing between the child's legs, she told her mother, "That's what David does with his finger, he did it for a long time and it hurt." Justiniano was convicted (the sentence is not revealed by the reported opinion), and he appealed.

The Washington Court of Appeals affirmed the admissibility of the mother's statement to Dr. Reimer about her daughter's statement. The mother was trying to obtain medical attention for her daughter because of the incident involving her boyfriend, and the appellate court found "the statements made to the doctor by the mother are the equivalent of statements made by the child to the doctor

---

[25] Although this is obviously a case of hearsay within hearsay, the court's analysis avoids or overlooks the Rule 805 dimensions of it, although it does evaluate each component for reliability.

and are admissible" under Washington's equivalent of Federal Rule 803(4).

(The child's statement itself was found to be admissible under Washington's "tender years" child-abuse hearsay statutory provision, RCW 9A.44.120, quoted in the opinion at footnote 2. As many similar states provisions do,[26] this statute provides admissibility for the hearsay statement of a young child – Washington's threshold is "under the age of ten" – describing an act of sexual contact if the court makes a determination of the reliability of the statement and, in the event the child cannot testify, if the statement is corroborated. Here the court determined the child was competent to remember and relate the truth, had no motive to lie, and made the statement without prompting or questioning, and her account was corroborated by her 10-year-old brother who testified that at about the time of the incident Jane told her mother about, he saw Justiniano with his hand in the little girl's pants.)

FRE 803(4) – Hearsay Exception: Declarant's Statement About Cause of Injury in Sexual Assault Prosecution Is Admissible if Pertinent to Diagnosis or Treatment

> **Rule 803. Hearsay Exceptions; Availability of Declarant Immaterial**
> The following are not excluded by the hearsay rule, even though the declarant is available as a witness:
>
> *(4) Statements for Purposes of Medical Diagnosis or Treatment.* Statements made for purposes of medical diagnosis or treatment and describing medical history, or past or present symptoms, pain, or sensations, or the inception or general character of the cause or external source thereof insofar as reasonably pertinent to diagnosis or treatment.

UNITED STATES v. IRON SHELL
633 F.2d 77 (8th Cir. 1980)

John Louis Iron Shell, Jr., was charged with assault with intent to commit rape in connection with his assault of a nine-year-old girl near his residence in Antelope, South Dakota, within the Rosebud Indian Reservation. At trial the prosecution called Dr. Mark Hopkins of the Indian Health Service, who testified over defense objection that Lucy told him, in answer to his questions during a medical examination, that "she had been drug [sic] into the bushes, that her clothes, jeans and underwear, were removed and that the man had tried to force something into her vagina which hurt. She said she tried to scream but was unable because the man put his hand over her mouth and neck." Lucy's own testimony consisted of long silences and "yes" responses to leading questions, which the trial court at least once directed the prosecution to limit. Iron Shell was convicted by a jury, and sentenced to serve a prison term of 17½ years.

On appeal, Iron Shell reiterated his argument (among several) that Dr. Hopkins' questions and Lucy's answers were not sufficiently connected to medical diagnosis and treatment to fall within Rule 803(4)'s exception to the hearsay rule. The Eighth Circuit Court of

---

[26]See *People v. Hammons, infra* p. 277, and *People v. Dunham, supra* p. 4.

Appeals affirmed. "The rationale behind the rule has often been stated. It focuses upon the patient and relies upon the patient's strong motive to tell the truth because diagnosis or treatment will depend in part upon what the patient says. It is thought that the declarant's motive guarantees trustworthiness sufficiently to allow an exception to the hearsay rule... This principle [also] recognizes that life and death decisions are made by physicians in reliance on such facts and as such should have sufficient trustworthiness to be admissible in a court of law.

"...A two-part test flows naturally from this dual rationale: first, is the declarant's motive consistent with the purpose of the rule; and second, is it reasonable for the physician to rely on the information in diagnosis or treatment.

"We find no fact in the record to indicate that Lucy's motive in making these statements was other than as a patient seeking treatment. Dr. Hopkins testified that the purpose of his examination was two-fold. He was to treat Lucy and to preserve any evidence that was available. There is nothing in the content of the statements to suggest that Lucy was responding to the doctor's question for any reason other than promoting treatment. It is important to note that the statements concern what happened rather than who assaulted her. The former in most cases is pertinent to diagnosis and treatment while the latter would seldom, if ever, be sufficiently related." The doctor testified that he needed the information Lucy provided so he would know where to examine Lucy and what to look for – and what not to bother looking for. Dr. Hopkins also said that he needed Lucy's statements "in deciding upon a course of treatment." That clinched it for the application of the exception.

FRE 803(4) – Hearsay Exception: Statement to Doctor Regarding Cause of Depression Is Not Excludable Just Because It Names Accused as Cause

> **Rule 803. Hearsay Exceptions; Availability of Declarant Immaterial**
> The following are not excluded by the hearsay rule, even though the declarant is available as a witness:
> *(4) Statements for Purpose of Medical Diagnosis or Treatment.* Statements made for purposes of medical diagnosis or treatment and describing medical history, or past or present symptoms, pain, or sensations, or the inception or general character of the cause or external source thereof insofar as reasonably pertinent to diagnosis or treatment.

STATE v. MOEN
786 P.2d 111, 309 Or. 45 (1990)

In Ronald Howard Moen's aggravated murder jury trial in Marion County, Oregon in the death of Moen's wife, Judith, and her mother, Hazel Chatfield, the state presented testimony of Dr. Daniel Davis Mulkey under Oregon's clone of Federal Rule 803(4). Dr. Mulkey repeated some of Chatfield's statements to him while he was treating her for high blood pressure, anxiety and depression. She answered Dr. Mulkey's questions about her anxiety and depression by describing Ronald Moen's presence in her home, his abusive conduct and her fears of him.

Moen was convicted and sentenced to death. He appealed, claiming among several grounds for reversal that Dr. Mulkey's testimony about Hazel Chatfield's statement should not have been admitted under the Rule 803(4) hearsay exception because her "motivation for giving the information is highly suspect" and Dr. Mulkey "did not specifically rely upon the statements as reasonably pertinent to his diagnosis of depression."

The Oregon Supreme Court affirmed the conviction and specifically upheld the admission of Dr. Mulkey's testimony about Chatfield's statements. In a very thoughtful, thorough analysis citing Kirkpatrick, Weinstein, Louisell & Mueller, the Oregon Rule's Legislative Commentary and several federal cases, the appellate court concluded, "Mrs. Chatfield made these statements as a patient to her treating physician during regularly scheduled visits to his office. The statements related directly to the severe emotional distress that she was suffering at the time of those visits. The depression that she experienced is a medically recognized illness that her physician had the training and experience to diagnose and to treat. Her complaints focused on her feelings of depression. Dr. Mulkey responded to her statements with clinical inquiries, a medical diagnosis, and a prescribed course of treatment.

"The trial court was entitled to conclude that the statements in question were 'made for purposes of medical diagnosis [and] treatment'" and that the statements "quite clearly described 'the inception or general character of the course [or] external source' of her continuing depression." To Moen's argument that Chatfield's statements were more in the nature of "accusations of personal fault," the court held that the argument "ignores the wording" of Rule 803(4), which "expressly authorizes the admission of statements concerning the 'cause [or] external source' of an illness, provided the statements are 'made for purposes of medical diagnosis or treatment' and are 'reasonably pertinent' to either endeavor. Mrs. Chatfield's statements concerning defendant communicated to Dr. Mulkey the ongoing cause of her situational depression. He used that information first, to diagnose, and, then, to treat her illness. The information and his professional skills permitted him to distinguish her depression from other forms of that illness and to prescribe specific treatment for it. The requirements of the rule are satisfied. The fact that the continuing cause of her illness was the presence and conduct of a named individual is not a basis for excluding the statements."

FRE 803(5)- Hearsay Exception: Law Enforcement Agent Report Is Admissible as Recorded Recollection

> **Rule 803. Hearsay Exceptions: Availability of Declarant Immaterial**
>
> The following are not excluded by the hearsay rule, even though the declarant is available as a witness:
>
> *(5) Recorded Recollection.* A memorandum or record concerning a matter about which a witness once had knowledge but now has insufficient recollection to enable the witness to testify fully and accurately, shown to have been made or adopted by the witness when the matter was fresh in the witness' memory and to reflect that knowledge correctly. If admitted, the memorandum or record may be read into evidence but may not itself be received as an exhibit unless offered by an adverse party.

UNITED STATES v. PICCIANDRA
788 F.2d 39 (1st Cir. 1986)

In 1974, Michael Picciandra established Natural Enterprises, Inc., ostensibly to engage in real estate ventures. On June 26, 1977, he participated in smuggling 10,000 pounds of marijuana into Buzzard's Bay, Massachusetts aboard the yacht *Muscavado*. The Coast Guard boarded and seized the yacht, but did not find Picciandra aboard. During July 1977, Picciandra delivered more than $145,000 to his lawyer. The money was disbursed to purchase real estate, a boat, and an airplane, yet Picciandra reported a taxable income of about $25,000, from his "lobster and fish" business.

Following the seizure of the yacht, DEA agent Francis Dever, posing as a drug dealer, met twice with Picciandra. Dever's report stated that Picciandra had admitted his participation in the smuggling venture. Picciandra was arrested in late 1978, but the complaint was dismissed. Subsequently, in 1981, the IRS began to investigate Picciandra for tax evasion. The IRS interviewed more than 60 witnesses and obtained voluminous documents. Picciandra was indicted for tax evasion. Following a 1984 trial, he was found guilty.

Picciandra appealed his conviction, claiming the District Court erred in admitting agent Dever's report as a recorded recollection. The First Circuit Court of Appeals affirmed the conviction, stating, "[a]t the time of trial, Dever could not remember the substance of his report that detailed a 1977 conversation in which Picciandra admitted his participation in the Muscavado smuggling venture...." The court held, "[t]he guarantee of trustworthiness is found in the reliability inherent in a record made while the events were still fresh in mind. We conclude that the district court did not err in admitting agent Dever's report made at the time of his conversation with Picciandra."

This is not really an end run around Rule 803(8)(B), which doesn't permit treating law enforcement documents as a reliable exception to the ban on hearsay statements in criminal cases. (The rule serves a preference for live, confront-able testimony.)[27] Dever was present at Picciandra's trial. He testified live. Per Rule 803(5) he would have been permitted only to read his report to the

---
[27] See *State v. Rivera, infra* p. 237.

jury, not hand it physically to them. (And, of course, the hearsay within the report was defendant's own statement, a party admission under Rule 801(d)(2)(A).)

FRE 803(5) – Hearsay Exception: Recorded Recollection Must Be Acknowledged as Accurate by Witness to Be Admissible

> **Rule 803. Hearsay Exceptions; Availability of Declarant Immaterial**
> The following are not excluded by the hearsay rule, even though the declarant is available as a witness:
>
> *(5) Recorded Recollection.* A memorandum or record concerning a matter about which a witness once had knowledge but now has insufficient recollection to enable the witness to testify fully and accurately, shown to have been made or adopted by the witness when the matter was fresh in the witness' memory and to reflect that knowledge correctly. If admitted, the memorandum or record may be read into evidence but may not itself be received as an exhibit unless offered by an adverse party.

STATE v. THOMPSON
397 N.W.2d 679 (Iowa 1986)

Stanley Dale Thompson stole Tamara Yezek's purse from the back room of a drugstore in Mason City, Iowa, then had his girlfriend, Lisa Werle, use the Visa card from it to make a purchase at a video store. (Thompson was identified from photos developed from film he had left at the drugstore before he was seen leaving the drugstore with the stolen purse.) He was charged with fraudulent use of a financial instrument under Iowa law.

At his trial the state called Lisa Werle, who professed a lack of memory as to who suggested she use the credit card and about anyone saying it should be used soon before it was reported stolen. The prosecuting attorney then showed her a copy of her pretrial deposition given a month after the crime took place. Werle said it did not refresh her memory. The prosecutor was then permitted over Thompson's hearsay objection to read from the deposition Werle's answer that Thompson "said that we should hurry because the card might be reported stolen soon and we should get there and get it done."[28] Thompson was convicted and sentenced as an habitual offender.

On his appeal, the Iowa Supreme Court found the admission of the deposition under the Iowa equivalent of Federal Rule 803(5) erroneous (although it affirmed the conviction because it held the deposition statement admissible under Iowa's Rule 801(d)(1)(A)). The state had failed to get Werle to acknowledge that the transcript accurately portrayed her knowledge at the time she gave it, and thus Rule 803(5) was not satisfied. "This deficiency is not supplied, as the State suggests, by Werle's testimony that she had attempted to testify truthfully at her deposition. The issue involved not only the accuracy of the statements which were made by the witness but also the accuracy of the written record of those statements made by the court reporter."

---

[28] The observant reader will note two levels of hearsay: the party admission within the ostensible recorded recollection. The court made no reference to Rule 805, however.

FRE 803(6) – Hearsay Exception: IRS Tax Records Are Admissible as Business Records Unless Specifically Shown to Be Untrustworthy

> **Rule 803. Hearsay Exceptions; Availability of Declarant Immaterial**
>
> The following are not excluded by the hearsay rule, even though the declarant is available as a witness:
>
> *(6) Records of Regularly Conducted Activity.* A memorandum, report, record, or data compilation, in any form, of acts, events, conditions, opinions, or diagnoses, made at or near the time by, or from information transmitted by, a person with knowledge, if kept in the course of a regularly conducted business activity, and if it was the regular practice of that business activity to make the memorandum, report, record, or data compilation, all as shown by the testimony of the custodian or other qualified witness, or by certification that complies with Rule 902(11), Rule 902(12), or a statute permitting certification, unless the source of information or the method or circumstances of preparation indicate lack of trustworthiness. The term "business" as used in this paragraph includes business, institution, association, profession, occupation, and calling of every kind whether or not conducted for profit.

UNITED STATES v. HAYES
861 F.2d 1225 (10th Cir. 1988)

The Internal Revenue Service claimed William L. Hayes did not file an income tax return for 1981, and he was charged with tax evasion and failure to file a return, a lesser included offense. At trial an IRS tax examiner, Dorothy Vest, testified that she searched Hayes' tax records for the years 1978-81 and found his returns for 1978, 1979 and 1980 but none for 1981, leading her to determine he had not filed one for that year. The government's Exhibit 5 at trial consisted of Certificates of Assessments and Payments (computer data evidence) showing Hayes' tax information for 1978-81, which were admitted over Hayes' "strenuous" objection as business records. Hayes objected that IRS records were untrustworthy. The jury convicted him of the lesser charge of willful failure to file a return, and he appealed.

Hayes had come under the influence of the kind of crackpot "tax advisers" who think there is a legal basis for asserting that the income tax is unconstitutional or doesn't apply to private citizens. (His defense to the willful tax evasion charge, apparently effective in the minds of the jurors, was that he was advised to invest in certain foreign trust organizations.)

The Tenth Circuit Court of Appeals affirmed his conviction. While Hayes had presented a series of 1985 articles from the Philadelphia Inquirer detailing anecdotal tales of "failures of IRS record keeping and computer systems generally, such as a loss of tax filings in 1985, the deliberate destruction of records, the mistaken destruction of tax returns, the erroneous granting of refunds, and typographical errors," the appellate court agreed with the trial court that "before the entire I.R.S. record keeping system could be shown unreliable or untrustworthy, some comparative evidence would have to be offered to show, for example, the percentage of lost documents." Besides, IRS employee Steven Ray testified to procedures at the Ogden, Utah Regional Service center where Hayes' returns were sent, and laid a strong foundation for the trial court's findings that the record keeping procedures in question were sufficiently trustworthy.

(The court also rejected Hayes' argument for exclusion under Rule 803(8)(B) and (C) because the records were not observations by law enforcement officials at the scene of a crime.)

FRE 803(6) – Hearsay Exception: Complaint Forms Received by Business Are Not Admissible as Business Records Because Not Made by Persons Acting Under Business Duty

> **Rule 803. Hearsay Exception; Availability of Declarant Immaterial**
>
> The following are not excluded by the hearsay rule, even though the declarant is available as a witness:
>
> **(6) Records of Regularly Conducted Activity.** A memorandum, report, record, or data compilation, in any form, of acts, events, conditions, opinions, or diagnoses, made at or near the time by, or from information transmitted by, a person with knowledge, if kept in the course of a regularly conducted business activity, and if it was the regular practice of that business activity to make the memorandum, report, record, or data compilation, all as shown by the testimony of the custodian or other qualified witness, or by certification that complies with Rule 902(11), Rule 902(12), or a statute permitting certification, unless the source of information or the method or circumstances of preparation indicate lack of trustworthiness. The term "business" as used in this paragraph includes business, institution, association, profession, occupation, and calling of every kind, whether or not conducted for profit.

THIRSK v. ETHICON, INC.
687 P.2d 1315 (Colo. App. 1983)

Walter Thirsk, Mack Whitaker and Billy Hollis separately sued Ethicon, Inc., claiming that during surgery they had each contracted an infection from a surgical bone wax manufactured by Ethicon that was contaminated by an organism called mycobacterium fortuitum. The infections led to injuries not specified in the reported opinion. The complaints sounded in products liability. The three cases were consolidated for trial. The jury rendered verdicts for the plaintiffs (amounts also not specified in the reported opinion), and Ethicon appealed.

The Colorado Court of Appeals reversed on other grounds, but instructed the trial court on remand that certain exhibits received during the first trial under the business records exception to the hearsay rule should not be admitted at the second. If, as seemed likely to the appellate court, certain Product Complaint Forms and Patient-Related Complaint Forms did not contain information transmitted by persons acting under a business duty to transmit such information (probably customer or patients, possibly medical personnel), the documents did not meet the requirements of Colorado's version of Federal Rule 803(6) and should not be admitted as business records.

(The court did note that under Colorado's Rule 105 the forms might be admissible not for the truth of their contents but "only to show that complaints were made," which might implicate the non-hearsay purpose of showing that the company was on notice.)

FRE 803(6) – Hearsay Exception: Computer Printouts Are Admissible Despite Failure of Business to Rely on Them

> **Rule 803. Hearsay Exceptions; Availability of Declarant Immaterial**
>
> The following are not excluded by the hearsay rule, even though the declarant is available as a witness:
>
> *(6) Records of Regularly Conducted Activity.* A memorandum, report, record, or data compilation, in any form, of acts, events, conditions, opinions, or diagnoses, made at or near the time by, or from information transmitted by, a person with knowledge, if kept in the course of a regularly conducted business activity, and if it was the regular practice of that business activity to make the memorandum, report, record, or data compilation, all as shown by the testimony of the custodian or other qualified witness, or by certification that complies with Rule 902(11), Rule 902(12), or a statute permitting certification, unless the source of information or the method or circumstances of preparation indicate lack of trustworthiness. The term "business" as used in this paragraph includes business, institution, association, profession, occupation, and calling of every kind, whether or not conducted for profit.

UNITED STATES v. CATABRAN
836 F.2d 453 (9th Cir. 1988)

When his three Sacramento waterbed stores experienced financial difficulties in June 1982, Lino Catabran filed for Chapter 11 bankruptcy protection. After most of the inventory and fixtures disappeared from two of the stores and were apparently disposed of at the third store in a going-out-of-business sale under a different business name ("Waterbed Liquidations" instead of the original "Bedder Nights"), the bankruptcy court in December ordered the Chapter 11 reorganization converted to a Chapter 7 liquidation. The trustee appointed by the court found less than $10,000 worth of merchandise and assets. Catabran and his vice-president, Jack Emmets, were charged with concealing assets in a bankruptcy.

At trial the government was allowed to admit general ledger computer printouts under the business records exception to the hearsay rule. "Qualified witnesses laid the foundation required by Rule 803(6). One of the bookkeepers, Miss Keys, testified that she put into the computer sales, inventory, payroll, and tax information on a current basis; that the printout accurately set forth that information; and that Bedder Nights produced these printouts as a regular practice each month. Ms. Keys also testified that she manually checked the information put into the computer for accuracy. Other witnesses provided similar testimony." Catabran objected that the printouts were not kept in the ordinary course of business because he did not rely on them for inventory purposes, and further that they contained inaccuracies and were therefore untrustworthy. The district court overruled these objections and admitted the printouts. Upon his conviction of two counts of concealing assets, Catabran appealed.

The Ninth Circuit Court of Appeals affirmed. The court held that Rule 803(6) "does not require that the business rely on the document in such a specific way," rather merely that it be "kept in the course of a regularly conducted business activity." The general ledger data contained in the printouts were maintained regularly and routinely. As to the inaccuracies claimed by Catabran, the settled rule is that generally this factor goes to weight, not admissibility.

(Catabran had also objected to the printouts as a "summary" under Rule 1006, inadmissible without the underlying documents. The court found the printouts to be the general ledger itself – and "the use of a computer to create the ledger does not change the result," the general admissibility of a business's general ledger.)

FRE 803(6) – Hearsay Exception: Regular Course of Business Does Not Include Preparation for Litigation for Business Records Exception

> **Rule 803. Hearsay Exceptions; Availability of Declarant Immaterial.**
> The following are not excluded by the hearsay rule, even though the declarant is available as a witness:
> *(6) Records of Regularly Conducted Activity.* A memorandum, report, or data compilation, in any form, of acts, events, conditions, opinions, or diagnoses, made at or near the time by, or from information transmitted by, a person with knowledge, if kept in the course of a regularly conducted business activity, and if it was the regular practice of that business activity to make the memorandum, report, record, or data compilation, all as shown by the testimony of the custodian or other qualified witness, or by certification that complies with Rule 902(11), Rule 902(12), or a statute permitting certification, unless the source of information or the method or circumstances of preparation indicate lack of trustworthiness. The term "business" as used in this paragraph includes business, institutions, association, profession, occupation, and calling of every kind, whether or not conducted for profit.

PALMER v. HOFFMAN
318 U.S. 109, 63 S. Ct. 477, 87 L. Ed. 645 (1943)

The engineer of a train involved in a grade crossing accident gave a formal statement two days later to an assistant superintendent of the railroad and to a representative of the Massachusetts Public Utilities Commission. By the time the lawsuit arising out of the accident came to trial, the engineer had died. The railroad offered the engineer's statement into evidence under the federal statute which is the direct predecessor of Rule 803(6), the business records exception to the ban on hearsay evidence.

The statute contained language very similar to current Rule 803(6): among several familiar requirements, the statement must have been "made in the regular course of any business... [if] it was the regular course of such business to make such... record.... "

The trial court sustained the plaintiff's objection to the introduction of the signed written record of engineer's statement. The United States Supreme Court agreed. Justice Douglas wrote for the court, "The business of the petitioners is the railroad business.... [The] primary utility [of employees' reports regarding accidents] is in litigating, not railroading." Therefore statements such as the engineer's "are not for the systematic conduct of the enterprise as a railroad business. Unlike payrolls, accounts receivable, accounts payable, bills of lading and the like, these reports are calculated for use essentially in the court, not in the business."

Although the court based its decision primarily on its reading of the words of the Congressional act and their "historic meaning," there is no doubt the justices mistrusted the reliability of records made principally for litigation. To broaden the application of the act to admit all memoranda any business regularly compiles (especially writings made in the course of paying or defending tort claims, which are also regular parts of most business enterprises' activities) would overlook the very theory of the rule: "[t]he probability of trustworthiness of records because they were the routine reflections of the day to day operations of a business...."

It is this skepticism of the trustworthiness of records kept for litigation purposes that led directly to the "unless" clause in Rule 803(6) that disqualifies business records from admissibility if "the source of information or the method or circumstances of preparation indicate lack of trustworthiness."

FRE 803(6), (7) – Hearsay Exception: Absence of Records of Payment Is Admissible to Prove Nonoccurrence of Payment

> **Rule 803. Hearsay Exceptions; Availability of Declarant Immaterial**
>
> The following are not excluded by the hearsay rule, even though the declarant is available as a witness:
>
> *(6) Records of Regularly Conducted Activity.* A memorandum, report, record, or data compilation, in any form, of acts, events, conditions, opinions, or diagnoses, made at or near the time by, or from information transmitted by, a person with knowledge, if kept in the course of a regularly conducted business activity, and if it was the regular practice of that business activity to make the memorandum, report, record, or data compilation, all as shown by the testimony of the custodian or other qualified witness, or by certification that complies with Rule 902(11), Rule 902(12), or a statute permitting certification, unless the source of information or the method or circumstances of preparation indicate lack of trustworthiness. The term "business" as used in this paragraph includes business, institution, association, profession, occupation, and calling of every kind, whether or not conducted for profit.
>
> *(7) Absence of Entry in Records Kept in Accordance With the Provisions of Paragraph (6).* Evidence that a matter is not included in the memoranda, reports, records, or data compilation, in any form, kept in accordance with the provisions of paragraph (6), to prove the nonoccurrence or nonexistence of the matter, if the matter was of a kind of which a memorandum, report, record, or data compilation was regularly made and preserved, unless the sources of information or other circumstances indicate lack of trustworthiness.

SHEYENNE VALLEY LUMBER CO. v. NOKLEBERG
319 N.W.2d 120 (N.D. 1982)

Sheyenne Valley Lumber Company of Leonard, N.D. sued carpenter Jorgen Nokleberg on an account the company claimed had a balance due of something over $13,000. The Lumber Company said it provided more than $26,600 in lumber and materials to Nokleberg, who performed services for Sheyenne that were worth just over $10,300. Nokleberg claimed he was not given sufficient credit for other services, overcharges by Sheyenne, returned materials and the like. A bench trial in Cass County District Court examined several months of the account's activities in painstaking detail, and resulted in a judgment for Sheyenne for just under $10,500. Both parties appealed to the North Dakota Supreme Court.

Amid a bewildering accumulation of commercial detail including some 950 invoices admitted at trial as business records, a $3,400 matter is of most use to this inquiry. The trial court had concluded that Sheyenne had proved it was entitled to some $5,545 for lumber and materials despite the fact that the 32 invoices representing those items, with the customary breakdown of specific material and jobs on which they were used, were missing and unavailable to the court, because Sheyenne's underlying bookkeeping records of these transaction were intact. Yet the court had also ruled that Nokleberg was not entitled to credit for labor on two construction jobs because Sheyenne claimed it had paid him for them, despite Sheyenne's failure to produce any business records of such payment even though it would have been expected to be reflected in business records had such payment been made. The court held that the trial court's judgment had to be modified to account for those credits due Nokleberg: If North Dakota's business records rules (substantially identical to their federal counterparts) are "to be applied consistently, the trial court should have credited the amounts on the Alvin Wahl machine shed and the Allen Braun barn as offsets to the amount Nokleberg owed Sheyenne.

"Sheyenne's owner conceded in his testimony that there was an agreement between Sheyenne and Nokleberg that Nokleberg was to be paid these amounts for labor on these projects. The records of Sheyenne fail to reflect that Nokleberg was paid or credited with these amounts.... It is apparent that credits for labor performed by Nokleberg were matters of which a memorandum, report, record, or data compilation was regularly made by Sheyenne. Therefore, the absence in Sheyenne's records of any indication that these amounts had been credited to Nokleberg is evidence that they were not so credited or paid."

FRE 803(6), (8)(B),(C) – Hearsay Exception: Report Ineligible for Admission as Public Record Because of Law Enforcement Personnel Exclusion Is Also Thereby Inadmissible as Business Record

> **Rule 803. Hearsay Exceptions; Availability of Declarant Immaterial**
>
> The following are not excluded by the hearsay rule, even though the declarant is available as a witness:
>
> *(6) Records of Regularly Conducted Activity.* A memorandum, report, record, or data compilation, in any form, of acts, events, conditions, opinions, or diagnoses, made at or near the time by, or from information transmitted by, a person with knowledge, if kept in the course of a regularly conducted business activity, and if it was the regular practice of that business activity to make the memorandum, report, record, or data compilation, all as shown by the testimony of the custodian or other qualified witness, or by certification that complies with Rule 902(11), Rule 902(12), or a statute permitting certification, unless the source of information or the method or circumstances of preparation indicate lack of trustworthiness. The term "business" as used in this paragraph includes business, institution, association, profession, occupation, and calling of every kind, whether or not conducted for profit.
>
> *(8) Public Records and Reports.* Records, reports, statements, or data compilations, in any form, of public offices or agencies, setting forth (A) the activities of the office or agency, or (B) matters observed pursuant to duty imposed by law as to which matters there was a duty to report, excluding, however, in criminal cases matters observed by police officers and other law enforcement personnel, or (C) in civil actions and proceedings and against the Government in criminal cases, factual findings resulting from an investigation made pursuant to authority granted by law, unless the sources of information or other circumstances indicate lack of trustworthiness.

STATE v. RIVERA
515 A.2d 182 (Del. Super. 1986)

Following their conviction by a jury of delivery of cocaine, Antonio Rivera and Angel M. Rivera filed a motion for a new trial, citing the admission of a state toxicology report under the Delaware business records exception.

The state forensic chemist who analyzed the substance found on the Riveras and who prepared the report was ill on the day of trial. The prosecution called another forensic chemist who worked in the same office, and who laid a competent foundation for the report's admission as a business record. The state apparently conceded by the time of the motion hearing post-trial that the report did not qualify for admission as a public record because of the exclusions in parts (B) and (C). The Superior Court for New Castle County held that the business records exception, under which the report seemed also to qualify, "does not open a back door for evidence excluded by Rule 803(8)." "Reports and records which fall within one of the exclusions to the public records exception and which by their nature raise confrontation issues, such as documents prepared for litigation or documents which require subjective evaluation of data or which lack indicia of trustworthiness, may not be admitted under Rule 803(6)." The Delaware Code of Evidence Committee had even anticipated the very situation posed here: "Rule 803(6) does not make admissible records created for the litigation such as the report of a medical doctor retained to examine a party at the request of the opposing party. *Likewise, a toxicologist's report on the presence of drugs would not be admissible because of Rule 803(8)*(emphasis added)."

Although Delaware's evidence code has a version of Rule 803(8) derived from the Uniform Rule rather than the Federal Rule, under either version the toxicology report is excluded: "A toxicologist's report...is a report requiring personal and not mechanical evaluation of data, is critical evidence of an essential element of the crime, and is necessarily prepared for use in the trial of a defendant charged with drug violations."

FRE 803(8)(C) – Hearsay Exception: Public Records Exception Includes Conclusions as Well as Factual Findings

> **Rule 803. Hearsay Exceptions; Availability of Declarant Immaterial**
> The following are not excluded by the hearsay rule, even though the declarant is available as a witness:
> *(8) Public Records and Reports.* Records, reports statements, or data compilations, in any form, of public offices or agencies, setting forth... (C) in civil actions and proceedings and against the Government in criminal cases, factual findings resulting from an investigation made pursuant to authority granted by law, unless the sources of information or other circumstances indicate lack of trustworthiness.

BEECH AIRCRAFT CORP. v. RAINEY
488 U.S. 153, 109 S. Ct. 439, 102 L. Ed. 2d 445 (1988)

Navy Lieutenant Commander Barbara Ann Rainey, a flight instructor, was killed in a plane crash along with her student pilot, Ensign Donald Bruce Knowlton, during touch-and-go exercises at Middleton Field, Alabama. The surviving spouses of Rainey and Knowlton brought a product liability action against Beech Aircraft, claiming the crash had been caused by a loss of engine power because of some defect in the plane's fuel-control system. Beech said pilot error had caused the crash. At trial each side offered expert testimony on the only disputed issue, causation.

Beech Aircraft offered into evidence a Navy investigative report about the accident organized into sections: "findings of fact," "opinions" and "recommendations." Although the report noted that the deaths of the two pilots and the destruction of the plane made it "almost impossible" to pinpoint the cause of the crash, it contained a detailed reconstruction of the accident based on the supposition of pilot error. It concluded that although it was impossible to rule out equipment malfunction, pilot error was the "most likely" cause. The trial court at first ruled that only the report's findings of fact would be admissible under the public records exception, Rule 803(8)(C). Just before trial the district judge decided to admit most of the "opinions" as well, except a few it deemed too speculative to be reliable.

Trial lasted two weeks and resulted in a verdict for defendant Beech Aircraft. Rainey appealed, and the Eleventh Circuit Court of Appeals reversed, holding that Rule 803(8)(C) does not encompass evaluative conclusions or opinions.

The United States Supreme Court reversed the Court of Appeals' decision, holding "statements in the form of opinions or conclusions are not by that fact excluded from the scope of [Rule] 803(8)(C)," thus addressing a long-standing conflict among the federal circuits on the question. The court found no significance in the omission from the rule of any reference to "opinions" which are expressly made admissible in the case of business records under Rule 803(6), noting that a common understanding of the meaning of "factual findings" would be "conclusion[s] by way of reasonable inference from the evidence." Looking to the legislative history of Rule 803(8)(C), the court found "no clear answer" in that the committees of the two Houses of Congress took "diametrically opposite positions" that were never reconciled. Because the Advisory Committee cited as illustrations of the proper application of the rule "reports that stated conclusions," the court came down on that side of the controversy.

The court noted that the so-called escape clause of the rule, "…unless the sources of information or other circumstances indicate lack of trustworthiness," is an adequate safeguard against the admission of unreliable evidence.

FRE 803(8) – Hearsay Exception: Police Report Is Admissible as Public Record When Offered by Accused in Absence of Specific Proof Demonstrating Report's Untrustworthiness

> **Rule 803. Hearsay Exceptions; Availability of Declarant Immaterial**
>
> The following are not excluded by the hearsay rule, even though the declarant is available as a witness:
>
> *(8) Public Records and Reports.* Records, reports, statements, or data compilations, in any form, of public offices or agencies, setting forth (A) the activities of the office or agency, or (B) matters observed pursuant to duty imposed by law as to which matters there was a duty to report, excluding, however, in criminal cases matters observed by police officers and other law enforcement personnel, or (C) in civil actions and proceedings and against the Government in criminal cases, factual findings resulting from an investigation made pursuant to authority granted by law, unless the sources of information or other circumstances indicate lack of trustworthiness.

UNITED STATES v. VERSAINT
849 F.2d 827 (3d Cir. 1988)

Delaware State Police conducted a valid no-knock search of a Seaford mobile home they suspected was the headquarters of a crack cocaine distribution operation. They found two guns and three pounds of cocaine and arrested the home's occupants, five Haitians and an American. Trooper Downes, who had made several undercover visits to the home and two drug buys, identified all but one of those arrested as persons who were present during one or both of the purchases he made there. All six were indicted by a federal grand jury. Cherubin Versaint, one of those arrested at the bust, was charged with distribution of crack and conspiracy.

At the joint trial of five defendants – one, the lone American, Amy Deal, had entered into a plea agreement and testified for the government – Downes' testimony placed Versaint at the mobile home when he made his buys. Deal also connected Versaint to the drug activities at the mobile home. Versaint offered into evidence the police report Downes prepared a month after the arrest that described one of his two undercover buys and named only Philistine Jean in connection with the buy. (Amy Deal's earlier statements to authorities also said only Philistine Jean was involved in the Downes buy; by trial she was able to "positively identify" Versaint as the person who sold drugs to Downes.) The trial court rejected the police report, saying under Rule 803(8)(C) it lacked the requisite trustworthiness.

The jury convicted Versaint on both counts, and he appealed. The Third Circuit Court of Appeals reversed, saying there was no affirmative indication that the report of Trooper Downes was untrustworthy. The district court had found the delay of a month in preparing the report significant, but the Third Circuit panel said the rule does not require the report to have been made at or near the time of the events described, as does Rule 803(6). Rule 803(8) presumes public officials perform their duties properly and conscientiously "without motive or interest other than to submit accurate and fair reports." To overcome the rule's presumption requires "an affirmative showing that the proffered evidence is untrustworthy." Such a showing was not made by the government here.

FRE 803(8)(B)- Routine, Mechanical Observations Not Part of Criminal Investigation When Made Are Not Excluded from Hearsay Exception Just Because Made by Law Enforcement Personnel

> **Rule 803. Hearsay Exceptions; Availability of Declarant Immaterial**
> The following are not excluded by the hearsay rule, even though the declarant is available as a witness:
>
> *(8) Public Records and Reports.* Records, reports, statements, or data compilations, in any form, of public offices or agencies, setting forth (A) the activities of the office or agency, or (B) matters observed pursuant to duty imposed by law as to which matters there was a duty to report, excluding, however, in criminal cases matters observed by police officers and other law enforcement personnel, or (C) in civil actions and proceedings and against the Government in criminal cases, factual findings resulting from an investigation made pursuant to authority granted by law, unless the sources of information or other circumstances indicate lack of trustworthiness.

UNITED STATES v. PUENTE
826 F.2d 1415 (5th Cir. 1987)

Roberto Puente testified before a federal grand jury that he had not been in Eagle Pass, Texas the night of a 1984 fire there that destroyed his family's auto supply business. He said he and his family drove his son's car to Monclova, Mexico that morning and stayed until the following evening. Government evidence including two witnesses contradicted Puente's testimony, and he was charged with four counts of knowingly making a false material declaration to a grand jury.

At his trial the government also introduced into evidence a computer printout generated by the Treasury Enforcement Communication System that indicated that Puente's son's car had crossed the border back into Texas from Mexico at 11:30 p.m. the night of the fire. Puente objected to the admission of the printout under Rule 803(8)(B), which allows public records as a hearsay exception but which excludes observations of law-enforcement personnel in criminal cases. Puente was convicted, and he appealed.

The Fifth Circuit Court of Appeals affirmed. The court first described the manner in which the TECS computer printouts are generated: "The Customs Service requires its employees to record in the TECS system the license plate number of every vehicle coming into the United States from Mexico at the Eagle Pass border checkpoint. As the automobile approaches the checkpoint, a Customs Service official routinely enters the license plate number into the TECS computer; the computer then scans its records to determine whether the vehicle is stolen or associated with other information—such as use in an earlier smuggling attempt – that would suggest special attention by the customs officers. If the computer search reveals no information, the automobile is allowed to proceed through the checkpoint. As the vehicle passes the official operating the TECS computer, that person verifies that the correct license number has been entered in the system by matching the license number on the automobile with that displayed on the computer screen. All the entries into the TECS system are later stored in a central system and retrieved as needed to prepare statistical reports on such topics as border traffic and vehicle multiple reentry."

While it conceded that Customs Service Officers are indeed "law enforcement personnel" within the meaning of Rule 803(8)(B), the court held against a "literal application" of the rule to this sort of "routine, objective" observation. The law enforcement personnel exclusion is supposed to apply to observations made "at the scene of a crime or in the course of investigating a crime," not to the "mechanical" registry of an "unambiguous factual matter." "The Customs Service officials who entered the license numbers of vehicles crossing the border into the TECS system have no motivation other than to 'mechanically register' this 'unambiguous factual matter.'"

FRE 803(9) – Hearsay Exception: Statement in Death Certificate That Decedent Was "Passenger" in Vehicle Is Not Admissible to Prove Who Was Driving

> **Rule 803. Hearsay Exceptions; Availability of Declarant Immaterial**
> The following are not excluded by the hearsay rule, even though the declarant is available as a witness:
>
> *(9) Records of Vital Statistics.* Records or data compilations, in any form, of births, fetal deaths, deaths, or marriages, if the report thereof was made to a public office pursuant to requirements of law.

STATE v. GOULD
704 P.2d 20 (Mont. 1985)

Dawn Marie Clough, 20, was killed in a one-vehicle accident a few miles north of Wolf Creek, Montana on I-15. James David Gould, who had been drinking all day and who owned the car, was charged with negligent homicide and driving under the influence of alcohol in her death. He claimed he "positively" remembered pulling over for a nap and turning the driving over to Clough. The couple were both thrown from the pickup. Highway Patrol Officer Gene Tinsley arrived on the scene of the accident and "conversed constantly" with Gould for half an hour to keep him awake. Gould answered Tinsley's questions that it was his truck, and that he had been driving. Gould later twice told the ambulance driver he was driving, too, once remarking that he never let anyone else drive his pickup. (On appeal from his conviction, Gould's counsel emphasized that none of the witnesses asked Gould specifically, "Were you driving *at the time of the accident?*") Gould's blood alcohol test result was .29 a couple of hours after the accident. The jury convicted Gould of both charges, and he was sentenced to three years in jail, all but six months suspended, and a $1,000 fine, on the negligent homicide charge, and 30 days in jail and a $300 fine on the DUI charged. He appealed.

One issue on appeal before the Montana Supreme Court, which affirmed Gould's conviction, concerned the admission into evidence at trial of Dawn Clough's death certificate as a record of vital statistics. The certificate contained the statement, "Decedent was a passenger in a pick-up truck which left the roadway and overturned. She was ejected from the vehicle." The court noted that to prove Clough's death not all statements on the certificate need be admitted. Because the coroner said he based the conclusion that she was a passenger on hearsay statements, the court said, "We conclude that the statement on the certificate that decedent was a passenger should have been excised prior to admission," but that the error was not grounds for reversal because "it confirmed in an insignificant way other evidence before the court."

FRE 803 (10) – Hearsay Exception: Certificates of County Clerks Stating No Voter Registration Records Were Found for Persons Who Signed Petitions Are Admissible to Invalidate Petitions

> **Rule 803. Hearsay Exceptions; Availability of Declarant Immaterial**
> The following are not excluded by the hearsay rule, even though the declarant is available as a witness:
> *(10) Absence of Public Record or Entry.* To prove the absence of a record, report, statement, or data compilation, in any form, or the nonoccurrence or nonexistence of a matter of which a record, report, statement, or data compilation, in any form, was regularly made and preserved by a public office or agency, evidence in the form of a certification in accordance with rule 902, or testimony, that diligent search failed to disclose the record, report, statement, or data compilation, or entry.

BARDACKE v. DUNIGAN
649 P.2d 1386, 98 N.M. 473 (1982)

New Mexico law provides that a candidate for statewide office who fails to receive 20% of the delegate vote can still appear on the primary election ballot, provided nomination petitions are filed at least 50 days before the primary and contain signatures of at least one percent of voters in each of 10 counties and at least three percent of voters statewide who voted in the last primary. Paul Bardacke, a candidate for the Democratic nomination for State Attorney General, filed suit in Santa Fe County District Court challenging the signatures filed by Thomas L. Dunigan, also vying for the nomination.

To prove that some 549 signatures were invalid (Dunigan's petitions only had 222 signatures to spare over the 4,523 he needed), Bardacke offered sworn certificates of county clerks around the state that for certain specific names on the petitions, "upon diligent search, no voter registration records could be found."[29] The district court considered these certificates under New Mexico Rule 803(10), identical to the federal rule, and found that as to 477 signatures of the 549 challenged, "the certificates were sufficiently reliable and trustworthy to establish that the names listed thereon were the names of persons who were not entitled to be counted" under New Mexico's election statutes.

Dunigan appealed. The New Mexico Supreme Court affirmed, holding the certificates admissible per Rule 803(10) as the district court had held. Other than to characterize the Rule 803(10) evidence offered by Bardacke as "insufficient," the court noted that Dunigan "failed to offer any further evidence regarding the accuracy of the certificates," which "offered adequate and substantial evidence" that Dunigan's petition contained 477 invalid signatures.

---

[29] These certificates were agreed by Dunigan to be "self-authenticating" domestic public documents under seal. See FRE 902(1), *United States v. Moore, infra* p. 304.

FRE 803(11) – Hearsay Exception: Statements of Financial Contribution to Church Are Not Personal Information Required for Admission as Religious Records

> **Rule 803. Hearsay Exceptions; Availability of Declarant Immaterial**
> The following are not excluded by the hearsay rule, even though the declarant is available as a witness:
> *(11) Records of Religious Organizations.* Statements of births, marriages, divorces, deaths, legitimacy, ancestry, relationship by blood or marriage, or other similar facts of personal or family history, contained in a regularly kept record of a religious organization.

HALL v. COMMISSIONER OF INTERNAL REVENUE
729 F.2d 632 (9th Cir. 1984)

The IRS challenged a $3,951 deduction claimed by William and Lorna Hall on their 1976 tax return. The money had been donated to something called the Church of The United Brotherhood ("CUB"), a congregation William Hall organized himself with two friends. It was chartered by the Universal Life Church, Inc. The congregation had no building, held no services and had no organizational documents save their charter. The Commissioner's office ruled that contributions to this "organization" did not qualify as tax-deductible charitable contributions, and the Tax Court upheld the ruling, including the imposition of a penalty for "disregard of Internal Revenue rules and regulations." Hall appealed.

The Ninth Circuit Court of Appeals affirmed the Tax Court ruling, holding that the tax-exempt status of a parent organization, here Universal Life Church, does not automatically carry over to local congregations like CUB. ("The evidence... established that the CUB served almost exclusively to funnel a rental allowance to its officers.") The Tax Court had excluded from evidence "an undated annual contribution statement from the Universal Life Church to prove that he had made contributions to a bona fide charity." Hall contended it should have been admitted under Rule 803(11) as religious records. The appellate court ruled that "Statements of contributions to a church do not constitute such personal information" as is required by the Rule. If the subject of the out-of-court record is not a fact of personal or family history "similar" to "births, marriages, or divorces," it does not qualify under this exception.

(The court also affirmed the Tax Court rejection of these records under the business records exception, Rule 803(6), because no proper foundation was laid for its admission as provided in the rule.)

FRE 803(12) – Hearsay Exception: Foreign Certificates of Birth, Death and Marriage Are Admissible to Prove Heirship

> **Rule 803. Hearsay Exceptions; Availability of Declarant Immaterial**
>
> The following are not excluded by the hearsay rule, even though the declarant is available as a witness:
>
> *(12) Marriage, Baptismal, and Similar Certificates.* Statements of fact contained in a certificate that the maker performed a marriage or other ceremony or administered a sacrament, made by a clergyman, public official, or other person authorized by the rules or practices of a religious organization or by law to perform the act certified, and purporting to have been issued at the time of the act or within a reasonable time thereafter.

MATUSZEWSKI v. PANCOAST
526 N.E.2d 80, 38 Ohio App. 3d 74 (1987)

When Joseph Keller died intestate in January 1983, a number of conflicting heirship claims were advanced. Mary Pancoast and Clemens Yawaski claimed as Keller's first cousin, the offspring of Keller's mother's brother, Frank Jaworski. About a year later, the claims of 12 additional cousins living in Czechoslovakia were filed, all the offspring of other siblings of Keller's mother. The referee of the Cuyahoga County Probate Court found that Joseph Keller died unmarried, and that his mother, Marianna Keller, nee Jaworski, had a sister, Anna Jaworski, and three brothers, Klement, Michal, and Frank Jaworski. The referee found that Joseph Keller had not two heirs, Pancoast and Yawaski, but 14 heirs, including the 12 lineal descendants of Anna, Klement and Michal Jaworski – Josef, Oldrich, Rudolf, Karel, Jindrich and Zdenek Nemec, Frantiska Folwarczna, Zdenka Dzidova, Emilie Oralkova, Karel Komender, Danuse Burkotova, and Jri Wisniowski. Pancoast and Yawaski's estate (he died while the case was pending) appealed.

The premise of their appeal was that the Probate Court erred in admitting marriage and baptismal certificates from Saint Clement Roman Catholic Church in Wieliczka, Poland to prove the marriage of Miciej and Wiktora Jaworski and the birth of their five children in order to show the lineage of the Czech claimants, and also in admitting several official birth, death and marriage certificates from the government of Czechoslovakia to prove the claimants were either children or grandchildren of Miciej and Wiktora Jaworski. The Ohio Court of Appeals, Cuyahoga County, affirmed, holding that the certificates were all admissible under Rule 803(12), having been authenticated as ancient documents under Rule 901(B)(8). (The certificates were also fully admissible as records of religious organizations, Rule 803(11), or, generically, as ancient documents, Rule 803(16).)

FRE 803(13) – Hearsay Exception: Postcard with Photograph and Statement of Identification Is Admissible as Inscription on Family Portrait

> **Rule 803. Hearsay Exceptions; Availability of Declarant Immaterial**
> The following are not excluded by the hearsay rule, even though the declarant is available as a witness:
> *(13) Family Records.* Statements of fact concerning personal or family history contained in family Bibles, genealogies, charts, engravings on rings, inscriptions on family portraits, engravings on urns, crypts, or tombstones, or the like.

MATTER OF ESTATE OF EGBERT
306 N.W.2d 525, 105 Mich. App. 395 (1981)

Renee Alice Unseld claimed to be the niece and hence sole heir of Charles Ernest Egbert, who died intestate in June 1978 at age 91. Egbert's two first cousins, Beatrice Bedenbaugh and Ernest D. Egbert, had earlier been determined to be his heirs at an uncontested proceeding; Unseld petitioned the Saginaw County Probate Court to set the earlier order aside. The probate court held that she failed to convince the court by a preponderance of the evidence that she was Charles Egbert's niece. Unseld's appeal to Saginaw County Circuit Court was denied, and she applied to the Michigan Court of Appeals, which granted leave to appeal.

The sole issue on appeal concerned the probate court's denial of Unseld's request to admit into evidence a picture postcard showing a photograph of a young girl, with handwriting stating: "Ren Robinson, My Sister, Daughter, Age About 3, /s/ Ernest Egbert." Unseld said the small girl was herself.

The Michigan Court of Appeals held that the photograph and its inscription were admissible under any one of three hearsay exceptions, the most obvious being Michigan's version of Rule 803(13) covering family records including "inscriptions on family portraits." (It was also admissible as an ancient document, Rule 803(16), and as a declarant-unavailable statement of family history under Rule 804(b)(4).) Although it was Unseld's lawyer's ineptitude with the more obscure hearsay exceptions that undoubtedly led the probate court to deny admission of the postcard, the appeals court noted that Rule 103(d) allows correction of "plain error" on appeal where, as here, "the excluded evidence, if given any weight at all, would be crucial and, perhaps, determinative of the lawsuit."[30] The court concluded "the better rule is that the trial court is bound to follow the law, whether or not it has been cited to the court."

---

[30] See, e.g., *Rojas v. Richards, supra* p. 7.

FRE 803(14),(15) – Hearsay Exception: Documents Affecting an Interest in Property Are Deeds, Mortgagees, Leases, Etc., But Do Not Include Affidavits of Heirship

> **Rule 803. Hearsay Exceptions; Availability of Declarant Immaterial**
>
> The following are not excluded by the hearsay rule, even though the declarant is available as a witness:
>
> *(14) Records of Documents Affecting an Interest in Property.* The record of a document purporting to establish or affect an interest in property, as proof of the content of the original recorded document and its execution and delivery by each person by whom it purports to have been executed, if the record is a record of a public office and an applicable statute authorizes the recording of documents of that kind in that office.
>
> *(15) Statements in Documents Affecting an Interest in Property.* A statement contained in a document purporting to establish or affect an interest in property if the matter stated was relevant to the purpose of the document, unless dealings with the property since the document was made have been inconsistent with the truth of the statement or the purport of the document.

COMPTON v. WWV ENTERPRISES
679 S.W.2d 668 (Tex. App. 1984)

In a suit to determine ownership to oil and gas interests in a 640-acre tract of land in Nolan County, Texas, plaintiffs and intervenors asserted claims as heirs of Martin W. Myers, who died in California in 1966, or as lessees of certain of his heirs. They sued M.L. Compton, Jr. who was the owner of the surface and part of the oil and gas rights. Mary Lee Hyde, Molly Hyde Blakeman, John S. Hyde, Oliver Franklin Warren, Bernice L. Erickson, Alta I. Bockey and Clifton V. Landmark all claimed to be relatives of Meyer: Erickson, Bockey, and Landmark as nieces and nephew, and the others as survivors of another niece, Gladys Landmark Hyde. WWV was a corporation/partnership that had received oil and gas leases from three of the listed relatives. They attempted to prove their relationships to Myers by offering into evidence three affidavits of heirship detailing the family histories of Myers and of Gladys Landmark Hyde. The Nolan County District Court admitted the affidavits and ruled for WWV and the relatives of Myers, and Compton appealed.

The Court of Appeals of Texas, Eastland, held the affidavit inadmissible. They should perhaps have been offered under the Texas version of Rule 804(b)(4), but no foundation was laid that the declarants (those who made the statements in the affidavits) were unavailable as required by that rule. As to Rule 803(14) and (15), urged on appeal as the proper basis for admission of the affidavits, the court held that those exceptions must be construed to relate to recitals or statements in deeds, leases, and mortgages "and the like," i.e., instruments that themselves create, modify or extinguish an interest in property, and not affidavits that could be admissible under Rule 804(b)(4).

Possibly because this case was decided shortly after Texas adopted its code of evidence rules, the appeals court decided to shape its ruling here in a spirit of helpfulness: "This

Court has the discretion to remand for new trial 'in the interest of justice' rather than rendering judgment that plaintiffs and intervenors take nothing.... The declarants who made the inadmissible affidavits can then testify in person or by deposition as to their family history under Rule 803(19). If proof is made of the declarants' unavailability under Rule 804(a), their affidavits would be admissible" under the Texas equivalent of Rule 804(b)(4).

FRE 803(14), (15) – Hearsay Exception: Judgment Establishing Creditor's Rights Is Admissible as Record of Those Rights

> **Rule 803. Hearsay Exceptions; Availability of Declarant Immaterial**
> The following are not excluded by the hearsay rule, even though the declarant is available as a witness:
>
> *(14) Records of Documents Affecting an Interest in Property.* The record of a document purporting to establish or affect an interest in property, as proof of the content of the original recorded document and its execution and delivery by each person by whom it purports to have been executed, if the record is a record of a public office and an applicable statute authorizes the recording of documents of that kind in that office.
>
> *(15) Statements in documents Affecting an Interest in Property.* A statement contained in a document purporting to establish or affect an interest in property if the matter stated was relevant to the purpose of the document, unless dealings with the property since the document was made have been inconsistent with the truth of the statement or the purport of the document.

GREYCAS, INC. v. PROUD
826 F.2d 1560 (7th Cir. 1987)

Lawyer-farmer Wayne Crawford, who had already "pledged most of his farm machinery to lenders," but who still needed money badly to keep his large downstate Illinois farm going, approached Greycas, Inc., an Arizona financial company. He offered to secure the large loan he sought with the farm machinery, neglecting to mention that most of it was already spoken for. Greycas agreed to lend Crawford more than $1,367,000 subject to Crawford submitting a letter from his own counsel stating no prior liens existed against the machinery. Crawford got his brother-in-law, Theodore S. Proud, to write him such a letter, which stated that Proud had "conducted a U.C.C., tax, and judgment search" and found all the farm equipment "free and clear of all liens or encumbrances."

Within a year after Greycas disbursed the money to Crawford, Crawford defaulted and committed suicide, and the farm machinery was sold at auction mostly for the benefit of the prior lenders who had perfected their liens. Greycas sued Proud for negligent misrepresentation and legal malpractice. Proud had never conducted the searches he said he did, and did not reveal to Greycas his relationship to Crawford. After a bench trial the U.S. District Court for the Southern District of Illinois entered a judgment for Greycas for $833,760 against Proud, who appealed.

The Seventh Circuit Court of Appeals had before it a number of issues, including the amount of damages. The court affirmed the verdict, saying, "in estimating what Proud's negligence had cost Greycas, the judge relied heavily on the state court's finding that Greycas' lien was subordinate to other liens. Proud complains that it was wrong to give collateral estoppel effect to a finding in a case to which he was not a party. But we do not understand the district judge to have been using the judgment to prevent further inquiry into the question of Greycas' damages. The state court's judgment determining the priority of the liens was merely some evidence of the degree to which Proud's misconduct had injured Greycas; for the injury depended on the size of the perfected liens that were prior to its lien. No one tried to prevent Proud from proving, if he could, that the judgment in the state court was erroneous and that Greycas' lien had actually enjoyed the priority that Proud had represented it to have. Proud offered no such evidence. His attack on the state court judgment must fail."

And, specifically addressing Proud's narrower hearsay objection, the appellate court held that "a judgment, insofar as it fixes property rights, should be admissible as the official record of such rights just like other documents of title" under Rule 803(14). "That was the use made of it by Greycas and the district judge: the state court judgment fixed Greycas' rights, equivalent to title, in Crawford's farm machinery."

FRE 803(15) – Hearsay Exception: Recital of Marital Status in Deeds Is Strong, Admissible Evidence of Facts Recited

> **Rule 803. Hearsay Exception; Availability of Declarant Immaterial**
>
> *(15) Statements in Documents Affecting an Interest in Property.* A statement contained in a document purporting to establish or affect an interest in property if the matter stated was relevant to the purpose of the document, unless dealings with the property since the document was made have been inconsistent with the truth of the statement or the purport of the document.

COMPTON v. DAVIS OIL CO.
607 F.Supp. 1221 (D.C. Wyo. 1985)

A quiet title action was brought in U.S. District Court in Wyoming to determine the ownership of a mineral estate in lands in Wyoming. Some $52,000 in oil royalties were deposited by Davis Oil Company pending resolution of the claims of various descendants of Dave Lewis. If he was married to Nettie Lewis at the time of his death in 1935, she was his sole heir and thus her granddaughter, Betty Compton, owned the mineral estate and the right to the royalty proceeds. If Dave Lewis was not married to Nettie Lewis when he died, "the property would have passed to his sister and five brothers," and title would have been held at the time of trial by some 10 individuals whose interests would have ranged from 1/24 to 1/6.

Lots of testimony about family memories and "common knowledge" among the family members was elicited at the bench trial. The evidence most persuasive to the trial judge appears to have been "recitals in the two warranty deeds executed by Dave and Nettie as husband and wife" in 1929 and 1930. There was a contention that because Nettie was Catholic she never divorced her first husband L.B. Johnson after he left her, and therefore never actually married Lewis nor her purported third or fourth husbands (John Busch and Bill Jewell) either. But the district court held the recitals in the deeds and "the conduct of the Lewis heirs over the course of many years prior to 1972 [the year one of the Lewis heirs filed an heirship certificate stating Dave Lewis was never married] was fully consistent with the recital in such instruments." The court noted that whether the statements in the deeds be admitted under Rule 803(15) or as ancient documents under Rule 803(16), "Statements in such ancient documents are admissible due to a rule of necessity as well as to the reliability of such evidence in comparison to any other form of available evidence.... Generally the declarant in such documents is not available to testify due to death, and even if not deceased, the declarant is practicably unavailable because of the inevitable loss of memory and confusion resulting from the passage of time. Generally, there will also be a scarcity of other available evidence probative of the matter asserted. Due to the lapse of time the rule reduces the preference for live testimony implicit in the hearsay rule. Eyewitness accounts of such events are likely to be less reliable than contemporaneous statements recorded in the ancient documents....

"In addition, recitations in ancient documents remove the risks of error in transmission of information by oral statements. This consideration is especially important where the passage of time tolls the memory and removes the statements from the context in which they were made. Also, such evidence is less likely to be affected by the forces generated by the litigation since they are made in a context where there is less reason to fear a lack of candor, distortion, whether conscious or unconscious, or even deliberate falsehood affected the statements made.

"Similarly, the exception to the hearsay rule concerning records and instruments affecting interests in property is based upon the reliability of such documents.... Such instruments are executed in relation to serious and carefully planned transactions, and the financial stake in the transaction, plus the obvious reliance upon the truth of statements made in such instruments by third parties are adequate to at least imply that the recitals in such instruments are trustworthy. The rule states that subsequent dealings inconsistent with the truth of the statements or purport of the document undermine the presumption of reliability.... Here the Lewis heirs, with full knowledge of the existence of the mineral estate, acted as if title to the property was in Nettie Lewis and her heirs between 1935 and 1972, a period of 37 years. They failed to assert any objection to her exercise of dominion over the property, and they did not attempt to exercise any dominion over the property on their own behalf until over a decade after Nettie's death. Unambiguous statements set forth in public records and made contemporaneously with the events at issue circumstantially establish that Nettie Lewis and Dave Lewis were husband and wife at least as early as 1929, and remained in that capacity until the time of his death in 1935."

FRE 803 (16) – Hearsay Exception: For Statement in Ancient Document to Be Admissible, Document Must Be More Than Mere Proposal to Settle Case Involving Disputed Facts

> **Rule 803. Hearsay Exceptions; Availability of Declarant Immaterial**
> The following are not excluded by the hearsay rule, even though the declarant is available as a witness:
> *(16) Statements in Ancient Documents.* Statements in a document in existence twenty years or more the authenticity of which is established.

MOORE v. GOODE
375 S.E.2d 549 (W. Va. 1988)

Widower Custer Waido Morris died without issue in September 1981 at the age of 76. His will left everything to his surviving brothers and sisters. The executrix of the will, Avis S. Moore, also the Clay County Clerk, listed the beneficiaries as Harry Morris, Goldie Douglas, Merle Rogers, Hallie Talley and Ruie Robertson, Morris's surviving brother and sisters, all born in wedlock to Isaac N. Morris. About a year later, Sarah Goode came forward claiming to be a half-sister to Morris, saying she had been born out of wedlock to Isaac Morris. Avis Moore filed suit for a determination of beneficiaries; Goode counterclaimed. The parties exchanged exhibits.

On the day set for trial in 1985, Goode's lawyer announced she had no additional evidence, and the Clay County Circuit Court entered summary judgment in favor of Morris's full siblings. Goode appealed.

One issue among many raised on appeal had to do with the trial court's refusal to admit into evidence a typed draft compromise agreement in connection with a paternity suit filed by Vesta Bishop against Isaac Morris in 1936 alleging that Morris was the father of Sarah Goode. The draft agreement offered into evidence in this case was not signed by Morris. The West Virginia Supreme Court of Appeals affirmed the decision below, rejecting the so-called agreement as an ancient document under West Virginia's Rule 803(16), identical to the federal rule. Although it was certainly old enough, there was a significant question of its "authenticity" at least as a purported recital of an agreement that Morris could be said to have acknowledged. "First, the document is not signed nor is there any evidence that it had ever been signed. Moreover, the content of the document is not a recital of facts that may be assumed to have been true at the time the document was made. Instead, the document purports to compromise a lawsuit which involved disputed facts about the paternity of a child. There is nothing in this document that indicates Isaac N. Morris acknowledged paternity, and nothing to show by way of signature that he acceded to it. We decline to accept it as within the ancient document hearsay exception."

FRE 803(16), 901(b)(8) – Hearsay Exception: Corporate Documents More Than Twenty Years Old, Found Where Expected and Appearing as Expected, Are Admissible as Ancient Documents

> **Rule 803. Hearsay Exceptions; Availability of Declarant Immaterial**
>
> The following are not excluded by the hearsay rule, even though the declarant is available as a witness:
>
> *(16) Statements in Ancient Documents.* Statements in a document is existence twenty years or more the authenticity of which is established.
>
> **Rule 901. Requirements of Authentication or Identification**
>
> *(a) General Provision.* The requirement of authentication or identification as a condition precedent to admissibility is satisfied by evidence sufficient to support a finding that the matter in question is what its proponent claims.
>
> *(b) Illustrations.* By way of illustration only, and not by way of limitation, the following are examples of authentication or identification conforming with the requirements of this rule:
>
> *(8) Ancient Documents or Data Compilation.* Evidence that a document or data compilation, in any form, (A) is in such condition as to create no suspicion concerning its authenticity, (B) was in a place where it, if authentic, would likely be, and (C) has been in existence 20 years or more at the time it is offered.

THREADGILL v. ARMSTRONG WORLD INDUSTRIES, INC.
928 F.2d 1366 (3d Cir. 1991)

The district court in this asbestos-liability suit on behalf of the widow and children of Walter Threadgill, who died of mesothelioma after long exposure to asbestos, refused to admit the famous "Sumner Simpson papers," corporate documents kept by the former president of Raybestos Manhattan.[31] "These documents, which have been considered with some frequency in the context of asbestos litigation, consist primarily of correspondence among a former president of Raybestos-Manhattan, Sumner Simpson, Johns-Manville's former in-house counsel Vandiver Brown, and others. The documents, originally produced by Raybestos-Manhattan in the course of nation-wide asbestos litigation, have been offered by various plaintiffs in other asbestos-related actions in an attempt to show that as early as the 1930s, asbestos manufacturers knew of the health hazards associated with asbestos and knowingly concealed those dangers. While many courts considering these documents have admitted them, others, responding to various defense objections, have not." The jury, unable to consider these documents, returned a verdict for the defendants.

On Threadgills' appeal to the Third Circuit Court of Appeals, the history of the Sumner Simpson documents was recounted: in a deposition given by William Simpson, the son of Sumner Simpson, testimony "establishes that Sumner Simpson was the president of Raybestos-Manhattan, Inc. from the 1930s until his death in the 1950s. William Simpson, who spent his career at Raybestos-Manhattan and also served as president, testified that he

---
[31] See *Lockwood v. AC & S, Inc., supra* p. 301, for another treatment of these papers.

was personally aware of the fact that Sumner Simpson had stored personal files in the Raybestos-Manhattan vault. The vault, in which William Simpson had seen documents filed, was secured by a combination lock, with access prior to 1969 limited to Sumner Simpson, William Simpson, two secretaries and the security guards. William Simpson never received reports of theft or tampering.

"In 1969, the box containing the papers at issue was moved to William Simpson's Bridgeport, Connecticut office where it remained secure in a closet until 1974. In 1974 the box was delivered to Raybestos-Manhattan's Director of Environmental Affairs, John Marsh. At some point between 1974 and 1977, Marsh told Simpson that the papers were relevant to asbestos disease and, in 1977, the papers were transferred to lawyers for Raybestos-Manhattan pursuant to a document production request in a then pending lawsuit.

"While the original documents remain in the possession of Raymark (the successor to Raybestos-Manhattan), copies were produced during discovery in this matter. The plaintiffs contend that the documents show that Johns-Manville had knowledge of health-related asbestos hazards and conspired with Raybestos-Manhattan to suppress information regarding these risks. Brief excerpts from these documents illustrate why the plaintiffs desire to have them admitted.

"In a letter dated September 25, 1935, written on 'Asbestos' magazine letterhead and signed 'A.S. Rossiter,' Rossiter wrote to Sumner Simpson at Raybestos-Manhattan asking whether Simpson would object to 'Asbestos' printing an article on the company's dust control procedures. The letter included the following:

"You may recall that we have written you on several occasions concerning the publishing of information, or discussion of, asbestosis and the work which has been and is being done, to eliminate or at least reduce it. Always you have requested that for certain obvious reasons we publish nothing, and naturally your wishes have been respected.

"A carbon copy of an October 1, 1935, letter from Bridgeport, Connecticut (Raybestos headquarters), to Vandiver Brown, general counsel for Johns-Manville, indicates that the Rossiter letter was enclosed. The copy, while unsigned, contains the word 'President' beneath the signature line. The initials 'SS-G' appear in the bottom left-hand corner of the copy. The letter, presumed to have been written or dictated by Sumner Simpson, and typed by Miss Garvey reads in part:

"'As I see it personally, we would be just as well off to say nothing about it until our survey is complete. I think the less said about asbestosis, the better off we are, but at the same time, we cannot lose track of the fact that there have been a number of articles on asbestos dust control and asbestosis in the British trade magazines. The magazine 'Asbestos' is in the business to publish articles affecting the trade and they have been very decent about not re-printing the English articles.'

"Vandiver Brown apparently received the Sumner Simpson letter as, on October 3, 1935, Brown wrote a letter to Simpson on Johns-Manville letterhead. This letter acknowledged receipt of the September 25 Rossiter letter and read as follows:

"'I quite agree with you that our interests are best served by having asbestosis receive the minimum of publicity. Even if we should eventually decide to raise no objection to the publication of an article on asbestosis in the magazine in question, I think we should warn the editors to use American data on the subject, rather than English. Dr. Lanza has frequently remarked, to me personally and in some of his papers, that the clinical picture presented in North American localities where there is an asbestos dust hazard is considerably milder than that reported in England and South Africa.'

"The plaintiffs contend that these documents indicate that certain asbestos manufacturers knew of the health hazards posed by asbestos and acted in concert to conceal those hazards."

The Third Circuit panel then held that the documents were authenticated under Rule 901(b)(8) and admissible as ancient documents under Rule 803(16): "Having reviewed the Sumner Simpson documents originally contained on the plaintiffs' exhibit list and the relevant portions of the original William Simpson deposition, we are convinced that on the basis of these materials alone, the plaintiffs have met their burden of establishing the *prima facie* authenticity of the documents. The Simpson deposition indicates to us that the manner of retaining the Sumner Simpson documents was consistent with what might have been expected. In view of this clear and unsuspicious history of custody... the papers are authentic under the standard of [Rule]901(b)(8). Defendants cannot put forward so much as a hint that these documents have been tampered with in any way. Nor in [our] perusal of the transcripts of the argument on similar motions in other asbestos litigation have [we] found any serious suggestion that the documents are fake or that they have been altered.... Once a document qualifies as an ancient document [under Rule 901(b)(8)], it is automatically excepted from the hearsay rule under Fed.R.Evid. 803(16)."

FRE 803(17) – Hearsay Exception: "Physicians Desk Reference" Is Not Admissible as Data Compilation Because It Contains Directions, Opinions, Suggestions and Recommendations

Rule 803. Hearsay Exceptions; Availability of Declarant Immaterial
The following are not excluded by the hearsay rule, even though the declarant is available as a witness:

(17) Market Reports, Commercial Publications. Market quotations, tabulations, lists, directories, or other published compilations, generally used and relied upon by the public or by persons in particular occupations.

GARVEY v. O'DONAGHUE
530 A.2d 1141 (D.C. App. 1987)

Diane R. Garvey sued Dr. J. Morgan O'Donaghue, Dr. Charles T. Gerber, and Dr. Joseph W. Giere for malpractice alleging they negligently prescribed and administered the antibiotic Tobramycin when she sought treatment for a sore throat that had quickly led to an ovarian abscess. She was admitted to Georgetown University Hospital where she was given Tobramycin and Cefoxiitin intravenously for two weeks. A few weeks after her discharge she said she noticed a ringing in her ears that did not improve despite extensive treatment. She blamed her condition, tinnitus, on the Tobramycin, "a highly toxic drug," and on the dosage and duration of its use she was prescribed. The

D.C. Superior Court jury's verdict was in favor of the physicians, and Garvey appealed.

One issue she raised was the trial court's refusal to permit her to admit into evidence pages of the Physicians Desk Reference (PDR) dealing with Tobramycin. The claim was that it was purely factual material and as such was admissible under Rule 803(17), for the "truth of the matter asserted"[32] in those pages. The District of Columbia Court of Appeals noted that "typically the publications covered by this exception to the hearsay rule are lists containing readily verifiable information such as telephone directories, price lists and the like," and cited two pre-Rules cases that admitted mortality tables as evidence of life expectancy under the same theory of reliability – the sheer routineness of inclusion in such quantities of like data, and the absence of a motive on the part of the compilers to fabricate. "In the instance of the PDR," held the appellate court, "interwoven among its factual statements are…directions, opinions, suggestions, and recommendations," thus removing the PDR from the category of lists and tables.

(The court then held that the trial court should have admitted the PDR, as well as package inserts from the Tobramycin, to establish, in conjunction with expert testimony, the proper standard of care – but that the error was harmless because "very nearly the same information [was] placed before the jury through another witness," here Garvey's medical expert Dr. Nicholas Criares.)

FRE 803(18) – Hearsay Exception: Treatise Cannot Be Used for Cross-Examination of Expert Unless Its Authority Is Established by Testimony of Some Expert During Trial

> **Rule 803. Hearsay Exceptions; Availability of Declarant Immaterial**
> The following are not excluded by the hearsay rule, even though the declarant is available as a witness:
>
> *(18) Learned Treatises.* To the extent called to the attention of an expert witness upon cross-examination or relied upon by the expert witness in direct examination, statements contained in published treatises, periodicals, or pamphlets on a subject of history, medicine, or other science or art, established as a reliable authority by the testimony or admission of the witness or by other expert testimony or by judicial notice. If admitted, the statements may be read into evidence but may not be received as exhibits.

MOLKENBUR v. HART
411 N.W.2d 249 (Minn. App. 1987)

After Leah Molkenbur took 40 Elavil tablets one day in December 1980, her parents drove her to St. Croix Valley Clinic, where Dr. Quinn prescribed Ipecac syrup to induce vomiting. She vomited but soon became incoherent and physically unbalanced, signs of toxic poisoning. Dr. Quinn sent her to Lakeview Memorial Hospital, where Dr. James F. Hart pumped out the contents of her stomach and inserted a breathing tube. "He also tried several medications to reduce the toxicity effects, elevate her blood pressure,

---
[32] See Rule 801(c).

and slow her heart rate," then rode in the ambulance with her as she was taken to St. Paul Ramsey Hospital. Shortly after her arrival she went into cardiac arrest for 30 minutes, causing her to suffer anoxic encephalopathy (brain damage from oxygen deprivation). She later brought an action for negligent care and treatment against both doctors, the St. Croix Valley Clinic and Lakeview Memorial Hospital. Lakeview was dismissed from the suit before trial, and the jury found the other defendants were not negligent in their treatment of Molkenbur. She appealed.

One evidentiary issue in her appeal concerned the trial court's refusal to let Molkenbur use a 1977 medical journal article on the treatment of Elavil overdoses to impeach Dr. Kingston, director of the Minnesota Poison Control Center, who testified as an expert witness for the defense.

The court affirmed, holding that under Minnesota's Rule 803(18), "a treatise cannot be used for cross-examination unless its authority is established, either through reliance by the expert during direct or reliance of any expert during the trial... Since neither Dr. Kingston nor *any other* expert in the lawsuit recognized this article as authoritative, the trial court properly refused to allow cross-examination based on it....

"Similarly, the trial court did not err in preventing appellant from questioning Dr. Bialka about an article that he did not recognize as authoritative. Appellant argues that she was not using the article to prove the truth of the matter asserted, but for impeachment purposes. Questioning regarding medical articles for impeachment is appropriate only if the Witness' opinion is based on the work or he recognizes the work as standard authority."

FRE 803(18) – Hearsay Exception: Statements in Articles May Be Read to Jury on Direct Examination if Expert Testifies to Their Reliable Authority

> **Rule 803. Hearsay Exception; Availability of Declarant Immaterial**
> The following are not excluded by the hearsay rule, even though the declarant is available as a witness:
>
> *(18) Learned Treaties.* To the extent called to the attention of an expert witness upon cross-examination or relied upon by the expert witness in direct examination, statements contained in published treatises, periodicals, or pamphlets on a subject of history, medicine, or other science or art, established as a reliable authority by the testimony or admission of the witness or by other expert testimony or by judicial notice. If admitted, the statements may be read into evidence but may not be received as exhibits.

STATE v. RANGITSCH
700 P.2d 382, 40 Wash. App. 771 (1985)

Kevin Danforth Rangitsch was charged with five counts of negligent homicide and one count of violation of the Uniform Controlled Substances Act (possession of cocaine). Rangitsch had been observed, both before and after the three-car, five-fatality accident he caused, acting in a way that suggested to trained observers that he was using cocaine. A later search of his home found traces of cocaine and drug paraphernalia. He was tried before a jury in Snohomish County and convicted of all six charges, and he appealed.

One of the seven issues he raised on appeal concerned the testimony of a Dr. Bonnell, who had had some pharmacological training and who had "done some reading on the effects of cocaine on human behavior." The prosecution used Dr. Bonnell... to testify on the effects of cocaine on Rangitsch's ability to drive a car,[33] and the doctor "relied on several statements in articles and in a monograph describing the effects of cocaine on human behavior and perception." He read to the jury from these texts over Rangitsch's objection, and on appeal the Washington Court of Appeals, Division 1, upheld this usage under Washington's equivalent of Federal Rule 803(18). "A witness permitted by the court to testify as an expert may rely on statements contained in treatises, periodicals, and pamphlets. These statements are not excluded by the hearsay rule, and they may be read into evidence provided the expert has testified to their reliable authority. Dr. Bonnell... first testified to their reliability as authority, thus qualifying the textual statements...." It is worth noting that the rules permit use of learned treatises not only to impeach a witness, but also in direct testimony of a witness to support his or her testimony.

FRE 803(19) – Hearsay Exception: Reputation Concerning Personal or Family History Includes Defendant's Reputation for Using a Certain Alias

> **Rule 803. Hearsay Exceptions; Availability of Declarant Immaterial**
> The following are not excluded by the hearsay rule, even though the declarant is available as a witness:
> *(19) Reputation Concerning Personal or Family History.* Reputation among members of a person's family by blood, adoption, or marriage, or among a person's associates, or in the community, concerning a person's birth, adoption, marriage, divorce, death, legitimacy, relationship by blood, adoption, or marriage, ancestry, or other similar fact of personal or family history.

UNITED STATES v. ALLEN
960 F.2d 1055 (D.C. Cir. 1992)

Maxwell Allen and James Casey were convicted of a number of drug charges. Among several grounds asserted on appeal by both, Casey claimed it was error to admit testimony that he also went by the name "Witcliff Rhoden," the name on an appointment card found in the bathroom ceiling (along with 9.5 grams of crack) of a house in Northwest Washington, D.C. where undercover police officers made controlled buys of crack before arresting Allen and Casey.

The District of Columbia Circuit Court of Appeals affirmed the convictions. The court called Casey's alias issue "an interesting question" noting, "One virtually always learns a name – even one's own – by being told what

---

[33]Reliance on this witness was upheld on appeal under Washington's Rule 702, despite his lack of a pharmacology specialty. "A physician is not incompetent to testify as an expert merely because he is not a specialist in the particular field of which he speaks."

it is.... Nevertheless, evidence as to names is commonly regarded as either not hearsay because it is not introduced to prove the truth of the matter asserted, or so imbued with reliability because of the name's common usage as to make any objection frivolous."

(While the testimony establishing that it was Casey's reputation to have used the alias "Witcliff Rhoden" may have been a good deal less than optimal, if its admission was error, "it was undoubtedly harmless. Casey was found hiding alone in an unlit, unusable bathroom within a few feet of both a bag of drugs consistent in size and appearance with the bag he had in his waistband during the undercover buy just moments before and, even more damningly, the very $20 bill the police had given him during that buy. Compared to that, the testimony regarding his alias was trivial.")

The whole question of names has troubled courts (although not, perhaps, very deeply) from the start. This rule seems as good a place as any to lodge its solution.

FRE 803(20) – Hearsay Exception: Out-of-Court Statement as to Lot Boundaries Must Be in Form of Reputation (General Consensus of Opinion), Not a Personal Observation

> **Rule 803. Hearsay Exceptions; Availability of Declarant Immaterial**
> The following are not excluded by the hearsay rule, even though the declarant is available as a witness:
> *(20) Reputation Concerning Boundaries or General History.* Reputation in a community, arising before the controversy, as to boundaries of or customs affecting lands in the community, and reputation as to events of general history important to the community or State or nation in which located.

GOODOVER v. LINDEY'S, INC.
757 P.2d 1290, 232 Mont. 302 (1988)

The 1944 plat of the Seeley Lake Shores Sites subdivision as filed with the Missoula County Clerk and Recorder was filled with errors. The northwest corner of Lot Two, owned by Pat M. Goodover, was relocated after years of observance of a wooden monument on the land by Lindey's, owner of Lots One and Three, after it had the legal description surveyed by R. David Schurian. According to this survey, Goodover's boathouse encroached the new line by several feet. Goodover filed an action for declaratory judgment that the long-observed boundary was correct. The Missoula County District Court determined the property line in favor of Goodover, and Lindey's appealed.

At trial Goodover had been allowed over objection to testify to a conversation he had with Jim Sullivan, a predecessor in title to Lot Two. Sullivan had told him a stake located four or five feet east of the boathouse marked the boundary of the lots in question. The Montana Supreme Court said Lindey's objection was "appropriate" under Montana's equivalent to Federal Rule 803(20) because Sullivan spoke of his own "personal observation" and experience, not a "general consensus of opinion" in the community as required by the rule. "In the case at bar, the rationale for excepting Goodover's testimony from the hearsay rule is not present. Goodover asserted Sullivan showed him where the property border marker existed. This assertion was presented as fact of personal observation. The reasoning behind the exception requires that the reputation of where Goodover's property line existed is reliable because 'there is a high probability that the matter underwent general scrutiny as the community reputation was formed' (quoting Weinstein). No evidence was presented regarding the reputation of the monument position. Lindey's objection was appropriate and should have been sustained."

But because the court found sufficient other reliable evidence of the boundary, the evidentiary error was held to be harmless, and the decision below was affirmed.

FRE 803(21) – Hearsay Exception: Character Evidence Must Be Admissible Under Another Substantive Rule (404, 405, or 608)

> **Rule 803. Hearsay Exceptions; Availability of Declarant Immaterial**
> The following are not excluded by the hearsay rule, even though the declarant is available as a witness:
> *(21) Reputation as to Character.* Reputation of a person's character among associates or in the community.

STATE v. JOHNSON
434 A.2d 532 (Me. 1981)

At the trial of Ronald Johnson in Lincoln County Superior Court for the murder of his mother, Verna Johnson, Johnson's friend and co-defendant, Steve Gillcash, who had pled guilty to the charge, testified for the defense. On cross-examination he said that on the night of the murder in March 1979, the two were both very drunk, went to the home of Johnson's mother together, and later left the state together, but that he had no other memory of the events of that night. He acknowledged, however, that his earlier statements to police and at his guilty plea hearing – in which he said he and Johnson jointly planned and participated in her murder – were true "as far as I can remember." The jury convicted Johnson, and he appealed.

The Maine Supreme Court considered a number of issues raised by Johnson on appeal. One involved the testimony of Robert Taylor, a fellow inmate of Gillcash. The defense called Taylor and without objection he testified that Gillcash told him in jail that Johnson was innocent and that Gillcash had killed Johnson's mother himself. "On cross-examination, the state's attorney asked Taylor, over the defendant's objection, whether it was the 'general consensus' and 'general feeling' in the prison that Gillcash was 'trying to cover for Johnson.' After first responding that Gillcash and Johnson were 'good friends' but that he did not know if Gillcash was trying to cover for Johnson, Taylor finally responded affirmatively. On redirect examination, Taylor repeated that he did not know."

The state high court agreed the statement should not have been admitted. If it was offered to impeach Gillcash, it needed to be evidence of Gillcash's character for untruthfulness. "Evidence that Gillcash was reputed to be covering for Johnson on a particular matter is not evidence of his general reputation for truthfulness."[34]

Applied properly, Rule 803(21) is only an answer to a hearsay objection, not to the various substantive hurdles that must be overcome for character evidence to be admissible. Conversely, every time a witness testifies to a person's reputation for a character trait under Rule 405(a), by way of Rule 404(a)(1), 404(a)(2), or 608(a), the court must be applying Rule 803(21) as well, to get past the hearsay nature of reputation: "They say..."

FRE 803(21) – Hearsay Exception: Reputation for Honesty Must Be in Community Larger Than Eighth Floor of County Jail to Be Admissible

> **Rule 803. Hearsay Exceptions; Availability of Declarant Immaterial**
> The following are not excluded by the hearsay rule, even though the declarant is available as a witness:
> *(21) Reputation as to Character.* Reputation of a person's character among associates or in the community.

FERGUSON v. STATE
675 P.2d 1023 (Okla. Cr. App. 1984)

Raymond N. Ferguson was charged in Tulsa District Court with first-degree murder and shooting with intent to kill in the shotgunning of his ex-wife, Virginia Sue Thomas, and her fiancé, Scott Turner. Turner died immediately; Thomas survived to identify Ferguson in court as the shooter. Ferguson called seven witnesses to establish an alibi defense. The jury convicted him, and he received two consecutive life sentences. Ferguson appealed.

The Court of Criminal Appeals of Oklahoma affirmed the conviction. One issue among several on appeal concerned the trial court's refusal to let Ferguson impeach a state witness with so-called dishonesty reputation testimony. Troy Birmingham was an inmate along with Ferguson in the county jail. Birmingham testified that Ferguson described the shootings to him and said he didn't know how he missed killing his wife. The defense called another county jail inmate, Dewey Jernigan, and tried to get Jernigan to testify to Birmingham's poor reputation for honesty "in the community of the Tulsa County jail."[35] The trial court sustained the prosecution's objection, and the appellate court upheld the ruling: "Jernigan had no knowledge of Birmingham's reputation in the community outside the jail. Although we do not conclude that a county jail may never qualify in itself as a 'community' in which one may establish a reputation which may be testified to, it is our opinion that in this case the eighth floor of the Tulsa county jail did not clearly qualify.... The six cells on the eighth floor of the Tulsa County jail are occupied at any given time by

---

[34] As to impeaching the hearsay statement of Gillcash offered by Johnson, the court said, "even if Gillcash's out-of-court statement was also hearsay, M.R. Evid. 806 permits impeachment of hearsay declarants only with evidence which would be admissible for those purposes if declarant had testified as a witness." See, e.g., *United States v. Wuagneux, infra* p. 282.
[35] Under Oklahoma's Rule 608(a).

eighteen to twenty-four inmates. This inmate population is transitory, constantly changing; it is not a stable group of people residing together for a substantial amount of time. It is our opinion that such a small constantly changing population is not clearly a community in which one inmate could become well-known and establish a reputation."

FRE 803(22) – Hearsay Exception: Judgment of Conviction Based on Guilty Plea Is Admissible as Party Admission

> **Rule 803. Hearsay Exceptions; Availability of Declarant Immaterial**
> The following are not excluded by the hearsay rule, even though the declarant is available as a witness:
> *(22) Judgment of Previous Conviction.* Evidence of a final judgment, entered after a trial or upon a plea of guilty (but not upon a plea of nolo contendere), adjudging a person guilty of a crime punishable by death or imprisonment in excess of one year, to prove any fact essential to sustain the judgment, but not including, when offered by the Government in a criminal prosecution for purposes other than impeachment, judgments against persons other than the accused. The pendency of an appeal may be shown but does not affect admissibility.

SAFECO INSURANCE COMPANY OF AMERICA v. McGRATH
708 P.2d 657, 42 Wash. App. 58 (1986)

In a restaurant parking lot in Bellevue one night in February 1980, attorney Thomas F. McGrath, Jr., intoxicated, shot Frederick R. Hayes in the neck, allegedly because Hayes "was approaching him in a menacing fashion." Nevertheless McGrath pled guilty to second degree assault, knowingly inflicting grievous bodily harm, in exchange for withdrawal of a second count and of a firearm charge that carried a mandatory five-year prison sentence. A year or so later, Hayes and his companion on the night of the shooting, Judy Frounfelter, filed a civil action against McGrath for damages arising out of the shooting, and McGrath called upon his insurers to defend the actions and indemnify any adverse judgment. Safeco was McGrath's homeowner's insurer; Lumberman's Mutual provided excess personal casualty liability coverage, and General Insurance Company insured McGrath's law firm.

The insurers filed an action in King County Superior Court against McGrath and his wife Terrell C. McGrath, Hayes and his wife and Frounfelter and her husband, seeking a declaratory judgment that they had no duty to defend or indemnify McGrath. Safeco's policy excluded from its coverage of bodily injury or property damage occurrences "bodily injury or property damage which is either expected or intended from the stand point of the insured." The trial court granted the insurers summary judgment, holding that McGrath's prior plea of guilty to criminal charges raises collateral estoppel on the issue of McGrath's intent, thereby putting this occurrence within the policy's exclusion. McGraths, Hayes and Frounfelters appealed.

The Washington Court of Appeals reversed and remanded, holding that an *Alford*[36]-type guilty plea, in which a defendant faced with

---
[36] *North Carolina v. Alford,* 400 U.S. 25, 91 S.Ct. 160, 27 L.Ed.2d 162 (1970).

the "powerful, coercive forces" of mandatory incarceration chooses to plead guilty to a reduced charge that holds a strong probability of a deferred or substantially suspended sentence, as here, does not present an appropriate setting for application of the doctrine of collateral estoppel. The court nonetheless held the plea of guilty itself to be admissible under Rule 803(22) as evidence of McGrath's admission that he acted intentionally under Rule 801(d)(2)(A). The plea, however – like all party admissions of whatever variety – is not to be viewed as "conclusive," so McGrath was held to be "entitled to present the jury with the facts surrounding his guilty plea." The issue of his intent was an open question for the jury.

FRE 803(23) – Hearsay Exception: Judgment of Citizenship Status Is Admissible to Prove Workers Were Aliens

> **Rule 803. Hearsay Exceptions; Availability of Declarant Immaterial**
> The following are not excluded by the hearsay rule, even though the declarant is available as a witness:
>
> *(23) Judgment as to Personal, Family, or General History, or Boundaries.* Judgments as proof of matters of personal, family or general history, or boundaries, essential to the judgment, if the same would be provable by evidence of reputation.

GRANT BROTHERS CONSTRUCTION CO. v. UNITED STATES
232 U.S. 647, 34 S. Ct. 452, 58 L. Ed. 776 (1914)

The government brought an action against Grant Brothers Construction Company of California to penalize it for violating the Alien Immigration Act by importing 45 workers from Mexico into the Territory of Arizona to work on a railroad line in October 1909. (Many more Mexican nationals came to work in Arizona on their own; the Act penalizes those who knowingly assist or encourage the importation of contract labor.) A jury rendered a judgment against the company for $45,000, "the prescribed penalty of $1,000 each" for the 45 violations of the Act. Grant Brothers appealed, and the Supreme Court of the Territory of Arizona affirmed. Grant Brothers appealed to the United States Supreme Court.

One issue on appeal concerned the adequacy of proof at trial that the 45 workers in question were citizens of Mexico. They had been hired by one agent, Rupelius, but upon entry at the border town of Naco were "taken into custody by an immigration inspector, and were examined before a board of special inquiry. The board found that they were alien contract laborers, ordered that they be excluded...." They returned to Hermosillo, then were induced by Rupelius and others to come back into the U.S. "Over the defendant's objection, the decision of the board of special inquiry was admitted in evidence as tending to prove that the forty-five men were aliens...." Grant Brothers Construction objected that it was hearsay, and because the company was not a party to that proceeding, the judgment was not binding upon them. The Supreme Court affirmed, observing that it was long established that "a judgment in a prior action is admissible, even against a stranger, as *prima facie,* but not conclusive, proof of a fact which may be shown by evidence of general reputation such as custom, pedigree, race, death and the like, and this because the judgment is usually more persuasive than mere evidence of reputation.... In principle, alienage is within the latter rule, and so the board's decision was properly admitted in evidence for the purpose stated."

The decision demonstrates the deep common law roots of many of the hearsay exceptions, here even of one of the exceptions usually regarded as somewhat obscure.

FRE 804 (a)(1) – Declarant Is Not "Unavailable" Because of Privilege Against Self-Incrimination Unless Court Has Issued Its Order Exempting Declarant from Testifying

> **Rule 804. Hearsay Exceptions; Declarant Unavailable**
> *(a) Definition of Unavailability.* "Unavailability as a witness" includes situations in which the declarant –
> (1) is exempted by ruling of the court on the ground of privilege from testifying concerning the subject matter of the declarant's statement;

PEOPLE v. ROSENTHAL
670 P.2d 1254 (Colo. App. 1983)

At Christina Rosenthal's murder trial in Adams County District Court the prosecution was allowed to present the testimony of Sheriff's Department investigator James Wilbourn to the effect that Rosenthal's companion, J.D. La Plant, had confessed to the murder of Ron Hardison. La Plant's out-of-court statement was admitted as a statement against interest under Colorado's Rule 804(b)(3), virtually identical to the federal rule. Rosenthal was convicted, and appealed on the question of the admission of La Plant's hearsay statement.

The Colorado Court of Appeals agreed with appellant that La Plant had not sufficiently been shown to be unavailable. The appellate court reversed her conviction, holding that the prosecution had to do more than simply assume that La Plant would invoke his Fifth Amendment privilege against testifying. "A declarant's assertion of a privilege does not result invariably in judicial approval thereof.... In this case, for example, La Plant at one point offered to waive his constitutional privileges against self-incrimination and to testify for the prosecutor in return for sentencing concessions by the prosecutor. No judicial ruling was requested or obtained here; hence, La Plant was not 'unavailable' pursuant to CRE 804(a)(1)."

Because the appellate court was easily able to dispose of the case on the preliminary question of the declarant's unavailability, it spared itself the harder task of weighing the extent to which the confession was in fact "at the time of its making... contrary to the declarant's... [penal] interest." Confessions often involve elements of reciprocal advantage to the accused, including reduced charges and sentences, or at least the accused's expectation of same. See Rule 804(b)(3).

FRE 804(a) – Hearsay Exceptions: Declarant Is Not "Unavailable" Where Proponent of Out-of-Court Statement Makes No Effort to Identify or Locate Declarant

> **Rule 804. Hearsay Exceptions; Declarant Unavailable**
>
> *(a) Definition of Unavailability.* "Unavailability as a witness" includes situations in which the declarant –
>
> (1) is exempted by ruling of the court on the ground of privilege from testifying concerning the subject matter of the declarant's statement; or
>
> (2) persists in refusing to testify concerning the subject matter of the declarant's statement despite an order of the court to do so; or
>
> (3) testifies to a lack of memory of the subject matter of the declarant's statement; or
>
> (4) is unable to be present or to testify at the hearing because of death or then existing physical or mental illness or infirmity; or
>
> (5) is absent form the hearing and the proponent of a statement has been unable to procure the declarant's attendance (or in the case of a hearsay exception under subdivision (b)(2), (3), or (4), the declarant's attendance or testimony) by process or other reasonable means.
>
> A declarant is not unavailable as a witness if exemption, refusal, claim of lack of memory, inability, or absence is due to the procurement or wrongdoing of the proponent of a statement for the purpose of preventing the witness from attending or testifying.

CUMMISKEY v. CHANDRIS, S.A.
719 F.Supp. 1183 (S.D.N.Y. 1989), aff'd 895 F.2d 107 (2d Cir. 1990)

While approaching the bar in the Dolphin Lounge on board the cruise ship S/S BRITANIS, Shirley Cummiskey slipped on wet tile and fell, injuring the fingers of her right hand. She sued the ship's operator, Chandris, S.A. and the owner, Ajax Navigation Co., in New York state court; the defendants removed the case to the federal district court for the Southern District of New York on the basis of diversity of citizenship.

To try to prove that the defendants had actual or constructive notice of the wet floor before her fall, Cummiskey offered into evidence the statement of an unidentified man dressed as an employee of the ship who allegedly said, "I am really sorry the floor is wet. I'm sorry," while assisting Cummiskey after her fall. Neither Cummiskey nor her traveling companions, Eileen and Tara Donohue, could identify the declarant more particularly than "medium-dark skin," speaking with an accent, a "foreigner," wearing a red or maroon uniform jacket, "like everybody else was wearing."

The trial judge held the declarant was not "unavailable" under Rule 804(a) because plaintiff had made no effort to identify him and "meet her foundational burden of establishing his unavailability." Although the court never identified the specific Rule 804(b) exception that would require unavailability of the declarant,[37] it

---
[37] The court in fact seems a bit confused, seeming to treat unavailability as a prerequisite to admitting the statement as an excited utterance, Rule 803(2). But as the court notes, the unavailability of the declarant, coupled with the offering party's inability to identify him, would make it difficult to admit the statement as an excited utterance because it would be hard to establish that the declarant had personally observed the startling event. It would be no less difficult to come up with independent evidence of agency for Rule 801(d)(2)(D).

264 Evidence Illustrated

seems likely the statement might have been offered as a statement against interest, Rule 804(b)(3). Summary judgment was entered for defendants.

FRE 804(b)(1) – Hearsay Exception: Grand Jury Testimony Is Inadmissible if Party Lacked Similar Motive to Develop It

Rule 804. Hearsay Exception; Declarant Unavailable

(a) Definition of Unavailability. "Unavailability as a witness" includes situations in which the declarant-

(1) is exempted by ruling of the court on the ground of privilege from testifying concerning the subject matter of the declarant's statement;...

(b) Hearsay Exceptions. The following are not excluded by the hearsay rule if the declarant is unavailable as a witness:

(1) Former Testimony. Testimony given as a witness at another hearing of the same or a different proceeding or in a deposition taken in compliance with law in the course of the same or another proceeding, if the party against whom the testimony is now offered, or, in a civil action or proceeding, a predecessor in interest, had an opportunity and similar motive to develop the testimony by direct, cross, or redirect examination.

UNITED STATES v. SALERNO
505 U.S. 317, 112 S. Ct. 2503, 120 L. Ed. 2d 255 (1992)

A New York federal grand jury indicted Anthony Salerno and six others for RICO[38] activities involving the New York construction industry, including the rigging of bidding on large Manhattan projects by influencing labor unions and controlling the supply of concrete. The indictments charged that the Genovese Family of La Cosa Nostra allocated contracts among six concrete companies forming a "Club."

Two owners of the Cedar Park Concrete Construction Corporation had testified before the grand jury under grants of immunity. Both Frederick DeMattheis and Pasquale Bruno repeatedly stated in response to government questions that Cedar Park did not participate in the Club.

At trial the government presented other evidence that suggested Cedar Park did participate in the Club and that the Family was a part owner of Cedar Park. Salerno and the other defendants attempted to introduce into evidence the grand jury testimony of DeMattheis and Bruno after they refused to testify at the trial on Fifth Amendment grounds.[39] The district court refused to admit the testimony under Rule 804(b)(1), former testimony, holding that the government's motive in examining witnesses before the grand jury was "far different" from its motive at trial.

The defendants were convicted of the RICO and other crimes. They appealed, and the Second Circuit Court of Appeals reversed. The appellate court held that

---

[38]Racketeer Influenced and Corrupt Organizations Act.
[39]They were thus "unavailable" under FRE 804(a)(1).

despite the government's dissimilar motive to develop the testimony, "adversarial fairness" requires disregarding the similar motive requirement of the rule "when the Government obtains immunized testimony in a grand jury proceeding from a witness who refuses to testify at trial."

The United States Supreme Court disagreed. Courts are not free to ignore the rule's provision that the party against whom the testimony is now being offered must have had a similar motive to develop the testimony at the hearing where it was originally given; that requirement does not "evaporate" (as the Second Circuit had said) just because it is defendants who are offering the grand jury testimony against the government, rather than the other way around.

(Because the Supreme Court believed both the District Court and the Court of Appeals had ruled on the question of the government's motive as a matter of law, they remanded the case for a factual determination whether the government indeed had a similar motive at trial as at the grand jury hearing.)

Justice Stevens wrote a vigorous dissent urging that as a matter of law the government does have a similar motive to develop its own witnesses' testimony in grand jury proceedings.

FRE 804(b)(1) – Hearsay Exception: Deposition from Earlier Case Against Party Is Inadmissible When Motive to Develop Testimony Was Different Based on Different Claims Against Party

> **Rule 804. Hearsay Exceptions; Declarant Unavailable**
>
> *(a) Definition of Unavailability.* "Unavailability as a witness" includes situations in which the declarant –
>
> (4) is unable to be present or to testify at the hearing because of death or then existing physical or mental illness or infirmity;...
>
> *(b) Hearsay Exceptions.* The following are not excluded by the hearsay rule if the declarant is unavailable as a witness:
>
> *(1) Former Testimony.* Testimony given as a witness at another hearing of the same or a different proceeding, or in a deposition taken in compliance with law in the course of the same or another proceeding, if the party against whom the testimony is now offered, or, in a civil action or proceeding, a predecessor in interest, had an opportunity and similar motive to develop the testimony by direct, cross, or redirect examination.

LOHRMANN v. PITTSBURGH CORNING CORP.
782 F.2d 1156 (4th Cir. 1986)

A shipyard pipefitter for 39 years, Frederick O. Lohrmann allegedly contracted asbestosis from prolonged contact with asbestos on the job, and retired because of pulmonary disability. He sued more than a dozen manufacturers and suppliers of asbestos and asbestos-related products on both negligence and strict liability theories. The defendants "contended that Lohrmann did not have asbestosis, but had emphysema, chronic bronchitis, and shortness of breath due to cigarette smoking." After plaintiff rested, the trial judge directed verdicts for Raymark Industries, Inc., Celotex Corporation, and Pittsburgh Corning Corp., leaving only Keene Corporation, Eagle-Pitcher Industries, Inc,. G.A.F. Corporation and A.C.& S., Inc. in the suit. (Other original defendants settled or were in bankruptcy proceedings.) The remaining defendants were let off the hook by the jury's verdict. Lohrmann appealed.

One of the issues raised before the Fourth Circuit Court of Appeals concerned the admissibility of a 1975 deposition given by Richard Gaze, deceased by the time of the Lohrmann trial.[40] The deposition was offered against defendant Pittsburgh Corning only and was not admitted.

Gaze had been deposed in connection with cases filed by two Pittsburgh Corning employees who had worked at its plant in Tyler, Texas. In affirming the district court's ruling, the appellate panel said the claims in that case involved "the hazardous effects of raw asbestos upon the health of plant workers exposed to the raw asbestos in a manufacturing environment. In the present case, the plaintiff is not a plant worker, but a pipefitter, who from time to time worked in close proximity to insulators and others using products containing asbestos after it had been processed. The state of the art as it relates to the health of persons exposed to asbestos products differs considerably for asbestos plant workers dealing with raw asbestos and for persons working in the vicinity of asbestos products. The cross examination of Gaze did not develop this distinction because such distinction was not relevant to the Tyler, Texas, cases...." Pittsburgh Corning, therefore, was held not to have had the same or similar motive to develop Gaze's testimony on cross-examination as it would have had in defending Lohrmann's action – despite the apparent similarity of the underlying causes of action.

FRE 804(b)(2) Hearsay Exception: Belief of Impending Death Is Necessary for Admissibility of Dying Declaration

> **Rule 804.**
> *(b) Hearsay Exceptions.* The following are not excluded by the hearsay rule if the declarant is unavailable as a witness:
> *(2) Statement Under Belief of Impending Death.* In a prosecution for homicide or in a civil action or proceeding, a statement made by a declarant while believing that the declarant's death was imminent, concerning the cause or circumstances of what the declarant believed to be impending death.

SHEPARD v. UNITED STATES
290 U.S. 96, 54 S. Ct. 22, 78 L. Ed. 196 (1933)

Zenana Shepard died a slow death by poisoning. Her husband, Army medical corps Major Charles Shepard, was charged with her murder. He was said to be in love with another woman and wished to marry her. The defense theory was suicide. Defense witnesses testified they had heard statements by Mrs. Shepard before her final illness "that she had no wish to live, and had nothing to live for, and... that she expected some day to make an end to her life."

---
[40] Thus, Gaze was "unavailable" per Rule 804(a)(4).

On rebuttal the government introduced, over the defense's hearsay objection, testimony by a nurse, Clara Brown, that two days after the onset of her illness Mrs. Shepard asked her to test a bottle of whiskey from her husband's bedroom closet that tasted and smelled strange, and from which she had taken a drink just before she collapsed. She explained, "Dr. Shepard has poisoned me." She died almost a month after this conversation. Defendant was convicted of murder, and he appealed.

The government's main argument was that Mrs. Shepard's words amounted to a dying declaration. (Its other contention, that the words rebutted the defense theory of a suicidal state of mind, was accepted by the Tenth Circuit Court of Appeals, but rejected out of hand by the United States Supreme Court: the words of Mrs. Shepard had not been offered at trial for that purpose, and in any event they were not about "her present thoughts and feelings, or even her thoughts and feelings in times past.") The nurse testified Mrs. Shepard also said she was not going to get well, that she was going to die.

Justice Cardozo wrote for the court that the statement did not qualify as a dying declaration because there was insufficient indication that the declarant spoke while believing her death was imminent. She seemed by the time of the conversation with the nurse to be recovering, and two weeks later, after a relapse and while her condition was grave, she said to one of her doctors, "You will get me well, won't you?" The Supreme Court said this hardly amounted to the "settled hopeless expectation... that death is near at hand... the consciousness of a swift and certain doom."

While "[t]here is no unyielding ritual of words to be spoken by the dying," and "despair of recovery may indeed be gathered from the circumstances if the facts support the inference," more is needed than a mere expectation of eventual death or a fear that death is possible.

Cases like *Shepard* may have been what prompted the drafters of the Rules to rename this exception the "Statement Under Belief of Impending Death," which is rather more neutral on the question of timing, at least, than some of Cardozo's poetry here.

FRE 804(b)(2) – Hearsay Exception: Court May Infer from Circumstances Attending Statement That Declarant Was Conscious of Impending Death

> **Rule 804. Hearsay Exception; Declarant Unavailable**
>
> *(a) Definition of Unavailability.* "Unavailability as a witness" includes situation in which the declarant –
>
> (4) is unable to be present or to testify at the hearing because of death or then existing physical or mental illness or infirmity;…
>
> *(b) Hearsay Exceptions.* The following are not excluded by the hearsay rule if the declarant is unavailable as a witness:
>
> *(2) Statement Under Belief of Impending Death.* In a prosecution for homicide or in a civil action or proceeding, a statement made by a declarant while believing that the declarant's death was imminent, concerning the cause or circumstances of what the declarant believed to be impending death.

PEOPLE v. SILER
429 N.W.2d 865, 171 Mich. App. 246 (1988)

Gordon Darwin called 911 for an ambulance. The tape of the call was introduced over a defense hearsay objection at William Harvey Siler's murder trial. The jury heard Darwin say, "I need an ambulance right away…. My heart's stabbed…. I've been stabbed in the heart…." When the dispatcher asked, "Who did it?" Darwin said, "Just come with the ambulance."

"Dispatcher: Who did it?
"Caller: A friend of mine.
"Dispatcher: Is he there?
"Caller: William Siler, yeah.
"Dispatcher: William Tyler.
"Caller: Siler, he's looking out for me in the meantime.
"Dispatcher: That would be apartment 514?
"Caller: 21 Weston, hurry please."

Twice more Darwin was heard saying, "Hurry with the ambulance." The call came in at 8:00 p.m.; by 9:30 p.m. Darwin had died at St. Mary's Hospital in Grand Rapids. Siler was convicted of second-degree murder and sentenced to a prison term of 15 to 30 years.

One issue raised in Siler's appeal to the Michigan Court of Appeals concerned the admissibility of Darwin's 911 tape. Siler contended Darwin had not sufficiently expressed a consciousness of impending death. The court affirmed the conviction. Contrary to Siler's protestations, Michigan's equivalent of Federal Rule 804(b)(2) does not make it "necessary for the declarant to have actually stated that he knew he was dying in order for the statement to be admissible as a dying declaration.

"Darwin called the emergency number, stating that he had been stabbed in the heart and that he needed an ambulance right away. Three times he repeated his request for an ambulance and told the police to hurry. A forensic pathologist testified that Darwin remained conscious for four to five minutes after the wound was inflicted. Approximately one and half hours later, he was pronounced dead without having regained consciousness. Taking these circumstances into account, we find that Darwin was conscious of impending death when he telephoned the emergency number. The tape recording reflects a dying declaration."

FRE 804(b)(3) – Hearsay Exception: Statement by Party's Deceased Predecessor in Title Is Admissible as Statement Against Interest

> **Rule 804. Hearsay Exceptions; Declarant Unavailable**
>
> *(b) Hearsay Exceptions.* The following are not excluded by the hearsay rule if the declarant is unavailable as a witness:
>
> *(3) Statement Against Interest.* A statement which was at the time of its making so far contrary to the declarant's pecuniary or proprietary interest, or so far tended to subject the declarant to civil or criminal liability, or to render invalid a claim by the declarant against another, that a reasonable person in the declarant's position would not have made the statement unless believing it to be true. A statement tending to expose the declarant to criminal liability and offered to exculpate the accused is not admissible unless corroborating circumstances clearly indicate the trustworthiness of the statement…

SACKETT v. ATYEO
552 N.W.2d 536, 217 Mich. App. 676 (1996)

When Duane and Violet Sackett bought their home in Lapeer, Michigan in 1962, Chester and Harriet White owned the house next door. A gravel driveway ran between the properties before branching off at a T. Sacketts and Whites shared the use of the gravel drive and split the costs of its maintenance.

After the Whites died, their home was purchased in 1990 by Scot Atyeo and Andrea Schroeder. Based on a stake survey they ordered just before the purchase, Atyeo and Schroeder believed they owned the entire driveway. After two years of friction with their neighbors, Atyeo and Schroeder put up a fence, based on the survey, which blocked the driveway.

Sacketts sued, claiming ownership of half the driveway under the doctrine of acquiescence. The trial court admitted into evidence statements made years earlier by Chester White to Sacketts and others to the effect that the boundary between the two lots ran right down the middle of the driveway. One of White's statements to that effect was made even after Sacketts had a survey done in 1972 that showed the entire driveway to be on White's property. Over objections that the statements were inadmissible hearsay, the trial court admitted them as statements against proprietary interest under Michigan Rule 804(b)(3).[41] (Thus Whites' acquiescence was long enough to bind their successor.)

The Michigan Court of Appeals affirmed, noting that a key element of the rule is that the declarant has to know at the time he speaks that the statement is against his interest. White's reference to the 1972 survey when he made one of the statements clinches his awareness that the statement was contrary to his proprietary interest, thus providing the reliability of the statement.

---

[41] The predicate of unavailability of the hearsay declarant was satisfied: White was deceased by the time of trial. The state rules applicable here are identical to FRE 804(a)(4) and FRE 804(b)(3).

FRE 801(c), 804(b)(3) – Question Can Be Statement Against Penal Interest

> **Rule 801.**
> *(c) Hearsay.* "Hearsay" is a statement, other than one made by the declarant while testifying at the trial or hearing, offered in evidence to prove the truth of the matter asserted.
>
> **Rule 804. Hearsay Exceptions; Declarant Unavailable**
> *(a) Definition of Unavailability.* "Unavailability as a witness" includes situations in which the declarant –
> (2) persists in refusing to testify concerning the subject matter of the declarant's statement despite an order of the court to do so; …
> *(b) Hearsay Exceptions.* The following are not excluded by the hearsay rule if the declarant is unavailable as a witness:
> *(3) Statement Against Interest.* A statement which was at the time of its making so far contrary to the declarant's pecuniary or proprietary interest, or so far tended to subject the declarant to civil or criminal liability, or to render invalid a claim by the declarant against another, that a reasonable person in the declarant's position would not have made the statement unless believing it to be true. A statement tending to expose the declarant to criminal liability and offered to exculpate the accused is not admissible unless corroborating circumstances clearly indicate the trustworthiness of the statement.

STATE v. SAUNDERS
491 N.E.2d 313, 23 Ohio App. 3d 69 (1984)

Robert L. Saunders was tried in Franklin County, Ohio for aggravated robbery of between $600 and $700 in coins from the managers of a laundromat after he had washed his clothes there for some time. Lynn Hines, the owner of a nearby motel where Saunders and a woman were staying, testified over a defense hearsay objection that some time after Saunders was seen going up to his room that night with a laundry basket, his companion came down to the office and inquired if Hines could use some spare change. Saunders was convicted by a jury, and he appealed.

Both sides appear to have badly misunderstood the hearsay issues on the appeal. The state contended the words of Saunders' companion were not hearsay, being a question and "not an assertion." Saunders' counsel seemed to think if it was hearsay it was automatically inadmissible.

The Court of Appeals of Ohio affirmed, along the way sorting out the issues admirably. The question can be taken as the equivalent of the assertion, "I have access to extra spare change." Nonetheless the question was admissible as a statement against the companion's penal interest, since it "tended to subject her to criminal liability as a participant in the robbery or for receiving stolen property." (As Ohio's evidence rule 804(b)(3) requires "corroboration" whether the statement is offered "to exculpate *or inculpate* the accused," unlike the Federal Rule, much of the opinion is devoted to "how much" corroboration is required. Not a lot, the court concluded.)

FRE 804(b)(3) – Hearsay Exception: Statement Against Penal Interest Offered to Exculpate Accused Must Be Corroborated and Must Strongly Indicate Trustworthiness

> **Rule 804. Hearsay Exceptions; Declarant Unavailable**
>
> *(b) Hearsay Exceptions.* The following are not excluded by the hearsay rule if the declarant is unavailable as a witness:
>
> *(3) Statement Against Interest.* A statement which was at the time of its making so far contrary to the declarant's pecuniary or proprietary interest, or so far tended to subject the declarant to civil or criminal liability, or to render invalid a claim by the declarant against another, that a reasonable person in the declarant's position would not have made the statement unless believing it to be true. A statement tending to expose the declarant to criminal liability and offered to exculpate the accused is not admissible unless corroborating circumstances clearly indicate the trustworthiness of the statement.

UNITED STATES v. SALVADOR
820 F.2d 558 (2d Cir. 1987)

Brothers Oscar and Roberto Salvador both declined to testify at their trial on charges of distribution and possession with intent to distribute cocaine and conspiracy to violate narcotics laws (with each other and with Juan Antonio Guzman). Oscar Salvador tried to offer into evidence Guzman's statement to an Assistant U.S. Attorney, given just prior to Guzman's guilty plea, that Oscar "was not an active participant in these things, that he did not know what was going on, that he was not a part of the deal." Guzman refused on Fifth Amendment grounds to testify at the Salvador trial.[42] The district judge refused to permit testimony about Guzman's statement. The Salvador brothers were convicted and sentenced to prison terms of four and eight years respectively.

Oscar Salvador appealed, and the Second Circuit Court of Appeals affirmed. Salvador argued that the statements strengthened the impression that Guzman had an insider's knowledge of the crimes, and that his statement was against his penal interest because it "displeased the prosecutor, threatened the plea agreement and might have led to an increased sentence." But the court concluded "the circumstances did not clearly corroborate either Guzman's trustworthiness or the truth of his statement." Too much government evidence existed that linked Oscar Salvador to the transaction in question for Guzman's statement to be "clearly" corroborated. And the circumstances of the making of the statement (possible motive to lie, lack of spontaneity, lack of a formal cooperation agreement) hardly suggest the kind of trustworthiness contemplated by Rule 804(b)(3).

---

[42] He was thus "unavailable" under Rule 804(a)(1).

272 Evidence Illustrated

FRE 804(b)(3) – Hearsay Exception: Admissibility of Statements Against Penal Interest Does Not Extend to Collateral Statements That Are Not Self-Inculpatory

> **Rule 804. Hearsay Exceptions; Declarant Unavailable**
>
> *(a) Definition of Unavailability.* "Unavailability as a witness" includes situations in which the declarant-
>
> *(2)* persists in refusing to testify concerning the subject matter of the declarant's statement despite an order of the court to do so;...
>
> *(b) Hearsay Exceptions.* The following are not excluded by the hearsay rule if the declarant is unavailable as a witness:
>
> *(3) Statement Against Interest.* A statement which was at the time of its making so far contrary to the declarant's pecuniary or proprietary interest, or so far tended to subject the declarant to civil or criminal liability, or to render invalid a claim by the declarant against another, that a reasonable person in the declarant's position would not have made the statement unless believing it to be true. A statement tending to expose the declarant to criminal liability and offered to exculpate the accused is not admissible unless corroborating circumstances clearly indicate the trustworthiness of the statement.

WILLIAMSON v. UNITED STATES
512 U.S. 594, 114 S. Ct. 2431, 129 L. Ed. 2d 476 (1994)

After Reginald Harris was stopped on a Florida highway and arrested for having 19 kilograms of cocaine in the trunk of his rental car, he was interviewed by Drug Enforcement Administration Agent Donald Walton by telephone. He claimed an unidentified Cuban gave him the cocaine for delivery to Fredel Williamson. Later in person Harris told the agent much the same story, but when Walton started to arrange a controlled delivery to Williamson, Harris stood up, said, "I can't let you do that," and said he'd lied about the Cuban. He said he was transporting the cocaine to Atlanta, with Williamson driving in front of him in another car. Williamson saw Harris get stopped, turned around, drove back past Harris and the police and must have seen Harris with his trunk open. Thus a controlled delivery would be impossible and likely dangerous for DEA agents. Although Agent Walton made no concrete promises to Harris about any specific reward or benefit for cooperating, he did promise to report Harris' cooperation to the Assistant U.S. Attorney.

At Williamson's trial, Harris refused to testify despite a grant of use immunity and a court order to testify. The district court ruled that Agent Walton could testify as to what Harris had told him under Rule 804(b)(3), statements against penal interest. Williamson was convicted, and on appeal the Eleventh Circuit Court of Appeals affirmed.

The United States Supreme Court, per Justice O'Connor, reversed and remanded, saying some parts of what Harris told Agent Walton were admissible but not all parts, because not every "statement" was strictly contrary to his penal interest. Taking the narrow definition of "statement" from Rule 801(a)(1) ("an oral or written assertion") rather than one dictionary alternative ("a report or narrative" – an "extended declaration") O'Connor wrote, "The fact that a person is making a broadly self-inculpatory confession does not make more credible the confession's non-self-inculpatory parts. One of the most effective ways to lie is to mix falsehood with truth, especially truth that seems particularly persuasive because of its self-inculpatory nature." Some of what Harris said might reasonably be taken as calculated to reduce his own criminal liability, especially the parts that implicated Williamson.

An analysis of each separate assertion in light of all the surrounding circumstances to determine if it possesses the reliability of a truly self-incriminatory statement may well promise a "fact-intensive inquiry," but the theoretical soundness of the rule demands such an undertaking.

FRE 804(b)(4) – Hearsay Exception: Statement of Personal or Family History Does Not Include Background Circumstances Leading Up to or Surrounding Birth or Death

> **Rule 804. Hearsay Exceptions; Declarant Unavailable**
>
> *(a) Definition of Unavailability.* "Unavailability as a witness" includes situations in which the declarant
>
> (1) is exempted by ruling of the court on the ground of privilege from testifying concerning the subject matter of the declarant's statement;…
>
> A declarant is not unavailable as a witness if exemption, refusal, claim or lack of memory, inability, or absence is due to the procurement or wrongdoing of the proponent of a statement for the purpose of preventing the witness form attending or testifying.
>
> *(b) Hearsay Exceptions.* The following are not excluded by the hearsay rule if the declarant is unavailable as a witness:
>
> *(4) Statement of Personal or Family History.*
>
> (A) A statement concerning the declarant's own birth, adoption, marriage, divorce, legitimacy, relationship by blood, adoption, or marriage, ancestry, or other similar fact of personal or family history, even though declarant had no means of acquiring personal knowledge of the matter stated; or
>
> (B) a statement concerning the foregoing matters, and death also, of another person, if the declarant was related to the other by blood, adoption, or marriage or was so intimately associated with the other's family as to be likely to have accurate information concerning the matter declared.

PEOPLE v. RAFFAELLI
701 P.2d 881 (Colo. App. 1985)

An autopsy on the two-month-old daughter of Robert J. Raffaelli revealed that the cause of her death five days after she was admitted, comatose, to a hospital was "a significant subdural hematoma." Raffaeli was charged with child abuse.

At his trial in Mesa County District Court, the prosecution was allowed over Raffaelli's objection to introduce into evidence several out-of-court statements made by his wife to a police detective and a caseworker. While she also made some statements to which Raffaelli did not object (that she had herself shaken the baby on four occasions, sometimes spanked the baby, and once while under her care the baby rolled off the kitchen table and landed on a chair),[43] the statements she made that Raffaelli objected to included allegations that he sometimes spanked the baby and would lose his temper, that he was holding the baby on his lap when she went limp and stopped breathing, and that on the day she was brought to the hospital she struck her head on the baby car seat when Raffaelli swerved the car to avoid a rock. Other objected-to statements by the wife concerned the "reasons for her marriage to defendant, and her feelings about her marriage as well as about her pregnancy and the birth of the child, plus her physical health and resulting medical treatment at the time of her pregnancy and the birth of the baby." The jury convicted Raffaelli of child abuse. He appealed.

The Colorado Court of Appeals reversed, holding the wife's out-of-court statements to which Raffaelli had objected to be inadmissible hearsay. The wife was unavailable under Rule 804(a)(1) because she refused to testify on grounds of her Fifth Amendment privilege against self-incrimination. But her statements implicating Raffaelli were not statements against her own penal interest, nor did they fall under any other Rule 803 or 804 hearsay exception. And her statements about the marriage generally or about the birth or death of the child did not qualify under Rule 804(b)(4): "The statements encompassed by this rule relate only to matters of pedigree such as date of birth, marriage, death, and the fact and degree of family relationships.... Thus, the fact that the baby died, the dates of her death and birth, and parentage are admissible under this hearsay exception. The statements relating to the condition of the baby, or the events and circumstances leading up to the death... or the circumstances surrounding the birth, were not admissible" under the rule.

FRE 804(b)(5) – Hearsay Exception: Accused Who Arranges Murder of Declarant Forfeits Objection to Admission of Declarant's Hearsay Statements

> **Rule 804. Hearsay Exceptions; Declarant Unavailable**
> *b) Hearsay Exceptions.* The following are not excluded by the hearsay rule if the declarant is unavailable as a witness:
>
> *(5) Forfeiture by Wrongdoing.* A statement offered against a party that has engaged or acquiesced in wrongdoing that was intended to, and did, procure the unavailability of the declarant as a witness.

UNITED STATES v. MASTRANGELO
693 F.2d 269 (2d Cir. 1982)

James Bennett would have testified against Richard Mastrangelo in Mastrangelo's trial on charges related to importing, with 11 co-defendants, 23.4 tons of marijuana and 499,000 methaqualone tablets in 1978, but on his way to the courthouse two days into

---

[43] Admissible under Colorado's equivalent of Rule 804(b)(3) as statements against penal interest made by an unavailable declarant (she refused to testify on Fifth Amendment grounds).

the trial, Bennett was chased and shot dead in the streets in Brooklyn. Bennett had sold Mastrangelo four trucks. The trucks, filled with the drugs, ended up being seized by federal narcotics agents. Later Mastrangelo was taped as he emphasized to Bennett that "You know what I mean Jim it's for your own good... I'll get back to you as far as anything [said]... ah reference to me..." if Bennett testified he sold the trucks to Mastrangelo.

Chief Judge Weinstein of the U.S. District court for the Eastern District of New York declared a mistrial and denied Mastrangelo's motion to bar reprosecution, finding that Mastrangelo had "either directly arranged for the killing of the witness" or acquiesced in it.

A second trial was held in which Bennett's grand jury testimony against Mastrangelo was admitted over Mastrangelo's hearsay objection.[44] He was convicted of possession, conspiracy, importation, and obstruction of justice charges, and he appealed.

The Second Circuit Court of Appeals affirmed the principle of forfeiture of objection by misconduct, but remanded for an evidentiary hearing on the issue of Mastrangelo's "waiver" of his hearsay objection. The appeals court held that the proper standard for finding Mastrangelo connected to the murder of Bennett would be a mere "preponderance of the evidence... [since] there is hardly any reason to apply a burden of proof which might encourage behavior which strikes at the heart of the system of justice itself." The court went out of its way to note that the hearing on the waiver of Mastrangelo's hearsay and confrontation clause objection "will be governed by [Rule] 104(a), which states that the exclusionary rules... do not apply at such proceedings. Thus, hearsay evidence, including Bennett's grand jury testimony, will be admissible, as will all other relevant evidence" including Bennett's tape of Mastrangelo's threats.[45] The court also held that "bare knowledge of a plot to kill Bennett and a failure to give warning to appropriate authorities" is enough to invoke the principle of forfeiture.

---

[44]As current FRE 804(b)(5) did not exist yet, the grand jury testimony was admitted under the residual exception, now numbered FRE 807.

[45]Admissible under FRE 801(d)(2)(A).

Hearsay Exception: Some States Recognize a "Tender Years" Exception in Child Sex Abuse Prosecutions

> **Mich.R.Evid. 803 A. Hearsay Exception; Child's Statement About Sexual Act**
>
> A statement describing an incident that included a sexual act performed with or on the declarant by the defendant or an accomplice is admissible to the extent that it corroborates testimony given by the declarant during the same proceeding, provided:
>
> (1) the declarant was under the age of ten when the statement was made;
>
> (2) the statement is shown to have been spontaneous and without indication of manufacture;
>
> (3) either the declarant made the statement immediately after the incident or any delay is excusable as having been caused by fear or other equally effective circumstance; and
>
> (4) the statement is introduced through the testimony of someone other than the declarant.
>
> If the declarant made more than one corroborative statement about the incident, only the first is admissible under this rule.
>
> A statement may not be admitted under this rule unless the proponent of the statement makes known to the adverse party the intent to offer the statement, and the particulars of the statement, sufficiently in advance of the trial or hearing to provide the adverse party with a fair opportunity to prepare to meet the statement.
>
> This rule applies in criminal and delinquency proceedings only.

PEOPLE v. HAMMONS
534 N.W.2d 183, 210 Mich. App. 554 (1995)

Kenneth Russell Hammons was charged in Livingston County Circuit Court in Howell, Michigan with first-degree criminal sexual conduct after allegedly inserting a finger, through her underwear, into his nine-year-old daughter's genital opening while she and her six-year-old brother were with Hammons for a post-divorce visitation weekend. The jury heard the little girl's testimony and that of her mother who recounted the girl's description to her of what her father had done to her. Her mother's testimony was admitted over objection under Michigan's Rule of Evidence 803A, commonly referred to as a "tender years" hearsay exception. Hammons was convicted of the charge, and he appealed.

One issue before the Michigan Court of Appeals was the admissibility of the mother's testimony about the daughter's out-of-court statement given the fact that "complainant did not relate the events that transpired to her mother for several days" after the occurrence. The appellate court said the delay was "excusable" under Michigan Rule 803A(3) "because of the nine-year-old complainant's fear of reprisal against her father, the defendant."[46] The court also observed that even if admitting the testimony was error, it was "harmless error," apparently because the daughter must have testified herself for her hearsay statement to be admissible under Michigan's rule.

Children's out-of-court statements about sexual misconduct present unique problems in criminal prosecutions. Although the Federal Rules of Evidence do not recognize

---
[46] In *People v. Dunham, supra* p. 4, a delay of eight to nine months was held excusable because of the child's fear of the accused.

any special mechanism for dealing with child-victims' hearsay, the states have adopted a variety of responses. Michigan's rule, seen in action in H*ammons* and *Dunham,* which admits the statements only under tight restrictions and then only as corroboration to the child's in-court testimony, is representative of a middle ground between extremes. The Federal Rules would be at one extreme end of the continuum, with no special accommodation; at the other extreme would be states whose "tender years" doctrine admits the statement even if the declarant has not testified – or which even requires the declarant to be unavailable, in the manner of the Rule 804(b) hearsay exceptions. Many states, without acknowledging a special accommodation for children's hearsay in these cases, stretch exceptions like Rule 803(4), the exception for statements for purposes of medical diagnosis or treatment, Rule 803(2), the excited utterance exception, or the residual exception, Rule 807, beyond recognizable dimensions. See, generally, Robert G. Marks, "Note: Should We Believe The People Who Believe The Children?: The Need For a New Sexual Abuse Tender Years Hearsay Exception Statute," 32 Harv. J. on Legislation 207 (1995).

(A structural problem – or advantage – with a corroboration-only rule is that the admission of the child's hearsay statement will always be in some sense cumulative, and when its admission is error, it will always be in some sense harmless error because it is not new information nor even, usually, the most persuasive source of it.)

FRE 805 – Hearsay Exception: If Each Hearsay Component of a Statement Containing Multiple Hearsay Statements Is Separately Admissible Under an Exception or Exemption, the Combined Statement Is Admissible

> **Rule 805. Hearsay Within Hearsay**
> Hearsay included within hearsay is not excluded under the hearsay rule if each part of the combined statements conforms with an exception to the hearsay rule provided in these rules.

UNITED STATES v. PORTSMOUTH PAVING CORPORATION
694 F.2d 312 (4th Cir. 1982)

When the Virginia federal district court jury could not agree on a verdict in the eight-day first trial of Portsmouth Paving Corporation, its president R. Curtis Saunders, Jr., three other corporations, and five other individuals for conspiracy to allocate contracts and rig bids in violation of the Sherman Act, a mistrial was declared and a second trial got underway in April 1981. The jury convicted Portsmouth, Saunders and some of the other defendants after a ten-day trial. Portsmouth was fined $400,000 and Saunders $30,000, and Saunders was sentenced to 120 days' imprisonment followed by three years' probation. They appealed.

One of several issues raised on appeal concerned the admission of hearsay within hearsay at trial. One small part of the evidence offered in support of the government's theory that for most of 20 years "the conspirators would trade projects among themselves by agreeing to withhold bids or to submit artificially high *'complementary'* bids" on scheduled and nonscheduled road resurfacing work in the Tidewater region, concerned a single telephone call. Robert Remington, manager of Sam Finley, Inc., a paving contractor involved in the conspiracy, testified as a government witness that he made a call to find out about another contractor's intentions. Over objection he was permitted to testify, "Well, I called Mr. Saunders' office, and the secretary said he wasn't in. And I said, 'You think you could get him on the car radio?' And she said, 'Yes, I'll try.' So a few minutes later she came back on the air and said, 'Mr. Saunders said that the air is clear in Chesapeake.'" Later in the trial, Elvin Ray Waterfield, of the Virginia Beach contractor Ashland-Warren, Inc., also involved in the conspiracy, recounted the same incident: from the doorway of Remington's office, he testified, he saw Remington hang up the phone. "Bob Remington laid down the phone and he said 'That was Curtis Saunders' secretary and she said that the sky was clear in Chesapeake,'" Waterfield said.

The Fourth Circuit Court of Appeals applied a Rule 805 analysis, taking each segment of the testimony separately. The statement attributed to Saunders was a party admission (he was a defendant in the suit) and thus admissible under Rule 801(d)(2)(A). The statement attributed to the secretary was deemed an agent admission under Rule 801(d)(2)(C)and (D), because there was ample independent evidence establishing an agency relationship between the secretary and the accused, Saunders: "First, Remington testified that he 'called Mr. Saunders' office.' Not only does this testimony authenticate the occurrence of the telephone call in accordance with the standard illustrated by Rule 901(b)(6), but the testimony also supports the inference that the one who answered the telephone was Saunders' agent. One would usually and properly assume upon the dialing of a business office phone number that the person who answers is employed by and has the authority to speak for the business.

"Second, Remington testified that 'the secretary' answered the call. That a businessman's secretary is an agent of the businessman for purposes of relaying messages to and from the businessman is common knowledge. Notwithstanding other testimony that casts some doubt on the accuracy of Remington's characterization of the answerer as a secretary, his description of the one with whom he spoke constitutes a portion of the necessary independent evidence.

"Finally, the two female employees in Saunders' office in 1975, the year that Remington made his call, testified that they occasionally answered the telephone and by radio relayed messages to and from Saunders. This testimony, in conjunction with that previously identified, virtually compels the conclusion that the woman to whom Remington spoke was an agent of Saunders with the authority to relay messages from Saunders to those who called his business office. Under the terms of Rule 801(d)(2)(D), the statement attributed to the woman, which was a simple declaration of what Saunders had said, concerned 'a matter' within the scope of her employment because part of her job entailed relaying messages from Saunders to business callers. That the woman's statement was 'made during the existence of the [agency] relationship' is an obvious corollary. Because the record contains the essential independent evidence of agency, the trial court did not err in admitting Remington's account of the telephone conversation."

As to Waterfield's account, "hearsay implications on a third level" are involved. "To paraphrase Waterfield, 'Remington said that the secretary said that Saunders said...'" The additional analysis is of Remington's statement. The appellate court said Remington's statement described an "event," the telephone conversation just completed; the statement was made "immediately after" he hung up the phone, i.e., after perceiving the event. Thus Waterfield's testimony about Remington's statement was admissible as a present sense impression under Rule 803(1). (The court found it unnecessary to decide whether Remington's statement was a co-conspirator admission under Rule 801(d)(2)(E).)

FRE 805 – Double Hearsay or Hearsay Within Hearsay Is Admissible Only if Both Statements Are Separately Admissible Under an Exception or Exemption

> **Rule 805. Hearsay Within Hearsay**
> Hearsay included within hearsay is not excluded under the hearsay rule if each part of the combined statements conforms with an exception to the hearsay rule provided in these rules.

HART v. O'BRIEN
127 F.3d 424 (5th Cir. 1997)

Following a law enforcement search of her home, Peggy Nell Hart spent more than two weeks in jail before marijuana possession charges against her were dropped. (She lived near – and often spent the night with – David Conine, who had a prior arrest for growing marijuana and operating a methamphetamine lab. Apparently sheriff's deputies also mistook her for a woman of the same name who was married to a Stanley Hart, a "known marijuana cultivator in Red River County," where she too lived.)

Hart filed suit against Red River County, two state narcotics officers, two sheriff's deputies, and an assistant county attorney from Lamar County, under 42 U.S.C. §1983 and Texas state law. The U.S. District Court for the Eastern District of Texas granted the county and one of the deputies summary judgment. On interlocutory appeal by the rest of the defendants, the Fifth Circuit Court of Appeals rendered judgment in favor of all the officials on the §1983 claims and in favor of the state narcotics officers on the state claims. Although the district court disavowed considering in its holding on the motions a deposition given by Peggy Nell Hart, the appeals court considered its evidentiary admissibility in its *de novo* review of the summary judgment motion. "Hart testified in her deposition that her neighbor had told Hart that, on the first day of Hart's detention, the neighbor had attempted to arrange for a bail bondsman to bail her out of jail. In addition, Hart testified that Shelly Dodson, a trustee at the Red River County jail, had told her that someone at the jail had informed the bail bondsman that Hart could not be released because of the federal hold. [Although the charge sheet from Hart's bail hearing listed 'Federal Hold' next to 'Bail is denied,' there was no federal detainer lodged against her.] Hart did not offer affidavits or deposition testimony from either her neighbor, Dodson, or the bail bondsman in opposition to defendants' summary judgment motion."

The appellate court held the statements to be inadmissible hearsay. In particular, "Hart's testimony concerning what Dodson told her about what a third-party said to a bail bondsman is inadmissible double hearsay...and does not otherwise fall within an exception to the hearsay rule." Hart would have to separately demonstrate grounds for admitting Dodson's statement and the statement of the third party for the combined statement to be admissible. Here no argument was made that either statement was admissible, much less both.

FRE 806, 613(b) – Extrinsic Evidence of Prior Inconsistent Statement Is Permissible Impeachment of Hearsay Declarant Despite Failure to Satisfy Foundational Requirements of FRE 613(b)

> **Rule 806. Attacking and Supporting Credibility of Declarant**
> When a hearsay statement, or a statement defined in Rule 801(d)(2) (C), (D) or (E), has been admitted in evidence, the credibility of the declarant may be attacked, and if attacked may be supported, by any evidence which would be admissible for those purposes if declarant had testified as a witness. Evidence of a statement or conduct by the declarant at any time, inconsistent with the declarant's hearsay statement, is not subject to any requirement that the declarant may have been afforded an opportunity to deny or explain. If the party against whom a hearsay statement has been admitted calls the declarant as a witness, the party is entitled to examine the declarant on the statement as if under cross-examination.
>
> **Rule 613. Prior Statements of Witnesses**
> *(b) Extrinsic Evidence of Prior Inconsistent Statement of Witness.* Extrinsic evidence of a prior inconsistent statement by a witness is not admissible unless the witness is afforded an opportunity to explain or deny the same and the opposite party is afforded an opportunity to interrogate the witness thereon, or the interests of justice otherwise require. This provision does not apply to admissions of a party-opponent as defined in Rule 801(d)(2).

SMITH v. FAIRMAN
862 F.2d 630 (7th Cir. 1988)

Gregory Smith was convicted in Cook County, Illinois Circuit Court of murder, attempted murder, home invasion, burglary, and armed violence in connection with the stabbing of Regina Tatton, the aunt of Smith's acquaintance Edward Boyle, during an attempt to steal Tatton's purse and/or a coin collection. On appeal, the Illinois Appellate Court and Supreme Court both affirmed most of the convictions. Smith brought a petition for a writ of habeas corpus in the district court for the Northern District of Illinois, but it was denied, and he appealed.

Among several issue raised before the Seventh Circuit Court of Appeals was the question of the propriety of excluding a prior inconsistent statement by Edward Boyle, offered by Smith to impeach a hearsay statement by Boyle that had been admitted at trial. Police Officer Stanley Wonsowicz testified that he went to the home where the stabbing had taken place and met Boyle at the door. Boyle told him, "I can't believe Greg Smith did it," and later, "Why don't you get that sonofabitch Greg."[47] Boyle died before Smith's state court trial.

---
[47] While the court was none-too-specific about the hearsay theory behind the admissibility of these remarks, Illinois's "res gestae" concept – roughly comparable here to an excited utterance – might well account for it.

The trial judge refused to let Smith's mother, Mrs. Henrietta Smith, testify that Edward Boyle had told her later that he wasn't sure who he'd seen on the night of the murder. The state contended that ruling was correct because one of the foundational elements necessary for admission of the statement was lacking, namely that Boyle had been given an opportunity to explain its significance, per Rule 613(b).

The court noted that Congress "specifically dispensed with this foundational requirement in drafting Rule 806," and held that since "Boyle was deceased, and because Mr. Smith was never given the opportunity to cross-examine Boyle regarding his hearsay statements to Officer Wonsowicz, this foundational requirement does not apply." The trial court's ruling was thus erroneous, and constitutionally so inasmuch as denial of the right to impeach Boyle, the dead declarant, amounted to a denial of the right of confrontation.[48]

(However, after assessing the impact the excluded evidence would have had on the jury, in context with all the other admitted evidence including a detailed confession by Smith, the court determined the error to have been harmless.)

FRE 806, 613(b) – Hearsay Declarant May Be Impeached with Prior Inconsistent Statement

Rule 806. Attacking and Supporting Credibility of Declarant
When a hearsay statement, or a statement defined in Rule 801(d)(2)(C), (D) or (E), has been admitted in evidence, the credibility of the declarant may be attacked, and if attacked may be supported, by any evidence which would be admissible for those purposes if declarant had testified as a witness. Evidence of a statement or conduct by the declarant at any time, inconsistent with the declarant's hearsay statement, is not subject to any requirement that the declarant may have been afforded an opportunity to deny or explain. If the party against whom a hearsay statement has been admitted calls the declarant as a witness, the party is entitled to examine the declarant on the statement as if under cross-examination.

Rule 613. Prior Statements of Witnesses
(b) Extrinsic Evidence of Prior Inconsistent Statement of Witness. Extrinsic evidence of a prior inconsistent statement by a witness is not admissible unless the witness is afforded an opportunity to explain or deny the same and the opposite party is afforded an opportunity to interrogate the witness thereon, or the interests of justice otherwise require. This provision does not apply to admissions of a party-opponent as defined in rule 801(d)(2).

UNITED STATES v. WUAGNEUX
683 F.2d 1343 (11th Cir. 1988)

An indictment charged George Wuagneux, CEO and controlling shareholder of a Hallandale, Florida construction company, with multiple counts of racketeering, embezzlement, mail fraud, and filing false income tax returns. A jury in the U.S. District Court for the Southern District of Florida convicted him on 11 counts. Among many

---
[48] See *Davis v. Alaska, supra* p. 152.

issues raised on appeal, Wuagneux raised a Rule 806 hearsay question.

In connection with the income tax evasion counts, Wuagneux had introduced the hearsay statement of his accountant, Joseph Spina, to another accountant, John Pitcher, to the effect that Spina was "surprised and concerned" that Wuagneux's tax return had not included income from an ownership interest in recreational leases from the Golden Horn Condominiums. Spina was reported to have said that he was aware of the income and presumed its omission from the return was either his fault or that of his employees. (Joseph Spina was himself under federal investigation in a separate proceeding, and his probable refusal to testify was ruled by the trial court to render him "unavailable" under Rule 804(a)(1).) Pitcher's testimony of what Spina said was admitted as a statement against interest under Rule 804(b)(3).

On rebuttal the government called IRS Agent Michalak to testify that Joseph Spina had told him some time before Wuagneux's returns were filed that Wuagneux "had disavowed any interest in the recreational leases." The trial judge admitted the testimony under Rule 806 over objection by Wuagneux that Spina was unavailable only because of the government's own refusal to grant Spina use immunity for his testimony. His attorney argued it would thus be "unfair" to apply Rule 806 to this kind of hearsay statement. The Eleventh Circuit Court of Appeals noted that had immunity "been granted and appellant was able to use Spina himself, presumably Michalak's testimony concerning Spina's inconsistent statement would still have been used to impeach his credibility. It is difficult see how the government unfairly took advantage of the decision not to offer Spina immunity...."

FRE 806, 608(a) – Impeachment of Witness Regarding Untruthfulness of Hearsay Statement of Non-Testifying Accused Opens Door to Rehabilitation of Accused's Truthful Character

> **Rule 806. Attacking and Supporting Credibility of Declarant**
>
> When a hearsay statement, or a statement defined in Rule 801(d)(2)(C), (D), or (E), has been admitted in evidence, the credibility of the declarant may be attacked, and if attacked may be supported, by any evidence which would be admissible for those purposes if declarant had testified as a witness. Evidence of a statement or conduct by the declarant at any time, inconsistent with the declarant's hearsay statement, is not subject to any requirement that the declarant may have been afforded an opportunity to deny or explain. If the party against whom a hearsay statement has been admitted calls the declarant as a witness, the party is entitled to examine the declarant on the statement as if under cross-examination.
>
> **Rule 608. Evidence of Character and Conduct of Witness**
>
> *(a) Opinion and Reputation Evidence of Character.* The credibility of a witness may be attacked or supported by evidence in the form of opinion or reputation, but subject to these limitations: (1) the evidence may refer only to character for truthfulness or untruthfulness, and (2) evidence of truthful character is admissible only after the character of the witness for truthfulness has been attacked by opinion or reputation evidence or otherwise.

UNITED STATES v. LECHOCO
542 F.2d 84 (D.C. Cir. 1976)

Napoleon Lechoco was a Philippine lawyer who moved with his wife to the United States. They were followed two years later by six of his seven children. He became convinced that his eldest son, 17, was being held as a political hostage, and entered the office of the Philippine Ambassador and demanded at gunpoint that his son be released. A member of the embassy staff was shot, and the Ambassador was handcuffed and held for some eight hours while extensive recorded telephone negotiations took place. Lechoco released the Ambassador and surrendered when he was assured the boy would be delivered to Washington.

Lechoco's kidnaping trial was held in two phases: a guilt phase, in which he presented no evidence, and then a sanity phase, much more crucial in that Lechoco contended only that he was not competent at the time of the offense. Lechoco did not testify in either portion of the trial. During this insanity phase, Lechoco presented testimony by three psychiatrists to the effect that due to a mental disease he had been unable to resist the impulse to act as he had. Each psychiatrist was "vigorously cross-examined" by the prosecution, mainly about the fact that the sole source of information each diagnosis was based on was what Lechoco had told them, "this man who wants to be acquitted in this case...and if what he was telling you was false, this would have to affect your diagnosis, wouldn't it?"

Defense counsel then tried to call a co-worker of Lechoco's to testify that Lechoco had a good reputation for truthfulness and honesty. The district judge sustained the prosecution's objection on grounds of irrelevance, and Lechoco was eventually convicted of the charges. He appealed.

The District of Columbia Circuit Court of Appeals reversed the verdict in the insanity phase and remanded the case for retrial on that issue. The court ruled that the truthfulness of the accused was relevant, even though he had not testified, because the prosecution had placed so much emphasis on the fact that the reliability of defense psychiatric testimony depended entirely on the credibility of the accused. For example, one of the doctors was asked, "would not a person in his situation charged with major offenses wanting to be acquitted by reason of insanity have a very good reason to try and fool or con you into a mental illness diagnosis?" The court thus found Lechoco's credibility – not as a witness but as a source of information relied on by witnesses – to be "of crucial importance…. His veracity goes to the heart of his guilt or innocence…." Since the government raised the issue in its cross-examination of the psychiatrist called by the defense, the court held that "opened the door for the introduction of testimony as to his reputation" for truthfulness.

In a footnote contemplating the remand hearing, the court also noted, "The defendant's statements to his psychiatrist fall within the statement to a physician exception to the hearsay rule embodied in Rule 803(4). As such, Mr. Lechoco's credibility was open to attack under Rule 806. The prosecutor's vigorous cross-examination represents the type of attack on credibility contemplated by the term 'otherwise' as contained in Rule 608(a). In light of this attack, the defendant is permitted by Rule 806 to present supporting credibility evidence notwithstanding his exercise of Fifth Amendment rights."

FRE 807 – Hearsay Exception: Necessary and Reliable Hearsay Not Covered by Categorical Exceptions Is Admissible Under Residual Exception

> **Rule 807. Residual Except**
>
> A statement not specifically covered by Rule 803 or 804 but having equivalent circumstantial guarantees of trustworthiness, is not excluded by the hearsay rule, if the court determines that (A) the statement is offered as evidence of a material fact; (B) the statement is more probative on the point for which it is offered than any other evidence which the proponent can procure through reasonable efforts; and (C) the general purposes of these rules and the interests of justice will best be served by admission of the statement into evidence. However, a statement may not be admitted under this exception unless the proponent of it makes known to the adverse party with a fair opportunity to prepare to meet it, the proponent's intention to offer the statement and the particulars of it, including the name and address of the declarant.

DALLAS COUNTY v. COMMERCIAL UNION ASSURANCE CO.
286 F.2d 388 (5th Cir. 1961)

The Dallas County courthouse tower in Selma, Alabama collapsed one Sunday morning in July 1957. Damage to the courthouse amounted to more than $100,000. Charred timbers and charcoal were found in the wreckage, which indicated to the state toxicologist who examined it for Dallas County that the tower had been struck by lightning. The county's policy with defendants covered fire and lightning damage. Several eyewitnesses claimed lightning had struck the courthouse a few days earlier.

The insurance company denied liability. Its investigators and engineers claimed that the courthouse tower had not been struck by lightning, that lightning could not have been responsible for the collapse, and that the courthouse tower collapsed "of its own weight." They attributed the collapse to "faulty design, poor construction, gradual deterioration of the structure, and overloading brought about by remodeling and the recent installation of an air-conditioning system... [partly] over the courtroom trusses." They testified that the charred timbers resulted from a long-ago fire.

The insurance company offered in evidence an unsigned article from the June 9, 1901 edition of the Morning Times of Selma, describing a fire in the courthouse tower earlier that morning. Such a fire would have accounted for the charred timbers found 56 years later. The county objected that the article was hearsay, not admissible under any recognized exception.[49]

The trial judge admitted it. The verdict was in favor of the insurance company.

Dallas County appealed, and the Fifth Circuit Court of Appeals held that the old newspaper article was reliable – more reliable, probably, than the aging recollections of any eyewitness to the fire still alive 58 years later – and necessary, being the only direct evidence of a courthouse fire. In holding that the newspaper article was admissible despite fitting into no "readily identifiable and happily tagged species of hearsay exception," the Fifth Circuit was acknowledging that there was still room for hearsay jurisprudence to evolve.

Dallas County is recognized as the conceptual ancestor of the catch-all (or residual) hearsay exception, Rule 807. In tracing the theory that some hearsay is reliable enough to be admissible back through Wigmore and his treatise on the common law history of hearsay, this case set the scene for the adoption of the ultimate example of flexibility within the law of evidence: provided the hearsay seemed trustworthy, and was necessary, the trial court had the discretion to apply "common sense."

---

[49] The business records exception was at the time considerably more narrowly drawn than present FRE 803(6). The article was not part of the *business* of newspapering. And the existing ancient documents exception probably covered only documents affecting an interest in property, such as deeds and wills, now the domain of FRE 803(15) which now has no such age requirement.

FRE 807 – Hearsay Exception: Hearsay Statement Offered Under Residual Exception Must Be Shown to Be Trustworthy

> **Rule 807. Residual Exception**
>
> A statement not specifically covered by Rule 803 or 804 but having equivalent circumstantial guarantees of trustworthiness, is not excluded by the hearsay rule, if the court determines that (A) the statement is offered as evidence of a material fact; (B) the statement is more probative on the point for which it is offered than any other evidence which the proponent can procure through reasonable efforts; and (C) the general purposes of these rules and the interests of justice will best be served by admission of the statement into evidence. However, a statement may not be admitted under this exception unless the proponent of it makes known to the adverse party sufficiently in advance of the trial or hearing to provide the adverse party with a fair opportunity to prepare to meet it, the proponent's intention to offer the statement and the particulars of it, including the name and address of the declarant.

UNITED STATES v. TRUJILLO
136 F.3d 1388 (10th Cir. 1998)

Charles Trujillo was charged with armed bank robbery, carrying a firearm during a crime of violence, and being a felon in possession of a firearm in connection with the October, 1991 robbery of the Del City branch of the Bank of Oklahoma. It wasn't until nearly five years later that he was finally indicted and tracked down in Grand Junction, Colorado.

At trial Trujillo's attorney sought to introduce two FBI summaries of witness statements that described the person who switched from a mini-van that was followed from the scene of the robbery by a customer to an Oldsmobile in which agents later found a paper bag containing over $5,000 stuck up in the wheel well. These statements described the person as having a full beard, which it is "undisputed" Trujillo did not have. The witnesses who gave those statements were not available at trial. The statements were offered by the defense under Rule 807's predecessor, Rule 804(b)(5).[50] The district court refused to admit the reports, finding that they lacked circumstantial guarantees of trustworthiness "equivalent" to those surrounding statements covered by the other 27 substantive hearsay exceptions. Trujillo was convicted and sentenced to five years' imprisonment as well as ordered to pay a fine and restitution.

On his appeal, the Tenth Circuit Court of Appeals affirmed Trujillo's conviction and upheld the exclusion of the FBI summaries. Because Congress intended the residual, or "catch-all," exception to be used "very rarely and only in exceptional circumstances," it follows that "the party offering the evidence bears a heavy burden of presenting the trial court with sufficient indicia of trustworthiness to trigger application of [the Rule]... When first proffered, defense counsel made no showing concerning the reliability or trustworthiness of the two FBI [form] 302 reports. He simply

---

[50] There used to be two identical residual exceptions, Rules 803(24) and 804(b)(5). This engendered no end of scholarly theorizing as to the difference between the two. Congress rendered the whole question moot when it consolidated the two as Rule 807, effective Dec. 1, 1997.

stated his desire to 'extricate' from the reports the fact the descriptions mentioned a beard. Nor did defense counsel elaborate on why the reports were inherently trustworthy when he presented the issue to the court a second time. What the trial court knew at the time was (1) as compared to Ms. Hendricks and Mr. Whitt, the unavailable witnesses had a limited opportunity to view the robber; (2) one of the proffered reports mistakenly describes Mr. Whitt, the retired gentleman who pursued the robber, as in his late twenties; (3) the subject of the second proffered report recalled seeing a maroon colored Dodge mini-van parked at the complex, whereas Mr. Whitt testified the van he followed to the parking lot was blue or greenish-blue; (4) an FBI 302 report inaccurately documented Ms. Hendricks' description of the robber; and (5) defense counsel had challenged the accuracy of an FBI 302 report that documented a conversation between Agent DeWitt and Agent Fitzpatrick.

"In sum then, the record reveals no self-evident, particularized guarantees of trustworthiness attributable to the proffered reports. Contrary to Mr. Trujillo's assertion on appeal, the reports were not corroborated in any real sense. Giving appropriate deference to the trial court's ability to weigh these circumstances first hand, we conclude the trial court did not abuse its discretion by excluding the two FBI 302 reports."

CHAPTER NINE
Article IX – Authentication and Identification

FRE 901(a) – Authentication: Testimony About Retrieval of Computer Printouts Combined with Expert Testimony Interpreting Them Is Sufficient for Admissibility

> **Rule 901. Requirement of Authentication or Identification**
> *(a) General Provision.* The requirement of authentication or identification as a condition precedent to admissibility is satisfied by evidence sufficient to support a finding that the matter in question is what its proponent claims.

UNITED STATES v. WHITAKER
127 F.3d 595 (7th Cir. 1997)

To help prove Frank Whitaker's role as the "right-hand man" and "second-in-command" in a large-scale marijuana importation and distribution ring centered in St. Louis and to prove the extent of its operations, the Government offered into evidence computer records of transactions. The computer records were seized from the residence of Gary Frost in Granite City, Illinois, which the organization was using as a storage and unloading site for the marijuana. FBI Special Agent Eric Daniel Clouse testified as an expert witness that "in his opinion the records pertained to a marijuana- trafficking business. The records contained an account named 'Me,' which, as Agent Clouse testified, referred to the person running the business and doing the transactions, and an account named 'Cruz,' which was [Ralph] Solis' nickname. [Solis was the alleged leader of the group.] The 'Cruz' account contained a notation that read 'Cash Gator $38,000' on October 16, 1993, which corresponded with a $38,000 reduction in the 'Me' account. A similar notation of 'Cash Gator $49,000' with a corresponding reduction in the 'Me' account also appeared on October 27, 1993. 'Gator' was Whitaker's nickname."

A jury in the Southern District of Illinois convicted Whitaker of conspiring to deliver about 2,000 kilograms of marijuana. He was sentenced to 15 years in prison and five years of supervised release. He was also ordered to forfeit more than $235,000 to the government. (Solis remained a fugitive, having jumped bail.) Whitaker appealed.

The first issue in Whitaker's appeal to the Seventh Circuit Court of Appeals concerned the printouts, which he argued were not sufficiently authenticated. He contended that "the prosecution failed to comply with the requirements of Rule 901(a) with respect to the computer printouts because it never supplied witnesses who had personal knowledge of the computer system's operation or who could confirm the accuracy of the input to and output from the computer." The appellate court affirmed, holding that between the testimony of FBI Special Agent Jay Keeven about retrieving the records from Frost's computer and obtaining the printouts, and Agent Clouse's testimony interpreting the records, the authenticity (and relevance) of the printouts were established under Rule 901(a). Although Agent Clouse was not a computer expert, his work for the FBI's Racketeering Analysis Unit in more than 400 drug and money-laundering cases qualified him to analyze the suspected drug records and interpret them in court.

FRE 901(a) – Authentication: For Testimony of Laboratory Analysis of Suspected Narcotic to Be Admissible, Prosecution Must Establish Continuous Chain of Custody Prior to Analysis to Connect Drug with Accused

> **Rule 901. Requirement of Authentication of Identification**
> *(a) General Provision.* The requirement of authentication or identification as a condition precedent to admissibility is satisfied by evidence sufficient to support a finding that the matter in question is what its proponent claims.

GRAHAM v. STATE
255 N.E.2d 652, 253 Ind. 525 (1970)

Junkie informant Willie Williams made a controlled buy of suspected heroin from Anthony Graham in an Indianapolis drugstore on November 22, 1966. He paid Graham 10 dollars and received a yellow Juicy Fruit gum wrapper, which he immediately turned over to waiting police officers. They noted a "white powder substance" in the tin foil and initialed it, then put it in a manila envelope. At police headquarters Sergeant Dora Ward ran a preliminary test on the powder and deposited it in the department's property room. Graham was arrested the following January 4 and charged with possession of heroin and sale of heroin.

At Graham's trial in Marion County Criminal Court, a laboratory analyst testified that the chemical received by the lab was heroin, despite Graham's attorney's objection that there was a six-day break in the chain of custody of the substance bought from Graham prior to its being sent to the lab. (On November 23, a Sergeant Elmore checked it out of the property room, and returned it November 29. No one testified as to why it was checked out, who had it during that time, or what may have happened to it, and no records disclosed these facts either.) The jury found Graham guilty of possession but not guilty of sale of heroin. He appealed.

The Indiana Supreme Court reversed, holding that the break in the chain of custody made it impossible to conclude beyond a reasonable doubt that the substance analyzed and found to be heroin was in fact the same substance Williams bought from Graham for police. The chain of custody concept is especially important "in the case of offenses such as the one before us where narcotics are involved. The danger of tampering, loss, or mistake with respect to an exhibit is greatest where the exhibit is small and is one which has physical characteristics fungible in nature and similar in form to substances familiar to people in their daily lives. The white powder in this case could have been heroin, or it could have been, for example, baking powder, powdered sugar, or even powdered milk. The burden on the state in seeking to admit such evidence is clear. Unless the state can show by producing records or testimony, the continuous whereabouts of the exhibit at least between the time it came into their possession until it was laboratory tested to determine its composition, testimony of the state as to the laboratory's findings is inadmissible.... What happened to the Juicy Fruit gum wrapper and its contents between November 23 and November 29 was not testimonially established. It would appear to be unreasonable and unrealistic to argue that the unaccounted for absence of a police exhibit of this nature for six days and six nights is not a complete break in the chain of evidence.

"Not until February 21, 1967, did the chemical examination take place which formed the basis for the expert testimony of the state's laboratory witness and the basis for the conviction. The fact that the chewing gum wrapper was identifiable as that acquired from appellant at the drugstore cannot cure the defective evidentiary chain of custody which preceded the laboratory experiments. Appellant was not convicted for possession of a chewing gum wrapper."

Although this is a pre-Rules case in a non-Rules state, the logic of the holding is identical to the reasoning in cases decided under Federal Rule 901(a) or a state clone: evidence "sufficient to support a finding" that suspected drugs seized from an accused are the same substance analyzed at the laboratory must include testimony or records establishing an unbroken chain of custody of the substance.

FRE 901(a) – Authentication: Physical Evidence Not Susceptible to Tampering Is Admissible if Evidence Is Sufficient for Judge to Find It Has Not Been Changed in Any Important Respect

Rule 901. Requirement of Authentication or Identification

(a) General Provision. The requirement of authentication or identification as a condition precedent to admissibility is satisfied by evidence sufficient to support a finding that the matter in question is what its proponent claims.

UNITED STATES v. HARRINGTON
923 F.2d 1371 (9th Cir. 1991)

Following a chase by police and shots fired at them by a man leaving the scene of a Gresham, Oregon armed bank robbery, officers arrested David Olon Harrington. They seized a blue bag he was holding that contained $8,759 in currency including bank "bait" bills, and a .357 caliber revolver that he tossed away at police direction. A police dog led the arresting officers to a shed near where Harrington was found, and they recovered six empty .357 cartridge cases, as well as a jacket and pants similar to what the fleeing suspect had been wearing. A jury in U.S. District Court for Oregon convicted Harrington of armed bank robbery, carrying a firearm during a crime of violence, and being a convicted felon in possession of a firearm.

On appeal, Harrington complained that the money, gun, casings and clothing introduced into evidence at trial were not properly authenticated. His defense had been that someone else robbed the bank, and gave him

$20 to "run if he saw a police car," and that he put the $20 in a pack of cigarettes he was carrying. The prosecution had called Officer Galen Tercek as a rebuttal witness. Tercek testified that, with others, he had seized the items from Harrington at his arrest and watched them being placed in an evidence bag by another officer. He identified all of the items from the bag, and testified he had not found "a $20 bill or any currency amounting to $20 in the cigarette pack or the blue bag." Tercek said he could not testify from memory what items had been placed in the bag, and that he was not the custodian of the bag. Harrington argued there was thus an insufficient chain of custody.

For evidence of this nature, the Ninth Circuit Court of Appeals held, "merely raising the possibility of tampering is not sufficient to render evidence inadmissible.... The possibility of a break in the chain of custody goes only to the weight of the evidence. In addition, the prosecution was not required to call the custodian of the evidence." The appellate court affirmed the conviction, although it reversed the sentence imposed because the court had improperly considered a psychiatric evaluation that contained confidential statements.

As another case[1] observed the following year, "The government is not required to maintain an eternal vigilance over all evidence in its custody. It is enough for its admissibility if the judge is satisfied that the relevant article has not, in all reasonable probability, been changed in any important respect. Once the judge admits the evidence, doubts about its identity go to its weight and are for the trier of fact to weigh and resolve."

FRE 901(b)(1) – Authentication: Real Evidence Is Admissible if Witness Testifies It Is Similar to Object Used

> **Rule 901. Requirement of Authentication or Identification**
> *(a) General Provision.* The requirement of authentication or identification as a condition precedent to admissibility is satisfied by evidence sufficient to support a finding that the matter in question is what its proponent claims.
> *(b) Illustrations.* By way of illustration only, and not by way of limitation, the following are examples of authentication or identification conforming with the requirements of this rule:
> *(1) Testimony of Witness With Knowledge.* Testimony that a matter is what it is claimed to be.

STATE v. KROEPLIN
266 N.W.2d 537 (N.D. 1978)

Cora Kroeplin was charged with reckless endangerment under circumstances manifesting an extreme indifference to human life. She was alleged to be the person seen shooting a rifle several times into the Buffalo Repair Shop where her husband Melvin, son Gary and their bookkeeper Lori Hill were inside. The .22 rifle thought to be used in the shooting was admitted into evidence over the defense's objection that there were insufficient foundation and authentication for its admissibility. A jury in Cass County District Court convicted Kroeplin. She was sentenced to 18 months

---
[1] *United States v. Pressley*, 978 F.2d 1026, 1028-29 (8th Cir. 1992).

at hard labor at the North Dakota State Penitentiary, and she appealed.

One of two issues Cora Kroeplin raised on appeal concerned the admission of the rifle. (The other was ineffective assistance of counsel.) The essence of her objection was that there was a break in the chain of custody. Melvin Kroeplin testified that sheriff's deputy Franck removed the gun, which he had bought for his son, from his home, and that it looked like the gun his wife had used. Lieutenant Larson testified that the next morning the gun was brought to his office by a jailer – he couldn't remember which one – and that it had a green tag on it identifying it. He then locked it in the evidence room where it remained until trial except for a brief period when it was sent to the FBI for testing.

The North Dakota Supreme Court affirmed the conviction and upheld the trial court's ruling admitting the rifle. Because eyewitness testimony established that Cora Kroeplin shot into the door of the shop with a rifle, "production of the specific rifle used was not essential to prove the charge against the defendant." That didn't make it improper to admit the rifle, however. And "in the admission of real evidence, impervious to change, such gun which is readily identifiable by its serial number and other characteristics, and which has been identified through testimony as being similar to the gun in question, a showing of a continuous chain of possession is not as important as it is with reference to items or objects which can easily be diluted, altered or even substituted." In that situation, the objection goes to the weight the jury should accord the exhibit, not to its admissibility, especially where, as here, the rifle was really only "circumstantial evidence corroborating the testimony of other witnesses."

FRE 901(b)(2) – Authentication: Handwriting Can Be Authenticated by Nonexpert Testimony That Witness Is Familiar with Writer's Handwriting Through Working Relationship with Writer

> **Rule 901. Requirement of Authentication or Identification**
> *(a) General Provision.* The requirement of authentication or identification as a condition precedent to admissibility is satisfied by evidence sufficient to support a finding that the matter is question is what its proponent claims.
> *(b) Illustrations.* By way of illustration only, and not by way of limitation, the following are examples of authentication or identification conforming with the requirements of this rule:
> *(2) Nonexpert Opinion on Handwriting.* Nonexpert opinion as to the genuineness of handwriting, based upon familiarity not acquired for purposes of the litigation.

STATE v. STOTTS
695 P.2d 1110, 144 Ariz. 72 (1985)

After conviction on his 1976 plea of guilty of armed aggravated assault in Pima County, Arizona, Superior Court in connection with a knife attack on a 15-year-old girl in an apparent attempted rape, James Stotts was placed on probation for 15 years so he could be returned to Washington where he was wanted as a parole violator. He had to report to the Western State Hospital in Fort Steilacoom, Wa. and complete a sex offender's treatment program.

By 1982 it was determined that he was untreatable and dangerous, and Washington returned Stotts to Arizona. The Arizona trial court revoked his probation and Stotts was sentenced to between 10 years and life in prison. He appealed.

One issue before the Arizona Supreme Court on Stotts' appeal concerned the authentication of most of the prosecution's documentary evidence, which came from Stotts' probation file. Although the appellate court affirmed the revocation of probation ("the trial court could have rationally concluded that appellant violated a condition of probation") and the sentence, it did find that with some of the documentary evidence admitted there was insufficient authentication. As to one exhibit, however, a decent illustration of handwriting authentication is presented. Two pages of exhibit 6 consist of reports by a Washington State Probation Officer, a Mr. Harris. Another probation officer from Washington, Mr. Stinson, gave testimony at the Arizona revocation hearing and said he recognized Harris' signature at the end of the reports.

The Arizona Supreme Court noted that in applying the state's counterpart of Federal Rule 901(b)(2), "Familiarity with a person's handwriting can be attained by working with that person over a period of time.... In the instant case, Stinson stated he had worked for the Washington State Adult Probation Department for six years. He also stated that Harris was his supervisor and that he recognized his signature. This testimony established a sufficient foundation pursuant to Rule 901(b)(2)." The court also held Stinson's testimony that he recognized Stotts' signature from having supervised him for four years was sufficient to authenticate the Agreement to Return (to Arizona) Stotts executed.

FRE 901(b)(3) – Authentication: Expert Testimony Comparing Signatures with Known Specimen of Accused's Handwriting Is Sufficient to Authenticate Signature for Admissibility

> **Rule 901. Requirement of Authentication or Identification**
>
> *(a) General Provision.* The requirement of authentication or identification as a condition precedent to admissibility is satisfied by evidence sufficient to support a finding that the matter in question is what its proponent claims.
>
> *(b) Illustrations.* By way of illustration only, and not by way of limitation, the following are examples of authentication or identification conforming with the requirements of this rule:
>
> *(3) Comparison by Trier or Expert Witness.* Comparison by the trier of fact or by expert witnesses with specimens which have been authenticated.

STATE v. REASONER
742 P.2d 1363, 154 Ariz. 377 (1987)

When Phoenix police officers arrested Randel Steven Reasoner at his residence on an outstanding car theft arrest warrant from Colorado, they noticed truck doors with missing identification numbers and a "chopped-up" truck cab, indicating to them "the presence of unlawful activity." They got a search warrant, returned and seized a number of items that led to several charges of theft, trafficking in stolen property, criminal damage and conducting an illegal enterprise.

At Reasoner's trial in Maricopa County Superior Court, the state attempted to prove that a lease they seized had been signed by Reasoner under the name "Randy Nichols." They called an expert documents examiner, who testified that "the lease for the residence at which appellant was arrested, the title for a Ford truck, and a bill of sale for the truck, obtained during the execution of the search warrant at the residence, were all signed by 'Randy Nichols.' The expert also testified these signatures were the same. The documents examiner further testified that those three documents were signed by the same person who signed the Arizona driver's license application in Exhibit 17, that also bore the signature of 'Randy Nichols.'"

Reasoner was convicted on all counts, and he appealed. Among several issues, he argued to the Arizona Court of Appeals that the documents bearing the signature "Randy Nichols" should not have been admitted. "Appellant argues there was no foundation to demonstrate that any of the signatures were his. However, appellant overlooks the fact that Exhibit 32, an Arizona driver's license bearing his picture and the signature of 'Randy Nichols' was admitted into evidence and, without objection, was stated to be a copy of Exhibit 17, the driver's license application. In Arizona, the driver's license application is photocopied to make the official license."

The appellate court affirmed, holding the authentication sufficient under Arizona's counterpart to Federal Rule 901(b)(3): "The trial court properly found that Exhibit 13 was identified as being in appellant's handwriting by a documents examiner who testified on behalf of the state. Exhibit 32, appellant's driver's license with his signature and photograph, was related to Exhibit 17, the application for the driver's license. The documents examiner testified that all of the signatures in the exhibit were similar. Testimony was offered to show that the lease, Exhibit 13, was seized during the execution of a search warrant and that the document was what the proponent claimed it represented. There was sufficient authentication under Rule 901...."

FRE 901(b)(4) - Authentication: Circumstantial Proof Is Permissible to Authenticate Writing

> **Rule 901. Requirement of Authentication of identification**
>
> *(a) General Provision.* The requirement of authentication or identification as a condition precedent to admissibility is satisfied by evidence sufficient to support a finding that the matter in question is what its proponent claims.
>
> *(b) Illustrations.* By way of illustration only, and not by way of limitation, the following are examples of authentication or identification conforming with the requirements of this rule:
>
> *(4) Distinctive Characteristics and the Like.* Appearance, contents, substance, internal patterns, or other distinctive characteristics, taken in conjunction with circumstances.

UNITED STATES v. WILSON
532 F.2d 641 (8th Cir. 1976)

Boyd Gray, Isreal Wilson and Brenda Brown were convicted of conspiracy to distribute heroin, based on nine overt sales they (along with an unindicted co-conspirator) made to federal narcotics agents in St. Louis.

On appeal the defendants contended that it had been improper for the government to introduce two notebooks and their contents in evidence because there was no proper foundation for them, no proper authentication linking them to defendants.

The Eighth Circuit Court of Appeals affirmed under Rule 901(b)(4). The activities mentioned and nicknames and codes used (e.g., "buttons" for heroin capsules, "Punkin" for Gray) in the notebooks, and the apartment where they were found, adequately made a "prima facie showing" of the notebooks' connection to defendants, and an informant also testified that it was defendants' drug transactions that made up a portion of the recorded information in the notebook. The contents of the notebooks themselves can be used to help determine their authenticity under Rule 901(b)(4).

FRE 901(b)(4) – Authentication: Link of Shipping Receipt to Accused Can Be Established with Circumstantial Evidence

> **Rule 901. Requirement of Authentication or Identification**
>
> *(a) General Provision.* The requirement of authentication or identification as a condition precedent to admissibility is satisfied by evidence to support a finding that the matter in question is what its proponent claims.
>
> *(b) Illustrations.* By way of illustration only, and not by way of limitation, the following are examples of authentication or identification conforming with the requirements of this rule:
>
> *(4) Distinctive Characteristics and the Like.* Appearance, contents, substance, internal patterns, or other distinctive characteristics, taken in conjunction with circumstances.

STATE v. BEST
703 P.2d 548, 146 Ariz. 1 (1985)

When a United Parcel Service clerk became suspicious of a parcel brought in for transport by a man who prepared a label with William Parker Best's name and address, she had a security officer note the license number of his car. (The plate traced back to Best's roommate.) A UPS supervisor discovered marijuana when he opened the package, and called the Department of Public Safety. A DPS officer checked the package and interviewed Best at his apartment. Best admitted he shipped the marijuana. He was charged and tried in Pima County Superior Court for unlawful transfer of marijuana. Upon his conviction, he appealed.

One issue on appeal concerned the admission into evidence at trial of the package shipping receipt. Best contended that the receipt was not properly authenticated to link it to him and was thus inadmissible. The Court of Appeals of Arizona affirmed, and said the foundation/authentication argument "borders on the frivolous, given the defendant's admission that he was the shipper and evidence to the same effect from his roommate. But even without that, it could be inferred that defendant wrote the documents from the fact that the receipt was recovered at his home and that the shipper departed in a car belonging to defendant's roommate. Under [Arizona's] Rule 901(b)(4)... authentication can be accomplished by circumstantial evidence."

FRE 901(b)(5) – Authentication: Witness Familiar with Voice of Accused Can Identify It on Tape Recording

> **Rule 901. Requirement of Authentication or Identification**
>
> *(a) General Provision.* The requirement of authentication or identification as a condition precedent to admissibility is satisfied by evidence sufficient to support a finding that the matter in question is what its proponent claims.
>
> *(b) Illustrations.* By way of illustration only, and not by way of limitation, the following are examples of authentication or identification conforming with the requirements of this rule:
>
> *(5) Voice Identification.* Identification of a voice, whether heard firsthand or through mechanical or electronic transmission or recording, by opinion based upon hearing the voice at any time under circumstances connecting it with the alleged speaker.

STATE v. WEST
345 S.E.2d 186, 317 N.C. 219 (1986)

After what she described as years of being raped by her stepfather, 14-year-old Kimberly Ann Hayes ran to a neighbor's home one morning when she was skipping school and told her story. The neighbor drove Kimberly to the family church; the preacher's wife told Kimberly's mother, and presently the sheriff's department was notified. Kimberly said her stepfather, Robert Lee West, threatened to hurt her and her mother if she ever told anyone.

West was tried on charges of rape in the first degree and sexual offense in the first degree. Over defense objection the prosecution was allowed to admit into evidence a tape recording found by the side of the road less than a mile from West's home. "The voice on the tape was identified by both Kimberly and her mother as being that of defendant. The voice described a sexual fantasy in which Kimberly was assaulted by several men, and it included the remark, 'I've been f_ _ _ _ _ _ her since she was eleven.'" West was convicted on both charges, and he appealed.

The Supreme Court of North Carolina affirmed the conviction, and held that the tape recording was properly authenticated by the identification of the voice as West's by Kimberly and her mother, as well as by the deputy sheriff who interviewed West, under North Carolina's Rule 901(b)(5), identical to the federal rule. "In addition, the tape's contents corroborate this identification testimony: the speaker mentions Kimberly's name and age and fantasizes about what he would like to do 'sometime when I know she's home by herself and her mama is gonna be at that plant.'" The court observed, "Properly authenticated, the contents of the tape comprise an admission" under the state version of Rule 801(d)(2)(A), and as such hold unquestionable relevance.

FRE 901(b)(6) – Authentication: Circumstantial Evidence Can Authenticate Identity of Telephone Caller to Corroborate Caller's Self-Identification

> **Rule 901. Requirement of Authentication or Identification**
>
> *(a) General Provision.* The requirement of authentication or identification as a condition precedent to admissibility is satisfied by evidence sufficient to support a finding that the matter in question is what its proponent claims.
>
> *(b) Illustrations.* By way of illustration only, and not by way of limitation, the following are examples of authentication or identification conforming with the requirements of this rule:
>
> *(6) Telephone Conversations.* Telephone conversations, by evidence that a call was made to the number assigned at the time by the telephone company to a particular person or business, if (A) in the case of a person, circumstances, including self-identification, show the person answering to be the one called, or (B) in the case of a business, the call was made to a place of business and the conversation related to business reasonably transacted over the telephone.

STATE v. HAMILTON
605 P.2d 1121, 185 Mont. 522 (1980)

At the Carbon County District Court trial of Edwin Grant Hamilton for the strangulation murder of his 75-year-old mother, Mabel Johnson, the prosecution introduced over objection testimony that the night of the murder the Red Lodge Police Department received a phone call. The dispatcher said, "This is the Red Lodge Police Department," but received no response, hearing instead the sound of "a couple of drunks arguing." The police listened in for half an hour, hearing a struggle between a male and a female, and finally the female "gasping for air and choking," and then the male saying at intervals, "Goddamnit, die. I am going to hell. Mamma, I am sorry. You all right, Mamma, huh? No, no, no, Mamma…. Die, you bitch…. Are you going to die or not?" and so forth. "As the officer continued listening, he heard what he thought was someone dialing the telephone on the other end of the line. The male voice then spoke into the receiver: 'Hang the goddamn phone up, I have to call my cousin. My mother is dead. She had a heart attack.' The officer inquired as to the party's name and address. The individual identified himself as Grant Hamilton of 207½ North Platt, a location only a block away from the police station." Officers went to the address, found Hamilton bruised and scratched, and his mother strangled to death. Hamilton was convicted by the jury of mitigated deliberate homicide, and he appealed.

The Montana Supreme Court affirmed the conviction, and specifically held that the phone-call testimony was admissible over Hamilton's contention that "there was no proper authentication or identification as a condition precedent to admissibility." Analogizing from Montana's equivalent of Rule 901(b)(6) – which, strictly speaking, applies literally only to phone calls placed, not to calls received – the court held that "circumstances… following a telephone conversation may serve to sufficiently identify a caller" and to corroborate his statement of self-identification to render the contents of the conversation fully admissible. "The conditions stated [in Rule 901(b)(6)] are examples only. In this case there are several confirming circumstances making it probable that defendant was in fact the speaker."[2]

FRE 901(b)(7), 803(8) – Authentication: EEOC Investigative Reports and Determination Are Admissible as Authenticated Public Records

> **Rule 901. Requirement of Authentication or Identification**
>
> *(a) General Provision.* The requirement of authentication or identification as a condition precedent to admissibility is satisfied by evidence sufficient to support a finding that the matter in question is what its proponent claims.
>
> *(b) Illustrations.* By way of illustration only, and not by way of limitation, the following are examples of authentication or identification conforming with the requirements of this rule:
>
> *(7) Public Records or Reports.* Evidence that a writing authorized by law to be recorded or filed and in fact recorded or filed in a public office, or a purported public record, report, statement, or data compilation, in any form, is from the public office where items of this nature are kept.
>
> **Rule 803. Hearsay Exceptions; Availability of Declarant Immaterial**
>
> The following are not excluded by the hearsay rule, even though the declarant is available as a witness.
>
> *(8) Public Records and Reports.* Records, reports, statements, or data compilations, in any form, of public offices or agencies, setting forth (A) the activities of the office or agency, or (B) matters observed pursuant to duty imposed by law as to which matters there was a duty to report, excluding, however, in criminal cases matters observed by police officers and other law enforcement personnel, or (C) in civil actions and proceeding and against the Government in criminal cases, factual findings resulting from an investigation made pursuant to authority granted by law, unless the sources of information or other circumstances indicate lack of trustworthiness.

GARCIA v. GLOOR
618 F.2d 264 (5th Cir. 1980)

Gloor Lumber and Supply, Inc., of Brownsville, Texas, had a rule that prohibited employees from speaking Spanish on the job unless they were dealing with customers who spoke Spanish. Hector Garcia, an employee there, was overheard by Alton Gloor, an officer and owner of the company, responding in Spanish to an inquiry by another Mexican-American employee in June 1975, and soon Garcia was fired. Garcia filed an Equal Employment Opportunity Act lawsuit in U.S. District Court for the Southern District of Texas challenging the rule and his firing as discriminatory on the basis of national origin.

The trial court ruled that the Gloor English-only rule did not discriminate on the

---

[2] Defendant's statements themselves, once his identity is authenticated, are admissible on a number of grounds, the most obvious being the party admission, see FRE 801(d)(2)(A).

basis of national origin and that Garcia was fired for a number of other reasons too. The Fifth Circuit Court of Appeals affirmed, but held that the district court had committed error, albeit a harmless one, in excluding certain EEOC investigative reports and determinations offered into evidence by Garcia. Although at trial the argument about the admissibility of the EEOC records had been "fought on the question of whether they were or were not business records" under Rule 803(6), the court held they were actually public records under Rule 803(8) and had been authenticated as such under Rule 901(b)(7), and were thus admissible. The appellate court also held that the trial court was correct in refusing to admit purported transcripts of Garcia's unemployment compensation claim hearing before the Texas Employment Commissioner's Appeals Tribunal because there had not been sufficient authentication.

It should be noted, as always with authentication rules, that the requirements of authentication are separate and distinct from any rules regarding substantive admissibility.

FRE 901(b)(8) – Authentication: Forty-Year-Old Corporate Papers Found in Likely Location Are Sufficiently Authenticated for Admissibility

> **Rule 901. Requirement of Authentication or Identification**
>
> *(a) General Provision.* The requirement of authentication or identification as a condition precedent to admissibility is satisfied by evidence sufficient to support a finding that the matter is question is what its proponent claims.
>
> *(b) Illustrations.* By way of illustration only, and not by way of limitation, the following are examples of authentication or identification conforming with the requirements of this rule:
>
> *(8) Ancient Documents or Data Compilation.* Evidence that a document or data compilation, in any form, (A) is in such condition as to create no suspicion concerning its authenticity, (B) was in a place where it, if authentic, would likely be, and (C) has been in existence 20 years or more at the time it is offered.

LOCKWOOD v. AC & S, INC.
722 P.2d 826, 44 Wash. App. 330 (1986)

Albert Lockwood worked in the Seattle shipyards from 1942 until 1972 as a rigger and boilermaker, repairing and renovating older ships. He retired at age 63, disabled with asbestosis. In 1982 Lockwood and his wife Dorothy joined the national asbestos litigation movement, suing Raymark (successor to Raybestos Manhattan, one of the principal manufacturer of asbestos insulating cloth), Pittsburgh Corning Corp. and 17 other asbestos textile manufacturers. Lockwood offered "substantial testimony" that many in the industry knew of the dangers of asbestos as early as the 1930s. Lockwood won a jury verdict in King County Superior Court of over $183,000 against the three defendants to go to trial, Raymark, Pittsburgh Corning and Standard Asbestos and Insulation Co. (the others settled or had been dismissed). After Pittsburgh Corning and Standard were granted new trials because a photo Lockwood had admitted into evidence had inadvertently not been disclosed during discovery, Raymark appealed the judgment to the Court of Appeals of Washington.

On appeal a major issue concerned the admissibility of the so-called "Sumner Simpson papers," some 6,000 documents collected by the president of Raybestos Manhattan, Sumner Simpson, consisting of reports and correspondence between Simpson and counsel for Johns-Manville Corporation and with editors of "Asbestos" magazine. The documents dated from the 1920s and were found in a storage area and an old safe in the 1970s.[3] Raymark contended they had not been sufficiently authenticated for admissibility. In a long footnote, the appellate court, which affirmed the verdict, found the papers had been properly authenticated as ancient documents under the Washington equivalent of Federal Rule 901(b)(8): "The court found no reasonable grounds for creating a suspicion concerning the authenticity of the papers and found them authentic as a matter of law; that they were located in a place where if authentic they would likely be; and that those which on their face indicated they were 20 years old or older were of that age and were authenticated. The factual basis for these findings was in the deposition of William Simpson, an officer of Raymark and son of the deceased Sumner Simpson. [Rule] 901(a) provides that evidence must be authenticated to be admissible and that authentication 'is satisfied by evidence sufficient to support a finding that the matter in question is what its proponent claims.' William Simpson's deposition provides sufficient evidence to support the findings in the order. We also find persuasive the host of federal and state courts which have admitted these same papers as authentic."

FRE 901(a),(b)(9) – Authentication: ATM Photograph of Accused Is Admissible Despite Failure to Meet Requirement for Witness with Knowledge of Accuracy of Process Producing Images

> **Rule 901. Requirement of Authentication or Identification**
>
> *(a) General Provision.* The requirement of authentication or identification as a condition precedent to admissibility is satisfied by evidence sufficient to support a finding that the matter in question is what its proponent claims.
>
> *(b) Illustrations.* By way of illustration only, and not by way of limitation, the following are examples of authentication or identification conforming with the requirements of this rule:
>
> *(9) Process or System.* Evidence describing a process or system used to produce a result and showing that the process or system produces an accurate result.

UNITED STATES v. REMBERT
863 F.2d 1023 (D.C. Cir. 1988)

Key evidence in the trial of Reginald Rembert for kidnapping, armed robbery and interstate transportation of a stolen vehicle was a set of photographs taken by ATM surveillance video cameras at the scene of one of the crimes. (There was other fairly compelling evidence linking Rembert to the 1987 "crime sprees," including positive eyewitness identifications by

---

[3]These papers figured prominently in much of the asbestos litigation, including *Lohrman v. Pittsburgh Corning, supra* p. 266. As for the papers' admissibility as ancient documents, see *Threadgill v. Armstrong World Industries, supra* p. 252.

the victims and some fingerprint evidence.) The jury convicted him, and he appealed.

The only issue an appeal to the District of Columbia Circuit Court of Appeals concerned the admission of the ATM surveillance photos. The photos were printed from film in the video recorder at the Sovran Bank in Seat Pleasant, Maryland. "The sole authenticating witness for the photos was Katie Wohlfarth, a supervisor in the loss control division of the bank, who testified that she was in charge of investigating questioned activities through the ATM machines. She testified that the machine-maintained records at the Seat Pleasant branch showed an unusual pattern of use associated with John Lynn's ATM card on July 26, 1987, at approximately 8:00 p.m. The machine's records indicated that the card had been entered ten times on that occasion and was retained by the machine on the tenth attempt. She further testified that video cameras are maintained at each of the three ATM machines at the Seat Pleasant location. A video recorder taped the view from each camera in sequence, rotating to the next camera, taking a photograph every three seconds. This videotaping process imprints the date and time at which the pictures were made on the resultant photographs. She then identified a strip of pictures which was admitted into evidence over Rembert's objection. She further testified that she had viewed the original videotape and the resultant photographs and that the photographs were fair and accurate depictions of what was on the videotape. The imprinted date and times on the photographs ranged from 8:04:22 p.m. until 8:13:30 p.m. on July 26, 1987. On cross examination, she testified that she had no personal knowledge of the events that transpired at the Seat Pleasant location on that date, and could not say from her own knowledge whether the photographs fairly and accurately depicted the scene and events at that time and place or not."

Rembert objected that Wohlfarth, the sponsoring witness, lacked personal knowledge of the scene depicted so as to be able to testify under Rule 901(b)(1) that the picture was fair and accurate. He further "persuasively contended" that Rule 901(b)(9)'s requirements were not met either, because Wohlfarth's "testimony did not really speak to the reliability of the process" that produced the pictures: "She testified rather as a custodian of the records without supplying evidence as to the type of camera used, its general reliability, the quality of its product, the purpose of its employment, the process by which it is focused, or the general reliability of the entire system."

But the appellate court noted that illustrations contained in Rule 901(b) are only that, and do not ban admission of evidence that does not precisely fit within one of the examples provided, as long as Rule 901(a) is satisfied. Noting that courts have continued to modernize their treatment of photographic evidence, the court held these ATM photos sufficiently authenticated and fully admissible as offered: "We conclude that the contents of photographic evidence to be admitted into evidence need not be merely illustrative, but can be admitted as evidence independent of the testimony of any witness as to the events depicted, upon a foundation sufficient to meet the requirements of Federal Rule of Evidence 901(a). In this case the circumstantial evidence provided by the victim witnesses as to the occurrences at the ATM machines, together with the testimony of Wohlfarth as to the loading of the cameras and the security of the film, coupled with the internal indicia of date, place, and event depicted in the evidence itself provide ample support for the District Court's exercise of its discretion.... The contents of the photos in the instant case supply any further need for authentication that the contact prints from the ATM machine may require on the present record."

FRE 902(1) – Authentication: Postal Service Certificate of Mailing Is Self-Authenticating, Needing No Extrinsic Foundational Testimony

> **Rule 901. Requirement of Authentication or Identification**
>
> *(a) General Provision.* The requirement of authentication or identification as a condition precedent to admissibility is satisfied by evidence sufficient to support a finding that the matter in question is what its proponent claims.
>
> **Rule 902. Self-Authentication**
>
> Extrinsic evidence of authenticity as a condition precedent to admissibility is not required with respect to the following:
>
> *(1) Domestic Public Documents Under Seal.* A document bearing a seal purporting to be that of the United States, or of any State, district, Commonwealth, territory, or insular possession thereof, or the Panama Canal Zone, or the Trust Territory of the Pacific Islands, or of a political subdivision, department, officer, or agency thereof, and a signature purporting to be an attestation or execution.

UNITED STATES v. MOORE
555 F.2d 658 (8th Cir. 1977)

Fred A. Moore, a postal service mail carrier, was tried on charges of detaining and delaying mail in St. Louis after he was seen dumping Normandy School District newsletters in a dumpster in August 1976. Eight counts altogether alleged that Moore did the same thing with several other bulk and individual mailings. A jury convicted him of all eight counts and he was given several concurrent 18-month prison sentences.

On his appeal to the Eighth Circuit Court of Appeals, one of a number of issues Moore raised concerned the admission in connection with Count VII of the government's Exhibit 13. Count VII charged him with detaining and delaying a magazine called "Postal Life," mailed by the U.S. Postal Service in Washington, D.C. to an addressee in St. Louis. Exhibit 13 was "a certification of mailing by the postal service of over 60,000 such pieces of mail from Washington under a 'postage and fees paid' label." Moore challenged its admissibility "on grounds of inadequate foundation because no witness identified the exhibits."

The appellate court affirmed Moore's convictions and specifically upheld the admissibility of Exhibit 13 under Rule 902(1): "The questioned exhibit bears a certification under formal seal of the United States Postal Service that said document constituted a true copy of the record retained in the official custody of the United States Postal Service.... For purposes of Fed.R.Evid. 902(1), the postal service is an agency of the United States.... Therefore, the certificate of the United States Postal Service, under seal and with a signature purporting to be an execution, constitutes a self-authenticated document needing no extrinsic evidence to sustain admissibility."

(Had a hearsay objection been posed, the exhibit would have been admissible under Rule 803(8) as a public record.)

FRE 902(2) – Authentication: No Certification of Delegation of Authority Is Necessary to Authenticate Custodian's Report That Firearms Registry Lacks Entry for Accused's Firearm

> **Rule 901. Requirement of Authentication or Identification**
>
> *(a) General Provision.* The requirement of authentication or identification as a condition precedent to admissibility is satisfied by evidence sufficient to support a finding that the matter in question is what its proponent claims.
>
> **Rule 902. Self-Authentication**
>
> Extrinsic evidence of authenticity as a condition precedent to admissibility is not required with respect to the following:
>
> *(2) Domestic Public Documents Not Under Seal.* A document purporting to bear the signature in the official capacity of an officer or employee of any entity included in paragraph (1) hereof, having no seal, if a public officer having a seal and having official duties in the district or political subdivision of the officer or employee certifies under seal that the signer has the official capacity and that the signature is genuine.

UNITED STATES v. COMBS
762 F.2d 1343 (9th Cir. 1985)

Michael Dwayne Combs was charged with possession of an unlawful, unregistered shortened-barrel Uzi rifle after two sheriff's deputies responded to complaints of illegal rapid-fire shooting by several individuals on private property near San Diego. He was convicted both of possession of an unlawful firearm that had been made from a rifle and of possession of an unregistered firearm having a barrel length of less than 16 inches. He was sentenced to 30 days in jail with the rest of two years suspended, and was placed on three years' probation. He appealed.

The Ninth Circuit Court of Appeals reversed the unlawful firearm conviction because of a bad jury instruction, but affirmed his conviction on the unregistered firearm count. Combs argued that it was error for the district court to admit into evidence on the government's motion a government report that no record of Combs' firearm existed in the official registry. M. Colleen Davis, a certified National Firearms Act specialist, wrote a certified report "in which she stated that she had custody and control of the National Firearms Registration and Transfer Record concerning the registration, importation, transfer and making of firearms and of approved applications to make and register firearms. In this report she certified that after a diligent search she found no evidence that the firearm described in the indictment had been registered to or lawfully acquired by Combs and no application by Combs to make and register a firearm.

"The report by Davis was not under seal, so the government had attached to the report a document under seal executed by Gary Schaible, Chief of the National Firearms Act Branch of the Bureau of Alcohol, Tobacco, and Firearms. In that document, Schaible stated that Davis had proper custody and control of the Firearms Registration and Transfer Record, that he was familiar with her signature, and that the signature on the report appeared to be true."

The appellate court concluded the report was properly admitted under Rules 803(10) and 902(2) as a certification of the absence of a public record of the registration of Combs' firearm. To Combs' more particular objection that "Schaible's certification that Davis has custody and control of the National Firearms Registration and Transfer Record does not certify that Davis has the 'official capacity' to act as required by Rule 902(2)." The court held that "Rule 902 required no certification of the *delegation of custodial authority* but that a signed certification by the public officer having actual legal custody was sufficient to satisfy the rule."

FRE 902(3),(4) – Authentication: Documents Generated By Foreign Government with Verifying Certificate Are Self-Authenticating as Foreign Public Documents; Private Documents Filed with Foreign Government Accompanied by Same Certificate Are Self-Authenticating as Public Record

> **Rule 902. Self-Authentication**
>
> Extrinsic evidence of authenticity as a condition precedent to admissibility is not required with respect to the following:
>
> *(3) Foreign Public Documents.* A document purporting to be executed or attested in an official capacity by a person authorized by the laws of a foreign country to make the execution or attestation, and accompanied by a final certification as to the genuineness of the signature and official position (A) of the executing or attesting person, or (B) of any foreign official whose certificate of genuineness of signature and official position relates to the execution or attestation or is in a chain of certificates of genuineness of signature and official position relating to the execution or attestation. A final certification may be made by a secretary of an embassy or legation, consul general, consul, vice consul, or consular agent of the United States, or a diplomatic or consular official of the foreign country assigned or accredited to the United States. If reasonable opportunity has been given to all parties to investigate the authenticity and accuracy of official documents, the court may, for good cause shown, order that they be treated as presumptively authentic without final certification or permit them to be evidenced by an attested summary with or without final certification.
>
> *(4) Certified Copies of Public Records.* A copy of an official record or report or entry therein, or of a document authorized by law to be recorded or filed and actually recorded or filed in a public office, including data compilations in any form, certified as correct by the custodian or other person authorized to make the certification, by certificate complying with paragraph (1),(2), or (3) of this rule or complying with any Act of Congress or rule prescribed by the Supreme Court pursuant to statutory authority.

UNITED STATES v. DOYLE
130 F.3d 523 (2d Cir. 1997)

Thomas Doyle and Robert Vance were charged with illegal exportation of technological products and conspiracy in violation of a 1986 Presidential Executive Order prohibiting trade with Libya. They were charged with supplying Lead Romac/Sieglar gas-type fuel pumps and other products to a Maltese company, Camarco International Limited, for ultimate use in land-based solar turbine engines operating in the oil fields of Libya. Their defense apparently was that they procured the parts for companies in Germany and Malta and elsewhere, and had no knowledge of where they ended up later. (Testimony by Richard Borden, an employee of Doyle's, suggested that when they received orders for parts sought for Libya, Doyle would redact the word "Libya" from the request and fax it to U.S. suppliers.)

Doyle and Vance were convicted of six counts. Doyle was sentenced to 15 months in prison followed by three years' supervised release and a $5,000 fine. Vance got five months in prison and three years' supervised release. They appealed.

Although the Second Circuit Court of Appeals reversed the judgment of conviction because of an egregiously erroneous jury instruction on the presumption of innocence, it did uphold the trial court's ruling that admitted documentary evidence from Malta. In response to international letters rogatory issued by Chief United States District Judge Peter C. Dorsey requesting records concerning the fuel pump shipments, "On December 1, 1993, Republic of Malta Deputy Attorney General Dr. Degaetano signed and certified as authentic numerous public documents of the Customs agency of Malta. The Government asserts that those documents which it offered at trial were generated in or collected by the Malta Customs agency in its official capacity. Further appended to the submission is a sworn statement of authenticity executed by Senior Malta Customs Inspector John Cauchi, sworn to under oath before Magistrate Dr. David Scicluna, and certification from the Assistant Attorney General of Malta. Finally, the United States Consul in the Republic of Malta certified that he received the letter rogatory and accompanying documents on December 10, 1993."

The trial court was correct that as to documents generated by the government of Malta, Rule 902(3) provided that they were self-authenticating. As to *private* business documents *collected* by the government of Malta, the court held the certification supplied was "clearly adequate" to satisfy Rule 902(4), providing for self-authentication of documents recorded or filed in a public office.

(In dealing with a separate objection to the admission of these documents as hearsay, the appellate court made an observation that must be kept in mind in dealing with all the authentication rules: "**It is axiomatic that authenticated evidence must still be admissible under the other rules of evidence....**")

FRE 902(4) – Authentication: Copy of State Court Judgment of Conviction Is Self-Authenticating in Prosecution for Possession of Firearm by Felon

> **Rule 902. Self-Authentication**
> Extrinsic evidence of authenticity as condition precedent to admissibility is not required with respect to the following:
> *(4) Certified Copies of Public Records.* A copy of an official record or report or entry therein, or of a document authorized by law to be recorded or filed and actually recorded or filed in a public office, including data compilations in any form, certified as correct by the custodian or other person authorized to make the certification, by certificate complying with paragraph (1), (2), or (3) of this rule or complying with any Act of Congress or rule prescribed by the Supreme Court pursuant to statutory authority.

UNITED STATES v. DANCY
861 F.2d 77 (5th Cir. 1988)

Willie Lee Dancy was charged in federal court in Texas with being a felon in knowing possession of a firearm. One of his defenses involved the government's proof that he was a convicted felon, which he claimed was insufficiently authenticated for admission into evidence. The proof was his "pen (penitentiary) packet" prepared by the California Department of Corrections, that consisted of copies of a criminal judgment and Dancy's fingerprint card. The defense argued that there was no showing the records were "actually recorded or filed in a public office." The trial court admitted the CDC records and a jury convicted Dancy. He appealed.

The Fifth Circuit Court of Appeals affirmed. Dancy's authentication argument was "meritless" because Rule 902(4) provides for self-authentication for official records "*or* of a document authorized by law to be recorded or filed," as alternative means, not as cumulative requirements. The pen packet documents were official records of the California Department of Corrections and as such were self-authenticating under the Rule.

(The court also dismissed Dancy's Rule 803(8) argument, saying "The rule excludes records that report the observation or investigation of crimes, not records that merely document routine, unambiguous factual matters."[4])

---

[4] See, e.g., *United States v. Puente, supra* p. 240.

FRE 902(5) – Authentication: Brochure Issued by District Housing Authority Is Self-Authenticating as Official Publication

> **Rule 902. Self-Authentication**
> Extrinsic evidence of authenticity as a condition precedent to admissibility is not required with respect to the following:
> *(5) Official Publications.* Books, pamphlets, or other publications purporting to be issued by public authority.

SILVERMAN v. BARRY
21 Fed. Rules Evid. Serv. 1003 (D.D.C. 1986), aff'd 845 F.2d 1072 (D.C. Cir. 1988)
(Unpublished Opinion)

Robert I. Silverman and partners sought to convert their District of Columbia apartment building at 3003 Van Ness Street to condominiums so they could sell it to the Van Ness South Tenants Association for $40,000,000. They obtained what purported to be the consents of as many as 344 tenants of the 603 living there, but the staff of the D.C. Department of Housing and Community Development was able to verify only 274 before the District's Rental Housing Conversion and Sale Emergency Act took effect in 1980. The Act effectively eliminated straight tenant consent conversions. Silverman's partnership was unable to obtain Department approval for the proposed conversion, and filed suit for damages equal to the difference between the proposed selling price to the VNSTA and what they were able to sell it for as a rental building, $27,000,000. They alleged a taking of their property in violation of the Due Process and Equal Protection Clauses, and a violation of the D.C. Home Rule Act. The U.S. District Court for the District of Columbia ruled against the partnership, and their appeal to the D.C. Circuit Court of Appeals was denied as well.

During trial an issue had come up concerning the authentication of some proffered evidence. A brochure issued by the D.C. Department of Housing and Community Development entitled, "Housing Problems, Conditions and Trends in the District of Columbia" was offered on the question of the background and purpose of the Department's regulation of condo conversion (which the District had regulated since 1976; co-op conversions had been regulated in the District since 1940). The district court held the brochure to be self-authenticating under Rule 902(5) as an official publication of the District.

FRE 902(6) – Authentication: Magazine Article Is Self-Authenticating

> **Rule 902. Self-Authentication**
> Extrinsic evidence of authenticity as a condition precedent to admissibility is not required with respect to the following:
> *(6) Newspapers and Periodicals.* Printed materials purporting to be newspapers or periodicals.

SNYDER v. WHITTAKER CORP.
839 F.2d 1085 (5th Cir. 1988)

Captain Andrew Allen and deckhand Robert Cameron died at sea when Allen's 75-foot shrimp boat *Texas Lady* sank in 40 feet of water after colliding with an ANR Pipeline drilling platform in the Gulf of Mexico in foggy weather in April 1983. Their personal representatives (Melanie Snyder and others) sued ANR, alleging it had not sounded its foghorn as required by Coast Guard regulations, and Whittaker Corporation, whose Desco Marine division had built the shrimper, claiming the hull was defectively designed and manufactured. "The gist of Snyder's case was that Whittaker's decision to build its shrimp boat hulls of two materials – balsa core material above the waterline and fiberglass laminate below – created weak points or 'stress spots' that allowed a small impact to cause a large hole." ANR settled on the final day of trial. The District court jury returned a verdict of $100,000 for the pain and suffering of each man, and more than $1,000,000 to Allen's family for loss of care, support and services, and lost inheritance.

One of Whittaker's points on appeal concerned the trial court's decision to admit a magazine article "lauding balsa-core material." Whittaker renewed its objection that the article was not properly authenticated. The Fifth Circuit Court of Appeals, which affirmed, noted that under Rule 902(6) no extrinsic evidence of authenticity is needed for "printed articles from periodicals," which are self-authenticating.

FRE 902(7) – Authentication: Inscription On Gun Indicating Country of Manufacture Is Admissible as Self-Authenticating

> **Rule 902. Self-Authentication**
> Extrinsic evidence of authenticity as a condition precedent to admissibility is not required with respect to the following:
> *(7) Trade Inscriptions and the Like.* Inspections, signs, tags, or labels purportating to have been affixed in the course of business and indicating ownership, control, or origin.

UNITED STATES v. ALVAREZ
972 F.2d 1000 (9th Cir. 1992)

With at least 14 criminal convictions under his belt already, Anthony Alexander Alvarez got into a row with the manager of San Diego's Sun Harbor Motel in April 1989 and fired his handgun. Alvarez's stepfather, Robert Brueggeman, had reported to police just the day before that Alvarez had stolen the gun from his home. Alvarez was arrested and charged with being an armed career criminal and a felon in possession of a firearm.

One of the elements of the felon-in-possession charge under 18 U.S.C. §922(g) is that the possession of the firearm be "in and affecting interstate or foreign commerce." To prove that the .32 caliber semi-automatic Astra Model 4000 Falcon pistol was manufactured in Spain, the government offered the pistol itself into evidence and pointed to the inscription, "Garnika, Spain" on the top of the pistol. The defense objected on hearsay and authentication grounds, but the trial court admitted the evidence. Alvarez was convicted quickly after a one-day trial, and was sentenced to 30 years' imprisonment.

On appeal to the Ninth Circuit Court of Appeals, Alvarez raised a number of issues, including the admissibility of the gun inscription. The appellate court, which reversed on sentencing issues, affirmed Alvarez's convictions and upheld the trial court's rulings on the gun inscription. Rule 902(7) does not require "extrinsic evidence of authenticity for inscriptions, signs, tags or labels which indicate workmanship, control or origin." (Nor was the inscription hearsay, but rather was a "mechanical trace" and thus a type of circumstantial evidence. Thus it was not an assertion under Rule 801(c).)

FRE 902(8) – Authentication: Notarized Affidavit of Personnel Officer That Accused Was Not Employed Is Admissible as Self-Authenticating

> **Rule 902. Self-Authentication**
> Extrinsic evidence of authenticity as a condition precedent to admissibility is not required with respect to the following:
> *(8) Acknowledged Documents.* Documents accompanied by a certificate of acknowledgment executed in the manner provided by law by a notary public or other officer authorized by law to take acknowledgments.

UNITED STATES v. M'BIYE
655 F.2d 1240 (D.C. Cir. 1981)

A native of Zaire, Honore M'Biye claimed to be employed as a consultant for the United Nations Industrial Development Organization when he applied for loans in 1980 from three D.C. area banks, National Bank of Washington, Hemisphere National Bank, and Riggs National Bank. M'Biye was charged and convicted on three counts of providing false information on loan applications made to federally insured banks. He appealed.

The only issue presented to the District of Columbia Circuit Court of Appeals was the admissibility of an affidavit by Kuo-ho Chang, Chief of Staff Services, Division of Personnel Administration, Office of Personnel Services of the United Nations Secretariat. Chang said in the affidavit that "as the responsible officer, [he] had caused a search to be conducted of U.N. and UNIDO personnel files and that the search 'did not uncover any indication that (Mr. M'Biye) had actually been employed' by either organization." M'Biye objected that the affidavit was hearsay and insufficiently authenticated.

The appellate panel affirmed, holding that the statements in the document were admissible under Rule 803(10) as evidence of the absence of public records, and further that the affidavit "fits squarely within Rule 902(8)" because it had been "executed and sworn to before a notary public of the State of New York." "Accordingly, the Rule 803(10) requirement of evidence 'in the form of the certification in accordance with Rule 902' was satisfied, and the Chang affidavit was properly admitted into evidence."

FRE 902(9) – Authentication: Checks Are Self-Authenticating as Commercial Paper in Check-Kiting Prosecution

> **Rule 902. Self-Authentication**
> Extrinsic evidence of authenticity as a condition precedent to admissibility is not required with respect to the following:
> *(9) Commercial Paper and Related Documents.* Commercial paper, signatures thereon, and documents relating thereto to the extent provided by general commercial law.

UNITED STATES v. LITTLE
567 F.2d 346 (8th Cir. 1977)

A check-kiting scheme that involved accounts in three separate banks resulted in indictments against James E. Little and I. L. Vaughn on eight counts of mail fraud. They were convicted on all eight charges, and they appealed.

The Eighth Circuit Court of Appeals affirmed. One issue concerned the admissibility of corporate checks that were supposed to be part of the scheme. The appellate court disposed of this issue "summarily." The checks were self-authenticating under Rule 902(9) as commercial paper.

FRE 902(10) – Authentication: Federal Statute Providing for Authentication of Foreign Business Records by Certificate Renders Foreign Bank Records Accompanied by Certificate Self-Authenticating

> **Rule 902. Self-Authentication**
> Extrinsic evidence of authenticity as a condition precedent to admissibility is not required with respect to the following:
> *(10) Presumptions Under Acts of Congress.* Any signature, document, or other matter declared by Act of Congress to be presumptively or prima facie genuine or authentic.

UNITED STATES v. STURMAN
951 F.2d 1466 (6th Cir. 1991)

Reuben Sturman led a group comprised of his son David A. Sturman, Ralph L. Levine, and Melvin Kaminsky that was in the business of production, sale and distribution of sexually explicit books and tapes, with "peep booths" at some of the individual business sites. They ran some 150 domestic corporations and five foreign corporations; despite listing many people as shareholders (some fictitious, some real people whose names were used without their knowledge or permission) "Reuben Sturman was the beneficial owner of most of the corporations." At their trial on charges of conspiracy to defraud the United States, and on Reuben Sturman's additional charges of tax evasion, filing false tax returns, and obstruction of justice, it was shown that "defendants used the corporations to conceal income. They transferred money between corporations in ways that made tracing income and expenses difficult. The defendants also skimmed money from some of the adult entertainment businesses. This money was then used to pay personal expenses or was transferred and deposited in Swiss bank accounts. These bank accounts were opened" to hide money and avoid taxes. A federal court jury in Ohio convicted all defendants on all charges brought, and they appealed.

One issue among many raised in their appeal to the Sixth Circuit Court of Appeals concerned the admissibility of "volumes of business records from seven foreign banks." The records were accompanied by 12 affidavits or certificates of authenticity. Although the defendants objected that allowing the records to be admitted on the certificates alone deprived them of the right of confrontation, the Sixth Circuit panel had no problem with the Congressional statute providing for admissibility in a criminal proceeding of foreign records that are certified to be the equivalent of business records.[5] The court noted that the Confrontation Clause works hand in hand with the hearsay exceptions to promote the same values. Technical objections to the certifications were dismissed summarily as "without merit."

In this case, the Act of Congress provided both an additional hearsay exception and a method of self-authentication to satisfy Rule 902(10). Congress intended to "dispense with the necessity of calling a live witness to establish authenticity" and thereby to facilitate criminal prosecutions where foreign records are needed.

FRE 903 – Authentication: Signed Employment Records Are Admissible Without Authenticating Testimony of Employee Who Signed Them

> **Rule 903. Subscribing Witness's Testimony Unnecessary**
> The testimony of a subscribing witness is not necessary to authenticate a writing unless required by the laws of the jurisdiction whose laws govern the validity of the writing.

McQUEENEY v. WILMINGTON TRUST COMPANY
779 F.2d 916 (3d Cir. 1985)

Francis J. McQueeney, a ship's second officer, claimed to have suffered a herniated cervical disc when an over-pressured water hose and the oil-slicked deck of the supertanker *TT Williamsburg* caused him to fall. He filed a Jones Act suit in June 1982 against Wilmington Trust Co., the owner of the tanker, and Anndep Steamship Corp.,

---

[5] Here it is 18 U.S.C. §3505 that makes foreign business records admissible on the same footing as domestic public records, i.e., without the need for a live witness. Compare FRE 803(6) with 803(8) and 902(4).

the operators. A federal district court jury in Pennsylvania awarded McQueeney over $300,000. The two defendants appealed.

Wilmington Trust and Anndep had sought to admit McQueeney's Sea Service Records into evidence. These are records the Coast Guard requires seamen to fill out at the end of each voyage. Each entry is signed both by the seaman and the master of the vessel and "records the time and place that the seaman began and finished his work, as well as the name of the ship and the nature of the voyage." The seaman keeps the original, with copies going to the master and to the Coast Guard. Wilmington Trust and Anndep offered the records to try to establish that McQueeney usually worked only four to six months a year so the jury could take that into account in assessing damages.

The trial court refused to admit the Sea Service Records because no testifying witness authenticated them. On this and other grounds[6] the Third Circuit Court of Appeals reversed and remanded. Citing Rule 903, the court held McQueeney's testimony unnecessary in light of the substantial circumstantial evidence tending to prove the records were authentic. The contents of the documents "tend to support their claim to authenticity" under Rule 901(b)(4); they were produced by McQueeney when the defense requested them during discovery; and the information in the records "although not secret by any means, was not widely held." The records should have been admitted.[7]

....

---

[6] The *McQueeney* case is considerably more well-known, and rightly so, for a pure relevance issue. Francis McQueeney was scheduled to be the only witness in his case; the morning of trial "McQueeney's counsel informed the court that he had just located an eyewitness to the accident, a fellow seaman of McQueeney's named Mauro De la Cerda, who was on board a ship in Freeport, Texas, and was therefore not able to appear as a witness. Counsel requested permission to depose De la Cerda," which was granted by the court. After De la Cerda was deposed and corroborated McQueeney's version of his fall "in all significant respects," defense counsel received crew lists from Anndep that showed De la Cerda wasn't even on board the *Williamsburg* until some months after the accident. McQueeney's counsel said he would not offer the deposition; defense attorneys announced they would offer it to show an attempted "fraud on the court." The trial court refused to allow its admission. Citing Wigmore, the Third Circuit panel ruled it should have been admitted: "Evidence of subornation of perjury is substantive evidence, not mere impeachment material; the inference that one may draw from the subornation does not depend upon anyone else's testimony. The fact that a party suborned perjury is what matters, not the ultimate success or failure of that subornation."

[7] McQueeney had signed what was written by others; the contents of the Sea Service Records therefore were admissible against him as adoptive admissions under Rule 801(d)(2)(b).

Rule 902. Self-authentication

Extrinsic evidence of authenticity as a condition precedent to admissibility is not required with respect to the following:

(11) *Certified domestic records of regularly conducted activity.* — The original or a duplicate of a domestic record of regularly conducted activity that would be admissible under Rule 803(6) if accompanied by a written declaration of its custodian or other qualified person, in a manner complying with any Act of Congress or rule prescribed by the Supreme Court pursuant to statutory authority, certifying that the record —

(A) was made at or near the time of the occurrence of the matters set forth by, or from information transmitted by, a person with knowledge of those matters;

(B) was kept in the course of the regularly conducted activity; and

(C) was made by the regularly conducted activity as a regular practice. A party intending to offer a record into evidence under this paragraph must provide written notice of that intention to all adverse parties, and must make the record and declaration available for inspection sufficiently in advance of their offer into evidence to provide an adverse party with a fair opportunity to challenge them.

(12) *Certified foreign records of regularly conducted activity.* — In a civil case, the original or a duplicate of a foreign record of regularly conducted activity that would be admissible under Rule 803(6) if accompanied by a written declaration by its custodian or other qualified person certifying that the record —

(A) was made at or near the time of the occurrence of the matters set forth by, or from information transmitted by, a person with knowledge of those matters;

(B) was kept in the course of the regularly conducted activity; and

(C) was made by the regularly conducted activity as a regular practice.

The declaration must be signed in a manner that, if falsely made, would subject the maker to criminal penalty under the laws of the country where the declaration is signed. A party intending to offer a record into evidence under this paragraph must provide written notice of that intention to all adverse parties, and must make the record and declaration available for inspection sufficiently in advance of their offer into evidence to provide an adverse party with a fair opportunity to challenge them.

CHAPTER TEN
Article X – Contents of Writings, Recordings and Photographs

FRE 1001(1) – Artist's Drawings Are "Writings" for Purposes of Original Writing Rule

> **ARTICLE X**
> **Contents of Writing, Recordings and Photographs**
> **Rule 1001. Definitions**
> For purposes of this article the following definitions are applicable:
> *(1) Writings and Recordings.* "Writings" and "recordings" consist of letters, words, or numbers, or their equivalent, set down by handwriting, typewriting, printing, photostating, photographing, magnetic impulse, mechanical or electronic recording, or other form of data compilation.
> **Rule 1002. Requirement of Original**
> To prove the content of a writing, recording, or photograph, the original writing, recording, or photograph is required, except as otherwise provided in these rules or by Act of Congress.

SEILER v. LUCASFILM, LTD.
808 F.2d 1316 (9th Cir. 1987)

Lee Seiler, a graphic artist whose specialty was science fiction figures (creatures and machines), claimed to have created beings called "Garthian Striders" in 1976 and 1977 and that Lucasfilm's 1980 movie *The Empire Strikes Back* infringed on his ownership of the figures by depicting "Imperial Walkers" which were based on Seiler's ideas. Seiler obtained his copyright in 1981 for the Garthian Striders, depositing "reconstructions" of the originals with the Copyright Office.

At a seven-day pre-trial evidentiary hearing Seiler showed the district court the "reconstructions" of his Striders that he proposed to show the jury in comparison with the Lucasfilm movie's Imperial Walkers. The court found that no originals predating the 1980 movie had been produced, that Seiler had lost or destroyed the originals of his creatures in bad faith (under Rule 1004(1)) and that therefore "no secondary evidence, such as the post-Empire Strikes Back reconstructions," was admissible under Rule 1002. The court granted Lucasfilm summary judgment and Seiler appealed.

One issue that figured prominently in the appeal before the Ninth Circuit Court of Appeals concerned the very applicability of the Original Writing Rule to this dispute. The appellate panel[1] held that Seiler's drawings were "writings" under Rule 1001(1), representing the "equivalent" of "letters,

---

[1] Which noted that "the rule requires not, as its common name implies, the best evidence in every case but rather the production of an original document instead of a copy" when its contents are at issue.

words or numbers." In a very thoughtful opinion, the court traced the historical role played by the rule and cited Wigmore and the Federal Rules Advisory Committee Notes in support of its expansion of the literal terms of the rule.

"The modern justification for the rule has expanded from prevention of fraud to a recognition that writings occupy a central position in the law. When the contents of a writing are at issue, oral testimony as to the terms of the writing is subject to a greater risk of error than oral testimony as to events or other situations. The human memory is not often capable of reciting the precise terms of a writing, and when the terms are in dispute only the writing itself, or a true copy, provides reliable evidence.... The contents of Seiler's work are at issue. There can be no proof of 'substantial similarity' and thus of copyright infringement unless Seiler's works are juxtaposed with Lucas' and their contents compared. Since the contents are material and must be proved, Seiler must either produce the original or show that it is unavailable through no fault of his own. Rule 1004(1). This he could not do.

"The facts of this case implicate the very concerns that justify the best evidence rule. Seiler alleges infringement by The Empire Strikes Back, but he can produce no documentary evidence of any originals existing before the release of the movie. His secondary evidence does not consist of true copies or exact duplicates but of 'reconstructions' made after The Empire Strikes Back. In short, Seiler claims that the movie infringed his originals, yet he has no proof of those originals.

"The dangers of fraud in this situation are clear. The rule would ensure that proof of the infringement claim consists of the works alleged to be infringed. Otherwise, 'reconstruction' which might have no resemblance to the purported original would suffice as proof for infringement of the original. Furthermore, application of the rule here defers to the rule's special concern for the contents of writings. Seiler's claim depends on the content of the originals, and the rule would exclude reconstituted proof of the originals' content. Under the circumstances here, no 'reconstruction' can substitute for the original.

"Seiler argues that the best evidence rule does not apply to his work, in that it is artwork rather than 'writings, recordings, or photographs.' He contends that the rule both historically and currently embraces only words or numbers.... To recognize Seiler's works as writings does not, as Seiler argues, run counter to the rule's preoccupation with the centrality of the written word in the world of legal relations. Just as a contract objectively manifests the subjective intent of the makers, so Seiler's drawings are objective manifestations of the creative mind. The copyright laws give legal protection to the objective manifestations of an artist's ideas, just as the law of contract protects through its multifarious principles the meeting of minds evidenced in the contract. Comparing Seiler's drawings with Lucas' drawings is no different in principle than evaluating a contract and the intent behind it. Seiler's 'reconstructions' are 'writings' that affect legal relations; their copyrightability attests to that.

"A creative literary work, which is artwork, and a photograph whose contents are sought to be proved, as in copyright, defamation, or invasion of privacy, are both covered by the best evidence rule.... We would be inconsistent to apply the rule to artwork which is literary or photographic but not to artwork of other forms. Furthermore, blueprints, engineering drawings, architectural designs may all lack words or numbers yet still be capable of copyright and susceptible to fraudulent alteration. In short, Seiler's argument would have us restrict the definitions of Rule 1001(1) to 'words' and 'numbers' but ignore 'or their equivalent.' We will not do so in the circumstances of this case.

"Our holding is also supported by the policy served by the best evidence rule in protecting against faulty memory. Seiler's reconstructions were made four to seven years after the alleged originals; his memory as to specifications and dimensions may have dimmed significantly. Furthermore, reconstructions made after the release of the Empire Strikes Back may be tainted, even if unintentionally, by exposure to the movie. Our holding guards against these problems."

FRE 1001(2),(3) – Diagnostic-Quality Copy of X-Ray Film May Be an Original for Purposes of Rules

> **ARTICLE X**
> **Contents of Writings, Recordings, and Photographs**
> **Rule 1001. Definitions**
> For purposes of this article the following definitions are applicable:
> (2) *Photographs.* "Photographs" include still photographs, X-ray films, video tapes, and motion pictures.
> (3) *Original.* An "original" of a writing or recording is the writing or recording itself or any counterpart intended to have the same effect by a person executing or issuing it. An "original" of a photograph includes the negative or any printout or other output readable by sight, shown to reflect the data accurately, is an "original."
> **Rule 1002. Requirement of Original**
> To prove the content of a writing, recording, or photograph, the original writing, recording, or photograph is required, except as otherwise provided in these rules or by Act of Congress.

UNITED STATES v. LEIGHT
818 F.2d 1297 (7th Cir. 1987)

Three weeks after his birth in December 1982 Daniel Leight was re-admitted to Chanute Air Force Base Hospital near Rantoul, Illinois with a skull fracture. An additional skull fracture was discovered during his many weeks of treatment for seizures. He died in March.

Daniel was the third child of Daniel and Karen Irene Shores Leight. The second, Kevin, had also died of head injuries at just over three months of age, in February 1981. Their first, Christopher, was treated for a month as an infant in 1979 for facial redness and blistering that Karen Leight attributed to a food allergy but that doctors diagnosed as a thermal burn.

Karen Leight was indicted for two charges of first degree murder. (It became a federal offense because it happened on a federal airbase.) The two counts were severed "because of the inherent prejudice that would result from trying the counts together," and she was tried for the murder of Daniel in December 1985. She contended the baby's injuries and death were accidental, at least partly caused by birth trauma. After a two-week trial Karen Leight was convicted of second degree murder and the following February 14 was sentenced to life in prison. She appealed.

A major component of Karen Leight's argument to the Seventh Circuit Court of Appeals concerned X-rays of the baby. She argued that a mistrial was required. "The government attempted to erase some grease-pencil marks from X-ray film taken of Daniel on January 14, 1983. In the process the government erased the emulsion off the film, completely obliterating the relevant part of the X-ray. This X-ray was at the crux of the dispute about whether Daniel suffered a second separate skull fracture or, instead, a branching fracture deriving from a single earlier injury," which could conceivably be accounted for by birth trauma. The defense argued that "this destruction of evidence mandates a mistrial because this pivotal issue – one injury or two – was forever obscured by the government's conduct."

The appellate court affirmed, noting, "It is regrettable, perhaps inexcusable, that the government destroyed the X-ray. But several diagnostic-quality copies of the X-ray existed, and they were introduced at trial. Karen has suggested that some anomaly in the original film or some aberration in a copy may have affected the quality of the copies used a trial. There are several reasons why Karen cannot prevail on this point.

"First, Federal Rule of Evidence 1001 states that an X-ray is a 'photograph' for evidentiary purposes and that an 'original of a photograph includes the negative or any print therefrom….' It may well be that a diagnostic-quality copy of X-ray film, therefore, is an 'original' for purposes of evidence law.

"Second even if the X-ray copy is not an 'original' but rather a 'duplicate,' Federal Rule of Evidence 1003 deems a duplicate admissible to the same extent as the original unless 'a genuine question is raised as to the authenticity of the original or… [unless] it would be unfair.'… The opponent of the evidence bears the burden of showing that a genuine issue exists as to its authenticity…. Karen offers only speculation that some relevant difference might exist between the original and the copies of the X-ray film. This is not a sufficient showing of a genuine issue as to authenticity or unfairness." Besides, there was ample expert medical testimony based on extensive records beyond the one X-ray "revealing multiple injuries separated in space and time."

FRE 1001(3),(4), 1003 – Photocopy of Altered Receipt Is Treated as Original When Accused Submitted Photocopy for Reimbursement of False Amount

> **ARTICLE X**
> **Contents of Writings, Recordings and Photographs**
> **Rule 1001 – Definitions**
> For purposes of this article the following definitions are applicable:
> *(3) Original.* An "original" of a writing or recording is the writing or recording itself or any counterpart intended to have the same effect by a person executing or issuing it. An "original" of a photograph includes the negative or any print therefrom. If data are stored in a computer or similar device, any printout or other output readable by sight, shown to reflect the data accurately, is an "original".
> *(4) Duplicate.* A "duplicate" is a counterpart produced by the same impression as the original, or from the same matrix, or by means of photography, including enlargements and miniatures, or by mechanical or electronic re-recording, or by chemical reproduction, or by other equivalent techniques which accurately reproduces the original.
> **Rule 1002. Requirement of Original**
> To prove the content of a writing, recording, or photograph, the original writing, recording, or photograph is required, except as otherwise provided in these rules or by Act of Congress.
> **Rule 1003. Admissibility of Duplicates**
> A duplicate is admissible to the same extent as an original unless (1) a genuine question is raised as to the authenticity of the original or (2) in the circumstances it would be unfair to admit the duplicate in lieu of the original.

UNITED STATES v. RANGEL
585 F.2d 344 (8th Cir. 1978)

Environmental Protection Agency employee Tiburcio Rangel submitted three vouchers to the agency for reimbursement of lodging expenses for business trips. To each he attached a photocopy of the customer copy of a Master Charge sales receipt. When the EPA checked up on these expenses they learned Rangel had altered the copies he submitted, and he was prosecuted for submitting a false instrument to defraud the government of $53.59. The jury convicted Rangel of the charge, and he was sentenced to serve two years' probation, pay a $700 fine, spend eight weekends in jail, and pay restitution.

On appeal to the Eighth Circuit Court of Appeals, Rangel challenged the admission into evidence at trial of the photocopies of the sales receipts he had submitted to the E.P.A., and of the merchant (carbon) copies, contending the original writing rule (called throughout this case, unfortunately, the "best evidence rule") required the "original" altered receipts. The appellate panel affirmed. As to the photocopies he had submitted, the court ruled, "the government had to prove the contents of the photocopy of the altered receipt since the photocopy, not the altered receipt, was identified as the document Rangel had submitted to support his demand for payment. Thus the photocopies were admitted as originals." And as to the admissibility of the merchant copies, the court concluded, "the merchants' copies were described by the district court as carbon copies of Master Charge sales slips, and as such were properly admitted as originals under Fed.R.Evid. 1001(3)." In any event, the court reasoned that if the exhibits were not "originals" under Rule 1001(3) then they were "duplicates" under Rule 1003 and thus just as admissible.

FRE 1002 – To Prove Result of Prior Litigation, Judgment Is Required to Be Admitted Into Evidence; Testimony About Result Is Inadmissible

> **Rule 1002. Requirement of Original**
> To prove the content of a writing, recording, or photograph, the original writing, recording, or photograph is required, except as otherwise provided in these rules or by Act of Congress.

UNITED STATES v. HUMPHREY
104 F.3d 65 (5th Cir. 1997)

Bruce Henry Humphrey and Fay Carolyn Humphrey, who ran a loan brokerage service called H&H Consultants, charged loan applicants up-front deposits in the neighborhood of $4,000, but "maintained no known bank accounts, choosing instead to use check cashing services to obtain cash from the deposits." They promised applicants there would be no more fees required. "Upon payment of the deposit, the applicant would receive a letter from a financial institution that conditioned any loan upon payment of a substantial amount of up-front money, generally between $7,500 and $15,000. Because this was contrary to the arrangement with the Humphreys, most applicants sought to have their deposit refunded and were refused. Other applicants paid the fee requested by the financial institution and still never received financing." Eventually the Humphreys were charged with 10 counts of mail fraud and wire fraud. They were convicted and sentenced to 41 months' imprisonment and three years of supervised release.

One of the issues they raised on appeal to the Fifth Circuit Court of Appeals was the exclusion of testimony from their former lawyer, James Dunn, about a civil lawsuit they had filed against him which they said had resulted in an award of commissions to them for "their loan-finding efforts." They offered this testimony "to establish their good faith and their lack of criminal intent in the operation of their business." In affirming the convictions, the court held that under Rule 1002, "the evidence regarding the prior successful action for commissions was properly excluded because the testimony of the lawyer was not the best evidence of the judgment.... The Humphreys offered no documentary proof of the judgment and, therefore, the exclusion of the testimony was not erroneous."

1002 – Law Enforcement Officer May Testify to Contents of Interview with Accused Despite Availability of Tape Recording of Interview

> **Rule 1002. Requirement of Original**
> To prove the content of a writing, recording, or photograph, the original writing, recording, or photograph is required, except as otherwise provided in these rules or by Act of Congress.

UNITED STATES v. FAGAN
821 F.2d 1002 (5th Cir. 1987)

A kickback scheme involving the use of leased boats to transport heavy equipment, crews and supplies to off-shore drilling rigs in the Gulf of Mexico resulted in Ralph Fagan paying Donald L. Riley, drilling superintendent for Texoma Production Co., some $165,000. As the scheme unraveled, Texoma filed a civil suit against Fagan, a criminal extortion complaint was filed by Fagan against Riley, and threats were made by Thomas Woolsey, a friend of Fagan's, against Riley concerning his testimony in the Texoma suit. Fagan was indicted on multiple counts of mail fraud and witness intimidation.

When Fagan had filed his criminal extortion complaint in Louisiana, he spoke at length with Chris Boudreau, a Lafourche Parish deputy sheriff. Boudreau taped the interview, in which Fagan described the kickback arrangement in some detail. Deputy Boudreau was called as a witness in Fagan's federal court trial, and over defense objections that the "best evidence" of the interview was the tape recording of it, testified to what Fagan had told him. Fagan was convicted of nine counts of aiding and abetting mail fraud, one count of witness intimidation and one count of transmitting a threat in interstate commerce. He appealed.

Among many issues raised on appeal, Fagan renewed his claims that admitting Deputy Boudreau's testimony about his interview with Fagan violated the so-called "best evidence" rule because of the availability of a tape recording of it. In affirming, the Fifth Circuit Court of Appeals, in a lengthy footnote, said the government "was not trying to show the contents of the tape but rather the contents of the *conversation*... (emphasis added)." Quoting from another case and McCormick, respectively, the court said, "Rule 1002 applies not when a piece of evidence sought to be introduced has been somewhere recorded in writing but when it is that written record itself that the party seeks to prove," and, "many facts may be proved without resort to writings which record them."

FRE 1002 – Insurance Policy Itself Need Not Be Produced to Prove Bank Was Insured at Time of Fraud

> **Rule 1002. Requirement of Original**
> To prove the content of a writing, recording, or photograph, the original writing, recording, or photograph is required, except as otherwise provided in these rules or by Act of Congress.

UNITED STATES v. SLIKER
751 F.2d 477 (2d Cir. 1984)

One essential element of each of the 15 counts of bank embezzlement, bank larceny and bank fraud in a federal indictment against John W. Sliker, John Carbone and Theodore "Bucky" Buchwald in a scheme involving checks issued by the non-existent "Bahrain Credit Bank" was that the victim bank, Merchants Bank, was insured by the Federal Deposit Insurance Corporation. "The only evidence offered [at trial] by the Government expressly addressed to proving this was the testimony of Richard Urbano, vice president and controller of Merchants Bank, that the bank's deposits 'are' FDIC insured." Carbone's attorney moved for dismissal at the close of the government's proofs arguing that the "best evidence rule"[2] required production of the FDIC insurance policy itself. The trial judge denied the motion. All three were convicted of bank embezzlement, bank larceny, interstate transportation of stolen property, falsification of bank records, and conspiracy, and sentenced to up to 10 years' imprisonment.

They appealed the convictions, raising numerous issues including the FDIC policy issue. "The proof required was proof of the fact of insurance and not of the contents of a writing" under Rule 1002, said the court, affirming the convictions, and that fact was established (if not optimally) by the testimony of Mr. Urbano, the bank officer.

FRE 1002 – Testimony of Witness Is Sufficient Without Written Invoices to Establish Cost of Goods Purchased

> **Rule 1002. Requirement of Original**
> To prove the content of a writing, recording, or photograph, the original writing, recording, or photograph is required, except as otherwise provided in these rules or by Act of Congress.

R&R ASSOCIATES, INC. v. VISUAL SCENE, INC.
726 F.2d 36 (1st Cir. 1984)

Visual Scene, Inc., a Florida import and wholesale distributor of sunglasses, contracted in 1974 to supply all the sunglasses requirements of R&R Associates, Inc., a New

---

[2]Throughout this volume the phrase "best evidence rule" appears with quotation marks around it, to indicate the author's contention that the phrase is an anachronistic, inaccurate and misleading substitute for what Rule 1002 really is, which is the "original writing rule." If we could get in the habit of calling it by its more accurate name there might be better trials, fewer appeals and fewer hopes futilely raised.

England corporation that distributes sunglasses to independent drugstores. By 1979 Visual Scene stopped accepting returns for credit of merchandise that R&R's customers found defective. R&R, whose $150,000 of business with Visual Scene now accounted for only one percent of Visual Scene's annual sales, sued Visual Scene for breach of contract, "alleging that defendant had breached its agreement with plaintiff by supplying defective and obsolete merchandise and by shipping merchandise plaintiff had not ordered. The complaint further alleged that the defendant failed to provide prompt shipment, thus creating excessive back orders, and had refused to allow plaintiff to return defective and obsolete merchandise for credit. The defendant counterclaimed for breach of contract, unfair competition, interference with a contractual relationship, palming off, and for monies due on a book account." A jury trial resulted in a $34,000 verdict for R&R, and Visual Scene appealed.

One issue raised before the First Circuit Court of Appeals was whether it had been proper for the trial court to permit the president of R&R, Thomas C. Smith, to testify "regarding the cost to plaintiff of procuring the allegedly defective sunglasses from defendant." Visual Scene contended the "best evidence rule" required R&R to produce original invoices to prove the cost. The appellate court affirmed, holding, "One need not read further than the opening clause of the Rule [1002] to detect the flaw in defendant's argument. For when President Smith testified that it cost plaintiff $31,850.19 to procure the allegedly defective merchandise, he was in no way attempting 'to prove the contents of a writing.' Rather, he was attempting by his own direct testimony to prove a particular fact: what it cost R&R to procure the merchandise. To be sure, plaintiff had in its possession written documentation that presumably supported President Smith's testimony. But, as the advisory committee note makes clear, Rule 1002 applies not when a piece of evidence sought to be introduced has been somewhere recorded in writing but when it is that written record itself that the party seeks to prove."

FRE 1003, 1001(4) – Copies Shown to Be Accurate Reproductions of Audio Tapes of Telephone Conversations Are Admissible as Duplicates

> **ARTICLE X**
> **Contents of Writings, Recordings, and Photographs**
> **Rule 1001 – Definitions**
> For purposes of this article the following definitions are applicable:
> *(4) Duplicate.* A "duplicate" is a counterpart produced by the same impression as the original, or from the same matrix, or by means of photography, including enlargements and miniatures, or by mechanical or electronic re-recording, or by chemical reproduction, or by other equivalent techniques which accurately reproduces the original.
> **Rule 1002. Requirement of Original**
> To prove the content of a writing, recording, or photograph, the original writing, recording, or photograph is required, except as otherwise provided in these rules or by Act of Congress.
> **Rule 1003. Admissibility of Duplicates**
> A duplicate is admissible to the same extent as an original unless (1) a genuine question is raised as to the authenticity of the original or (2) in the circumstances it would be unfair to admit the duplicate in lieu of the original.

UNITED STATES v. DiMATTEO
716 F.2d 1361 (11th Cir. 1983)

A sizeable quantity of marijuana was flown into the U.S. from Colombia and Haiti in April 1980 in a DC-6 and loaded into trucks. DEA agents seized the marijuana and later arrested Richard DiMatteo, Morris Kessler, and James Suggs, who had conspired together in the presence of DEA undercover agents and informants to import the grass. They were charged with a variety of offenses arising out of the transaction. DiMatteo and Kessler "tried to show that they had been attempting to establish legitimate business ventures," and to that end Kessler introduced into evidence, apparently without objection by the government, a recording of a phone call to an informant named Miller. "The government in turn introduced duplicates of other recordings made by informant Miller in which Kessler discussed the drug transaction, rather than a legitimate business deal." They were convicted, and appealed.

Although the Eleventh Circuit Court of Appeals reversed on other grounds, it upheld the trial court's ruling admitting the duplicates of the Miller-Kessler tape. The tapes introduced into evidence at trial were copies made by the DEA, and Miller testified they were "exact recordings of conversations that were on the original tapes." So the requirement of accurate reproduction was met; therefore the tapes introduced fit the definition of Rule 1001(4) for "duplicates." And as to Kessler's objection that there might be some inaccuracy because of the process of re-recording the tapes, the court held, "the burden of raising an issue as to the authenticity of the original is on the party opposing admission.... We do not believe that Kessler ever met his burden of raising a genuine issue as to the authenticity of the originals. Furthermore, even if he had done so, Miller's testimony that the duplicates accurately reproduced the conversations would have been a sufficient response." Thus under Rules 1001(4) and 1003 the duplicate tapes were fully admissible.

FRE 1004 – Witness May Testify to Contents of Brochure Destroyed by Fire to Establish Warranty

> **Rule 1004. Admissibility of Other Evidence of Contents**
>
> The original is not required, and other evidence of the contents of a writing, recording, or photograph is admissible if –
>
> *(1) Originals Lost or Destroyed.* All originals are lost or have been destroyed, unless the proponent lost or destroyed them in bad faith; or
>
> *(2) Original Not Obtainable.* No original can be obtained by any available judicial process or procedure; or
>
> *(3) Original in Possession of Opponent.* At a time when an original was under the control of the party against whom offered, that party was put on notice, by the pleadings or otherwise, that the contents would be a subject of proof at the hearing, and that party does not produce the original at the hearing; or
>
> *(4) Collateral Matters.* The writing, recording, photograph is not closely related to a controlling issue.

NEVILLE CONSTRUCTION COMPANY v. COOK PAINT AND VARNISH COMPANY
671 F.2d 1107 (8th Cir. 1982)

Sparks or slag from a welder used in the vehicle shop owned by Neville Construction Co. ignited the Coro-foam insulation in the walls in July 1976 and destroyed the building in minutes. The sprayed-on insulation manufactured by Cook Paint and Varnish Company had been represented by the installer, Thomas Kreis, as being flame retardant; Kreis had given Neville a Cook brochure making the same representation. "Neither Kreis nor the brochure from Cook indicated that the insulation should be covered by paneling or other building material." Neville sued Cook on theories of negligence and express warranty, and the parties stipulated to damages of $80,000 if liability were found. The jury found for Neville, and the trial court denied Cook's motions for judgment N.O.V. and for a new trial. Cook appealed.

Cook had objected to the testimony of Dennis Neville about the fire retardance claims in the brochure, contending the "best evidence" of the contents of the brochure would be the brochure itself. Neville testified that the brochure he had been given was destroyed in the fire. The Nebraska federal district court allowed Neville to testify about the brochure. On appeal the Eighth Circuit Court of Appeals affirmed the verdict, and specifically upheld the ruling on Neville's testimony about Cook's brochure under Rule 1004.

"Cook contends that that because the witness had identified a brochure similar to the one destroyed in the fire it was incumbent upon the Nevilles to introduce that brochure as a duplicate. Cook's argument lacks merit. Because Cook successfully objected to the admission of the similar brochure, it now cannot complain that that document provided the only proper evidence of the contents of the brochure destroyed in the fire. Moreover, the Federal Rules of Evidence recognize no degrees of secondary evidence to prove the contents of a writing that has been lost or destroyed.... The court, therefore, properly admitted the testimony of Dennis Neville as secondary evidence of the contents of the brochure destroyed in the fire."

FRE 1005 – Photocopy of Automobile Certificate of Title Is Admissible in Absence of Claim of Inaccuracy

Rule 1005. Public Records

The contents of an official record, or of a document authorized to be recorded or filed and actually recorded or filed, including data compilations in any form, if otherwise admissible, may be proved by copy, certified as correct in accordance with Rule 902 or testified to be correct by a witness who has compared it with the original. If a copy which complies with the foregoing cannot be obtained by the exercise of reasonable diligence, then other evidence of the contents may be given.

UNITED STATES v. RODRIGUEZ
524 F.2d 485 (5th Cir. 1975)

During the trial of Jose Rodriguez on charges of importing and possessing with the intent to distribute 1105 pounds of marijuana, one of the facts the government wanted to establish, in order to prove the marijuana was in the constructive possession of Rodriguez, was that he was the owner of the car in which it was discovered. To that end the government offered into evidence a photocopy of an automobile certificate of title listing Rodriguez as the owner. DEA Agent Lawrence made the copy from state records. The defense objected that the copy was both hearsay and not properly authenticated. The U.S. District Court for the Southern District of Texas admitted the copy. After Rodriguez was convicted, he appealed.

The Fifth Circuit Court of Appeals affirmed. The photocopy of the title certificate was admissible under both Rule 1003 and Rule 1005.[3] Under Rule 1003 no claim was raised that either the copy or the original record was inaccurate; "in fact, Rodriguez never denied ownership of the vehicle." And under Rule 1005, "vehicle registration is a matter of public record... Agent Lawrence testified that the government's Exhibit 1 was a copy of the official vehicle registration certificate, made by him from the original. Although the prosecutor did not specifically inquire whether it was a 'correct' copy, Agent Lawrence's failure to indicate otherwise must be taken as an indication that the copy was an accurate duplicate of the original. In the face of this substantial compliance with Rule 1005, the appellant has no legitimate grievance."

---

[3] The Federal Rules of Evidence had not gone into effect at the time of the trial of this case. The court noted that the new rules "merely codified existing laws."

FRE 1006, 803(6) – Summaries of Admissible Business Records Are Admissible if Original Records Are Too Voluminous to Be Conveniently Examined

> **Rule 1002. Requirement of Original**
>
> To prove the content of a writing, recording, or photograph, the original writing, recording, or photograph is required, except as otherwise provided in these rules or by Act of Congress.
>
> **Rule 1006. Summaries**
>
> The contents of voluminous writings, recordings, or photographs which cannot conveniently be examined in court may be presented in the form of a chart, summary, or calculation. The originals, or duplicates, shall be made available for examination or copying, or both, by other parties at reasonable time and place. The court may order that they be produced in court.
>
> **Rule 803. Hearsay Exceptions; Availability of Declarant Immaterial**
>
> The following are not excluded by the hearsay rule, even though the declarant is available as a witness:
>
> *(6) Records of Regularly Conducted Activity.* A memorandum, report, record, or data compilation, in any form, of acts, events, conditions, opinions, or diagnoses, made at or near the time by, or from information transmitted by, a person with knowledge, if kept in the course of a regularly conducted business activity, and if it was the regular practice of that business activity to make the memorandum, report, record, or data compilation, all as shown by the testimony of the custodian or other qualified witness, or by certification that complies with Rule 902(11), Rule 902(12), or a statute permitting certification, unless the source of information or the method or circumstances of preparation indicate lack of trustworthiness. The term "business" as used in this paragraph includes business, institution, association, profession, occupation, and calling of every kind, whether or not conducted for profit.

FORD MOTOR COMPANY v. AUTO SUPPLY COMPANY, INC.
661 F.2d 1171 (8th Cir. 1981)

Ford Motor Company sued Harold H. Karp and two businesses he owned and controlled, H.K. Auto Supply, Inc., and Auto Supply Company, Inc., in U.S. District Court for Nebraska for trademark infringement. They bought parts, put Ford's trademark on the parts and boxes they were shipped in, and distributed them as genuine Ford parts. Karp did not contest these allegations; his only argument was "that the parts were purchased from the same suppliers which sell parts to plaintiff and thus could not be categorized as counterfeit parts likely to cause confusion among retail customers as to either quality or source of origin." The district court entered partial summary judgment for Ford in September 1977, finding the defendants liable for trademark infringement, false designation of origin, and copyright infringement under federal statutes and for unfair business practices under Nebraska state law. The court then conducted a hearing on damages. It found actual damages of $1,700,000 and doubled that figure under the trademark statute and added $200,000 in attorney's fees. The court rendered a final judgment of $3,600,000 and granted Ford a permanent injunction against Karp and his companies. They appealed.

The main basis for the actual damages figure had been "Exhibit 30," a summary "single sheet statement of sales and costs of the five specific parts involved in this litigation for the years 1972-1975." The summary was prepared by Terrence Marrs, financial analysis department manager of Ford's parts and service division, who "testified in detail concerning the origin of the figures and summary,...the Product Line Profitability Analysis," an annual compilation of performance by product lines. The PLPA is itself a summary of actual business records, all kept in the ordinary course of business.

The Eighth Circuit Court of Appeals affirmed the verdict and upheld the admissibility of Exhibit 30 under Rules 1006 and 803(6). Under Rule 1006, "a summary, if drawn from data that is inadmissible, likewise must be excluded.... The question of whether the PLPAs are admissible and therefore a proper source for the exhibit 30 summary can be answered by Rule 803(6). That rule allows admission of a record or data compilation, in any form, of events made at or near the time by a person with knowledge if kept in the course of a regularly conducted business activity and if it was the regular practice of that business to make the data compilation. This showing is required to be made by the custodian or other qualified witness.

"By its terms Rule 803(6) encompasses the PLPA. They are a record or data compilation made at the end of the business year. Marrs testified, and it is undisputed, that the PLPAs were kept in the course of regularly conducted business and that it was an annual practice to prepare these financial statements.Further, the rule expressly permits these elements to be shown by a 'qualified witness's as opposed to the custodian. Marrs, as manager of the financial analysis department, was certainly a qualified witness."

Satisfaction of the foundational requirements for Rule 803(6) therefore supplied nearly all of the foundation needed for the summary under Rule 1006.

FRE 1006 – Summaries of Inadmissible Evidence Are Likewise Inadmissible

Rule 1002. Requirement of Original

To prove the content of a writing, recording, or photograph, the original writing, recording, or photograph is required, except as otherwise provided in these rules or by Act of Congress.

Rule 1006. Summaries

The contents of voluminous writings, recordings, or photographs which cannot conveniently be examined in court may be presented in the form of a chart, summary, or calculation. The originals, or duplicates, shall be made available for examination or copying, or both, by other parties at reasonable time and place. The court may order that they be produced in court.

UNITED STATES v. JOHNSON
594 F.2d 1253 (9th Cir. 1979)

Lowell F. Johnson, Joe S. Agers and W. Shelley Richey were indicted, with two other people, for mail fraud in connection with an alleged "elaborate land sale fraud" that involved Thunderbird Valley Corporation. Thunderbird was alleged to have "assigned spurious mortgages to third parties…[and] used the same lots as security on two or more instruments without telling the creditors of other claims against the lots… [There were] a great number of such double mortgages and assignments to the point where it was beyond inadvertence."

At trial the government called a Mr. Harbert, a postal inspector, to give testimony in support of a summary he had prepared from records seized from Thunderbird Valley's offices. The records purported to show "80 double assignments out of 260 files of transactions perused." Defense counsel objected that there was no foundation laid for the admissibility of the underlying records being summarized. After an extended discussion, the trial court admitted the summary because the defense had been given advance notice that the summary would be offered and an opportunity to inspect them: "You had an opportunity to look. That's the problem, though, and evidently you didn't. You didn't care to." The exhibit was admitted, and the defendants were convicted of 24 counts, one for "each…check mailed to an assignee of a spurious or defaulted mortgage." Each defendant was sentenced to four years' imprisonment and $24,000 in fines. They appealed.

The Ninth Circuit Court of Appeals reversed on the issue of the admissibility of Harbert's summary. Under Rule 1006, the appellate court ruled, "The district court erred in not requiring the proponent of the summary to establish a foundation. It was incorrect to suggest that the opponents had the burden of determining that a foundation was lacking…. The purpose of Rule 1006 is to allow the use of summaries when the volume of documents being summarized is so large as to make their use impractical or impossible; summaries may also prove more meaningful to the judge and jury… Such a rationale imports that instead of using a summary, the proponent of the summary could introduce the underlying documents upon which the summary is based. "Moreover, requiring the proponent to show the admissibility of the underlying materials is necessary to protect the integrity of the Federal Rules. In the instant case, the Government argued that notification of opposing counsel obviated the need to show that the underlying material fell within an exception to the hearsay rule. We do not believe that Congress intended that counsel could abrogate other restrictions on admissibility like the hearsay rule by the use of summaries; we cannot read Rule 1006 as preempting the other Rules.

"Finally, Congress placed Rule 1006 not in the Article of the Federal Rules dealing with exceptions to the hearsay rule, Article VIII, but rather in the Article dealing with 'Contents of Writings, Recordings and Photographs,' Article X. While the Government argues that this Article X Rule abrogates the hearsay limitations of Article VIII, the Article X provisions more properly deal with the 'best evidence' problems arising from the use of material other than originals. See Fed.R.Evid 1002. And when Congress intended to provide an exception to the hearsay rule for materials which it also exempted from the best evidence rule in Article X, it did so by a provision in Article VIII. For example, Rule 1005 provides that public records may be proved with other than the original under some circumstances. Rules 803(8),(9), and (10), however, provide the hearsay exception for various types of public records. Similarly, Rule 1007 allows the use of secondary materials to prove the contents of testimony or a written admission of a party. But Rule 801(d)(2) provides that admissions are not subject to the hearsay rule.

In claiming that Rule 1006 provides an exception from both the 'best evidence' rule for summaries and the hearsay rule for the underlying materials, the Government (and the district court) misapprehended this congressional scheme."

The Ninth Circuit panel cited Weinstein, Wigmore and a pre-rules case to the same effect.

Finally the court held the record insufficient to establish that the records were either business records under Rule 803(6) or party admissions under Rule 801(d)(2)(A).

FRE 1007 – Production of Original Release Is Not Required if Plaintiff Admits Executing One

> **Rule 1002. Requirement of Original**
> To prove the content of a writing, recording, or photograph, the original writing, recording, or photograph is required, except as otherwise provided in these rules or by Act of Congress.
>
> **Rule 1007. Testimony or Written Admission of Party**
> Contents of writings, recordings, or photographs may be proved by the testimony or deposition of the party against whom offered or by that party's written admission, without accounting for the nonproduction of the original.

B.D. CLICK COMPANY, INC. v. UNITED STATES
614 F.2d 748 (Ct. Cl. 1980)

B.D. Click Co. was awarded a contract to build a storage building at Laredo Air Force Base, Texas for just under $25,000. Typical of government contracts, it contained dozens of pages of specifications, including 11 pages of specs for a sprinkler system. A detail of a drawing showed only the outside connections and alarms for the sprinkler system, and Click contended that it was only required to install those. The government's contracting office argued that the contract required installation of the whole system. Click said the installation was an add-on, for which it was entitled to be paid an extra $3,000. Click filed a claim for the $3,000 only after accepting the final payment for the contract price and signing a release on June 3, 1971, so the claim was denied. Click said it signed the release "under duress in that the contracting officer and another official of the Government threatened that otherwise the company's record with the Government would be ruined and it would not be awarded any future government contracts."

Click filed an appeal of the denial with the Armed Services Board of Contract Appeals. The Board denied the appeal. Click then instituted proceedings in the Court of Claims; both sides moved for summary judgment.

One of Click's contentions was that the Board should not have concluded that Click had signed a release, inasmuch as no signed release was offered into evidence by the government. The Court of Claims noted that Click no fewer than half-a-dozen separate times made reference in written documents to the fact that it had signed the release. (It dismissed the "under duress" contention as "without merit.") In light of Rule 1007, the nonproduction of the original release by the government was "immaterial": the court held "the record shows overwhelmingly that the plaintiff signed a release," thus barring its claims.

FRE 1008 – Judge Must Determine Whether There Is Prima Facie Evidence Supporting Document's Authenticity, Then Jury Must Determine Sufficiency of Authenticating Facts and Weight to Accord Document

> **Rule 1008. Functions of court and Jury**
>
> When the admissibility of other evidence of contents of writings, recordings, or photographs under these rules depends upon the fulfillment of a condition of fact, the question whether the condition has been fulfilled is ordinarily for the court to determine in accordance with the provisions of Rule 104. However, when an issue is raised (a) whether the asserted writing ever existed, or (b) whether another writing, recording, or photograph produced at the trial is the original, or (c) whether other evidence of contents correctly reflects the contents, the issue is for the trier of fact to determine as in the case of other issues of fact.

FOX v. PECK IRON AND METAL COMPANY, INC.
25 Bkrtcy. Rptr. 674 (S.D. Cal. 1982)

Perennially cash-short Scrap Disposal, Inc., of National City, California, worked out an arrangement with Julius Peck, owner of Peck Iron and Metal Company, Inc. of Richmond, Virginia. Peck was seeking tax-deferred exchanges with other scrap-metal operations, while Scrap Disposal needed money. In 1976, Scrap arranged to transfer most of its assets to Peck and lease them back; Scrap received $1.6 million. Peck also sold a baler shear machine to Scrap for $445,000. The arrangement was that at the end of the lease Scrap could repurchase all the property involved for $2,045,000 or that Peck could insist on the reconveyance. Rental payments totalled more than $276,000 or something over $7,600 per month, for the three years of the lease. Subsequent modifications increased the amounts.

A few months after the lease was up, Scrap gave notice of its intention to repurchase the assets subject to the agreement, then filed for bankruptcy protection under Chapter 11. Within a couple of months, in July 1980, Scrap Disposal and Joseph N. Fox, the appointed trustee, filed a complaint against Peck claiming that "even though the transactions were denominated a sale of Scrap's assets to Peck with a leaseback to Scrap,... this was actually a disguised financing arrangement," a violation of California state financing laws and leading to payments to Peck that amounted to unlawful preferential distributions.

The major evidentiary issue in the case involved the admissibility of Exhibit 24, alleged to be a photocopy of a document representing a "side arrangement" between the parties that reflected almost $400,000 in additional, "off the books" payments to Peck. The Bankruptcy Judge in the Southern District of California held that under Rules 1008 and 901, there was sufficient *prima facie* evidence to support the admissibility of the document, although because this was a bench trial the judge as trier of fact found the witness supporting the exhibit insufficiently trustworthy to credit the document.

(On the strength of lots of other evidence, however, the Bankruptcy Court held that the transaction was a loan, not a sale and leaseback, and that the interest involved exceeded that permitted by California usury laws. The trustee was allowed to recover some $565,116 in excess payments made by Scrap to Peck.)

Index and Tables

INDEX

Citation to a topic to the first page of a case includes its mention on subsequent pages of the same case.

A

Absence of business record, 235, 236
Absence of public record, 243, 306, 313
Acknowledged document, 313
Admissibility,
  determining outside of jury presence, 11, 12
Admissions,
  adoptive, 165, 166, 191, 200, 201, 202, 203, 315
  against government, 206, 207
  agent, 198, 199, 205, 206, 264, 265, 279
  as exceptions vs. nonhearsay, 201
  authorized, 204, 205
  co-conspirator, 193, 209, 210,211
  during plea discussions, 76, 77, 78, 79
  during settlement negotiations, 74
  direct, 82, 102, 164, 191, 197, 198, 199, 200, 218, 230, 261, 262, 279, 298, 300
  guilty plea, 261, 262
  non-binding, 198, 199, 201, 203
  personal knowledge, 191
  silence, 165, 166, 202, 203
Affirmation, 119, 120
Ancient documents,
  authentication, 245, 246, 252, 253, 254, 301, 302
  hearsay, 245, 246, 250, 251, 252, 253, 254
"Any tendency," 25
Applicability of Rules, 1, 2, 276
Attorney-client privilege, 8, 9, 98, 99, 100, 101, 102, 103, 104, 105, 106, 107, 161, 162
Authentication,
  acknowledged document, 313, 314
  ancient documents, 245, 246, 252, 253, 254, 301, 302
  certified copies, 307, 308, 309
  chain of custody, 290, 291, 292
  circumstantial proof, 296, 297, 299, 300
  commercial paper, 313
  comparison, 295, 295
  computer records, 289, 290
  distinctive characteristics, 297
  exemplar, 294, 295
  expert witness, 289, 294, 295
  foreign public documents, 245, 307
  generally, 289-315
  handwriting, 193, 293, 294
  newspapers and periodicals, 311
  official publication, 310
  person with knowledge, 292, 293
  physical evidence, 292, 293
  presumptions under statute, 313, 314
  process or system, 302, 303
  public documents, 243, 304, 305, 307, 308
  public records, 300, 301, 309, 313
  real evidence, 292, 293
  self-authentication, 243, 304-314
  subscribing witness, 314, 315
  telephone conversations, 279, 299, 300
  trade inscriptions, 311, 312
  transcripts of taped conversations, 6
  voice identification, 13, 14, 298
  witness with knowledge, 292, 293

B

Balancing test, 34, 92, 93, 94, 95, 96, 144, 149
Baptismal certificates, 245
Belief of impending death, 10, 11, 197, 267, 268, 269
Best Evidence Rule, See Original Writing Rule
Bias, 80, 84, 123, 130, 131, 132, 133, 135, 136, 154
"Bootstrapping," 39, 40, 46
Boundaries, 258, 259
Burden of proof, 21, 26, 33, 64, 130
Business records, 2, 176, 231, 232, 233, 234, 235, 237, 238, 244, 286, 302, 313, 314, 330

C

Capacity of witness, 128, 129, 130, 134, 137, 138, 157
Certified copies of public documents, 307, 308, 309
Chain of custody, 290, 291, 292
Character,
  civil case, 40, 41, 54, 56, 59, 62
  criminal case–accused, 39, 40, 43, 49, 51, 52, 53, 54, 93, 142, 143, 259, 260, 261
  criminal case–victim, 40, 41, 42, 44, 58, 60, 61
  cross–examination, 39, 40, 53, 54, 55
  essential element of case, 42, 44, 56, 58, 59, 60, 61
  generally, 39-61
  habit and, 41, 62, 65
  "opening the door", 39, 40, 54
  opinion testimony, 39, 40, 42, 44, 54, 55, 141
  other crimes, wrongs, or acts, 4, 5, 38-65, 120, 137, 138, 140, 141, 142, 143
  reputation testimony, 41, 42, 43, 44, 53, 141, 259, 260, 261
  truthfulness, 3, 4, 137-153
Child witness, 111
  tender years hearsay exception, 4, 226, 277
Circumstantial evidence, 24, 199, 296, 297, 299, 300, 315
Co-conspirator, 193, 209, 210, 211
Collateral and non-collateral, 4, 156
Commercial paper, 313
Commercial publications, 254, 255
Comparison by expert, 294, 295
Competency,
  child as witness, 111
  faulty memory, 115
  hypnotically induced testimony, 117, 118, 119
  judge as witness, 121, 122, 123
  juror as witness, 123, 124, 125, 126, 127
  interpreter, 112, 113, 120, 121
  state law governing, 113, 114
Completeness, rule of, 17

Compromise, 50, 70, 71, 72, 73, 74
Computer records, 233, 289, 290
Conditional relevancy, 11, 13, 14
Conduct evidence, 2, 3, 4, 5, 38-66, 93, 94, 95, 96, 120, 137, 138, 140, 141, 142, 143
Confrontation clause, 90, 125, 136, 153, 202, 212, 213, 219, 314
Confusion of jury, 27, 37
Construction of Rules, 2, 3, 4, 17
Credibility,
   of hearsay declarant, 281, 282, 283, 284, 285
   of witness, 3, 4, 12, 15, 25, 26, 27, 34, 43, 55, 86, 90, 127-154, 163, 164, 165, 166, 195, 196
Cross-examination,
   character witness, 39, 40, 53, 54, 55, 142, 143
   collateral and non-collateral, 156
   good faith basis, 54, 142, 143
   impeachment, 127-154, 163-166, 281-285
   limits on, 155,156
   of expert witness, 135
   prior act of misconduct, 39, 40
   prior conviction, 143-153
   scope and extent, 128, 158
Current state of mind, 25, 45, 58, 220, 221, 222, 223, 224

D

"Daubert" test, 179, 180, 204
Dead Man's Statutes, 113, 114
Destruction of evidence, 200
Distinctive characteristics, 297
Documents affecting interest in property, 247, 248, 249, 250
Domestic documents not under seal, 305
Domestic documents under seal, 243, 304
Door opening, 39, 40, 285
Double level hearsay, 200, 215, 218, 225, 278, 279, 280, 281
Duplicates, Original Writing Rule, 318-322, 326, 327
Dying declaration, 10, 11, 197, 267, 268, 269

E

Evaluative report, 237, 238
Excited utterance, 212, 215, 217, 218, 219, 220, 278
Exclusion of witnesses, 168, 169, 170
Exemplar, 294, 295
Expert witness,
   authentication, 289, 294, 295
   bases of opinion, 178-187, 225
   court-appointed, 186, 187
   cross-examination of, 135
   "Daubert" test, 179, 180, 204
   general scientific acceptance, 112, 179, 180
   generally, 177-187
   helpfulness requirement, 177, 178
   opinions by, 177-187
   qualification of, 178, 179, 180, 257
   subject of testimony, 177, 178, 179, 180, 181, 182, 183, 184
Extrinsic evidence, 2, 3, 124, 129, 133, 138, 166, 281, 282

F

Facilitated testimony, 112, 113
Family records, 246, 247
Forfeiture of hearsay objection, 275, 276

Foreign public documents, 307
Form of question, 54, 55
Former testimony, 230, 265, 266, 267
"Frye" test, 112, 179, 180
Function of court and jury,
   generally, 10, 11, 12, 13, 14
   Original Writing Rule, 333, 334

G

General scientific acceptance, 112, 179, 180
Guilty plea of co-defendant, 15

H

Habit, 41, 62, 63, 64, 65
Handwriting, 193, 293, 294, 295
Harmless error, 7, 14, 18, 60, 64, 114, 131, 136, 145, 211, 212, 255, 258, 259, 278, 282, 301
Hearsay,
   admission by party-opponent, 82, 165, 166, 191, 193, 197-211, 218, 230, 264, 279, 298, 300, 315
   circumstantial evidence, 189, 190, 200
   definition of, 25, 189, 190, 191, 192, 193, 201, 271, 312
   effect on listener, 191, 232
   forfeiture by wrongdoing, 275, 276
   generally, 189-288
   impeachment, 260, 261, 281, 282, 283, 284, 285
   mechanical traces, 312
   nonverbal conduct, 189, 190
   pretext offerings, 200
   prior consistent statement, 195, 196
   prior identification of a person, 196, 197
   prior inconsistent statement, 163, 164, 165, 166, 167, 194, 195, 230, 281, 282, 283
   prior statement by witness, 194-197, 230
   reliance on by expert witness, 181
   res gestae, 281
   state of mind, 189, 190, 220, 221, 222, 223, 224
   statements offered for nonasserted inference, 189, 190
   verbal act, 9, 192, 193
   within hearsay, 200, 215, 218, 225, 278, 279, 280, 281
Hearsay exceptions,
   absence of business record, 235, 236
   absence of public record, 243, 306, 313
   ancient document, 245, 246, 250, 251, 252, 253, 254, 286, 301, 302
   baptismal certificate, 245
   belief of impending death, 10, 11, 197, 267, 268, 269
   boundaries, 258, 259
   business records, 231, 232, 233, 234, 235, 237, 238, 244, 286, 301, 313, 314, 329, 330
   "catch-all," 9, 197, 225, 278, 285, 286, 287, 288
   commercial publication, 254, 255
   credibility of hearsay declarant, 281-285
   current state of mind, 220, 221, 222, 223, 224
   double level hearsay, 200, 215, 218, 225, 278, 279, 280, 281
   dying declaration, 10, 197, 267, 268, 269
   evaluative report, 237, 238
   excited utterance, 212, 215, 217, 218, 219, 220, 278, 281
   family records, 246, 247, 274, 275
   forfeiture by wrongdoing, 275, 276
   former testimony, 230, 265, 266, 267
   hearsay within hearsay, 200, 215, 218, 225, 278, 279, 280, 281
   history, 246, 247, 248, 257, 262, 274

interest in property, 247, 248, 249, 250, 286
judgment of personal history, 262, 263
judgment of previous conviction, 261, 262
learned treatises, 255, 256, 257
market report, 254, 255
marriage certificate, 245
medical diagnosis or treatment, 212, 224, 225, 226, 227, 228, 278, 285
misconduct as waiver of objection, 275, 276
multiple level hearsay, 200, 215, 218, 225, 278, 279, 280, 281
necessity as basis, 221
personal or family history, 247, 257, 258, 262, 274, 278
plan, 220, 221
predecessor in title, 270
present sense impression, 213, 214, 215, 216, 280
prior conviction, 261, 262
prior testimony, 230, 265, 266, 267
property, 247, 248, 249, 250, 286
public records, 229, 232, 237, 238, 239, 240, 241, 300, 301, 304, 309, 313
recent perception, 197
recorded recollection, 218, 229, 230
records of regularly conducted activity, 231, 232, 233, 234, 235, 237, 238, 244, 286, 301, 330
religious organizations, 244
reputation as to character, 259, 260, 261
residual exception, 9, 197, 225, 278, 285, 286, 287, 288
spontaneous declaration, 212
state of mind, 220, 221, 222, 223, 224
statement against interest, 263, 264, 265, 270, 271, 272, 273, 274, 283
statement of intent, 220, 221
tender years, 4, 226, 277, 278
unavailability, 202, 212, 213, 246, 263, 264, 265, 267, 272, 278, 283
vital statistics, 242
Hearsay within hearsay, 200, 215, 218, 225, 278, 279, 280, 281
History, 246, 247, 248, 257, 262, 274
Husband–wife privilege, 106, 107, 108, 109
Hypnotically induced testimony, 117, 118, 119

I

Identity, 49
Impeachment, 2, 3, 26, 46, 67, 68, 80, 127-153, 163, 164, 165, 166, 260, 261, 281, 282, 283, 284, 285
Inadmissible evidence,
improper suggestion to jury, 6
proper use in preliminary determination, 9
reliance by expert, 181
use in refreshing memory, 158, 159, 160
Insurance, liability, 79, 80, 81, 82, 83, 84
Intent, 46, 47, 50, 86, 120, 145, 220, 221
Interpreter, 112, 113, 120, 121
Interrogation by judge, 167, 168

J

Judge as witness, 121, 122, 123
Judge, interrogation by, 167, 168
Judgment in previous civil case, 50, 51
Judgment of previous conviction, 261, 262
Judicial notice, 19, 20
Juror as witness, 123, 124, 125, 126, 127
Jury instruction, 47, 126

K

Knowledge, 53, 86, 120, 190

L

Lawyer–client privilege, 8, 9, 98, 99, 100, 101, 102, 103, 104, 105, 106, 107, 161, 162
Lay witness,
opinions, 171-176
Leading questions, direct examination, 195
Learned treatises, 256, 257
Liability insurance, 79, 80, 81, 82, 83, 84
Limiting instructions, 15, 16, 47, 128, 149, 153, 165
Logical relevance, 25

M

Market report, 254, 255
Marriage certificate, 245
Medical and similar expenses, 75
Medical diagnosis or treatment, 212, 224, 225, 226, 227, 228, 278, 285
Miscellaneous proceedings,
nonapplicability of Rules, 1
Misconduct as waiver of hearsay objection, 275, 276
Motion in limine, 8, 29, 32, 67, 83, 93, 95, 140, 144, 217, 221
Motive, 46, 47, 50, 82, 131
Multiple level hearsay, 200, 215, 218, 225, 278-281

N

Names, 257, 258
Newspapers and periodicals, 311
"No harm, no foul," 54, 141
Nonprosecution of accused, relevance, 32, 33

O

Oath, 119, 120
Objection,
error in admitting, 7
error in excluding, 5
forfeiture, 275, 276
generally, 7
motion in limine, 8, 29, 32, 95, 217
offer of proof, 5, 6
waiver, 16, 92, 275, 276
Offer of compromise, 50, 70, 71, 72, 73, 74
Offer of proof, 5, 6
Offer to pay medical expenses, 75
Official publication, 310
Opinion testimony,
character, 39, 40, 42, 44, 54, 55, 141
court–appointed experts, 186, 187
experts, 177-187
lay witnesses, 171, 172, 173, 174, 175, 176, 293, 294
truthfulness, 141
Order of proceedings, 155
Original Writing Rule,
application of rule, 220, 317-334
artwork as "writing", 317, 318
duplicates, 318, 319, 320, 321, 322, 326, 327
excuses for nonproduction, 220, 318, 327, 328
function of court and jury, 333, 334

generally, 317-334
nature of an original, 318, 319, 320, 321, 322
other evidence of content, 220, 327, 328
photographs, 319, 320
public records, 328
requirement of an original, 220, 318, 319, 320, 321, 322, 323, 324, 325, 326, 327, 328, 332, 333
secondary evidence, 220, 327
summaries, 234, 329, 330, 331, 332
testimony or written admission, 332, 333

Other crimes, wrongs or acts, 4, 5, 38, 39, 40, 41, 42, 44, 46, 47, 48, 49, 50, 51, 52, 53, 54, 55, 56, 57, 58, 59, 60, 61, 62, 63, 64, 65, 120, 137, 138, 140, 141, 142, 143

Other claims by plaintiff, 29
lack of prior claims, 31

P

Past recollection recorded, 215, 229, 230
Past sexual behavior, 11, 12, 85, 86, 87, 88, 89, 90, 91, 92
Payment of medical expenses, 75
Personal knowledge, 115, 116, 191
Personal or family history, 247, 257, 258, 262, 274, 275
Photographs, as prejudicial, 36
illustrative or substantive evidence, 303
Original Writing Rule, 319, 320
Physical evidence, 291, 292, 293
Plain error, 4, 7, 8, 16, 246
Plan, 47, 51, 52, 53, 53, 220, 221
Plea bargaining, 76, 77, 78, 79
Polygraph examination,
willingness to take, 33, 34
results inadmissible, 34, 138, 139
Prejudicial evidence, 4, 7, 8, 27, 30, 31, 33, 34, 35, 36, 38, 47, 53, 54, 93, 94, 95, 96, 114, 127, 128, 132, 136, 139, 144, 148, 149, 206, 212, 222
Preliminary questions,
conditional relevancy, 11, 12, 13, 14
court only, 9, 11, 12, 13
generally, 9, 13
Preparation, 47
Present sense impression, 213, 214, 215, 216, 280
Preservation of error, 5, 6, 16, 92
Presumptions,
effect of rebutting, 23
generally, 21-24
governed by state law, 24
rebuttable, 21, 22, 23
Prior act of misconduct, 4, 5, 38, 39, 40, 41, 42, 46, 47, 48, 49, 50, 51, 52, 53, 54, 55, 56, 57, 58, 59, 60, 61, 93, 94, 95, 96, 120, 137, 138, 140, 141, 142, 143
Prior act of sexual misconduct, 93, 94, 95, 96
Prior consistent statement, 195
Prior conviction,
by plea of nolo contendere, 148
details admissible to rebut
witness account, 147
dishonesty or false statement, 149, 150
felony, 143, 144, 145, 146, 147, 148, 151
generally, 124, 143, 144, 145, 146, 147, 148, 149, 150, 151, 152, 153
hearsay, 261, 262

impeachment by evidence of, 143, 144, 145, 146, 147, 148, 149, 150, 151, 152, 153
juvenile adjudication, 152, 153
"mere fact" method, 145, 146
ten years elapsed, 151
Prior dishonest acts, 140, 141, 142, 143, 149
Prior identification of person, 195, 196
Prior inconsistent statement,
extrinsic evidence, 163, 164, 165, 166, 281, 282
foundation, 163, 164, 165, 166, 167, 194
generally, 163, 164, 165, 166, 167, 194, 195
hearsay declarant, 281, 282, 283
impeachment vs. substantive use, 195
inconsistency, 163, 164, 194, 195
lack of recollection, 163, 164, 194, 195
own witness, 194, 195
prior disclosure, 166, 167
Prior statement by witness, 194-197, 230
Prior testimony, 230, 265, 266, 267
Privilege,
attorney-client, 8, 9, 98, 99, 100, 101, 102, 103, 104, 105, 106, 107, 161, 162
procedural aspects, 98, 99, 101
psychologists, 109, 110
self-incrimination, 18, 88, 97, 263, 273
social workers, 109, 110
spousal communication, 107, 108
spousal testimonial, 106, 107, 109
waiver of, 8, 9, 107, 161, 162
Probability evidence, 36, 37
Process or system, authentication, 302, 303
Property, 247, 248, 249, 250, 286
Psychotherapist-patient privilege, 109, 110
Public records,
authentication, 300, 301, 309
hearsay, 229, 232, 237, 238, 239, 240, 241, 300, 301, 304
Original Writing Rule, 328

R

Real evidence, 193, 292, 293
Rebuttal, 25, 56, 120, 132, 155, 220
Recorded recollection, 215, 229, 230
Recordings, 14, 16
Records of regularly conducted activity, 231, 232, 233, 234, 235, 237, 238, 244, 286, 301, 313, 314, 340
Redirect examination, scope of, 157, 158
Refreshing recollection, 117, 118, 119, 158, 159, 160, 161, 162
Relevance,
acquittal of accused, 33, 46, 47
and social policy, 67-84
as distinct from conclusiveness, 25
nonprosecution of accused, 32, 33
polygraph examination, 33, 34
sufficiency for admissibility, 25, 27
vs. prejudice, 27, 34, 35, 37, 47, 48, 94, 95, 96, 128, 144, 148
Religious beliefs, 43, 153, 154
Religious organizations, 243
Remainder of related statements, 16, 17
Reputation testimony,
character, 41, 42, 43, 44, 53, 54, 55, 259, 260
truthfulness, 141, 260, 261, 284

Res gestae, 281
Residual hearsay exception, 9, 197, 225, 278, 285, 286, 287, 288
Routine practice, 66
Rule of Completeness, 17
Rules of evidence, applicability, 1, 2, 276

S

Scientific reliability, 112
Self–authentication,
    acknowledged document, 313, 314
    certified copies, 307, 308
    commercial paper, 313
    domestic documents not under seal, 305
    domestic documents under seal, 243, 304
    foreign public document, 307
    generally, 304-315
    newspapers and periodicals, 311
    official publication, 310
    presumptions under statute, 313, 314
    subscribing witness, 314, 315
    trade inscriptions, 311, 312
Self-defense,
    knowledge or belief of accused, 25, 44, 58
    character of victim, 61
Separation of witnesses, 168, 169, 170
Settlement, 50, 70, 71, 72, 73, 74
Sex offenses,
    accused's prior offenses, 93, 94, 95, 96
    victim's reputation, 86, 87, 88
    victim's sexual history, 11, 12, 85, 86, 87, 88, 89, 90, 91, 92
Similar happenings, 28, 29, 30, 31
    nonoccurrence, 28, 31
Social policy and relevant evidence, 67-110
Spontaneous declaration, 212
State of mind, 25, 45, 58, 220, 221, 222, 223, 224
Statement against interest, 263, 264, 265, 270, 271, 272, 273, 274, 283
Statement of intent, 220, 221
Subscribing witness, 314, 315
Subsequent remedial measures, 67, 68, 69, 70
Summaries, 234, 329, 330, 331, 332

T

Telephone conversations, 299, 300
Trade inscriptions, 312

U

Unavailability, 202, 212, 213, 246, 263, 264, 265, 272, 278, 283

V

Vital statistics, 242
Voice identification, 13, 14, 200, 298
Voir dire, 84, 111

W

Witnesses,
    competency, 111, 113, 114
    exclusion and separating, 168, 169, 170
    expert, 177-187, 289, 294, 295
    failure to call, 26
    facilitated testimony, 112, 113
    faulty memory, 115
    lay, 171, 172, 173, 174, 175, 176
    personal knowledge, 115, 116
    refreshing recollection, 117, 118, 119, 158, 159, 160, 161, 162
    subscribing, 314, 315
Wrongdoing, forfeiture of hearsay objection, 275, 276

X

X–rays, 319, 320

TABLE OF CASES

c = cited in main text *n = cited in footnote*

A

Aaron, State v. (NM 1984), 123
Abel, United States v. (US 1984), 132
AC & S, Lockwood v. (Wa App 1986), 301
Ahrens, United States v. (CA 8 1976), 21
Alaska, Davis v. (US 1974), 152, n 282
Alford, North Carolina v. (US 1970), c 261
Allen, United States v. (CA DC 1992), 257
Allison, State v. (NC 1983), 184
Alosa, United States v. (CA 1 1994), 193
Allstate Ins. Co., Bunion v. (ED Pa 1980), 29
Alvarez, United States v. (CA 9 1992), 311
Amaral, United States v. (CA 9 1973), 177
Anderson, Perrin v. (CA 10 1986), 40
Anthony, United States v. (CA 10 1991), 175
Archambeau, State v. (SD 1983), 186
Arizona, Miranda v. (US 1966), c 57, c 166
Armstrong World Industries,Inc., Threadgill v.
 (CA 3 1991), 252, n 302
Atyeo, Sackett v. (Mi App 1996), 270
Auble, State v. (Ut 1988), 221
Auto Supply Co., Inc., Ford Motor Co. v. (CA 8 1981), 329

B

B.D. Click Co., Inc. v. United States (Ct Cl 1980), 332
Balsys, United States v. (US 1998), 97
Barber v. Ponte (CA 1 1985), 19
Bardacke v. Dunigan (NM 1982), 243
Barela, State v. (NM App 1982), 196
Barnier v. Szentmiklosi (CA 6 1987), 138
Barry, Silverman v. (D DC 1986), 310
Battle v. Unites States (CA DC 1965), 128
Batts, United States v. (CA 9 1977), n 3
Bazan, State v. (NM 1977), 42
Beamon v. State (Wi 1980), 197
Beech Aircraft Corp. v. Rainey (US 1988), 238
Bell Helicopters Textron, Inc., Rocky Mountain Helicopters,
 Inc. v. (CA 10 1986), 58
Bergeron v. State (Wi 1978), 211
Berroyer v. Hertz (CA 3 1981), 155
Best, State v. (Az App 1985), 297
Bhandari v. First National Bank of Commerce
 (CA 5 1987), 71
Biaggi, United States v. (CA 2 1990), 78
Bishop v. State (Ok Cr App 1978), 156
Boeing Airplane Co. v. Brown (CA 9 1961), 68, n 80
Boughton, Kelly's Auto Parts, No. 1, Inc. v. (CA 6 1987), 32
Brady v. Maryland (US 1963), c 131
Brand v. Brand (CA 2 1986), 113
Bratton, United States v. (CA 5 1989), 127
Brewer, State v. (Me 1985), 26
Bright, Unites States v. (CA 5 1979), 53
Brown, Boeing Airplane Co. v. (CA 9 1961), 68, n 80
Buchanan, United States v. (CA 10 1989), 131

Buckhart, United States v. (CA 10 1972), 52
Bulthuis v. Rexall Corp. (CA 9 1985), 224
Bunion v. Allstate Ins. Co. (ED Pa 1980), 29
Burdge, State v. (Or 1983), 169
Burke v. State (De 1984), 168
Burkey v. Ellis (ND Al 1979), n 208, 208
Burlington Northern RR Co. v. Nebraska (CA 8 1986), 176
Byrd, United States v. (CA 7 1984), 108

C

Cameron County v. Velasquez (Tx App 1984), 198
Campbell, United States v. (CA 5 1996), 8
Cardinal, United States v. (CA 6 1986), 89
Carlson, People v. (Co 1986), 223
Carlson, State v. (Oh App 1986), 44, n 58
Carter v. Wiese Corp. (Ia App 1984), 182
Case, State v. (NM 1984), 216
Catabran, United States v. (CA 9 1988), 233
Cessna Aircraft Co., Monger v. (CA 8 1987), 24
Cessna Aircraft Co., Radke v. (CA 8 1983), 143
Chandris, S.A., Cummiskey, v. (SD NY 1989), 264
Charmley v. Lewis (Or 1986), 64
Charter v. Chleborad (CA 8 1977), 80, n 84
Chleborad, Charter v. (CA 8 1977), 80, n 84
Chnapkova v. Koh (CA 2 1993), 140
Cincinnati Ins. Co., Murphy v. (CA 6 1985), 33
City of Chicago, Wilson v. (CA 7 1993), 145
City of Hartford, Ricketts v. (CA 2 1996), 13
City of West Palm Beach, Fox v. (CA 5 1967), 121
Click Co., Inc., B.D., v. United States (Ct Cl 1980), 332
Cole v. Tansy (CA 10 1991), 219
Collins, People v. (Ca 1968), 36
Collins v. Wayne Corp. (CA 5 1980), 135
Combs, United States v. (CA 9 1985), 305
Commercial Union Assurance Co., Dallas County v.
 (CA 5 1961), 285
Commissioner of Internal Revenue, Hall v.
 (CA 9 1984), 244
Commissioner of Internal Revenue, Hudspeth v.
 (CA 9 1990), 73
Commonwealth, Griswold v. (Va App 1995), 20
Compton v. Davis Oil Co. (D Wy 1985), 249
Compton v. WWV Enterprises (Tx App 1984), 247
Cook Paint and Varnish Co., Neville Const. Co. v.
 (CA 8 1982), n 220, 327
Covington v. Sawyer (Oh App 1983), 204
Crain Bros., Inc., Dobbins v. (WD Pa 1976), 79
Cummiskey v. Chandris, S.A. (SD NY 1989), 264

D

Dallas County v. Commercial Union Assurance Co.
 (CA 5 1961), 285
Dancy, United States v. (CA 5 1988), 309
Daniel, United States v. (CA 5 1992), 151

Dann, Legille v. (CA DC 1976), c 23
Dannenberg, Fox v. (CA 8 1990), 5
Daubert v. Merrell Dow Pharmaceuticals, Inc. (US 1993), 179, n 204
Davenport, United States v. (CA 9 1985), 142
Davis Oil Co., Compton v. (D Wy 1985), 249
Davis v. Alaska (US 1974), 152, n 282
Delaware v. Van Arsdall (US 1986), 136
Delkamp, Scientific Applications, Inc. v. (ND 1981), 206
Dependency of Penelope B,., In re (Wa 1985), 189
De Soto, United States v. (CA 7 1989), 177
DeTella, Henderson v. (CA 7 1996), 129, n 138
DiMatteo, United States v. (CA 11 1983), 326
DiPaolo, United States v. (CA 2 1986), n 129, 137
Dobbins v. Crain Bros., Inc. (WD Pa 1976), 79
Doe v. United States (CA 4 1981), 85, c 88
Doyle, United States v. (CA 2 1997), 307
Doyle v. Ohio (US 1976), 165
Dunham, People v. (Mi App 1992), 4, n 148, n 226, n 277, c 278
Dunigan, Bardacke v. (NM 1982), 243
Dunn, Saudi-Arabian Airlines Corp. v. (Fl App 1983), 200

E

Egbert, Matter of Estate of (Mi App 1981), 246
Ellis, Burkey v. (ND Al 1979), n 208, 208
Ellis, State v. (Ne 1981), 150
Emmons, United States v. (CA 10 1994), 190
Estate of Egbert, Matter of (Mi App 1981), 246
Ethicon, Inc., Thirsk v. (Co App 1983), 232

F

Fagan, United States v. (CA 5 1987), 323
Fairman, Smith v. (CA 7 1988), 281
Ferguson v. State (Ok Cr App 1984), 260
Firemen's Fund Ins. Co. v. Thien (CA 8 1995), 154
First National Bank, Freidus v. (CA 8 1991), 71
First National Bank of Commerce, Bhandari v. (CA 5 1987), 71
First State Bank of Denton v. Maryland Casualty Co. (CA 5 1990), 213
Ford Motor Co. v. Auto Supply Co., Inc. (CA 8 1981), 329
Ford Motor Co., Redman v. (SC 1969), 183
Forehead v. Galvin (Ne 1985), 185
Fowler, United States v. (CA 5 1979), 119
Fox v. City of West Palm Beach (CA 5 1967), 121
Fox v. Dannenberg (CA 8 1990), 5
Fox v. Peck Iron and Metal Co., Inc. (Bkrty, SD Ca), 333
Freidus v. First National Bank (CA 8 1991), 72
French v. Sorano (Wi 1976), 63
Frye v. United States (CA DC 1923), c 112, c 179
Fuller, United States v. (CA 8 1989), 45, n 120

G

Galvin, Forehead v. (Ne 1985), 185
Garcia v. Gloor (CA 5 1980), 300
Garfole, State v. (NJ 1978), 48
Garvey v. O'Donaghue (CA DC 1987), 254
General Foods Corp., Reeves v. (CA 5 1982), c 23
Gilliland, United States v. (CA 10 1978), 39
Gloor, Garcia v. (CA 5 1980), 300
Gonzalez, United States v. (CA 2 1984), 74
Goode, Moore v. (WV 1988), 251
Goodover v. Lindey's, Inc. (Mt 1988), 258
Gould, State v. (Mt 1985), 242

Govt. of Virgin Islands v. Mujahid (CA 3 1993), 15
Govt. of Virgin Islands v. Petersen (CA 3 1977), 43
Graham v. State (In 1970), 290
Grand Jury Subpoena, In re (CA 5 1991), 101
Grand Trunk Western RR Co., Hewitt v. (Mi App 1983), 214
Grant Bros. Construction Co. v. United States (US 1914), 262
Green v. State (Tx Cr App 1992), 10
Greycas, Inc. v. Proud (CA 7 1987), 248
Griswold v. Commonwealth (Va App 1995), 20
Guardia, Unites States v. (CA 10 1998), 93

H

Hall v. Commissioner of Internal Revenue (CA 9 1984), 244
Halloran v. Virginia Chemicals, Inc. (NY 1977), 62
Hamilton, State v. (Mt 1980), 299
Hammons, People v. (Mi App 1995), n 4, n 226, 277
Harakis, Panas v. (NH 1987), 56
Hare, United Sttes v. (CA 8 1995), 77
Harrington, United States v. (CA 9 1991), 290
Hart, Molkenbur v. (Mn App 1987), 255
Hart v. O'Brien (CA 5 1997), 280
Hartman v. Opelika Machine & Welding Co. (Fl App 1982), 69
Hawkins v. United States (US 1958), c 106
Hayes, United States v. (CA 10 1988), 231
Henderson v. DeTella (CA 7 1996), 129, n 138
Henze, State v. (Ia 1984), 181
Hertz, Berroyer v. (CA 3 1981), 155
Hewitt v. Grand Truck Western RR Co. (Mi App 1983), 214
Hickman, United States v. (CA 6 1979), 167
Hicks Co., Higgins v. (CA 8 1985), 28
Higgins v. Hicks Co. (CA 8 1985), 28
Hillmon, Mutual Life Ins. Co. v. (US 1892), 220
Hines v. Joy Mfg. Co. (CA 6 1988), 31
Hoffman, Palmer v. (US 1943), 234
Home Ins. Co. v. Spears (Ar App 1979), 75
Hudspeth v. Commissioner of Internal Revenue (CA 9 1990), 73
Hugo's Skateway, Johnson v. (CA 4 1991), 50
Humphrey, United States v. (CA 5 1997), 322

I

Illinois, White v. (US 1992), n 202, 212, n 219
In re Dependency of Penelope B. (Wa 1985), 189
In re Grand Jury Subpoena (CA 5 1991), 101
In re the Yoder Company (CA 6 1985), 22
Iron Shell, United States v. (CA 8 1980), 226

J

Jaffee v. Redmond (US 1996), 109
Johnson v. Hugo's Skateway (CA 4 1991), 50
Johnson, State v. (Me 1981), 259
Johnson, United States v. (CA 9 1979), 330
Joy Mfg. Co., Hines v. (CA 6 1988), 31
Judd v. Rodman (CA 11 1997), 91
Justiniano, State v. (Wa App 1987), 225

K

Keiser, United States v. (CA 9 1995), n 58, 60
Kelly's Auto Parts, No. 1, Inc. v. Boughton (CA 6 1987), 32
Knapp v. State (Ind 1907), 25
Koh, Chnapkova v. (CA 2 1993), 140
Kotsimpulos, State v. (Me 1980), 27
Kozlowski v. Rush (Id 1992), 83

344 Evidence Illustrated

Krezdorn, United States v. (CA 5 1981), 51
Kroeplin, State v. (ND 1978), 292
Kurtz, Progressive American Ins. Co. v. (Fl App 1987), 66

L

Lechoco, United States v. (CA DC 1976), 284
LeCompte, United States v. (CA 8 1997), 95
Legille v. Dann (CA DC 1976), c 23
Leight, United States v. (CA 7 1987), 319
Lewin v. Miller Wagner & Co., Ltd. (Az App 1986), 217
Lewis, Charmley v. (Or 1986), 64
Lewis v. State (De 1980), 174
Liebman, United States v. (CA 3 1987), 100
Lindey's, Inc., Goodover v. (Mt 1988), 258
Lindstrom, United States v. (CA 11 1983), 133
Little, United States v. (CA 8 1977), 313
Local 512, Warehouse & Office Workers Union v. NLRB (CA 9 1986), n 9, 192
Lockwood v. AC & S, Inc. (Wa App 1986), 301
Lohrman v. Pittsburgh Corning Corp. (CA 4 1986), 266, n 302
Loof v. Sanders (Ak 1984), 173
Lucasfilm, Ltd., Seiler v. (CA 9 1987), 317
Luz P., Matter of (NY App 1993), c 113

M

Maceo, United States v. (CA 5 1991), 122
Malady, United States v. (CA 8 1992), 141
Maniccia, State v. (Ia App 1984), 199
Manufacturers Life Ins. Co., Wilmington Trust Co. v. (CA 5 1980), 130
Maryland, Brady v. (US 1963), c 131
Maryland Casualty Co., First State Bank of Denton v. (CA 5 1990), 213
Mastrangelo, United States v. (CA 2 1982), 275
Matter of Estate of Egbert (Mi App 1981), 246
Matter of Luz P. (NY App 1993), c 113
Matuszewski v. Pancoast (Oh App 1987), 245
Mauldin v. Upjohn Co. (CA 5 1983), 153
Mayans, United States v. (CA 9 1994), 120
M'Biye, United States v. (CA DC 1981), 312
McCrary-El v. Shaw (CA 8 1993), 116
McGrath, Safeco Ins. Co. of America v. (Wa App 1986), 261
McLaughlin, United States v. (CA 9 1981), 166
McQueeney v. Wilmington Trust Co. (CA 3 1985), 314
Merrell Dow Pharmaceuticals, Inc., Daubert v. (US 1993), 179, n 204
Miller v. Szelenyi (Me 1988), 82
Miller Wagner & Co., Ltd., Lewin v. (Az App 1986), 217
Mills, People v. (Mi 1995), 35
Mintle v. Mintle (Wyo 1988), 59
Miranda v. Arizona (US 1966), c 57, c 166
Moen, State v. (Or 1990), 227
Molkenbur v. Hart (Mn App 1987), 255
Monger v. Cessna Aircraft Co. (CA 8 1987), 24
Monks, United States v. (CA 9 1985), 201
Monsanto, United States v. (CA 2 1991), 1
Moore, United States v. (CA 8 1977), n 243, 304
Moore v. Goode (WV 1988), 251
Morrissey v. Welsh Co. (CA 8 1987), 81
Murphy v. Cincinnati Ins. Co. (CA 6 1985), 33
Mutual Life Insurance Co. v. Hillmon (US 1892), 220
Mujahid, Govt. of the Virgin Islands v. (CA 3 1993), 15
Muzyka v. Remington Arms Co., Inc. (CA 5 1985), 67

N

NLRB, Local 512, Warehouse & Office Workers Union v. (CA 1986), n 9, 192
Napier, United States v. (CA 9 1975), 218
Nebraska, Burlington Northern RR Co. v. (CA 8 1986), 176
Neville Construction Co. v. Cook Paint and Varnish Co. (CA 8 1982), n 220, 327
Nokleberg, Sheyenne Valley Lumber Co. v. (ND 1982), 235
North Carolina v. Alford (US 1970), c 261
Nye, State v. (Me 1988), 222

O

O'Brien, Hart v. (CA 5 1997), 280
O'Donaghue, Garvey v. (CA DC 1987), 254
Ohio, Doyle v. (US 1976), 165
Old Chief v. United States (US 1997), 38
Oliphant, People v. (Mi 1976), 46, n 52, n 120
Oloyede, United States v. (CA 4 1992), 99
Opager, United States v. (CA 5 1979), 2
Opelika Machine & Welding Co., Hartman v. (Fl App 1982), 69

P

Palmer v. Hoffman (US 1943), 234
Panas v. Harakis (NH 1987), 56
Pancoast, Matuszewski v. (Oh App 1987), 245
Payan, United States v. (CA 5 1993), n 169
Peck Iron and Metal Co., Inc., Fox v. (Bkrty, SD Ca), 333
Penelope B., In re Dependency of (Wa 1985), 189
People v. Carlson (Co 1986), 223
People v. Collins (Ca 1968), 36
People v. Dunham (Mi App 1997), 4, n 148, n 226, n 277, c 278
People v. Hammons (Mi App 1995), n 4, n 226, 277
People v. Mills (Mi 1995), 35
People v. Oliphant (Mi 1976), 46, n 52, n 120
People v. Petersen (Ca App 1972), 163
People v. Raffaelli (Co App 1985), 274
People v. Rosenthal (Co App 1983), 263
People v. Siler (Mi App 1988), n 10, 269
Perrin v. Anderson (CA 10 1986), 40
Peters, SEC v. (CA 10 1992), 54
Petersen, Govt. of Virgin Islands v. (CA 2 1977), 43
Petersen, People v. (Ca App 1972), 163
Peyro, United States v. (CA 8 1986), 115
Picciandra, United States v. (CA 1 1986), 229
Pittsburgh Corning Corp., Lohrman v. (CA 4 1986), 266, n 302
Platero, United States v. (CA 10 1995), 11
Ponder v. Warren Tool Corp. (CA 10 1987), 30
Ponte, Barber v. (CA 1 1985), 19
Portsmouth Paving Corp., United States v. (CA 4 1982), 278
Praegitzer, Smith v. (Id 1988), 171
Pressley, United States v. (CA 8 1992), n 292
Progressive American Ins. Co. v. Kurtz (Fl App 1987), 66
Proud, Greycas, Inc. v. (CA 7 1987), 248
Puente, United States v. (CA 5 1987), 240, n 309
Pzeradski v. Rexnord, Inc. (Mi App 1982), 205, n 206

R

R.A.B v. State (Fl App 1981), 159
R & R Associates, Inc. v. Visual Scene, Inc. (CA 1 1984), 324
Radke v. Cessna Aircraft Co. (CA 8 1983), 143
Raffaelli, People v. (Co App 1985), 274

Rainey, Beech Aircraft Corp. v. (US 1988), 238
Ramada Development Co. v. Rauch (CA 5 1981), 70
Rangel, United States v. (CA 8 1978), 321
Rangitsch, State v. (Wa App 1985), 256
Rauch, Ramada Development Co. v. (CA 5 1981), 70
Reasoner, State v. (Az App 1987), 294
Redman v. Ford Motor Co. (SC 1969), 183
Redmond, Jaffee v. (US 1996), 109
Reeves v. General Foods Corp. (CA 5 1982), c 23
Rembert, United States v. (CA DC 1988), 302
Remington Arms Co., Inc., Muzyka v. (CA 5 1985), 67
Rexall Corporation, Bulthuis v. (CA 9 1985), 224
Rexnord, Inc., Pzeradski v. (Mi Ap 1982), 205, n 206
Richardson, Rojas v. (CA 5 1983), 7, n 246
Ricketts v. City of Hartford (CA 2 1996), 13
Rivera, State v. (De Sup 1986), n 229, 237
Robertson, United States v. (CA 5 1976), 76
Robinson, United States v. (CA 4 1986), 172
Rocky Mountain Helicopters, Inc. v. Bell Helicopters Textron, Inc. (CA 10 1986), 58
Rodman, Judd v. (CA 11 1997), 91
Rodriguez, United States v. (CA 5 1975), 328
Rojas v. Richardson (CA 5 1983), 7, n 246
Roman, State v. (Me 1993), 111
Rosenthal, People v. (Co App 1983), 263
Rush, Kozlowski v. (Id 1992), 83

S

Sackett v. Atyeo (Mi App 1996), 270
Safeco Ins. Co. of America v. McGrath (Wa App 1986), 261
Salazar, State v. (Mn 1980), 172
Salerno, United States v. (US 1992), 265
Salvador, United States v. (CA 2 1987), 272
Samaritan Health Services, Inc. v. Superior Ct. (Az 1984), 161
Sanders, Loof v. (Ak 1984), 173
Sanders, United States v. (CA 4 1992), 144, n 148, n 149
Santos, United States v. (CA 2 1967), 207, n 208
Saudi Arabian Airlines Corp. v. Dunn (Fl App 1983), 200
Saunders, State v. (Oh App 1984), 271
Saunders, United States v. (CA 4 1991), 87
Sawyer, Covington v. (Oh App 1983), 204
Scientific Applications, Inc. v. Delkamp (ND 1981), 206
SEC v. Peters (CA 10 1992), 54
Seiler v. Lucasfilm, Ltd. (CA 9 1987), 317
77,819.10 Acres of Land, United States v. (CA 10 1981), 178
Shaw, McCrary-El v. (CA 8 1993), 116
Shepard v. United States (US 1933), n 10, 267
Sheyenne Valley Lumber Co. v. Nokleberg (ND 1982), 235
Siler, People v. (Mi App 1988), n 10, 269
Silverman v. Barry (D DC 1986), 310
Sliker, United States v. (CA 2 1984), 324
Smedra v. Stanek (CA 10 1951), 191
Smith v. Fairman (CA 7 1988), 281
Smith v. Praegitzer (Id 1988), 171
Snyder v. Whittaker Corp. (CA 5 1988), 311
Sonny Mitchell Center, United States v. (CA 5 1991), 148
Sorano, French v. (Wi 1976), 63
Spears, Home Ins. Co. v. (Ar App 1979), 75
Stanek, Smedra v. (CA 10 1951), 191
Stanton v. Stanton (US 1975), n 107
State of Nebraska, Burlington Northern RR Co. v. (CA 8 1986), 176
State v. Aaron (NM 1984), 123
State v. Allison (NC 1983), 184

State v. Archambeau (SD 1983), 186
State v. Auble (Ut 1988), 221
State v. Barela (NM App 1982), 196
State, Beamon v. (Wi 1980), 197
State, Bergeron v. (Wi 1978), 211
State v. Bazan (NM 1977), 42
State v. Best (Az App 1985), 297
State, Bishop v. (Ok Cr App 1978), 156
State v. Brewer (Me 1985), 26
State v. Burdge (Or 1983), 169
State, Burke v. (De 1984), 168
State v. Carlson (Oh App 1986), 44, n 58
State v. Case (NM 1984), 214
State v. Ellis (Ne 1981), 150
State, Ferguson v. (Ok Cr App 1984), 260
State v. Garfole (NJ 1978), 48
State v. Gould (Mt 1985), 242
State, Green v. (Tx Cr App 1992), 10
State, Graham v. (In 1970), 290
State v. Hamilton (Mt 1980), 299
State v. Henze (Ia 1984), 181
State v. Johnson (Me 1981), 259
State v. Justiniano (Wa App 1987), 225
State, Knapp v. (In 1907), 25
State v. Kotsimpulos (Me 1980), 27
State v. Kroeplin (ND 1978), 292
State, Lewis v. (De 1980), 174
State v. Maniccia (Ia App 1984), 199
State v. Moen (Or 1990), 227
State v. Nye (Me 1988), 222
State, R.A.B. v. (Fl App 1981), 159
State v. Rangitsch (Wa App 1985), 256
State v. Reasoner (Az App 1987), 294
State v. Rivera (De Sup 1986), n 229, 237
State v. Roman (Me 1993), 111
State v. Salazar (Mn 1980), 172
State v. Saunders (Oh App 1984), 271
State v. Stotts (Az 1985), 293
State v. Thompson (Ia 1986), 230
State, Van Hattan v. (Ak App 1983), 194
State v. Warden (Ks 1995), 112
State v. West (NC 1986), 298
State, Williamson v. (Ak App 1984), 210
State, Wilson v. (Ar 1982), 158
State v. Woodson (WV 1989), 57
State v. Yslas (Az 1984), 209
Stotts, State v. (Az 1985), 293
Straach, United States v. (CA 5 1993), 126
Sturman, United States v. (CA 6 1991), 313
Sumner, United States v. (CA 8 1997), 94
Superior Court, Samaritan Health Services, Inc. v. (Az 1984), 161
Sutherland, United States v. (CA 5 1981), 6
Sutton, United States v. (CA DC 1986), 16
Swanson, United States v. (CA 8 1993), 147
Swidler & Berlin, United States v. (US 1998), 103
Swinton, United States v. (CA 8 1996), 124
Szelenyi, Miller v. (Me 1988), 82
Szentmiklosi, Barnier v. (CA 6 1987), 138

T

Tansy, Cole v. (CA 10 1991), 219
Taylor, United States v. (CA 8 1979), 157
Tedder, United States v. (CA 4 1986), 102
Thien, Firemen's Fund Ins. Co. v. (CA 8 1995), 154

Thirsk v. Ethicon, Inc. (Co App 1983), 232
Thompson, State v. (Ia 1986), 230
Threadgill v. Armstrong World Industries, Inc. (CA 3 1991), 252, n 302
Tome v. United States (US 1995), 195
Toney, United States v. (CA 5 1980), 149
Trammel v. United States (US 1980), 106, n 108, c 109
Trujillo, United States v. (CA 10 1998), 287

U

United States v. Abel (US 1984), 132
United States v. Ahrens (CA 8 1976), 21
United States v. Allen (CA DC 1992), 257
United States v. Alosa (CA 1 1994), 193
United States v. Alvarez (CA 9 1992), 311
United States v. Amaral (CA 9 1973), 177
United States v. Anthony (CA 10 1991), 175
United States, B.D. Click, Co., Inc. v. (Ct Cl 1980), 332
United States v. Balsys (US 1998), 97
United States, Battle v. (CA DC 1965), 128
United States v. Batts (CA 9 1977), n 3
United States v. Biaggi (CA 2 1990), 78
United States v. Bratton (CA 5 1989), 127
United States v. Bright (CA 5 1979), 53
United States v. Buchanan (CA 10 1989), 131
United States v. Buckhart (CA 10 1972), 52
United States v. Byrd (CA 7 1984), 108
United States v. Campbell (CA 5 1996), 8
United States v. Cardinal (CA 6 1986), 89
United States v. Catabran (CA 9 1988), 233
United States v. Combs (CA 9 1985), 305
United States v. Dancy (CA 5 1988), 309
United States v. Daniel (CA 5 1992), 151
United States v. Davenport (CA 9 1985), 142
United States v. De Soto (CA 7 1989), 177
United States v. DiMatteo (CA 11 1983), 326
United States v. DiPaolo (CA 2 1986), n 129, 137
United States, Doe v. (CA 4 1981), 85, c 88
United States v. Doyle (CA 2 1997), 307
United States v. Emmons (CA 10 1994), 190
United States v. Fagan (CA 5 1987), 323
United States v. Fowler (CA 5 1979), 119
United States, Frye v. (CA DC 1923), c 112, c 179
United States v. Fuller (CA 8 1989), 45, n 120
United States v. Gilliland (CA 10 1978), 39
United States v. Gonzalez (CA 2 1984), 74
United States, Grant Bros. Const. Co. v. (US 1914), 262
United States v. Guardia (CA 10 1998), 93
United States v. Hare (CA 8 1995), 77
United States v. Harrington (CA 9 1991), 290
United States, Hawkins v. (US 1958), c 106
United States v. Hayes (CA 10 1988), 231
United States v. Hickman (CA 6 1979), 167
United States v. Humphrey (CA 5 1997), 322
United States v. Iron Shell (CA 8 1980), 226
United States v. Johnson (CA 9 1979), 330
United States v. Keiser (CA 9 1995), n 58, 60
United States v. Krezdorn (CA 5 1981), 51
United States v. Lechoco (CA DC 1976), 284
United States v. LeCompte (CA 8 1997), 95
United States v. Leight (CA 7 1987), 319
United States v. Liebman (CA 3 1987), 100
United States v. Lindstrom (CA 11 1983), 133
United States v. Little (CA 8 1977), 313

United States v. Maceo (CA 5 1991), 122
United States v. Malady (CA 8 1992), 141
United States v. Mastrangelo (CA 2 1982), 275
United States v. Mayans (CA 9 1994), 120
United States v. M'Biye (CA DC 1981), 312
United States v. Monks (CA 9 1985), 201
United States v. Monsanto (CA 2 1991), 1
United States v. Moore (CA 8 1977), n 243, 304
United States v. McLaughlin (CA 9 1981), 166
United States v. Napier (CA 9 1975), 218
United States, Old Chief v. (US 1997), 38
United States v. Oloyede (CA 4 1992), 99
United States v. Opager (CA 5 1979), 2
United States v. Payan (CA 5 1993), n 169
United States v. Peyro (CA 8 1986), 115
United States v. Picciandra (CA 1 1986), 229
United States v. Platero (CA 10 1995), 11
United States v. Pressley (CA 8 1992), n 292
United States v. Portsmouth Paving Corp. (CA 4 1982), 278
United States v. Puente (CA 5 1987), 240, n 309
United States v. Rangel (CA 8 1978), 321
United States v. Rembert (CA DC 1988), 302
United States v. Robertson (CA 5 1976), 76
United States v. Robinson (CA 4 1986), 172
United States v. Rodriguez (CA 5 1975), 328
United States v. Salerno (US 1992), 265
United States v. Salvador (CA 2 1987), 272
United States v. Sanders (CA 4 1992), 144, n 148, n 149
United States v. Santos (CA 2 1967), 207, n 208
United States v. Saunders (CA 4 1991), 87
United States v. 77, 819.10 Acres of Land More or Less (CA 10 1981), 178
United States, Shepard v. (US 1933), n 10, 267
United States v. Sliker (CA 2 1984), 324
United States v. Sonny Mitchell Center (CA 5 1991), 148
United States v. Straach (CA 5 1993), 126
United States v. Sturman (CA 6 1991), 313
United States v. Sumner (CA 8 1997), 94
United States v. Sutherland (CA 5 1981), 6
United States v. Sutton (CA DC 1986), 16
United States v. Swanson (CA 8 1993), 147
United States v. Swidler & Berlin (US 1998), 103
United States v. Swinton (CA 8 1996), 124
United States v. Taylor (CA 8 1979), 157
United States v. Tedder (CA 4 1986), 102
United States, Tome v. (US 1995), 195
United States v. Toney (CA 5 1980), 149
United States, Trammel v. (US 1980), 106, n 108, c 109
United States v. Trujillo (CA 10 1998), 287
United States, Upjohn Co. v. (US 1981)), 105
United States v. Valdez (CA 5 1984), 117
United States v. Versaint (CA 3 1988), 239
United States v. Whitaker (CA 7 1997), 289
United States, Williamson v. (US 1994), 273
United States v. Wilson (CA 8 1976), 296
United States v. Wiseman (CA 1987), n 20, 203
United States v. Wuagneux (CA 11 1988), n 260, 282
United States v. Zolin (US 1989), 98
Upjohn Co., Mauldin v. (CA 5 1983), 153
Upjohn Co. v. United States (US 1981), 105

V

Valdez, United States v. (CA 5 1984), 117
Van Arsdall, Delaware v. (US 1986), 136

Van Hattan v. State (Ak App 1983), 194
Velasquez, Cameron County v. (Tx App 1984), 198
Versaint, United States v. (CA 3 1988), 239
Virginia Chemicals, Inc., Halloran v. (NY 1977), 62
Visual Scene, Inc., R & R Associates, Inc. v. (CA 1 1984), 324

W

WWV Enterprises, Compton v. (Tx App 1984), 247
Warden, State v. (Ks 1995), 112
Warren Tool Corp., Ponder v. (CA 10 1987), 30
Wayne Corp., Collins v. (CA 5 1980), 135
Welsh Co., Morrissey v. (CA 8 1987), 81
West, State v. (NC 1986), 298
Whittaker Corp., Snyder v. (CA 5 1988), 311
Whitaker, United States v. (CA 7 1997), 289
White v. Illinois (US 1992), n 202, 212, n 219
Wiese Corporation, Carter v. (Ia App 1984), 182
Williamson v. State (Ak App 1984), 210
Williamson v. United States (US 1994), 273
Wilmington Trust Co., McQueeney v. (CA 3 1985), 314
Wilmington Trust Co. v. Mfrs. Life Ins. Co. (CA 5 1980), 130
Wilson v. City of Chicago (CA 7 1993), 145
Wilson v. State (Ar 1982), 158
Wilson, United States v. (CA 8 1976), 296
Wiseman, United States v. (CA 1 1987), n 20, 203
Woodson, State v. (WV 1989), 57
Wuagneux, United States v. (CA 11 1988), n 260, 282

Y

Yoder Company, In re (CA 6 1985), 22
Yslas, State v. (Az 1984), 209

Z

Zolin, United States v. (US 1989), 98

TABLE OF RULES

Citations to state rules are listed under their Federal Rule counterparts.

Rule	Pages
101	1
102	2, 3, 4, 17
103(a)	4, 5, 6, 16, 148
103(c)	6, 7, 83, 84
103(d)	5, 7, 8, 246
104(a)	9, 10, 11, 12, 13, 98, 99, 276
104(b)	11, 12, 13, 14
105	15, 47, 149, 153, 232
106	16, 17, 18
201	19, 20, 203
301	21, 22, 23
302	24
401	25, 26, 27, 28, 29, 30, 31, 32, 33, 34, 35, 36, 78, 132
402	94
403	7, 27, 29, 30, 31, 33, 34, 35, 36, 38, 50, 80, 93, 94, 95, 96, 127, 128, 132, 136, 138, 143, 144, 145, 147, 148, 149, 180, 207, 222
404(a)	39, 40, 41, 42, 43, 44, 45, 48, 50, 51, 52, 53, 54, 61, 93, 142, 259, 260
404(b)	4, 45, 46, 47, 48, 50, 51, 52, 53, 61, 93, 95, 120, 142, 145
405(a)	39, 40, 41, 42, 43, 44, 45, 53, 54, 55, 56, 57, 58, 59, 60, 61, 93, 142, 259, 260
405(b)	42, 44, 56, 57, 58, 59, 60, 61
406	41, 62, 63, 64, 65, 66
407	67, 68, 69, 80
408	50, 70, 71, 72, 73, 74
409	75
410	76, 77, 78, 79, 148
411	75, 79, 80, 81, 82, 83, 84
412	11, 12, 85, 86, 87, 88, 89, 90, 91, 92, 93
413	93, 94
414	94, 95, 96
501	97, 98, 99, 100, 101, 102, 103, 104, 105, 106, 108, 109, 161
601	111, 112, 113, 114, 115
602	115, 116, 117, 118
603	119, 120
604	120
605	121, 122, 123
606	123, 124, 125, 126, 127
607	26, 127, 128, 129, 130, 131, 132, 133, 135, 136, 137, 140, 150, 152
608(a)	80, 138, 141, 259, 260, 284, 285
608(b)	2, 3, 4, 133, 137, 138, 140, 142
609(a)	93, 124, 143, 144, 145, 146, 147, 148, 149, 150, 152
609(b)	151
609(d)	152, 153
610	43, 153, 154
611	128, 155, 156, 157, 158, 195
612	158, 159, 161, 162
613	132, 163, 164, 165, 166, 167, 194, 195, 281, 282
614	167
615	168, 169
701	171, 172, 173, 174, 175, 176
702	6, 36, 177, 178, 179, 180, 257
703	176, 180, 181, 182
704	183
705	184, 185
706	180, 186
801(a),(b),(c)	25, 160, 189, 190, 191, 192, 193, 199, 200, 201, 203, 204, 205, 206, 211, 271, 273
801(d)(1)	194, 195, 196, 197
801(d)(2)(A)	76, 82, 102, 164, 191, 197, 198, 199, 202, 203, 218, 230, 262, 279, 298, 300, 331, 332
801(d)(2)(B)	165, 191, 200, 201, 203, 315
801(d)(2)(C)	198, 204, 205, 279, 312
801(d)(2)(D)	206, 207, 208, 264, 279
801(d)(2)(E)	193, 209, 211, 280
803(1)	213, 214, 215, 216, 280
803(2)	210, 212, 215, 217, 218, 219, 264, 278
803(3)	220, 221, 222, 223, 224
803(4)	212, 224, 225, 226, 227, 278, 285
803(5)	215, 229, 230
803(6)	231, 232, 233, 234, 235, 237, 238, 240, 244, 286, 301, 314, 329, 330, 332
803(7)	235
803(8)	229, 232, 237, 238, 239, 240, 241, 300, 301, 304, 309, 314, 331
803(9)	242, 331
803(10)	243, 306, 313, 331
803(11)	224, 245
803(12)	245
803(13)	246
803(14)	247, 248, 249
803(15)	247, 248, 249, 250
803(16)	245, 246, 250, 251, 252, 254
803(17)	254, 255
803(18)	255, 256, 257
803(19)	248, 257
803(20)	258

Rule	Pages
803(21)	259, 260
803(22)	261, 262
803(23)	262
[Mi 803A]	4, 226, 277
804(a)	10, 213, 248, 263, 264, 265, 266, 267, 269, 270, 271, 272, 273, 274, 275, 283
804(b)	213, 264, 278
804(b)(1)	266
804(b)(2)	10, 197, 267, 268, 269
804(b)(3)	263, 270, 271, 272, 273, 275, 283
804(b)(4)	246, 247, 248, 274, 275
804(b)(5)	275, 276
[Proposed (deleted) 804(b)(2)]	197
805	200, 215, 225, 230, 278, 279, 280
806	260, 281, 282, 283, 284
807	9, 197, 276, 278, 285, 286, 287
901(a)	13, 252, 289, 290, 291, 292, 293, 294, 296, 297, 298, 299, 300, 301, 302, 303, 305, 333
901(b)(1)	292, 303
901(b)(2)	293, 294
901(b)(3)	294, 295
901(b)(4)	296, 297, 315
901(b)(5)	298
901(b)(6)	279, 299
901(b)(7)	300, 301
901(b)(8)	245, 252, 254, 301, 302
901(b)(9)	302, 303
902(1)	243, 304
902(2)	305, 306
902(3)	307, 308
902(4)	307, 308, 309, 314
902(5)	310
902(6)	311
902(7)	311, 312
902(8)	312, 313
902(9)	313
902(10)	313
902(11)	316
902(12)	316
903	314, 315
1001(1)	317, 318
1001(2)	318, 320
1001(3)	318, 320, 321, 322
1001(4)	321, 326, 327
1002	220, 317, 318, 321, 322, 323, 324, 325, 326, 329, 330, 331, 332
1003	320, 321, 322, 326, 327, 328
1004	220, 318, 327
1005	328, 331
1006	234, 329, 330, 331, 332
1007	331, 332
1008	333
1101	1, 99
U.S. Const., 5th Am	97, 101, 121, 263, 275, 285
U.S. Const., 6th Am	101, 136, 153, 202, 212,